The Continuing Voice of Jesus

CHRISTIAN PROPHECY AND THE GOSPEL TRADITION

The Continuing
Voice of Jesus

M. EUGENE BORING

WESTMINSTER/JOHN KNOX PRESS Louisville, Kentucky

A previous edition of this work was published in
Great Britain by Cambridge University Press in 1982
under the title *Sayings of the Risen Jesus.*

Book design by Publishers' WorkGroup

Published by Westminster/John Knox Press
Louisville, Kentucky

PRINTED IN THE UNITED STATES OF AMERICA

9 8 7 6 5 4 3 2 1

Library of Congress Cataloging-in-Publication Data

Boring, M. Eugene.
  The continuing voice of Jesus : Christian prophecy and the gospel
tradition / M. Eugene Boring.
      p.   cm.
  Rev. ed. of : Sayings of the risen Jesus. 1982.
  Includes bibliographical references and index.
  ISBN 0–664–25184–6

  1. Jesus Christ—Words. 2. Bible. N.T. Gospels—Criticism,
interpretation, etc. 3. Prophecy (Christianity) I. Boring, M.
Eugene. Sayings of the risen Jesus. II. Title.
BS2555.6.P72B67   1991
226'.015—dc20   90–47608

To Karen

Contents

PART TWO
A Profile of Early Christian Prophecy

PART THREE
Prophetic Sayings of the Risen Jesus in the Gospels

10

Abbreviations

AGJU	Arbeiten zur Geschichte des antiken Judentums und des Urchristentums
ANRW	*Aufstieg und Niedergang der römischen Welt*
ATANT	Abhandlungen zur Theologie des Alten und Neuen Testaments
BETL	Bibliotheca ephemeridum theologicarum lovaniensium
BU	Biblische Untersuchungen
BWANT	Beiträge zur Wissenschaft vom Alten und Neuen Testament
BZ	*Biblische Zeitschrift*
DBSup	*Dictionnaire de la Bible, Supplément*
EKKNT	Evangelisch-katholischer Kommentar zum Neuen Testament
ErFor	Erträge der Forschung
ExpTim	*Expository Times*
FRLANT	Forschungen zur Religion und Literatur des Alten und Neuen Testaments
HNT	Handbuch zum Neuen Testament
HTKNT	Herders theologischer Kommentar zum Neuen Testament
HTR	*Harvard Theological Review*
ICC	International Critical Commentary
Inter	Interpretation
JBL	*Journal of Biblical Literature*
JJS	*Journal of Jewish Studies*
JRelS	*Journal of Religious Studies*
JSNT	*Journal for the Study of the New Testament*
JSNTSup	Journal for the Study of the New Testament—Supplement Series
JTS	*Journal of Theological Studies*

KBANT	Kommentare und Beiträge zum Alten und Neuen Testament
KEK	Kritisch-exegetischer Kommentar über das Neue Testament
LTK	*Lexicon für Theologie und Kirche*
NovT	*Novum Testamentum*
NovTSup	Novum Testamentum, Supplements
NTD	Das Neue Testament Deutsch
RAC	*Reallexikon für Antike und Christentum*
RGG	*Die Religion in Geschichte und Gegenwart*
SAC	Studies in Antiquity and Christianity
SBB	Stuttgarter biblische Beiträge
SBLDS	Society for Biblical Literature Dissertation Series
SBS	Stuttgarter Bibelstudien
SBT	Studies in Biblical Theology
SJT	*Scottish Journal of Theology*
SNTSMS	Society for New Testament Studies Monograph Series
SUNT	Studien zur Umwelt des Neuen Testaments
TDNT	G. Kittel and G. Friedrich, eds., *Theological Dictionary of the New Testament*
THNT	Theologischer Handkommentar zum Neuen Testament
TU	Texte und Untersuchungen
TZ	*Theologische Zeitschrift*
UNT	Untersuchungen zum Neuen Testament
WMANT	Wissenschaftliche Monographien zum Alten und Neuen Testament
WUNT	Wissenschaftliche Untersuchungen zum Neuen Testament
ZNW	*Zeitschrift für die neutestamentliche Wissenschaft*
ZTK	*Zeitschrift für Theologie und Kirche*

Preface

This book began as a revision of my monograph *Sayings of the Risen Jesus* (Cambridge: Cambridge University Press, 1982), with which it still has much in common. As the revision proceeded, however, it became clear that a complete rewriting was needed.

The present volume is both more and less than a new edition of *Sayings of the Risen Jesus*. It is *less* in that much of the documentation and detailed argument of the previous work is eliminated or strongly reduced. Only a few samples are given for the reader who is interested in how the book's conclusions might be supported with evidence and argument. This may be beneficial both to readers who question whether there is any hard evidence to support such views as are here advocated, as well as to readers who might tend to overestimate the foundation on which scholarly conclusions rest.

But this book, though less technical than its predecessor (it assumes a reading knowledge of English alone, for example), is also *more* than the previous monograph. It takes into consideration the literature and study since 1979, especially the major works on Christian prophecy that have appeared in the meantime (especially Hill, Aune, and Forbes; see bibliography) and the intensive study of the sayings of Jesus in the Jesus Seminar directed by Robert W. Funk, the International Q Seminar directed by James M. Robinson, and the multitude of individual works such as Sato on Q and prophecy. It responds to the major alternative approaches and conclusions such as those of Riesner and the recent resurgence of conservatism of the Tübingen scholars. This book is more readable than its predecessor, directed to a more general readership. The previous work was concerned with method and evidence in order to make a scholarly case. The present work does not neglect those concerns but is also concerned with the theological issues inherent in the phenomenon of Chris-

tian prophecy and is more oriented to the understanding of this phenomenon and these texts in the life of the church.

I complete this work with gratitude to Davis Perkins, John G. Gibbs,
and Cynthia Thompson of Westminster/John Knox Press for their acceptance of the initial proposal and encouragement along the way, and
to Edward J. McMahon and Lana N. Byrd of Texas Christian University
for able research assistance and secretarial work. The book is dedicated
to Karen Boring, whose love and encouragement have sustained this and
all my efforts, and whom I also like a lot.

1

Introduction: The Continuing Voice of Jesus in the Early Church

THE JESUS WHO SPOKE AND SPEAKS

Christians have always heard in the Gospels the voice of a real person from the historical past: Jesus of Nazareth, who called disciples in Galilee, taught, healed, helped, and was crucified under Pontius Pilate in Jerusalem in the first century C.E. Christians have always heard in the Gospels an authentic voice addressing them in their own present, the contemporary address of the resurrected and exalted Lord who still calls to discipleship. Without reflection or analysis, the immediate Christian experience of reading the Gospel texts points both to the reality of a past historical figure and the reality of a present address by one who still lives.

This double dimension of immediate Christian experience corresponds to the nature of the Gospels. A careful analysis reveals to the student both a pre-Easter and a post-Easter dimension to the church's remembrance of Jesus preserved and witnessed to in the Gospel texts. They preserve the memory and impact of what Jesus actually said and did. Yet the variations and modifications of those sayings of Jesus contained in the Gospels do not represent a defect of the Gospels, as though the church had attempted to remember "what actually happened" and "what Jesus actually said" but had failed. The various forms of the Gospel tradition point to the continual reinterpretation of these sayings in the post-Easter church to express the continuing word of Jesus to the church in changed circumstances.

An even more careful and analytical look at the sayings of Jesus as they were handed on and around in the churches before the Gospels were written has convinced many scholars that the distinction we now too easily assume was rarely made in earliest Christianity—the distinction between what Jesus "really" said during his ministry in Galilee and Jerusalem, and what was said after Easter in his name, as earlier sayings were

15

expanded and modified, and new sayings were spoken in the name and authority of the risen Jesus. Within the prophetic community new sayings of the risen Jesus appeared, traditional ones were prophetically modified to express the present voice of the risen Lord, and were transmitted along with historically authentic sayings of Jesus of Nazareth. The Gospels themselves already point not only "backward" to the "Jesus of history" but "upward" and "outward" to the heavenly Lord who continues to address his church after Easter and is present in its mission to the world (Mark 13:11; Matt. 23:34; 28:16–20; John 16:12–15).

CHRISTIAN PROPHETS AND THE SAYINGS OF JESUS: THE ISSUE

The early church thus used the name "Jesus" and such christological titles as "Christ" and "Lord" to refer both to the historical figure Jesus of Nazareth and to the risen Lord of the church's faith. Accordingly, such phrases as "word(s) of Jesus" and "saying(s) of the Lord" had a potential ambiguity from the very beginning.

On the one hand, "word(s) of the Lord" could refer primarily to "historical" sayings, as for example in Luke 22:61; Acts 20:35; or 1 Corinthians 11:23–25. Such sayings are here called "historical" not because they necessarily represent a verbatim report of what Jesus of Nazareth once actually said but because they are represented in their present narrative frameworks as the words of a past historical figure. They may have been subject to additions or modifications in the course of the traditioning process or conceivably may have been created from whole cloth. But the saying is transmitted in the community and reported in the New Testament as something that the pre-Easter Jesus once said, and it is by virtue of this purported setting in the life of Jesus that the saying is here called "historical."

On the other hand, such a phrase as "word(s) of the Lord" may refer to the post-Easter address of the exalted Lord to the community, spoken, for example, through a Christian prophet, as in the Apocalypse. Sayings of Christian prophets may comprise not only new, post-Easter revelations; they may also take up and re-present words from the tradition, including pre-Easter words of Jesus of Nazareth. They are here called "prophetic" because they are presented in the community not as what Jesus once said but as what the post-Easter exalted Lord now *says*. The difference is between the "word of the Lord" as *report* and *address.*

Christian prophets who continued to speak in Jesus' name played a major role in early Christianity and in the formation of the New Testament. It is well known that prophets were key figures in the history of Israel and the development of the Hebrew Bible. Unfortunately, however, the prophetic component of early Christianity is often overlooked.

Early Christianity was a prophetic movement. Prophets form a major line of continuity between Israel, Judaism, and the church, both historically and theologically. "Without this rebirth of prophecy, there would have been no Jesus movement, no Gospels, and thus no Christianity."[1]

How did the earliest church deal with this ambiguity of the tradition in Jesus' sayings? Did early Christians in fact make the distinction between "historical" and "prophetic" sayings, hearing them as different kinds of sayings of Jesus and keeping them in separate categories? Is this distinction partly or entirely a modern one? To the extent that this distinction existed at all prior to the Gospels, was it blurred, intentionally or unintentionally, with the result that there was fluid interchange between "historical" and "prophetic" sayings?

THE ALTERNATIVES

This problem, and alternative answers to it, first clearly emerged in New Testament studies with the advent of the discipline of form criticism, which concentrated on an analysis of the oral tradition between Jesus and the Gospels. Early in this century, the two leading pioneers of form criticism, Rudolf Bultmann and Martin Dibelius, gave opposite answers to the question of whether the early church distinguished between "historical" and "prophetic" sayings of Jesus. Bultmann[2] saw a fluid interchange between these two types of tradition. In this discussion I will call this the "fluid-tradition" view. Dibelius[3] saw a firm distinction made by the earliest church between "historical" and "prophetic" sayings of Jesus, which I will call the "controlled-tradition" view.

New Testament study has come a long way since the pioneer form critics Bultmann and Dibelius—so far, in fact, that informed readers might wonder at the wisdom of rehashing the issues debated by form critics of a past generation. Literary criticism presently dominates Gospel studies in America and has attracted much interest in Europe, where the historical paradigm still prevails.[4] The shift to literary criticism and its emphasis on the meaning of the final form of the text as a whole is in a certain sense to be celebrated. But this does not mean the abandonment of the questions related to the tradition behind the Gospels, including the

---

1 Migaku Sato, *Q und Prophetie. Studien zur Gattungs- und Traditionsgeschichte der Quelle Q,* 411.

2 *The History of the Synoptic Tradition* (German first edition 1921).

3 *From Tradition to Gospel* (German first edition 1919).

4 As examples of recent interest in literary approaches to the Gospels in Germany, see Ferdinand Hahn, ed., *Der Erzähler des Evangeliums. Methodische Neuansätze in der Markusforschung,* SBS 118/119 (Stuttgart: Katholisches Bibelwerk, 1985), and Reinhold Zwick, *Montage im Markusevangelium. Studien zur narrativen Organisation der ältesten Jesuserzählung,* SBB 18 (Stuttgart: Katholisches Bibelwerk, 1989), which includes an extensive bibliography.

question of the historical Jesus. It is passing strange that at the same time literary studies of the final form of the Gospels have been in the ascendancy, study of the historical Jesus has experienced a renewal, sometimes at the same hands. (Several members of the Jesus Seminar directed by Robert W. Funk are also leaders in the newer literary approaches to the Gospels, e.g., John Dominic Crossan, Vernon Robbins, Brandon Scott, Robert Tannehill, and, of course, Funk himself.)

What has been neglected in recent study is the period *between* Jesus and the Gospels. For this crucial period in the development of early Christianity and the formation of the Gospels, the appropriate starting point is still that of the classical form critics, Bultmann and Dibelius, and the issues that divided them. It is now recognized that there were problems with their assumptions and methods (see Kelber below). But to explore the issue of how the words of Jesus were transmitted in the post-Easter but pre-Gospel oral period, we must first return to the fundamental parting of the ways that occurred in the earliest days of form critical study of the sayings material in the Gospels.

Form criticism as practiced by both Bultmann and Dibelius was attacked from the beginning by those who were afraid it undermined the historical truth of the Gospels.[5] The more recent, and more serious, objections have come from the point of view of modern linguistics[6] and studies in orality. Werner Kelber lists seven points on which the assumptions of classical form critics must be considered suspect: (1) "Easter faith as watershed and point of departure for the tradition"; (2) "the notion of the original form and its compulsory development into progressively more complex and hybrid formations"; (3) "collective consciousness as the shaping force both of oral materials and gospel textuality"; (4) "the concept of 'setting in life' as the sociological determinant of oral forms"; (5) "the heuristic value of the categories of Palestinian versus Hellenistic"; (6) "and the thesis of an intrinsic gravitational or teleological pull toward the gospel composition," by which Kelber means the form critics' assumption that the transition from the oral tradition to Gospel composition was in continuity with the preceding period and its almost automatic and inevitable result. (7) "More than anything else . . . [form criticism's] failure to appreciate the actuality of living speech as distinct from written texts."[7]

I consider all of these except the first to be important corrections to

---

5 E.g., B. S. Easton, *The Gospel Before the Gospels,* and E. F. Scott, *The Validity of the Gospel Record.*

6 Erhardt Güttgemanns, *Candid Questions Concerning Gospel Form Criticism: A Methodological Sketch of the Fundamental Problematics of Form and Redaction Criticism.*

7 See especially Werner Kelber, *The Oral and Written Gospel: The Hermeneutics of Speaking and Writing in the Synoptic Tradition, Mark, Paul, and Q,* 8.

the form critical approach, and they are taken into account in the discussion of the relation of Christian prophets to the tradition of Jesus' words in Part Three below. While Bultmann emphasized lack of continuity between Jesus and the church and continuity between the oral tradition and the written Gospels, Kelber sees continuity between the oral teaching of Jesus and the oral tradition of his words in the church and a break in continuity at the transition from orality to textuality.

In my own view, Bultmann and the form critics were correct in emphasizing the importance of the Easter event for the stream of tradition that proceeds from Jesus to the Gospels. While there may have been "Jesus movements" in Palestine after Jesus' death for which the resurrection faith played only a minimal role or none at all,[8] these would not have been the circles that transmitted the traditions that became textualized in the canonical Gospels. Nor would they have been the groups in which Christian prophets who spoke in the name of the risen Jesus would have been active. Defining Christian prophecy as I do, I find it difficult to understand Kelber's claim that after the crucifixion, "irrespective of Easter faith, Jesus could thus continue his role as proclaimer and assume presence in prophetic words. Because the oral medium is exceptionally equipped to appropriate authoritative presence, Easter will hardly have caused the irrevocable christological rupture Bultmann envisioned."[9] But there is a great difference in whether words of Jesus are understood as the remembered words of a past historical figure who is now dead, or understood as spoken in the present by one who still lives. Early Christian prophecy proceeding from within and on the basis of this latter view, presupposed faith in the resurrection and a difference between "pre-Easter" and "post-Easter," though this Easter event need not be thought of as a "christological rupture." On the other hand, Kelber is correct that the transition from oral tradition to written text was a transformation of major importance that was not merely the inevitable result of the momentum of the tradition itself (see chapter 13 below).

The contours of the debate have thus been sharpened by recent study, but the discussion has continued to the present along the lines first marked out by the "classical" form critical studies of Bultmann and Dibelius. Since these two perspectives on the tradition have been so influential on later study, including contemporary discussions not always aware of their own roots, each view needs to be brought into sharper focus.

---

8 In addition to Kelber, see James M. Robinson, "The Jesus Movement in Galilee: Reconstructing Q," 4–5; and Burton L. Mack, *A Myth of Innocence,* 78–97.

9 *Oral and Written Gospel,* 20.

Dynamic, Open Tradition and the Legacy
of Rudolf Bultmann

Bultmann was convinced that form criticism must go beyond observations on form and lead to historical judgments regarding the authenticity of the material being examined. His approach was to assume that the synoptic tradition of Jesus' words was church material and to place the burden of proof on those who argued for its authenticity. Only material that is distinctively non-Jewish and non-Christian can safely be attributed to Jesus.[10] Only a few sayings survived Bultmann's examination. He never made an exhaustive list but in one study listed a total of forty-one verses (about three pages of Greek text!) of sayings he considered authentic.[11] Bultmann's procedure left him with a large amount of church formulation on his hands that called for explanation.

Christian prophets were brought into the discussion by Bultmann to help explain how it could be that so many sayings of Jesus were created by the church. Although not the first to suggest that part of the Gospel sayings tradition originated as the sayings of Christian prophets,[12] Bultmann was certainly the first to bring the phenomenon of Christian prophecy into conjunction with that of the growth of the Gospel tradition in any comprehensive way. He did not, however, begin with a study of the phenomenon of Christian prophecy as such and thereby become convinced that Christian prophets contributed sayings to the Gospel tradition but seems to have hit upon Christian prophecy as he sought an explanation for the creativity of the church. Whether this was serendipity or rationalization is still debated.

Bultmann tended to make generalizations about the "utterances of the Spirit" and "sayings of the risen Lord" in order to account for the wholesale expansion of the tradition that he believed he saw. Only rarely did he identify particular sayings as oracles of Christian prophets. He never gave supporting evidence as to why a particular saying should be considered the product of Christian prophecy rather than some other kind of secondary expansion such as scribal, midrashic, didactic, or redactional. This is due in part to the fact that Bultmann's hypothesis regarding

---

10 See his *History of the Synoptic Tradition*, 5, 105, 205; *Jesus and the Word*, 13.

11 "The Study of the Synoptic Gospels," in *Form Criticism* (New York: Harper & Brothers, [1934] 1962), 61–63.

12 The earliest specific suggestion known to me that a Gospel saying originated as Christian prophecy is that of Timothy Colani in 1864, who suggested that the apocalyptic discourse now attributed to Jesus in Mark 13:5–30 originated as the oracle that, according to Eusebius, *Ecclesiastical History* 3.5, warned the Jerusalem church to flee from the impending destruction of the city in 65 C.E. (*Jésus Christ et les croyances messianiques de son temps*, 202–203). A few similar suggestions can be found in the late-nineteenth-century works of H. J. Holtzmann, Hermann Gunkel, Hermann von Soden, and especially Alfred Loisy, but none of these were developed. It was Rudolf Bultmann who first developed this suggestion into a program.

Christian prophets did not grow out of his study of the texts but was brought in to help justify his negative conclusions regarding the historicity of the bulk of the sayings tradition. But there was another factor in the development of his view that may be evaluated more positively, namely, his view of the tradition.

Bultmann believed that the early church generally regarded the tradition of the words of Jesus as the vehicle of the voice of the *risen* Lord. Not only were Jewish and Hellenistic materials that originally had nothing to do with Jesus commandeered and incorporated into the tradition to express the message of the exalted Christ, even authentic dominical sayings were not heard as the recorded teaching of a past historical figure but as the voice of the exalted Lord. The common denominator for authentic pre-Easter sayings and various types of post-Easter material, including oracles of Christian prophets, was "word of the (risen) Lord," not "sayings of (the historical) Jesus." Thus Bultmann believed that the church, with full awareness of what it was doing, incorporated new material into its tradition of dominical sayings and that it was never concerned to keep these in separate categories. This common basis for the tradition facilitated interchange between its various elements; sayings of the historical Jesus could be heard as sayings of the risen Lord and vice versa.

Since Bultmann saw the tradition itself as a vehicle of the Spirit and oriented toward the risen Lord, this permitted him to operate without a sharply focused definition of Christian prophetism. He never defined Christian prophecy, nor did he attempt to characterize Christian prophets. It is not clear whether he equated such expressions as "word of the risen Lord" and "Christian prophecy," or whether he regarded the latter as a more specific phenomenon than the former. He seemed to draw no clear line between (1) charismatic prophets consciously delivering oracles in the name of the risen Lord, (2) the more "ordinary" preaching of the gospel, and (3) the promulgation of the tradition/word of the risen Lord in the community at large. All came under the one rubric: "word of the (risen) Lord."

Bultmann's seminal idea became widely accepted, so that in scholarly literature one readily finds sayings of Jesus attributed to Christian prophets. The most complete catalog was made by David Aune for the 1975 Seminar on Early Christian Prophecy, listing a total of 115 different synoptic passages totaling 449 verses considered prophetic by one or more of 28 scholars. A 1977 supplement lists an additional 21 passages totaling 73 verses, and an additional 17 scholars, for a grand total of 136 sayings, 572 verses, and 45 scholars.[13] Many of these scholars are stu-

---

13 "Christian Prophets and the Sayings of Jesus: An Index to Synoptic Pericopae Ostensibly Influenced by Early Christian Prophets," in *SBL 1977 Seminar Papers*, 131–142. The Supplement was privately distributed.

dents, directly or indirectly, of Bultmann and have developed his original insights in two directions.

First, Bultmann's idea that it is the risen Lord who speaks in every level of the tradition has been consciously adopted and reflectively elaborated as a hermeneutical principle by individual scholars such as Julius Schniewind and Herbert Leroy[14] and became one of the foundational principles of the post-Bultmannian stream known as the New Hermeneutic.[15] The vague line that separated historical and prophetic sayings in Bultmann's understanding of the early Christian tradition has disappeared entirely. The question of which sayings are authentic has become a second-rate question (Schniewind). Analogously, the blurred distinction between Christian prophets and other members of the *pneuma*-charged early church likewise has evaporated.

Ernst Fuchs portrayed the early church as having prophets whose words were sometimes added to the tradition as words of Jesus but says such prophets were not the only ones who spoke the authentic post-Easter word of Jesus. Fuchs understood Christian believers to be those who were grasped by the fact that "Jesus had brought God into language." "*Whoever* [emphasis mine] understood himself out of this situation would bring Jesus Christ into language."[16] What was unclear in Bultmann has become explicit in Fuchs: the goodly fellowship of the prophets has become coextensive with the Christian community; the prophetic phenomenon can simply be identified with "the event of preaching."

Ernst Käsemann developed Bultmann's insight in another direction and was his most productive student in giving substance to the suggestion that Christian prophets are responsible for parts of the sayings tradition. Unlike Schniewind and Fuchs, he did this not by further softening the focus of Bultmann's insight until it diffused into the whole tradition and the whole community but by attempting to sharpen the focus to reveal the phenomenon of prophecy more clearly, to differentiate it from other elements in the community, and to give evidence of the prophetic origin of sayings in particular cases. Although Käsemann sometimes continued the Bultmannian practice of simply declaring secondary logia to be prophetic without more ado, in one important group of sayings—"sentences of holy law"—he offered some evidence for his assertions.[17]

---

14 Julius Schniewind, *Das Evangelium nach Markus*, 3–5, 132; Herbert Leroy, *Jesus Überlieferung und Deutung*.

15 Ernst Fuchs, "Das Sprachereignis in der Verkündigung Jesu, in der Theologie des Paulus und im Ostergeschehen," in *Zum hermeneutischen Problem in der Theologie. Die existentiale Interpretation*.

16 Ibid., 303.

17 The thesis was developed and defended in a series of essays now printed together

Static, Controlled Tradition and the Legacy
of Martin Dibelius

An alternative to Bultmann's way of viewing the development of the sayings tradition was offered at the outset from within the form-critical school by Martin Dibelius and has been continued by his successors. Dibelius believed there were basically two types of sayings material that circulated in the early church: (1) the tradition of the words of the historical Jesus and (2) "sayings of Christian exhortation," which were "regarded as inspired by the Spirit or by the Lord." He terms the former category "regulatory" and the latter "inspirational."[18] Although the "regulatory" materials were amplified by homiletical additions and modifications to keep the tradition relevant to changing situations, these additions were minimal and did not change the basically historical character of the tradition. Dibelius thinks the regulatory sayings were more rigidly fixed than the "Haggadic" narrative material. This fixation occurred in the 40s of the first century, under the control of eyewitnesses, so that the tradition of Jesus' sayings, thought of as legal material, was set apart from the "inspirational" sayings.[19] Jesus' words continued to be heard as the authoritative word of the teacher of Nazareth given in the past, a kind of Christian *Halakah.*

The "inspirational" materials existed alongside the regulatory sayings but in clear distinction from them. These "inspirational" sayings might include sayings of Christian prophets but apparently only to a minimal extent. They are mostly Christian parenesis, infused with the "spirit" of the Lord but not generally thought of as sayings of the risen Jesus in any prophetic way, and unlikely to be "mistaken" for a saying of Jesus. Only once in all his writings did Dibelius make prophetic speech a constituent part of that preaching which was the "beginning point of all inspired production in early Christianity," and even here the bare mention of Christian prophecy was not developed or followed up.[20]

Although Dibelius saw the early church as attempting to keep the two types of sayings materials separate, he considered it inevitable that occasionally one would be mistaken for the other, so that there was some interchange between the two traditions, and a post-Easter hortatory saying "through the Spirit" would be "mistaken" for an authentic regulatory

---

in *New Testament Questions of Today:* "Sentences of Holy Law in the New Testament" (1954); "The Beginnings of Christian Theology" (1960); and "On the Subject of Primitive Christian Apocalyptic" (1962).

18 *Tradition to Gospel,* 241–242.

19 Ibid., 242, 293, 295, 298.

20 *Botschaft und Geschichte. Gesammelte Aufsätze von Martin Dibelius*, vol. 1: *Zur Evangelienforschung*, 221.

word of the historical Jesus. Dibelius gave no examples of this principle, labeled it "error," and said that the number of "genuine" words of Jesus was increased by only a "few spurious ones."[21]

Dibelius assumed this view of the tradition as a working hypothesis and never presented a specific rationale for it. Dibelius seems to have been misled by the present structure of our New Testament, which contains the sayings tradition of Jesus in the pre-Easter framework of the Gospels and reflects the parenetic materials in the Letters. On this anachronistic basis, Dibelius posited two quite separate channels of transmission for the two types of material. There is a bit of irony in the fact that one of the founders of the discipline that turned our attention to the pre-Gospel form of the tradition should still tend to think of the sayings tradition as enclosed in the "life of Jesus" framework, when it was precisely the work of scholars such as Dibelius himself that first let us see how the material functioned and was heard as it circulated as individual units and collections before Mark first put them into an explicit pre-Easter framework. *The achievement of Mark, in creating the narrative framework of the Gospel form and thereby binding the word of the Lord to the pre-Easter Jesus, has not been sufficiently appreciated* (see chapter 13).

However, Dibelius's assumption of separate channels of transmission for "regulatory" and "inspirational" sayings is still no cause to think of them as isolated from each other, since he posited the same setting in the life of the church, the teaching ministry, for both kinds of material. Dibelius is sometimes misunderstood and falsely accused of making "preaching" the one setting in the church's life for all elements of the tradition. But preaching was a broad and flexible category for him that included among other types of communication "didactic preaching" and "catechumen instruction."[22]

The basic reason for Dibelius's arguing that the "authentic" tradition of Jesus' words was not "contaminated" to any considerable extent by post-Easter formation of the church seems to be that he imagined the former to be a rather rigidly formed tradition, fixed quite early, and under the control of eyewitnesses. There is a certain tension between Dibelius's view of the manner in which he conceived most of the tradition from and about Jesus to have been handed on, by "unliterary men awaiting the end of the world,"[23] and the transmission process he envisaged for the sayings of Jesus. To support his view Dibelius would have needed to have

---

21 *Tradition to Gospel,* 241.

22 Ibid., 14, 15; see 27.

23 Ibid., 61. But, as Rainer Riesner points out, already Qumran and Paul demonstrate that fervent eschatological expectation and concern to hand on a sacred tradition need not be alternatives but can be complementary dimensions of religious community (*Jesus als Lehrer. Eine Untersuchung zum Ursprung der Evangelien-Überlieferung,* 496).

posited some sort of trained academy of repeaters who kept watch over the purity of the tradition from the beginning.

Some scholars sensed this problem and have attempted to correct it by positing just such a setting in the life of the church for the transmission of the tradition. The idea that Jesus taught in rabbinic style and that his disciples memorized his sayings like rabbinic students has emerged fairly often before and alongside the classical form critical view.[24] Harald Riesenfeld and his student Birger Gerhardsson made the most sustained attempt to argue that the tradition of Jesus' words was handed on in a carefully guarded rabbinic fashion from the time of Jesus until its incorporation into the Gospels.[25] They based their argument almost entirely on analogies from the rabbinic material, rather than on the materials in the Gospels themselves. The rabbinic materials and transmission procedures to which they appeal are generations later than Jesus and the Gospels. The concern for verbatim repetition of a received tradition did not develop until the second century.[26] Their occasional attempts to support their case from the New Testament were sometimes painful, e.g., when they argued that the phrase "to visit Cephas" in Galatians 1:18 means Paul submitted to an "ordination examination" at the hands of Peter, who tested whether Paul had utilized his "three years in Arabia" to unlearn his rabbinic Torah and replace it with the memorized tradition from Jesus.

An openness to the general view proposed by Riesenfeld and Gerhardsson has been expressed by some,[27] but for the most part, the attempt to fill in the gap between Jesus and the Gospels with a Christian rabbinic academy that transmitted a carefully guarded tradition has met with severe criticism.[28] Some researchers, especially Jewish scholars, rather than regarding rabbinic transmission as an alternative to the form-critical approach, applied form criticism to the rabbinic materials themselves. The result was that the rabbinic materials seem to have

---

24 Riesner, *Jesus als Lehrer,* 40–54, documents details of these efforts.

25 Harald Riesenfeld, *The Gospel Tradition and Its Beginnings;* Birger Gerhardsson, *Memory and Manuscript: Oral Transmission and Written Transmission in Rabbinic Judaism and Early Christianity.* Gerhardsson's first reply to his critics is represented by *Tradition and Transmission in Early Christianity;* his most recent statements of the thesis are *Die Anfänge der Evangelientradition* and "Der Weg der Evangelien-Tradition," in *Das Evangelium und die Evangelien,* ed. Peter Stuhlmacher, 79–102.

26 So Jacob Neusner, *Early Rabbinic Judaism,* 85. A. J. Saldarini, " 'Form Criticism' of Rabbinic Literature," dates this even later, not prior to the third century.

27 E. g., David Dungan, *The Sayings of Jesus in the Churches of Paul,* 141–143; Riesner, *Jesus als Lehrer;* A. F. Zimmerman, *Die Urchristlichen Lehrer. Studien zum Tradentenkreis* der didaskaloi *im frühen Urchristentum,* 23.

28 E.g., Morton Smith, "A Comparison of Early Christian and Early Rabbinic Tradition," *JBL* 82 (1963): 169–176, and somewhat more positively, W. D. Davies, "Reflections on a Scandinavian Approach to 'the Gospel Tradition,' " Appendix 15 of *The Setting of the Sermon on the Mount,* 464–480.

experienced a similar kind of modification and expansion as the Gospel traditions.[29] Riesner has recently responded with a detailed study arguing that not only rabbinic education, but education in general was a matter of memorization in New Testament times, so the issue of "rabbinic transmission" is beside the point.[30]

Even if the view of a Christian rabbinic academy extending from Jesus to the Gospels could be made tenable, there is still room within such a theory to allow for prophetic expansion of the tradition. Gerhardsson states:

> We must take into account that at least some teachers—and haggadists in particular—placed special emphasis on certain of their sayings, delivering them with particular care just because they considered them to be particularly "wise" words which they had "received" in moments of inspiration. The critical attitude of the Tannaitic and Amoraic rabbis to new prophetic revelation and the like ought not to be allowed to obscure this phenomenon.[31]

Early Christianity was not nearly so suspicious of prophetic phenomena as the rabbinism posited by Gerhardsson, so the tradition of Jesus' words could have been augmented by prophetic sayings even if transmitted in a Christian rabbinic structure. There is thus no basis for an a priori denial of the prophetic expansion of the sayings tradition on the basis of the tradition process itself, however it is conceived.

ISSUES AND CHALLENGES OF THE PRESENT DEBATE

Evidence

The Bultmannian tradition has been accused of assuming what is to be proved and seeking to establish the case by assertion and repetition.[32] The charge is justified. Christian prophets cannot be called in as a solution to the problem posed by the apparent prolific productivity of the community as long as their role is simply assumed. Fritz Neugebauer has shown the fallacy of the formula "not from Jesus, therefore from a Christian prophet" often implicit—and sometimes even explicit—in such discussions.[33] *Any new attempt to deal with the problem of Christian prophecy and*

---

29 So, e.g., Saldarini, "Form Criticism," and Neusner, "The Formation of Rabbinic Judaism: Yavneh [Jamnia] from A.D. 70 to 100."

30 *Jesus als Lehrer*, 97–245.

31 *Memory and Manuscript*, 178. Gerhardsson documents this and gives further literature.

32 E.g., by David Hill, "On the Evidence for the Creative Role of Christian Prophets," 273. See also *New Testament Prophecy*, 160–185.

33 Fritz Neugebauer, "Geistsprüche und Jesuslogien."

the Gospel tradition should realize that it will be expected to provide evidence for its assertions, derived from the study of the prophetic phenomenon in early Christianity.

The Traditioning Process

A second issue that has emerged concerns the nature of the pre-Gospel traditioning process. It had already become apparent in the earliest form-critical studies of Dibelius and Bultmann that the view one has of the tradition and the traditioning process between Jesus and Mark is a significant factor in whether or not one sees Christian prophets as having added to the sayings tradition. Thus É. Cothonet, for example, in one of the most complete discussions of Christian prophecy available, treats the question of the role of prophets in the formation of the Gospel tradition very briefly and dismisses it somewhat peremptorily because of the role he believes the apostles and tradition to have played in early Christianity.[34] Other scholars also express objections, not on the basis of a study of the alleged prophetic logia themselves but on the view of the tradition process implied by the theory. E. F. Scott presented a romanticist picture of how the purity of the tradition was maintained. He speaks imaginatively of those who would "perceive at once, by the very turn of phrase, whether any given utterance was really in character. No saying would find its way into the record unless it bore the intrinsic marks of the language of Jesus. Some one would certainly be present at every meeting who would know the facts and would protest against any statement that was plainly wrong."[35]

We shall see that there is a valid instinct at work here, for the community did test potential additions to the tradition as to their appropriateness in representing who Jesus was and the meaning of the Christ-event, so that not just anything was accepted. Yet Scott's picture of omnipresent eyewitnesses guarding the purity of the tradition is utterly incredible. Likewise Vincent Taylor's oft-quoted quip that "If the [Bultmannian] Form Critics are right, the disciples must have been translated to heaven immediately after the resurrection"[36] is more rhetoric than reason.

Still and all, the advocates of this point of view from Dibelius to the present have made it clear that any theory of prophetic expansion of the tradition implies a theory not only about Christian prophecy but about the nature of the tradition process itself. Some scholars, for example, are quite comfortable with the view that Christian prophets drew sayings of Jesus *from* the tradition, which they re-presented as sayings from the risen Lord, adding to them and modifying them to make them more relevant to changing situations, but reject the idea that entirely new sayings were

---

34 É. Cothonet, "Prophétisme dans le Nouveau Testament," in *DBSup* 8.
35 *The Validity of the Gospel Record*, 141, 161.
36 *The Formation of the Gospel Tradition*, 38.

created, which were then added *to* the tradition.[37] These scholars fail to make clear whether the tradition process is supposed to have had some means of accepting altered and expanded (peshered) sayings *back* into the tradition and distinguishing these from sayings created *de novo,* which it refused to accept, or whether Christian prophets themselves are supposed to have expressed their oracles only in the form of modified traditional sayings. This only illustrates that, for the most part, generalizations have been made on all sides of the discussion without the issues having been focused sharply enough to facilitate clear debate. While there is presently no consensus about the nature of the traditioning process and the relation of Christian prophets to it, if any, some things relevant to our present study may be confidently stated:

1. While the spectrum of opinion on the issue is wide, even the view that sees the tradition as most rigidly controlled still allows for the possibility of prophetic expansion, as indicated in the discussion of Riesenfeld, Gerhardsson, and Riesner above.

2. *All parties in the debate still tend to see the material too much through post-Markan eyes. It was Mark who first put the units of sayings material into a firm pre-Easter framework as an element in his creation of the Gospel form.* Thus Neugebauer's protest that words of the risen Jesus would not have been confused with words of the historical Jesus because the genres "Gospel" and "apocalypse" are essentially different is well taken but anachronistic.[38] Prior to Mark's creation of a comprehensive narrative framework for the sayings, they circulated and were proclaimed and heard as "sayings of Jesus," but Jesus was both the Jesus "back there" in history and the Jesus "up there" in heaven who was present and addressed his church through Christian prophets. If we want to see how the "sayings of the Lord" were proclaimed and heard in pre-Markan Christianity, our only sources are Q and Paul. Of our New Testament documents, only the letters of Paul let us see directly how the tradition of Jesus' words was handled in (at least one stream of) pre-Markan Christianity. This must be done on the basis of Pauline usage as a whole, not by the citing of isolated texts.

3. *Nothing is settled by appealing to 1 Corinthians 7:10–40.* This is the favorite proof-text in support of the view that the early church kept the historical tradition of Jesus' words and the post-Easter revelations strictly separate. A typical comment is from Scott: "A line was drawn from the first between the interpretations given by the Spirit and . . . the tradition

---

37 E.g., David Hill in the works cited above, and James D. G. Dunn, *Jesus and the Spirit,* and "Prophetic 'I-Sayings' and the Jesus Tradition: The Importance of Testing Prophetic Utterances Within Early Christianity."

38 Neugebauer's objection in "Geistsprüche und Jesuslogien" goes back as far as Dibelius (see above) and has been repeated most recently by Riesner, *Jesus als Lehrer,* 9.

which had been received from the Lord Jesus. . . . This was the position of Paul, and it was shared, we may be sure, by the whole church."[39] On the other hand, some scholars argue that all the sayings referred to in 1 Corinthians 7 are from the risen Lord, not from the historical Jesus.[40] David Dungan presents a curiously mixed view. After insisting that it is Paul who inserts the qualifying clause into the midst of the traditional saying in verse 11a, he continues: "It is most interesting to observe Paul's scrupulous concern with the difference between *halakoth* of the Lord and his own, his conservatism as to 'expanding' existing sayings of the Lord to fit new situations."[41]

Further discussion of the bearing of this text on the relation between Christian prophecy and the Gospel tradition should keep in mind:

(a) There is no consensus on the extent to which, if at all, Paul understands himself to be "quoting" a traditional saying of the historical Jesus.[42] (b) There is no agreement on how Paul sees this text—as a word of a past authority figure, as the exalted Lord speaking through a traditional saying, or as a combination of these. (c) The relation of the traditional element to the element added by Paul remains unclear. (d) *Especially* the extent to which we can generalize from this text to the purported practice of "the early church" in maintaining a strict separation between traditional and prophetic words is minimal. Who would be willing to generalize from Paul's (lack of) treatment of the miracle stories about Jesus to "the practice of the early church"?

4. A more illuminating example is 1 Thessalonians 4:15–17. Although what we have here is most likely an oracle of a Christian prophet, some would see it as—in Paul's view, and/or in actuality—a pre-Easter saying of Jesus. But that the matter is even debated should indicate the ambiguity of whether any given isolated dominical saying is even purportedly pre- or post-Easter. On the other hand, when it is sometimes asserted that sayings such as 1 Corinthians 7:10; 9:14; and 11:24–25, usually assumed to have been understood by Paul as from the pre-Easter Jesus, were in fact understood by him as revelations of the exalted Lord illustrates the same point: in the early decades of the church isolated sayings of the Lord were not always clearly identified as to their alleged point of origin. It may be that Mark, for his own good reasons to be discussed later in this book, first forced this issue upon us. But if we would see the matter as it was in the period with which we are concerned and

---

39 Scott, *Validity*, 73. The argument is repeated most recently by Riesner, *Jesus als Lehrer*, 11.

40 E.g., Werner Kramer, *Christ, Lord, Son of God,* SBT (Naperville, Ill.: Alec R. Allenson, 1966), 160; Ernst Benz, *Paulus als Visionär*, 37, 113.

41 *Sayings of Jesus*, 100.

42 See also Sato, *Q und Prophetie*, 8.

hear the sayings of Jesus as they were heard in the first four decades of the church's life, we must learn to bracket out the necessity of immediately trying to hear a saying in *either* a pre-Easter *or* a post-Easter frame of reference, for this imposes an alien categorization on the materials. *Any new attempt to deal with the problem of Christian prophecy and the Gospel tradition must be explicitly concerned with the relation of prophets to the tradition process.*

The Character of the Prophetic Phenomenon

A third issue that has emerged from the debate of the last generation concerns the relation of the specific phenomenon of Christian prophecy to the general presence of the Spirit in earliest Christianity. The Bultmann school is charged with a vagueness in its view of what prophecy was and how it functioned. Gerhard Delling insists that we should distinguish carefully between prophetic revelations through the *Spirit,* which he finds in, e.g., 1 Corinthians 15:51 and Romans 11:25, and words of the risen *Jesus,* which purportedly could blend in with the Gospel tradition. As we shall see, it is quite true that there are prophetic revelations not in the form of first person statements in which Jesus is the speaker, and such oracles are not likely to be taken as sayings of either the pre- or post-Easter Jesus. Delling insists that research attend to such distinctions as are made in Acts, which distinguishes the Spirit's addressing someone and utterances of the glorified Lord. But it should be noted that the distinction between the Spirit and the risen Jesus is blurred in both Paul (e.g., 2 Cor. 3:18; Rom. 8:9–10) and Acts (e.g., 2:33–34; 16:6–10), as well as in our clearest example of Christian prophecy (Rev. 2:1, see also 2:7; Rev. 2:8, see also 2:11; and each of the messages to the seven churches in chapters 2–3).

The issue may be illustrated by one final point: Neugebauer argues that in the first-century Palestinian situation prophetic material was never anonymous but was always handed on under the name of its author, so that the nature of prophetic speech precludes its being confused with the traditional words of the historical Jesus. Though, as we shall see, Neugebauer's argument points to an important issue, the assertion itself is false for two reasons:

1. While it is true that prophetic *books* always circulated under the name of a prophet rather than anonymously, this does not mean that all the individual prophetic sayings in the book were from the prophet whose name the book bears, as the prophetic books themselves amply illustrate.[43] More than half of the sayings in "Isaiah," for instance, were not

---

43 Sato, *Q und Prophetie,* 7.

spoken by the historical Isaiah of Jerusalem but by his later disciples. The tradition was loathe to preserve anonymous sayings as anonymous sayings but placed them in a collection bearing the name of the "founder" of the stream of tradition that resulted in the prophetic book. This is analogous to what happened as oracles of Christian prophets were finally contained within the sayings collections and narratives attributed to Jesus.

2. Christian prophetic oracles were not actually anonymous but were often spoken in the name and with the ego of the risen Jesus, and thus were always considered his sayings, not those of the prophet (see chapter 9). The valid and important aspect of Neugebauer's argument is his charge that Bultmann and his students asserted considerable prophetic expansion of the tradition of Jesus' words without making any careful study of what prophetic utterance itself was like in the first century. This was a defect of Bultmann's approach, for he backed into a consideration of Christian prophets without making a study of them *from* which his hypothesis might more legitimately have proceeded. *Any new attempt to deal with the issue of Christian prophecy and the Gospel tradition should define its terms and characterize the prophetic phenomenon as exactly as possible, making historical distinctions.*

The present study investigates the relevant material in early Christian literature to determine what data there are to support the following hypotheses:

1. Christian prophets were present in the early church prior to the writing of the Gospels.

2. They delivered utterances that were heard and transmitted as sayings of the risen Jesus.

3. Such sayings were incorporated into the tradition of sayings of the historical Jesus and with other sayings purporting to be from the pre-Easter Jesus.

4. Some of these sayings of the risen Jesus that found their way into the Gospel tradition may be identified with a fair degree of probability.

5. A history of the interplay between sayings of the risen Jesus and the tradition of Jesus' words can be discerned. Such a history, noting the major moments in the interaction between the traditions of the exalted Lord and the historical Jesus, is important for understanding not only the sayings themselves but also the Gospel forms in which they are now contained.

Much is at stake in the truth of this hypothesis. The nature of the Gospels and how they are to be interpreted in the church are related to how one answers these questions. The answer cannot be given lightly but must be a result of careful step-by-step study. The next steps must include a clear definition of terms (chapter 2); a survey of the prophetic phenomenon in the context of early Christianity (chapter 3); an examination of the variety of ways Christian prophecy is reflected in the early Christian sources themselves (chapter 4); and a discussion of how these sources may be used to bring the picture of early Christian prophets into sharper focus (chapter 5).

PART ONE

THE REDISCOVERY
OF CHRISTIAN
PROPHECY

2

What Is "Christian Prophecy"?

DEVELOPING A WORKING DEFINITION

This discussion has long been plagued by lack of clear definitions. If one is not clear what he or she means by "prophecy" and "prophets," almost any saying or document in Christian history, past or present, can be labeled "prophetic." Modern religious leaders who are suspicious of charismatic phenomena but want to claim the biblical prophets as their heroes can consider the essence of "prophetic" ministry to be championing the cause of the oppressed in the name of social justice, as in Protestant liberalism, or simply identify "prophecy" and "preaching with authority," so that "every real preacher is a prophet,"[1] as in some conservative streams of Protestantism. Antoinette Clark Wire has exposed the modern liberal Protestant tendency to domesticate the Christian prophet, "who turns out to be what we would call a preacher."[2]

The discussion of prophecy in early Christianity has likewise been clouded by unclear definitions. Thus David Hill, though he claims to borrow the definition worked out by the Society of Biblical Literature's Seminar on Early Christian Prophecy,[3] in fact uses the vague phrases "pastoral preaching" and "exhortatory teaching" as his working definition, which allows him to designate Paul's sermon in Acts 13, all of Paul's

---

1 J. W. McGarvey, *Short Essays in Biblical Criticism* (Cincinnati: Standard Publishing Co., 1910), 118.

2 Antoinette Clark Wire, "Prophecy and Women Prophets in Corinth," in *Gospel Origins and Christian Beginnings,* 134–150.

3 This Seminar met annually 1973–77, with M. Eugene Boring as the first chairperson, succeeded by David E. Aune. Its reports are found in the *Society of Biblical Literature Seminar Papers* (Missoula: Scholars Press, 1973–77). The essay on definition is from the 1973 session of the Seminar: M. Eugene Boring, " 'What Are We Looking For?' Toward a Definition of the Term 'Christian Prophet.' "

letters, and the Letter to the Hebrews as "prophecy."[4] Walter Houston's 1973 Oxford dissertation uses "creative manipulator of traditions" as his definition, which allows him to consider Matthew, Mark, and Luke *all* to be prophets![5] Likewise Wayne Grudem's 1978 Cambridge dissertation makes reception and delivery of edifying discourse crucial in his definition, so that "revelation" but not "inspiration" is the sine qua non of prophecy, which means that one could "prophesy" without being aware of the fact.[6]

It is unfortunate that research on early Christian prophecy has proceeded thus far without any generally accepted definition of terms. There is, however, a certain correspondence here to the loose and varied usage of the terms for prophetic phenomena in the Hellenistic world.[7] A glance at the entry on "prophecy" in the standard dictionary of ancient Greek[8] will reveal that in the world into which Christianity was born the terms *prophet, prophecy, prophesy,* and *prophetic* did not function univocally but were used with reference to a variety of figures and functions. "Prophet" was used not only to mean one who speaks for a god and interprets the god's will to human beings but also for the cultic official keepers of the oracle (at Branchidae), for members of the highest order of the priesthood (in Egypt), for herbalists and quack doctors, for the interpreters of the oracles of the *mantis* (Plato, *Timaeus* 72a), and hence derivatively for poets as such (see Titus 1:12, of Epimenides), and then metaphorically of proclaimers in general, including the announcer at the games.

On the other hand "prophet" and related words represented only one set of terms used for the claim to communicate messages from the gods, with other designations such as "seer," *mantis,* and "sibyl" being used in related and overlapping ways. To a limited extent, this is also true of the New Testament itself, where prophetic terminology is not used

---

4 *New Testament Prophecy,* 105, 126, 129, 138, 143–144. See my critique in *JBL* (1981): 300–301.

5 Walter Houston, *New Testament Prophecy and the Gospel Tradition,* 282.

6 Wayne A. Grudem, *The Gift of Prophecy in 1 Corinthians,* 139–144; see his later statements in *The Gift of Prophecy in the New Testament and Today.* In both books Grudem distinguishes two types of prophets in the New Testament, "those with absolute authority of words" and those without it, and laments the fact that New Testament scholars have generally restricted prophecy to the former. The twin concerns of the doctrine of verbal inspiration of Scripture and the importance of the phenomenon of prophecy as a reality in the contemporary church seem to hover in the background of all Grudem's discussion (see *Gift of Prophecy in 1 Corinthians,* 33, 110–113). The prophets of the Old Testament and the Apostles of the New Testament, i.e., the writers of Scripture, were verbally inspired, but the prophets of the New Testament were not, nor, on the model of New Testament prophets, need contemporary church prophets claim verbal inspiration (*The Gift of Prophecy in the New Testament and Today,* 17–114).

7 On this the 1927 comprehensive study by Erich Fascher, *PROPHĒTĒS. Eine sprach- und religionsgeschichtliche Untersuchung,* is still indispensable.

8 Henry George Liddell and Robert Scott, *A Greek-English Lexicon,* rev. ed., eds. Henry Stuart Jones and Roderick McKenzie (Oxford: Clarendon Press, 1953), 1539–1540.

with consistent meanings although the range is not so wide as in the Hellenistic world generally.

This situation makes it imperative that any discussion of early Christian prophecy be prefaced by a definition of terms. This, of course, is no claim to settle in advance what Christian prophecy "really" is. A preliminary definition of terms is simply a necessary step to facilitate communication. In the present study we are concerned to investigate the phenomenon represented by those Christians in the early church who spoke new sayings of Jesus in the name of the risen Lord and their influence on the developing Gospel tradition. The definition needed here, then, should seek to define, in functional terms, this phenomenon with which we are concerned rather than to analyze the usage of a word group in a body of literature. Some studies of early Christian prophecy have been too dominated by the occurrence or nonoccurrence of the word "prophet." It has been assumed that the most viable procedure is to accumulate all the instances of the occurrence of the prophet/prophecy word group, reduce their usages to a least common denominator, and use the result as the definition of "prophet." This procedure is something of a guard against arbitrary definitions, but it is more appropriate to the making of a dictionary than to the study of a phenomenon. Since the phenomenon we wish to study is not always bound to a particular terminology, and vice versa, we must not limit our study to the texts that use the prophet/prophecy vocabulary. Especially to be avoided is the procedure of gathering up all the instances of the prophet/prophecy word group, listing the characteristics of the persons thereby indicated, and using the resulting composite as definitive for the meaning of "prophet."

A functional, phenomenological definition, as proposed here, also excludes the procedure of choosing one source that portrays prophets in a certain manner and using this portrayal as the normative picture of Christian prophecy. David Hill, for instance, lets 1 Corinthians 14 be definitive for what Christian prophecy "really" was and then on this basis raises the question as to whether the Apocalypse should in fact be called Christian prophecy. This would be analogous to using 2 Samuel and 1 Kings as the normative sources from which to derive a definition of "prophet" *(nabi')* and then on this basis questioning whether Jeremiah can in fact be called a prophet. Likewise to be avoided is a definition in terms of the content of the prophetic utterance itself, such as predictive or antiestablishment elements. It may be that there are characteristic items of content that the oracles of early Christian prophets have in common, but this is a judgment that should be withheld prior to resolving the issue of who belongs to the category "prophet."

Similarly, if we wish to examine prophetism as a function and phenomenon in early Christianity, we should not define "prophet" initially in terms of an "office." The relation of prophets to apostles, teachers, and other ministers of the word is a matter that must be discussed as the phenomenon is brought to sharper focus, but it can remain an open question in preliminary definitions. Our initial working definition should, therefore, be brief, simply stating the sine qua non function of the prophet. The following is my initial working definition: *The early Christian prophet was an immediately inspired spokesperson for the risen Jesus, who received intelligible messages that he or she felt impelled to deliver to the Christian community or, as a representative of the community, to the general public.* It was these figures in the early church who might have promulgated oracles that could have been incorporated into the Gospel tradition as sayings of Jesus or who might have influenced the developing tradition in other ways. These are the persons I have in mind in using the word "prophet," whether or not the prophet/prophecy terminology is used of them or by them. In order to be as clear as possible, some terms in this definition need to be elaborated.

CLARIFYING THE TERMS

"Inspiration" may be used in a variety of senses. By "immediately inspired" I intend to indicate that the prophet claims that what he or she is saying or writing represents the present, immediate voice of the deity. No statement about the state of consciousness in which the prophet receives the oracles is intended. Nor is the definition intended to exclude the prophet's utilization of sources, traditional materials, or the reflections of the prophet himself or herself, all of which may be involved in the personal formulation and delivery to the community of what he or she perceives to be directly revealed from the risen Lord.

By using the term "risen Jesus" in the definition, I do not intend to draw any sharp distinction among Christian prophets who portray themselves, or are portrayed, as speaking for God, the risen Jesus, or the Holy Spirit. In early Christianity in general, and particularly in the prophetic experience, these were not always distinguished (Rom. 8:9–10; Rev. 1:1–2; 2:1, 7, etc.). If Revelation is representative of Christian prophecy on this point, "word of the risen Jesus" tended to modulate into and be indistinguishable from "word of God" or "word of the Spirit" (see chapter 4, "Revelation").

The uniqueness and importance of the phrase "spokesperson for the risen Jesus" in our definition will be clarified by the examination of alleged parallels. I offer three examples from the ancient world, one each from the pagan, Jewish, and Christian traditions, and one example of alleged modern parallels.

1. Plutarch refers to "prophets of Epicurus."[9] Fascher indicates that

---

9 *On the Pythian Oracles* c. 7 = 397c (see Fascher, *PROPHĒTĒS*, 21).

not only Epicurus but Plato and other philosophers had groups of "prophets" who carried on their teaching after their death, and suggests: "Since the dead philosopher could be thought of as belonging to the divine world, . . . this expression contains a cultic overtone."[10] Similarly, in discussing the discourses of the Fourth Gospel, B. H. Streeter toys with the idea that Plato's promulgation of discourses that he places in the mouth of his deceased teacher Socrates is something of a parallel to the prophetic phenomenon in the New Testament.[11] But no one, Fascher and Streeter included, would suggest that Plato intended to claim that the recently martyred Socrates was now exalted and speaking to his "prophet" Plato, who communicated the message he thus received in the *Dialogues*. Plato's writing of discourses for Socrates is rather to be seen as a literary phenomenon, his attempt to delineate what Socrates would have said, a development of his teaching on the horizontal level, going back to the inspiration of the historical Socrates and thus properly attributed to him in some sense. The relation of the Pastorals to Paul is thus a better analogy to this than is that of the Fourth Gospel to Jesus. It was an elaboration of the dead teacher's doctrine, not "the word of the exalted Socrates," that was proclaimed by his "prophets."

David Aune discusses the phenomenon that after their death some philosophers occasionally appeared to people in dreams and gave oracles or instruction that was later considered a part of the authentic teaching of the philosopher himself.[12] Aune rightly argues that this is evidence that in the Hellenistic world posthumous oracles could receive the same authority as the teaching delivered during the life of the philosopher and that such sayings could be assimilated to the body of sayings and teaching associated with a particular individual. This is an important observation in regard to the thesis pursued in this book. Aune is also correct, however, in maintaining that this phenomenon is not a parallel to Christian prophets receiving oracles from the risen Jesus since the "oracles" are received in dreams by nonprophetic figures. That is, the phenomenon is an example of the many claims to have received information from the world of the dead in dreams, seances, and such, not an example of prophecy as defined here.

2. Sigmund Mowinckel has argued that a phenomenon similar to Christian prophetism was present in the transmission and expansion of the sayings of the Old Testament prophets. He argues that this is seen especially in the Servant Songs of Second Isaiah, for here, he maintains, is to be found a cultic circle of disciples who met after the sacrificial death of their teacher

---

10 Fascher, *PROPHĒTĒS*, 21, 52.
11 *The Four Gospels: A Study of Origins*, 369–374.
12 *Prophecy in Early Christianity and the Ancient Mediterannean World*, 235–236.

in which the life, death, and saving significance of the Servant would be preached . . . with his resurrection. Here it would be natural to put into the mouth of the Servant words about the promises associated with his call . . . and, as it were, to allow him to appear himself in the prophetic circle and proclaim the conviction which God had given him and was now giving them, that his cause would triumph, and would lead to Israel's conversion, ingathering, and restoration, and to the spread of true religion among all the people. This cultic interpretation enables us to understand the use of the first person in the Second and Third Songs.[13]

Mowinckel contends that "there are other examples in the history of religion of a central figure of this type being introduced as speaking in the first person in a cultic circle," but the examples he gives are all dependent on the Christian tradition.

In response to this, it must first be said that Mowinckel's view as a whole suggests that the relationship of Jesus and the early church has been read back into the Old Testament materials. But even if he is correct in his understanding of the relationship of the disciples of Second Isaiah to their dead teacher, we still do not have a real parallel to early Christian prophetism, for it is inconceivable that the disciples of Second Isaiah would put their dead master—even if "resurrected"—in the place of the deity in the prophetic experience, though this is exactly what happened in the case of Jesus and the early church. To the disciples of Second Isaiah, "the LORD says" (e.g., 49:5) could never mean "our dead and exalted teacher says" but only "Yahweh says," as in the Old Testament prophetic idiom universally. The tradition of Second Isaiah is rather a matter of an imaginative prophetic continuation of the earthly teacher's message in which Yahweh alone is regarded as the agent who inspires the prophets to speak. There is thus no parallel here to the distinctive element in early Christian prophetism.

3. Neither is there a parallel to the Christian prophetic phenomenon in the pseudepigraphical production of literature in the name of a past revered figure, as happened for example in the deutero-Pauline letters. In the Pastorals or Colossians, a figure from the historical past addresses other figures in the historical past, within some fictive there-and-then framework.[14] This is not what happens in Christian prophecy. Early

---

13 Sigmund Mowinckel, *He That Cometh* (Nashville: Abingdon Press, 1954), 152–153; compare *Prophecy and Tradition: The Prophetic Books in the Light of the Study of the Growth and History of the Tradition*, passim, esp. 67–77.

14 This aspect of the issue is neglected in Frank Witt Hughs, *Early Christian Rhetoric and 2 Thessalonians*, 86–89, who thus tends to blur the distinction between pseudepigraphical production of letters in Paul's name and the voice of the exalted Jesus in Christian prophecy. The same is true of Allen Brent, "Pseudonymity and Charisma in the Ministry of the Early Church," who relates the production of pseudonymous letters to the phenomenon

Christianity did produce pseudepigraphical letters in Jesus' name, e.g., the Letters of Jesus to Abgar, king of Edessa.[15] Even if their author wanted to use this literary genre to allow "Jesus" to address his contemporary concerns, the form still exhibits a fictitious Jesus in a fictitious narrative framework addressing other fictitious people of the past. The contemporary reader "overhears" the Jesus in the story addressing others but is not directly addressed by the exalted Lord in his or her own time. There is thus no parallel to Christian prophecy in the Christian pseudepigrapha.

4. The same is true when we turn to alleged modern parallels. Robert R. Hahn suggests that the traditions concerning Hiawatha, the founder of the Iroquois Dekaniwideh cult, came to be distorted in the course of their transmission. In particular, "there was an eventual failure to distinguish between a saying thought to have been received by divine revelation, and words actually spoken by a historical individual."[16] He compares this to the expansion of the Jesus tradition by Christian prophets. But (a) in the case of the Hiawatha tradition, it was a centuries-long process of expansion, while in Christianity it happened immediately and then died out; (b) in early Christianity it was not a matter of "confusing" two strands of tradition its bearers attempted to keep separate; (c) the increments to the Hiawatha tradition were mostly narrative rather than sayings; and (d) unlike early Christianity, there was no prophetic revelatory gestalt in which Hiawatha played the role of the deity. The essential point with regard to all alleged parallels is simply that Christian prophetism presupposes a Christology that is not found elsewhere.

Integral to the definition of Christian prophecy is the phrase "the Christian community." This phrase is intended to distinguish the prophet from the mystic, on the one hand, and the magicians and fortune tellers of whatever sort (even if these were also sometimes called "prophets") who claim to dispense supernatural information to individuals, on the other. Prophecy as here defined is a church phenomenon (see chapter 6). This does not mean that it is necessarily a congregational, cultic phenomenon—this question is to be left open. But it does indicate that the figures who claim our interest in this study have their setting in the life of the Christian community (and that their oracles are related to the life and affairs of that community) rather than being free-lancers who speak to individuals on personal matters. As our definition indicates, this does not

---

of Christian prophecy, as did Kurt Aland, "The Problem of Anonymity and Pseudonymity in the Christian Literature of the First Two Centuries."

15 See Edgar Hennecke and Wilhelm Schneemelcher, eds., *New Testament Apocrypha,* 1:437–444.

16 Robert R. Hahn, "Post-Apostolic Christianity as a Revitalization Movement: Accounting for Innovation in Early Patristic Traditions," 61–62.

mean that prophets spoke only in the cultic setting of Christian worship to insiders who already belonged to the Christian community. We shall see that prophets also addressed the public at large, but they did this not as "inspired" individuals but as representatives of the Christian community who spoke on its behalf as well as in behalf of the risen Jesus. Thus there is not only an indispensable christological aspect to Christian prophecy but a necessary ecclesiological one as well.

Christian prophecy as defined above is also specifically intended to be distinguished from three related phenomena in early Christianity although each of these three is sometimes included in discussions of Christian prophecy:

1. The specific phenomenon of early Christian prophecy is to be distinguished from the general "prophetic" character that the early Spirit-filled Christian community possessed. The matter cannot be settled by appealing to Acts 2:4, 16–21, and claiming that "it is a specific mark of the age of fulfillment that the Spirit does not only lay hold of individuals but that all members of the eschatological community without distinction are called to prophesy."[17] To be sure, it was universally assumed in early Christianity that all Christians possessed the Spirit. There were, in fact, many circles in which the equation prevailing in some settings of early Judaism, "Holy Spirit" = "Spirit of prophecy," had an enduring influence. The prophet in the strict sense is not as sharply marked off from the rest of the community as in the Old Testament and Judaism.

The emergence of such a community, in which every member did have a kind of prophetic potential, does make the identification of prophetic figures in the strict sense more difficult. But there is ample evidence that even those early Christians, such as Paul and Luke, who affirmed that every member of the community was empowered by the Spirit (Acts 2:38, 19:1–7; 1 Cor. 12:3, 13) still did not regard every Christian as a prophet, even though both associate the Spirit with prophecy (Acts 2:17–18; 13:1–2; 19:6; 21:10–11; 1 Thess. 5:19–20; Rom. 12:6; 1 Corinthians 14 throughout, especially v. 37). On the contrary, both Paul and Luke distinguished the general gift of the Spirit from the specific manifestation of prophecy (Acts 13:1; 11:27–28; 15:32; 21:9–11; 1 Cor. 12:29; 14:29).

2. Similarly, the specific phenomenon of early Christian prophecy is to be distinguished from the general phenomenon of the risen Lord's speaking through the sayings of Jesus handed on in the tradition of the church. Since the earliest days of form criticism, it has been rightly urged that the tradition of Jesus' sayings, containing both authentic sayings

---

17 Gerhard Friedrich, *"Prophētēs," TDNT* 6:848–849.

from the historical Jesus and the church formulations circulating in the name of Jesus, was often heard in the early church not as the remembered words of a great figure of the past but as the present word of the exalted Lord. Both Dibelius and Bultmann affirmed this despite their differences on other issues. This would have been true regardless of whether the tradition was repeated by a genuinely prophetic figure or not—it was something inherent in the nature of the tradition when combined with the community's faith in Jesus as the risen Lord.

Christian prophets were not the only members of the early Christian community who expanded the tradition of Jesus' sayings by modifying old sayings and creating new ones. A comparison of the way Jesus' sayings appear in the oldest Gospel, Mark, with Matthew and Luke, will reveal a multitude of redactional modifications and expansions on the part of the later evangelists. We must assume that in the period prior to the oldest Gospel this same type of redactional expansion occurred, and that in the oral period performancial variations and expansions were typical. It was standard practice in biographical and historical works to compose appropriate speeches and place them in the mouth of the protagonist.[18] Likewise Josephus composes long and moving speeches for his heroes, sometimes with no historical kernel at all. The powerful speech of Eleazar addressing the defenders of Masada, for instance, must be entirely the work of Josephus since there was no way he could have had reports of what was said just before the fall of Masada, Eleazar and all his hearers having committed suicide.[19]

In accord with the accepted practice of the times, early Christian teachers and composers did not hesitate to modify and expand the tradition of Jesus' sayings, to allow the Jesus of the narrative to address the readers' situation more directly. Such changes and expansions seemed all the more appropriate in the perspective of the church's faith in Jesus' resurrection—the sayings were not the legacy of a dead rabbi but the continuing voice of the living Lord. But this general contemporizing mode in which the tradition was generally heard in the early church must not be equated with, or confused with, the phenomenon of Christian prophecy as defined above.

3. And, finally, the specific phenomenon of early Christian prophecy is to be distinguished from the general phenomenon of the living Christ who speaks through Christian preaching and testimony. Several New Testament scholars simply identify "prophecy" and "preaching."[20] Enthusiasts for preaching who are suspicious of charismatic phenomena,

---

18 Thucydides 1.22.

19 Josephus, *Jewish War* 7. 323–336.

20 E.g., Heinrich Schlier, "Die Verkündigung im Gottesdienst der Kirche," in *Die Zeit der Kirche*, 259.

and who want to have Paul on their side, are inclined to cite 1 Corinthians 14 as identifying prophecy with any discourse that is intelligible and edifying, i.e., with preaching (see 1 Cor. 14:3–4, 19). They fail to notice that the subject in 1 Corinthians 12–14 as a whole is charismatic speech. Paul is here contending against the Corinthians' too-high valuation of a glossolalia that he regards as individualistic, unintelligible, and disruptive. Over against this, Paul commends charismatic speech that is intelligible and beneficial to the community as a whole, namely prophecy. While prophecy, in contrast to glossolalia, was intelligible and edifying, it does not follow that he considered all intelligible and edifying speech to be prophecy (see chapters 7 and 8). The consensus of New Testament scholarship on Paul's understanding of prophecy is well represented by the words of James D. G. Dunn:

> For Paul prophecy is a word of revelation. It does not denote the delivery of a previously prepared sermon; it is not a word that can be summoned up to order, or a skill that can be learned; it is a spontaneous utterance, a revelation given in words to the prophet to be delivered as it is given (1 Cor. 14:30). At this point Paul stands wholly within the (Hebraic) tradition of prophecy as inspired utterance.[21]

There are several streams of Christian theology that understand preaching in a way sometimes thought to be akin to Christian prophecy.[22] This popular theological conception of preaching is expressed, for example, in Karl Adam's dictum that "Christ speaks in the sermon of every country priest."[23] But this is a theological understanding of the nature of the preaching event and of the text that is heard in the sermon. It moves on another plane than our discussion here, involving other categories than those we are using in dealing with a particular history-of-religions phenomenon in the first few Christian generations. The exponents of this understanding of the nature of the preaching event would affirm that it may happen irrespective of whether the preacher understands himself or herself in prophetic terms as we have defined them above. Indeed, this "prophetic" understanding of the preaching event usually assumes that the preacher's self-understanding is far removed from that of such a prophet and that nothing like "immediate inspiration" is involved.

This means that the Christian minister should not claim to be a Christian prophet in the sense used in this book. The Christian minister

---

21 *Jesus and the Spirit*, 228.

22 Dietrich Bonhoeffer, *Act and Being* (New York: Harper & Row, 1956), 142; Karl Barth, *Church Dogmatics* (Edinburgh: T. & T. Clark 10⌐⌐-69), 1:91, 205–206, 235, 320; Karl Adam, *The Spirit of Catholicism* (New York: Doubleday, 1935), 11–13, 58, 159.

23 Ibid., 22.

has the responsibility inherent in his or her calling to be prophetic in the common sense of that term: to oppose unjust power structures in the name of Christ who is champion of the poor and the oppressed, to proclaim justice and righteousness as the will of God even at the cost of personal sacrifice, to stand against the cultural enslavement of the faith in the name of the living God, to be a voice to the culture rather than an echo of its values. Ministry in the name of Jesus Christ is inherently prophetic in this sense. Every minister has a prophetic vocation in this sense. But that is very different from claiming to be, or aspiring to be, a prophet in the same sense as those immediately inspired spokespersons for the risen Lord of earliest Christianity who spoke in the first person for the risen Christ and whose oracles were sometimes included in the synoptic tradition of Jesus' words. The Sunday morning sermon, however "prophetic" it may be in terms of content, is a different genre from "sayings of the risen Jesus," just as the twentieth-century pastor and the first-century Christian prophet, in the perspective of the historical study of religious phenomena, represent two different types of religious leaders. Just as the modern minister's task is not to be an *apostle* but to be *apostolic,* i.e., to be committed to the apostolic faith rather than to an heretical alternative to it, so the minister's task today is not to be a prophet but to let the canonical prophets of the Old and New Testament be heard in such a way that they address the real world of the contemporary hearer in the confidence that the risen Lord of the church founded on apostles and prophets is able thereby to make his own voice heard.

Yet understanding the phenomenon of Christian prophecy to mean simply preaching has caused some blurring of the lines that separate preaching from prophecy per se. One finds, for example, C. K. Barrett interpreting John 16:8 as referring to "the spirit-inspired utterances of Christian preachers."[24] Should one conclude that Barrett understands this text as referring to Christian prophets as we have defined them or only that the Spirit, in the view of the Fourth Gospel, is active in the normal preaching activity of the church? This latter view has been advocated especially by Bultmann and others in his wake[25] and may be partially responsible for the failure of the majority of Johannine scholars even to consider the possibility that John intends to picture the ministry of Christian prophets (in the strict sense) in his own community (see chapter 4, "The Gospel and Letters of John"). Thus the question of

---

24 *The Gospel According to St. John,* 406.
25 Rudolf Bultmann, *Theology of the New Testament,* 2:88–90; Eduard Schweizer, *"Pneuma," TDNT* 6:443; Siegfried Schulz, *Komposition und Herkunft der johanneischen Reden,* 147.

definition leads to the question of which sources may be used for reconstructing the lineaments of early Christian prophecy.

NARROWING AND SHARPENING THE FOCUS
OF THE INVESTIGATION

Prophecy continued in what became the main stream of the church until the outbreak of the "new prophecy" by Montanus and his followers in the middle of the second century C.E. caused the emerging Catholic church to distance itself from prophetic claims. Our concern here, however, is not to write a comprehensive history of prophetic phenomena for all of early Christianity. Rather, our interest is focused on those prophets in earliest Christianity who may have influenced the tradition of Jesus' sayings that led to the formation of the Gospels.

Assuming that the Q material began to congeal in written form by 50 C.E. and was virtually complete by 70, and that a substantial element of the materials peculiar to Matthew ("M") and Luke ("L") also antedate 70, the only materials in the canonical Gospels later than 70 are the later strata of "M" and "L" of the traditions, the later elements of the Johannine tradition, and the redactional compositions of the evangelists themselves. The events of 70 C.E. in Palestine thus form something of a watershed in the development of Christian prophecy. The first fixation of the materials in writing brought an end to the fluid interplay between traditional sayings and new revelations that had prevailed during the oral period of 30–70. The enclosure of the sayings of Jesus within a narrative framework created or sharpened the distinction between sayings attributed to the pre-Easter Jesus and revelations of the risen Lord. This means that after 70 it would have been more difficult for prophetic oracles to be accepted into the developing canonical tradition of Jesus' words in the written Gospels than before. Further, the war in Judea and the destruction of Jerusalem in 70 tended to precipitate a fixation of the traditions.

Our inquiry has something of a geographical limitation as well. Since our interest is concentrated on the interplay between early Christian prophecy and the developing tradition of Jesus' words, we are interested primarily in those prophets who stood within that tradition of sayings of Jesus that emanated from Palestine and spread from there into the Hellenistic world. By "early Christian prophets," then, I mean Christian prophets in that stream of tradition that emanated from Jesus and the earliest Jesus movements in Palestine, who spoke in Jesus' name in the period 30–90, with most of the prophetic activity with which we are concerned occurring in the first generation after Jesus' death, 30–70.

How can we bring these figures within the range of our historical vision? We would like to have video or audio recordings of an early

Christian worship service in which prophets spoke.[26] Failing that, we would like to have a detailed transcript and description by a trained reporter attempting to preserve and describe the phenomenon for future generations. We would like to have windows through which we could listen and look directly into the world of early Christianity and discern the features of the prophet.

There are no such clear windows constructed for the benefit of later historians. We have no direct sources for those prophets who may have contributed to the Gospel tradition except as their sayings may now be contained in the Gospels as sayings of Jesus. No one in the first two centuries wrote to provide information for the efforts of later historians to reconstruct the history of the early church. What we have are various documents from the Hellenistic and Jewish context from which this history emerged and within which it developed, as well as the Christians' own writings, in which the phenomenon we are seeking to understand is incidentally reflected and refracted as in a prism. If we can know anything at all about early Palestinian Christian prophets, our reconstruction must be based on indirect sources. Used with critical care, these sources may yet allow us to see aspects of this phenomenon. These sources may be divided into sources that reflect the nature of prophecy in the Hellenistic world that formed the context for the church's life and mission, and writings from within the church itself. We will explore each of these in turn.

---

26 We have these for modern Pentecostal services, so that researchers into the meaning of charismatic phenomena in contemporary Christianity have primary data with which to work.

3

Prophecy Before and Alongside the Church

We may legitimately seek illumination on the figure of the early Christian prophet from any material in the Hellenistic world that has significant points of contact with any of the features of prophecy as defined above. Apart from Christian documents, these comprise three categories of materials: Gentile and Jewish prophecy of the Hellenistic period, and the pictures of prophetic phenomena contained in the Hebrew scriptures adopted by the church as its Bible.

PROPHECY IN THE HELLENISTIC GENTILE WORLD

A few members of the early history-of-religions school argued that early Christian prophecy was derived from pre-Christian Hellenistic prophecy,[1] but that argument has been effectively refuted and will not concern us here.[2] Nonetheless, the student of Christian origins cannot proceed as though early Christianity existed in a vacuum. Neither synagogue nor church introduced prophets to the Hellenistic world. The inspired spokesperson for the gods, the oracle giver, the ecstatic mouthpiece for the deity was a familiar figure to the Greco-Roman populace. Many gods could speak through their prophets, of whom Apollo was only one of the more active. There were many shrines where the

---

1 E.g., Hans Leisegang, *Der Heilige Geist. Das Wesen und Werden der mystisch-intuitiven Erkenntnis in der Philosophie und Religion der Griechen*, and *Pneuma Hagion: Der Ursprung des Geistsbegriffs der synoptischen Evangelien aus der griechischen Mystik*.

2 Prior to Leisegang's work, Hermann Gunkel's *Die Wirkungen des heiligen Geistes. Nach der populären Anschauung der apostolischen Zeit und nach der Lehre des Apostels Paulus* had already made a convincing case that earliest Christianity was pneumatic before it ever adapted itself to the wider Hellenistic world. C. K. Barrett later refuted Leisegang point by point in *The Holy Spirit and the Gospel Tradition*.

gods could be consulted by means of the oracle, of which Delphi was only the most famous.

In the Hellenistic culture, prophecy was located within the broad spectrum of devices by which information from the world of the gods was transmitted and received. There was a tradition at least as old as Plato that distinguished *artificiosa divinatio* and *naturalis divinatio*. The former refers to divination by technical means such as the interpretation of dreams and reading the will of the gods from the flight of birds and the livers of sacrificed animals, while the latter refers to communication of a message from the gods by inspired speech, often received in trance, ecstasy, or vision.[3] Greek prophecy was not always ecstatic. The spectrum of prophetic experiences ranged from ecstatic raging through trance-like loss of consciousness to sober declaration of the message from the god. Plutarch describes (*On the Cessation of Oracles* 431d–438e) the Pythia at Delphi as inhaling the vapors from a fissure in the earth, becoming "inspired," and delivering unintelligible utterances that were then translated by the "prophets." The account is now widely considered legendary, but it at least expresses an image of prophecy popular among the masses. In other descriptions, the Pythia became inspired by drinking from the sacred spring and then delivered intelligible oracles herself. Probably different practices occurred at different times and places, even in the history of one oracle center such as Delphi. Plato's description (*Timaeus* 71–72) of the mantic behavior of the agents of revelation and the translation of their utterances into intelligible speech by the prophets has perhaps been too influential in the scholarly assessment of Greek prophecy, causing scholars to think of "Greek" prophecy in only one mode.

Generalizations about prophecy in the Greco-Roman world should be avoided, but in a context where early Christian prophecy is being explored, some features that were often characteristic of Hellenistic prophecy may be noted, with preliminary points of comparison and contrast to prophecy in early Christianity.

1. Prophecy in the Hellenistic world was almost always a response to inquiries in which human beings took the initiative and was subject to manipulation, rather than the result of the spontaneous inspiration by the deity. Based on the texts and analysis in H. W. Parke and D. E. W. Wormell,[4] David Aune calculates that less than 5 percent of the Delphic oracles were spontaneous.[5] Christopher Forbes points out that only one of Aune's twenty-eight instances that comprise his 5 percent is later than the third century B.C.E., which suggests that in the period of early Chris-

---

3 Aune, *Prophecy*, 24 and 349 n.9.
4 *The Delphic Oracle* (Oxford: Oxford University Press, 1956).
5 *Prophecy*, 66.

tianity spontaneous prophecy initiated by the deity was virtually absent from the Hellenistic world.[6]

This is in contrast to the New Testament, where prophecy is at God's initiation. The New Testament knows of only one attempt to determine the will of God by manipulation, the selection of Judas's successor in Acts 1:15–26 by the casting of lots. Nothing comes of Matthias, the one who is chosen by this means, and the incident is cast in the shadow of Pentecost and the gift of the prophetic Spirit that immediately follows in Luke's story. It is a "church" without the Spirit that resorts to such devices. It is not clear whether Luke sees this as representing the practice of Israel, now superseded in the age of the Spirit (cf. Num. 27:21; 1 Sam. 14:41), or a contrast to pagan divination such as the oracle of Herakles, where the will of the gods was learned by casting dice (*Pausanias* 7.25.10).

2. In the Hellenistic world inspired oracular prophecy was often thought to be a phenomenon mostly or entirely limited to the classical past, rather than present experience. In this it was somewhat like the view common in Judaism (see below). But early Christianity experienced the rebirth of the classical, scriptural phenomenon in its own life and worship.

3. Prophecy was a part of the general public cultural scene, available to any interested person. In early Christianity, on the other hand, prophecy was a function of a particular religious community and was directed to a group of insiders.

4. Prophecy was generally directed to the needs and inquiries of individuals, revealing the will of the deity or future information concerning their personal lives. Typical inquiries were "Shall I marry?" and "Shall I lend money?" When the topic had to do with religious concerns, they were typically institutional and cultic, that is, still a matter of public concern. In early Christianity on the other hand, the subject matter typically dealt with the religious mission of the community in the world.

5. Greco-Roman prophecy was typically institutionalized and bound to particular places. But early Christianity had no oracle shrines. Prophecy was related to the congregation and particular persons within it, not to particular sites.

6. Hellenistic prophetic oracles were often intentionally ambiguous. Heraclitus's remark with reference to the Delphic oracle is characteristic: *Oute legei, oute kryptei, alla sēmainei* ("She neither reveals nor conceals but signifies"). But clarity was the hallmark of Christian prophecy (1 Cor. 14:8!).

---

6 Christopher Forbes, "Prophecy and Inspired Speech in Early Christianity and Its Hellenistic Environment," 369.

7. In the Hellenistic world, prophecy was often concerned with the future, that is, the short-range historical "secular" future. Nothing like eschatology was typical for the content of Hellenistic prophecy. Early Christian prophets, as we shall see, operated within the eschatological horizon of God's plan for history and interpreted the present in the light of the ultimate eschatological future.

8. Hellenistic oracles were generally brief and expressed in metrical form. Here, Christian prophecy often has more in common with its Hellenistic context, though revelations of Christian prophets were not necessarily either brief or metrical.

9. Collections of oracles were made and preserved for later generations, who interpreted them with reference to their own situation. This was also the case with Christian prophets, and it is an important prophetic feature with reference to the issue of the relation of Christian prophets to the Gospel tradition.

PROPHECY IN FIRST-CENTURY JUDAISM

The Christian prophets in whom we are interested derive from a Jewish-Christian stream of tradition that began in Galilee and Jerusalem; then spread through Palestine and Syria, with a concentration in Antioch; then spread into the rest of the Hellenistic world. This tradition often made contact with Jewish synagogues and drew its imagery and understanding of prophecy from its roots in the Hebrew scriptures and Palestinian Judaism.[7] The prophetic spirit was alive in the Judaism from which Christianity was born. To be sure, in some circles the dominant view was that prophecy had ended in the time of Ezra or Alexander and would not return until the eschatological age (e.g., *Song of Songs Rab.* 8:9–10; *Numbers Rab.* 15:10; *b. Yoma* 9b, 21b; *t. Sota* 13:2; *Aboth* 1). This dogma has been accepted at face value and generalized to include all first-century Judaism by some Christian scholars (hence the later idea of the "four hundred silent years" between Malachi and John the Baptist).

In actuality, first-century Judaism knew no dearth of prophetic figures, in the sense of persons who claimed to speak the word of God by inspiration. Except for the cases of John the Baptist and Jesus, who were incorporated into the Christian stream of history, the New Testament presents only minimal and indirect evidence for contemporary Jewish prophecy (cf. John 11:51; Acts 13:6). There is massive evidence for first-century Jewish prophecy, however, from the Jewish sources themselves.

---

7 Cf. Gerhard Dautzenberg, *Urchristliche Prophetie,* 303.

The variety and pervasiveness of prophetic phenomena in first-century Judaism have been documented by others,[8] so I will only illustrate with some samples.

Josephus

Josephus (37–c.100 c.e.) wrote our only comprehensive history of the Jewish people during the period of the church's beginnings. Although Josephus sometimes seems to accept the rabbinic theory that prophecy was limited to the biblical period (*Against Apion* 1:40–41), contemporary Jewish prophets in fact play a prominent role in his history (*Jewish War* 1.78–80; 2.112–113; 2.159; 2.259–263; 6.283–288; 6.300–309; *Antiquities* 13.311–313; 14.172–176; 15.3–4; 15.370; 17.345–348; 20.97–99; 20. 168–172). The term "prophet" is used in several senses by Josephus, who applies it to Zealot prophets and Essene seers, as well as to folk prophets among the people, especially during the critical period of the war and siege of Jerusalem 66–70 c.e. The result is that it is not always clear that he refers to persons characterized by the claim to be inspired spokespersons for God.

It is equally clear, however, that he does describe such people, though for his own political purposes he sometimes describes them as "false prophets." Josephus claimed that during the 66–70 war he presented himself to the conquering Roman commander, Vespasian, as a messenger sent from God to announce that he would be the new Roman emperor (*Jewish War* 3.400–402). Without using the word, he thus claimed to be a prophet himself. That the prophetic phenomenon was alive in first-century Judaism is illustrated in Josephus's account of Joshua (Jesus) ben Ananiah, an unlettered peasant who began in 62 constantly to repeat an oracle of doom against the city, and continued despite insults and torture to repeat his oracle until the last days of Jerusalem in 70, when he was killed by a Roman projectile (*Jewish War* 6.300–309).

Philo

Hellenistic Judaism too had prophets in its ranks. Within the extant materials deriving from the Hellenistic synagogue, Philo of Alexandria, a contemporary of Jesus and Paul, offers the most information concerning the prophetic phenomenon. If Philo was aware of the tradition of the cessation of prophecy, he ignored it. Prophecy had been available to every good Israelite and was still available to "every worthy man" (*Who Is the Heir?* 259). Like other Hellenistic Jews (cf., e.g., Wisd. Sol. 7:27),

---

8 E.g., Rudolf Meyer, *"Prophētēs," TDNT* 6:812–828; Joseph Blenkinsopp, "Prophecy and Priesthood in Josephus"; Werner Forster, "Der Heilige Geist im Spätjudentum"; Richard A. Horsley with John S. Hanson, *Bandits, Prophets, and Messiahs,* 247ff.

Philo understood all the religious leaders in Israel's history in prophetic terms and understood prophecy in Hellenistic terms, using the complete range of the vocabulary of Greek ecstatic experience to portray biblical prophets. Moses and Abraham were prophets, and the Pentateuch was a collection of oracles.

Like Josephus, Philo never explicitly calls himself a prophet, but his extraordinarily frequent discussions and detailed descriptions of the prophetic experience strongly suggest that he was describing a contemporary phenomenon he had observed in the synagogue, and indeed that he himself experienced a kind of inspiration akin to the prophetic (cf., e.g., *On the Migration of Abraham* 35; *On the Cherubim* 27; esp. *Who Is the Heir?* 259–260). How representative Philo is of Hellenistic Judaism generally and how his discussions of prophecy in particular are to be interpreted are both disputed points. From the Palestinian Jewish sources we learn that Christianity was born in a context where prophecy was alive; from Philo and other Hellenistic Jewish sources, such as elements of the Sibylline Oracles, we learn that Christianity spread into a Hellenistic world where prophecy existed to some extent before and alongside it in the Hellenistic synagogue.

The Rabbis

The rabbis, too, testify to the fact that the prophetic spirit was alive and well in that Judaism from which Christianity was born. The heavenly voice, called the *Bath Qol* ("daughter of a voice") to distinguish it from the claim to prophetic revelation, was heard even by those rabbis who believed that prophecy had ceased and that the *Bath Qol* could not take precedence over the traditional Halakah. Gamaliel is reported to have received revelations from the Holy Spirit (= the Spirit of Prophecy); Johanan b. Zakkai prophesied to Vespasian that he would become emperor; and other rabbis gave inspired predictions of mundane events in the short range future. Though by no means a major element in rabbinic religious experience, a significant number of prophetic phenomena may be documented even in those circles where the dogma of the end of prophecy might be expected to have been most influential.

Qumran and Other Apocalyptic Groups

The dogma of the end of prophecy with Ezra seems to have been less influential outside rabbinic circles. Since prophetic phenomena occur, despite the dogma, even among the rabbis, we should not be surprised to find an abundance of evidence for prophets and prophecy among the Zealots, Essenes, and other apocalyptically oriented groups, as well as in first-century Jewish folk religion in general (though conspicuously absent among the Sadduccees). Ulrich Müller has convincingly argued that it was the prophetic circles behind the production of some Jewish apocalypses that kept alive Old Testament prophetic forms, which were then taken over by early Christian prophets.[9]

Qumran illustrates the presence of prophecy in one apocalyptic Jewish fringe group that believed it lived in the last days within which the gift of prophecy had been renewed. The Teacher of Righteousness functioned as a prophet. The presence of prophecy at Qumran has been denied because the word *nabi'* ("prophet") was never applied to the Teacher or anyone else in the sect, or because the community was so oriented to rigid structure, study of Scripture, and keeping of the Law that the prophetic spirit could find no place. Each of these objections is wide of the mark. The former objection simply illustrates the fallacy of binding the phenomenon of prophecy to a particular vocabulary. The absence of the word *nabi'* is not due to the absence of prophecy but to the theology of the sect that reserved the term exclusively for the prophets of scripture and for the eschatological prophet yet to come. The latter objection presupposes that prophecy can only exist in the absence of structured authority, an assumption not borne out by our sources. The Qumran community manifests a combination of ardor and order, charismatic immediacy and organizational rigidity, not unlike some early Christian communities.

The Teacher of Righteousness is a first-century Jewish prophet analogous to an early Christian prophet in our definition. The Habakkuk Commentary portrays him as one who speaks from the mouth of God (*1QpHab* 2:2–3), who is taught by God himself, who has poured out the divine Spirit upon him (*1QpHab* 7:4–7). In the Qumran Psalms (1QH) "the most distinctive individual element is the consciousness of having received a divine revelation," even according to Millar Burrows, who (because the *word* is not found!) regards prophecy as absent from Qumran.[10] Although the Teacher's oracles derive from the interpretation of scripture, they are not seen as an "uninspired" comment, however correct, upon an "inspired" text, but as themselves the word of God to and about the present. Thus Gerd Jeremias translates 1QH 2:2, "What comes out of his mouth is the word of God."[11] The Teacher's charismatic enlightenment obviously results in a message that must be shared with the community.

---

9 *Prophetie und Predigt im Neuen Testament. Formgeschichtliche Untersuchungen zur urchristliche Prophetie.*

10 Millar Burrows, *More Light on the Dead Sea Scrolls* (New York: Viking Press, 1958), 381. Gerd Jeremias offers an extensive rationale and evidence for the prophetic character of the Teacher of Righteousness in *Der Lehrer der Gerechtigkeit*. Wayne Grudem rejects this identification and gives supporting bibliography in *The Gift of Prophecy in First Corinthians*, 23, but rightly sees it is a matter of definition. The Teacher qualifies as a prophet according to my definition.

11 *Lehrer der Gerechtigkeit*, 81.

We may regard the Qumran materials as having originated within a community that experienced the reality of prophecy, a community in the same locale as and contemporary with early Christianity. In particular, we may regard the writings of the Teacher of Righteousness as those of a prophet. As in early Christianity, prophecy was related to the interpretation of the scripture and to the eschatological theology of the community.

John the Baptist

The first prophet described in the New Testament is John the Baptist, also mentioned in Josephus, though Josephus does not call him a prophet (*Antiquities* 18:116–119). John's career was contemporary with, and in some respects like, that of Jesus: he was a popular charismatic figure who created eschatological excitement, was alienated from conventional culture, was critical of the established authorities and suffered death at their hands, and had a community of disciples that continued to revere him after his death (Mark 6:17–29 par. 9:11–13 par. Luke 1:5–80; 3:2–20 par.; Luke 7:18–35 par.; John 1:19–36; Acts 19:1–7). As a result, the Christian tradition, which could not ignore him, was at pains to fit him into a Christian understanding of the founding events and to show his subordination to Jesus.

This means that the portrait of the historical John cannot be read off the surface of the New Testament text as an instance of first-century Jewish prophecy that we can directly observe but must be disentangled from the later layers of Christian interpretation. Some early Christians came to terms with John by interpreting him as Elijah, understood as the forerunner of the Messiah (Matt. 17:9–13, but contrast John 1:21). It is thus difficult to determine, for example, if John's strange dress is historical reminiscence or the later effort to describe him as Elijah (compare Mark 1:6 and 2 Kings 1:8). Luke in particular is intent on describing John as belonging to the prophets of Israel described in the Hebrew Bible (3:10–14, peculiar to Luke).

Still, it is clear that John was a prophet conscious of a direct call by God, who called for repentance on the basis of the eschatological judgment in the near future (Luke 3:7–9 par.). John's baptism could well be understood in the category of the symbolic actions of the prophets. He expected an eschatological "mighty one" who would execute the fiery baptism of God's judgment on those who had not received his baptism with water as the sign and seal of their repentance. John is thus pictured in the New Testament as belonging to the prophetic line of biblical prophets but as "more than a prophet," i.e., the eschatological prophet who serves as the immediate forerunner and herald of the final act of God's saving history (Luke 7:26 par.).

Jesus of Nazareth

All four canonical Gospels picture Jesus as a prophet. He is regarded as a prophet not only in the eyes of the people and his accusers (Matt. 16:14; 21:11, cf. 26:68; Mark 6:15; 8:28; 14:65; Luke 7:16; 9:8, 19; John 4:19; 9:17), but, in one of the few sayings preserved in all four Gospels, he applies the proverb of the prophet rejected in his native land to himself (Matt. 13:57; Mark 6:4; Luke 4:24, cf. 13:33; John 4:44). Moreover, Jesus is pictured as receiving a vision at the beginning of his ministry corresponding to a prophet's call (Mark 1:10–11; cf. Isa. 6:1–10, and the role that 6:9–10 plays in the Gospel's accounts of Jesus' ministry, Mark 4:10–12 par.). The Spirit that he received in baptism would be understood in a Jewish context as the Spirit that made one a prophet. When challenged on his claim to authority, Jesus is portrayed by Mark as appealing to his baptism by John, i.e., as understanding it as his call and authorization to act in God's stead with prophetic authority (Mark 11:27–33 par.).

The Jesus of the Gospels speaks in behalf of God in a way that seems blasphemous to his opponents (Mark 2:5–7 par.; John 5:30). He claims to possess the Holy Spirit (= the Spirit of prophecy) and pronounces those who resist it to be guilty of eternal sin (Mark 3:28–29). He does not use the characteristic prophetic legitimization formula of the biblical prophets, "Thus says the Lord . . ." but speaks with the immediate authority of a divine commission, expressing his prophetic self-consciousness in formulae such as "Amen [truly], I say to you" and "I have come to . . . ," even as he uses prophetic forms such as beatitudes and pronouncements of judgment (e.g., Mark 3:28–29 par.; Matt. 5:3–11 par.; Luke 6:24–26). Jesus' authority is not the derived authority of the scribe but the immediate authority of the inspired prophet (Mark 1:22; Matt. 7:29).

Though the Jesus of the Gospels never explicitly says anything like "I am a prophet," he clearly places himself in the prophetic line (Matt. 23:37–39; Luke 13:34–35). He performs symbolic actions in the manner of the prophets of Israel such as the messianic entry into Jerusalem (Mark 11:1–11 par.), the cursing of the fig tree (Mark 11:12–14), and the cleansing of the temple (Mark 11:15–17). Jesus is described as having apocalyptic visions of the fall of Satan (Luke 10:18) and even of delivering prolonged apocalyptic discourses (Mark 13:3–37; Luke 17:20–37).

First-century Judaism's understanding that the true prophet was characterized by persecution and death may have provided the context or key for Jesus' understanding of his own destiny in prophetic terms, as reflected in the passion predictions in the Gospels (Mark 8:31; 9:31; 10:32–33). For Luke in particular, "prophet" is not a mistaken, preliminary, or minor category, but a major category of his christological thought: Jesus is indeed the eschatological prophet promised in the scriptures (Luke 24:19; Acts 3:22–23, 7:37; cf. Deut. 18:15–18), who specifically identifies the Spirit that empowers him as the prophetic Spirit of Isaiah 61:1–2 (Luke 4:16–21).

Yet if in the case of John the Baptist the historical figure of the prophet John is covered with layers of Christian interpretation, this is all the more true in the case of Jesus. Was the historical Jesus a prophet, or does "prophet," i.e., "eschatological prophet," the final messenger from God before the End, belong to the early layers of Christian interpretation of the significance of Jesus? This is a complex issue that properly belongs in the large and growing body of research on the historical Jesus. Our concern in this study is with the phenomenon of prophecy in the early church, for which Jesus, John, and first-century Jewish prophets formed part of the immediate background and context.

Here I can only state that Christian scholars of the most varied theological positions have generally agreed that the New Testament's picture of Jesus as prophet is historical bedrock. Conservative and evangelical Christians, while affirming the "higher" christological titles as more important in interpreting the theological significance of Jesus, have nonetheless concurred in asserting that the historical Jesus was also a prophet.[12] Liberal theologians, while considering other titles such as "Son of God" to be later church interpretation, have celebrated Jesus as the prophet of social justice.[13] Rudolf Bultmann's agnosticism about the historical Jesus did not extend to his doubting that Jesus was a prophet,[14] and his students who returned to the ("new") quest of the historical Jesus found "prophet" to be the key category.[15] Some recent American study of the sayings tradition has suggested or argued that the prophetic picture of Jesus was a church construction, and that Jesus was in actuality more like a Cynic sage than a Jewish prophet,[16] but the majority of scholarship would see two prophetic figures, John and Jesus, at the beginnings of the Christian movement.

---

12 Joachim Jeremias, *New Testament Theology*, vol. 1: *The Proclamation of Jesus*, 42–75; 250–257; James D. G. Dunn, *Christology in the Making*, 137; *Jesus and the Spirit*, 44–61.

13 Walter Rauschenbusch, *A Theology for the Social Gospel* (Nashville: Abingdon Press, 1917); Harry Emerson Fosdick, *The Modern Use of the Bible* (New York: Macmillan Co., 1924); Morton Scott Enslin, *The Prophet from Nazareth* (New York: McGraw-Hill Publishing Co., 1961).

14 *Jesus and the Word*, 26, 121–122; *Theology of the New Testament*, 1:20, 27.

15 Günther Bornkamm, *Jesus of Nazareth*, 45; Hans Conzelmann, *Jesus*, 49–50.

16 Robinson, "The Jesus Movement in Galilee," 4–5; John S. Kloppenborg, *The Formation of Q*; Burton L. Mack, *A Myth of Innocence*; John Dominic Crossan, *In Fragments: The Aphorisms of Jesus*.

PROPHECY IN THE BIBLE OF
THE EARLY CHURCH

When the church adopted the Hebrew scriptures as its own, it also adopted an understanding of the nature of prophecy and pictures that characterize the "true" prophet. It is thus clear that the Old Testament as used in early Christianity would often have had an influence on how prophecy was thought of, especially in those circles that understood the gift of prophecy present in the church as the eschatological outpouring of that same prophetic spirit that had inspired the Old Testament prophets. As will be apparent below, there are many points of contact between prophecy as it is understood in the Old Testament and as it is expressed in early Christianity. It is too simple, however, to claim that Christian prophecy is "biblical," "Israelite," or "Jewish," in contrast to "Greek" or "Hellenistic," for both these streams were complex realities, as was early Christian prophecy, and the streams did not always flow in separate channels.

The three categories of materials discussed above have been introduced as the relevant background and context for understanding early Christian prophecy, not because they may be used as direct sources in the reconstruction of its characteristics. Christian prophecy must be portrayed from Christian sources. This is not to dismiss history-of-religions study out of hand but to insist that we should not first form our ideas of prophecy and prophets from non-New Testament or non-Christian sources, then impose these ideas on Christian materials. Christian prophecy as defined above is sufficiently different from anything outside the church as to exclude our trying to understand it as *simply* a subheading under prophecy in the Hellenistic world in general. In formulating our characterization, we need to be aware of materials from and about prophets in the Old Testament, Judaism, and Hellenism, as these circulated in the Hellenistic world. Christian prophecy is not utterly discontinuous from non-Christian prophecy. After the main contours of the picture of early Christian prophets have been drawn on the basis of Christian sources, non-Christian materials may be used in a secondary and analogical way for illustration and illumination.

4

Prophecy in the Prism
of Early Christian
Literature

CHRISTIAN PROPHECY IN PAUL AND
THE PAULINE CHURCHES

Paul's letters are valuable sources for the reconstruction of early Christian prophecy for five reasons: (1) They are our *earliest* Christian documents, containing our earliest references to Christian prophecy. (2) They contain our only first-hand observer's *description* of prophecy in the Pauline churches—seen and interpreted, to be sure, through Paul's own understanding of the nature of prophecy. (3) They contain our only canonical *discussion* of prophecy. (4) They portray Paul's *own* prophetic self-understanding. (5) They contain *prophetic formulae and oracles* from Paul himself and other early Christian prophets.

Our earliest New Testament document concludes with a Pauline exhortation not to despise prophesying, 1 Thessalonians 5:19–21. Paul appears as the advocate of the prophetic gift. Brief as it is, this instruction of Paul is important in that it shows that prophecy is already present at the earliest point at which we can observe the Hellenistic church, indeed, that it has already undergone a certain development, the stages of which can be charted: initial appearance of prophecy at Thessalonica, some sort of problem or excesses that caused at least some of the Thessalonians to reject or disdain it, and Paul's promotion of their reevaluation and critical acceptance of it. But, here as elsewhere, Paul reports nothing concrete about the content of the preaching of prophets.

Our most extensive discussion of Christian prophecy is found in 1 Corinthians 12–14. If one attempts to filter out what can be learned about prophecy in the Corinthian congregation from the comments Paul makes from his own perspective, the following items emerge:

- Prophecy occurred at Corinth as one item of a cluster of extraordinary religious phenomena, as the whole discussion makes clear.
- The Corinthians' term for these phenomena seems to have been *pneumatika* ("spiritual" [things]), for which Paul substituted his own term, *charismata* ("gifts"), which expressed his theological understanding of these phenomena as the gift of the deity for the benefit of the church, rather than merely a fascinating eruption of the spirit world into human experience.
- The Corinthians had experienced analogous religious spiritual phenomena prior to their becoming Christians (12:2) and were inclined to understand their Christian experience in terms of their pre-Christian history.
- In the worship setting, someone claiming to speak in the power of the Spirit had said "Jesus be cursed" (12:3), which had given rise to a pointed question to Paul concerning what could count as authentic speech inspired by the Spirit.
- The Corinthians, in contrast to Paul, understood the spiritual phenomena individualistically (12:7).
- Prophecy was a kind of inspired speech distinct from glossolalia on the one hand, in that it was expressed in intelligible language and glossolalia was not (14:2–3), and from the "word of knowledge" and "word of wisdom" on the other, in that it was more directly inspired and less like ordinary human speech (12:8–10). On the scale of how "ecstatic" it is, prophecy thus stands between glossolalia and the word of wisdom and knowledge. There was some distinction among the varieties of charismatic speech phenomena, both for the Corinthians and for Paul. Yet the terminology is not exactly precise. In 14:6, for example, prophecy is distinguished from "revelation" just as it is from "teaching" and "knowledge." But in 14:26 and 30–31, "revelation" and "prophecy" seem to be identified.
- Though every member of the congregation, women as well as men (11:5), has the potential to exercise the prophetic function (14:5, 24), prophets are a distinct, identifiable group within the congregation (12:10). The group of actual prophets includes both men and women.[1]

---

1 1 Corinthians 11:5 makes it clear that the prophetic group at Corinth included women. Paul's typical generic use of the masculine pronoun throughout chapter 14 (3, 4, 37, 38) obviously includes women. The halfway measures of the Revised English Bible's effort to express this in more inclusive language actually obscures Paul's inclusiveness: ". . . if anyone prophesies, he is talking to men and women" (14:3). The New Revised Standard Version preserves Paul's inclusiveness on this point. 1 Corinthians 14:34–35 is widely considered a later interpolation representing the same stream of tradition as 1 Timothy 2:11–12.

- Prophecy is associated with "knowing mysteries" (13:2).
- Prophecy as speech inspired by the spirit was considered by the Corinthians a kind of involuntary possession (14:26–33).

As in 1 Thessalonians, Paul's statements have a polemical tone, again revealing Paul as the advocate of prophecy, this time over against an inappropriately high valuation of glossolalia at the expense of prophecy. There is little indication of the content of the Corinthian prophets' oracles to be gleaned from this passage. Its primary value for our reconstruction is rather that it permits us to examine Paul's own extended discussion of the nature of Christian prophecy, portraying how *he* understood it.

The brief reference to prophecy in Romans 12:3–8 is valuable in that it is not addressed to a situation where prophecy is, in Paul's estimation, misunderstood or devalued. Rather than polemics, a fundamental assumption of Paul's comes to expression here, namely that wherever there is a church, the Holy Spirit is at work, and wherever the Spirit is, there is to be found a (the?) principal manifestation of the Spirit, the gift of prophecy. Indeed, prophecy is the only constant in Paul's "lists" of charismatic gifts (1 Cor. 12:8–11, 28–30; 13:1–2; Rom. 12:6–8) and, when the gifts are "ranked," prophecy appears second only to apostleship or, from another point of view, love. These texts from three different letters, taken together, show that Paul is not forced into discussing prophecy by its occurrence in his churches, and that for him it is not a "problem" to be dealt with but a constituent part of church life.

Is Paul himself to be numbered among the early Christian prophets? The importance of definition becomes apparent once more in determining how this question is to be answered. If prophecy is defined functionally as above, then Paul is a prophet, for he is an immediately inspired spokesman for the risen Lord, who receives revelations that he is impelled to deliver to the Christian community (cf., e.g., 1 Cor. 2:13; 5:3–4; 7:40 [and, in the light of this "postscript," cf. the preceding verses]; 14:6, 37; 2 Cor. 2:17; 12:1–9, 19; 13:3; Gal. 1:12; 2:2; 1 Thess. 2:13; 4:1–2, 15–17).

To be sure, Paul never calls himself "prophet," nor is he called such by others. However, it is function, not label, that is important. The absence of the title in Paul's case is accounted for by his insistence that he is an "apostle." But the figure of the apostle in the early church, and especially in Paul, is modeled largely on the role of the prophet in Israel as God's representative, who has been called and commissioned by God himself. Paul's account of his call in Galatians 1:15–16 is replete with prophetic allusions and shows that he understands himself in the succession of prophets. "Apostle" is frequently paralleled by "servant," the meaning of which, when Paul uses it of himself, extends beyond its general meaning in reference to all Christians and expresses his claim to the same office as that held by those Old Testament "servants of God," the prophets. Further, Paul does not use "apostle" in the sense of one charismatic gift among many—not even the chief one—but as an office that comprehends the other charismatic gifts, including prophecy, in itself. As an apostle he speaks in tongues (1 Cor. 14:6, 18) and works miracles (2 Cor. 12:12; Gal. 3:5); as an apostle he can and does prophesy (1 Cor. 14:6; 1 Thess. 4:15–17). Paul Minear has made an extensive case that for Paul the apostolic office was grounded on the prophetic gift.[2]

The fact that Paul was a prophet does not mean, however, that Paul's letters are to be seen en bloc as Christian prophecy. It is true that a general prophetic standpoint characterizes all of Paul's preaching and writing. It is the word of the crucified and risen Jesus that comes to speech in Paul's writings. But this hardly means that material from Paul's letters may be quoted indiscriminately as examples of early Christian prophecy. Rather, we must sort out the variety of ways in which the prophetic nature of Paul's ministry has impressed itself upon his letters. There are principally three of these.

1. Paul's prophetic self-understanding is occasionally reflected in his letters only incidentally, by his vocabulary, manner of expression, and choice of materials. Just as a scribe or priest will incidentally adopt a scribal or priestly style and use scribal or priestly materials, even when not dealing with scribal or priestly lore, so Paul the prophet may reflect his prophetic viewpoint in those passages where he is neither discussing prophecy, nor quoting prophetic revelations per se. For example, 1 Thessalonians 4:7–9, a passage of general parenesis, has a number of words and concepts particularly appropriate to prophetic ministry: the note of "solemn forewarning," the idea of divine calling, the idea that to reject the warning is not simply to reject the human messenger but to reject the God who sent him, the reference to the Holy (= prophetic) Spirit, the idea that the hearers have no need to be instructed because they are all "taught by God." In 1 Corinthians 4:1, in describing himself as among the "servants of Christ and stewards of the mysteries of God," Paul incidentally gives a description of Christian prophets. The unusual use of "hearing"—Greek *akoē* (in Gal. 3:2, 5 and Rom. 10:17–18)—for the prophetic message, meaning the same as *kērygma*, is best understood as a technical term of prophetic origin. The Romans passage has additional prophetic overtones: (a) "the message that is preached comes from the word of Christ" (JB), reading "of Christ" with the best MSS and taking it as at least a *semi-subjective* genitive; (b) the prophetic connotation of the word for "voice," *phthongos* (cf. the cognate forms *phthengomai* in Acts

---

2 Paul S. Minear, *New Testament Apocalyptic*, 102.

4:18, and *apophthengomai* in Acts 2:14; 26:25); (c) and the general thrust of the passage to the effect that people do not take the preaching task on themselves but are *sent*. All these are expressions of the prophetic point of view. The capital illustration of this kind of material in Paul is 1 Corinthians 2:6–16, which is often regarded as an expression of prophetic consciousness. Although these verses are not a prophetic oracle per se, their subject and background is the prophetic revelation that lives in Paul's mission.

2. A second, concrete way in which Paul's prophetic self-understanding has impressed itself on his letters is found in the number of prophetic forms and formulae that Paul uses even when he is not quoting a prophetic oracle. Extensive sections of his writings sometimes seem to be shaped, consciously or unconsciously, by forms that have their home in prophetic speech. A comprehensive and detailed study of this aspect of Paul's writing style has appeared in a monograph by Ulrich Müller.[3] Müller's argument is as follows: Paul was a prophet, acquainted with prophetic speech in the congregation. He did not write his letters but spoke them orally, bringing his congregation before his mind's eye as he spoke. One would therefore expect Paul's oral style of prophetic address to influence the form and style of his letters. This is confirmed when we find prophetic formulae in his letters, formulae that are recognized as prophetic because of their occurrence in the Old Testament, in Jewish prophecy, and in Christian prophecy as we otherwise know it.

Müller is careful to delineate the criteria by which he picks out prophetic elements in Paul's letters, a kind of methodological care almost unknown in discussions of Christian prophecy. These criteria are: (a) introductory and authorization formulae, (b) function and content, i.e., material that represents a divine decision to be delivered to the community, (c) traditional speech forms of prophets (Old Testament, Jewish, Christian), (d) the congruency of the text in question with our picture of early Christian prophecy as we otherwise know it, (e) the congruency of the text with oral prophetic speech patterns, (f) a sudden departure from the literary style of the context. Müller's use of these criteria shows how pervasive prophetic speech was in Paul's letters, including both prophetic oracles and the incidental fragments of prophetic forms that are not a part of a prophetic oracle per se.

3. Most valuable of all the types of prophetic material that may be isolated in Paul's letters are those passages where we probably have the inspired revelations of Paul himself or of some other early Christian prophet. The list of oracles claimed by various scholars to be prophetic that can be gleaned from the literature on Paul is rather extensive: Ro-

---

3 *Prophetie und Predigt.*

mans 8:19–22; 11:25–26, 31–32; 13:11–14; 16:17–20; 1 Corinthians 3:17; 7:10, 29–31; 11:23–25; 12:3; 13:13; 14:38; 15:20–29, 51–52; 16:22; 2 Corinthians 5:20–21; 11:13–15; 12:9; Galatians 1:9–10; 5:21b; Philippians 2:6–11; 3:17–4:1; 1 Thessalonians 2:15–16; 3:4; 4:2–6, 15–17; 5:1–11 (2 Thess. 2:3–12; 3:6, 10, 12). Although many of these verses do bear certain marks of Christian prophecy as we will characterize it below and express something of Paul's prophetic self-consciousness, in most instances a convincing case has not been made for the verses concerned being in fact the oracle of some Christian prophet. Thus most of these passages would seem rather to belong to our categories (a) and (b) above. There are three passages, however, that have repeatedly been acknowledged as prophetic oracles on the basis of form, style, and content: Romans 11:25–26, 1 Corinthians 15:51–52 and 1 Thessalonians 4:15–17.

Paul's prophetism was once widely regarded as being of a piece with Hellenistic prophecy generally. More recent study has correctly observed that Paul's understanding of prophecy is not simply a reflection of prophetic phenomena as experienced in his churches but stands in tension with it. Already in 1 Thessalonians 5:19–20, but especially in the running debate of 1 Corinthians 12–14, Paul is exalting a kind of prophecy that he advocates over against an understanding of prophecy in his churches. The criticism of Paul by his opponents in 2 Corinthians 10:10; 11:6 probably represents their charge that he lacked facility in extemporaneous speaking, which facility was the mark of the true pneumatic. For the Corinthian prophets, the Spirit was irresistible, but for Paul the spirits of the prophets were under the control of the prophets themselves (1 Cor. 14:32). For the Corinthians, the prophet was autonomous, but for Paul the community as a whole must weigh and "confirm" what is said (1 Cor. 14:29). The Corinthians espoused a super-realized eschatology, against which Paul advocated the old Jewish-Christian apocalyptic understanding kept alive by Christian prophets (1 Corinthians 15). The Corinthians had rejected the category "new people of God" and had substituted an individualistic anthropology, but Paul's understanding of spiritual gifts is corporate, so that their only purpose is edification of the whole body of Christ, the church (1 Cor. 12:7, 27–28; 14:4, 12).

This tension between Paul's understanding of prophecy and that of his churches can best be explained by the fact that Paul did not merely reflect the understanding of prophecy current in his Hellenistic environment but stood in a prophetic tradition. This tradition has its roots in the Old Testament–Jewish understanding of prophecy and represents the understanding of prophecy and prophets as they were manifest in some streams of the early Palestinian church. Paul has been influenced by this tradition, which was a major factor in molding his own concept of prophecy.

This can be documented by concrete illustrations, e.g., when rabbinic

Judaism's understanding of Numbers 12:6–8 in terms of prophecy is explicitly reflected in 1 Corinthians 13:12.[4] It is also supported by specific evidence that when Paul presents his views of prophecy over against the Corinthians, he is drawing on traditional material. The listing "first apostles, second prophets, third teachers" in 1 Corinthians 12:28, for instance, seems not to be formulated ad hoc, but to represent a fragment of an earlier church order with Palestinian-Syrian connections.[5] It stands out from its context as a traditional element by the facts that (1) the first three elements are enumerated, but not the others; (2) the first three are offices or agents, the others are functions; (3) the first three are hierarchically prioritized, the others not—and this in a letter that specifically opposes such hierarchical distinctions (e.g., 12:23); (4) teachers are mentioned only here in the authentic Pauline corpus; (5) the person and tense of the verbs changes at verse 28, suggesting the introduction of a traditional fragment; and (6) the syntax of the sentence itself suggests that the first three items represent traditional material inserted here, the series of Greek particles *de . . . epeita . . . epeita* being unexpected. The close association of prophets and teachers reminds one of Acts 13:1–2, which is also a traditional list, and both may derive from the Antioch church, which itself had Palestinian roots.

Paul is pictured in Acts as having been in close association with prophetic figures of the early Palestinian church: Barnabas (Acts 4:36; 13:1–15:40, esp. 13:1–2; Gal. 2:1, 9, 13; 1 Cor. 9:6); Silas/Silvanus (Acts 15:22, 32; 15:40–18:17; 2 Cor. 1:19; 1 Thess. 1:1 [2 Thess. 1:1]); Agabus, the daughters of Philip, and other anonymous prophets (Acts 11:27–30; 21:9–14; cf. 16:6; 20:23; 21:4). Although some details of the Acts representation may have been colored by legend or Lukan *Tendenz,* there is no reason to deny this picture as a whole. Further, Paul's obvious preference for prophecy among the gifts of the Spirit in the discussion in 1 Corinthians 14 expresses the point of view dominant in Palestinian-Jewish Christianity, in which the Spirit is preeminently the Spirit of prophecy. The particular contrasts between Paul's understanding of the prophetic gift and that of the Corinthians must have made him appear as something of a traditionalist to them. Paul's connection with this prophetic tradition probably extends even to the occasional preservation and transmission of an oracle that originated in early Palestinian prophecy.

---

4 Dautzenberg, *Urchristliche Prophetie,* 176, 180.
5 Cf. Zimmermann, *Lehrer,* 107.

THE PAULINE TRADITION CONTINUED

Colossians, Ephesians, and the Pastorals may be expected to portray prophecy as it was understood in the Pauline churches of the second and third generation, either as a reflection of prophetic phenomena contemporary with the later authors or as a projection of what they imagined these phenomena to have been in Paul's time. It is possible, however, that even these late products of developing Pauline Christianity may contain some memories and impressions of the ministry of Christian prophets in earlier times.

Colossians: Prophecy Forgotten or Ignored

It is strange that there is no specific reference to prophecy in Colossians. "Spirit" is used only twice, both times of the human spirit. "Spiritual" in 1:9 and 3:16 suggests "inspired" insights and songs, but they are not related to Christian prophets. The references to "love" and "body" seem to reflect an awareness of the subject matter of 1 Corinthians 12–14 but without interest in the subject of charismatic phenomena. Prophetic speech seems not to have been a concern of the author of Colossians.

Ephesians: Prophets Remembered
and Admired

Although Ephesians is very dependent on Colossians, incorporating most of its text, the Pauline concern for prophecy reemerges. The three explicit references to prophets in Ephesians are all to Christian prophets rather than to Old Testament figures. This is clearly the case in 3:5 and 4:11, where a church context is specified, but is hardly less obvious in 2:20, where word order and the fact that both "apostles" and "prophets" are embraced under one article argues for church prophets.

It is just as clear, however, that these are not prophets in the time contemporary with the author but belong to a period already past. In 3:5, the revelation given to the prophets calling for a startling new departure is now something presupposed and celebrated but no longer debated. In 2:20 prophets are regarded, along with the apostles, as forming an essential part of the founding generation of the church but not necessarily a part of its present ministry. The reference to prophets in 4:11 should be seen within the temporal framework assumed by the author, representing "Paul's" time, but not the author's, who no longer knows either apostles or prophets personally. The manifold charismatic gifts of Paul's own time are here reduced to apostles, prophets, evangelists, and pastor-teachers as representative of the whole group enumerated in 1 Corinthians 12–14 and Romans 12. Since apostles and prophets belong to the "founding" period, the ministry in the author's own church seems to be composed of "evangelists" and "pastors" and "teachers," the latter probably thought of as one office, "pastoral teachers."

The earlier charismatic ministry is remembered with gratitude, but it is only a memory and has given way to a more structured, ordered ministry in the later Pauline churches. No materials are preserved in Ephesians that originated as the oracles of the earlier charismatics. There is no awareness that the existence of prophets in the earlier church was a problem as well as a blessing. The author is simply grateful that in the early days of the church the exalted Christ bestowed this gift upon the young church. *The memory persists even in the author's time that a theological decision of momentous import, the decision to include the Gentiles within the church, was not based on the teaching of the historical Jesus but was a matter of post-resurrection revelation* "in the spirit" to apostles and prophets (3:5).

This fading away of the prophetic gift, strictly defined, seems to have happened without a crisis, without any suspicion or denigration of the prophetic phenomena. This is seen not only in the reverence in which he holds the earlier prophets but in the fact that the author's vocabulary concerning revelation and the spirit is related to the earlier prophetic vocabulary, though no longer limited to the prophetic phenomenon per se (e.g., 1:9, 17). Expressions originally at home in the circles of Christian prophets have been broadened to describe the Christian life generally. This means that the author stands in a tradition in which Christian prophecy was once active, the effects of which can still be perceived to some minimal extent in this later deposit.

The Pastoral Letters: Orthodoxy Replaces Prophecy

Likewise in the Pastorals, prophecy is primarily a remembered phenomenon from the Pauline past, rather than a vital part of the Pastor's own church. There may still be some stirrings of the prophetic spirit manifest in the references in 1 Timothy 1:18, 4:14, and 2 Timothy 1:14, but if these refer to the time of the author and are not simply embellishments portraying Timothy's ministry in accord with its assumed time frame, then the gift of prophecy is regarded with more than a bit of suspicion. The point seems to be that the prophetic charisma should lead to regular ordination and, in fact, operates properly only within the legitimately ordained channels and in connection with the deposit of tradition that "has been entrusted to you/me" (1 Tim. 6:20, 2 Tim. 1:12, 14). The references to prophecy in 1 Timothy 1:18 and 4:14 belong to the fictive world of "Paul"; they do not reflect the actual world of the Pastor's church where strictly "objective" criteria are used for the qualifications for ministers (1 Timothy 3).

The dearth of reference to the Spirit, so frequent in Paul, has significance not only for the question of authorship but in illustrating the non-pneumatic nature of the Pastor's situation. The chief function of the ministry is the teaching of orthodox doctrine, handing on the tradition of the past, not the reception of new "words of the Lord," or the charismatic interpretation of scripture or the sayings of Jesus. Claims that prophetic oracles are found in the Pastorals are uniformly unsupported by evidence. The prophetic spirit is considered incompatible with the emphasis on "divine order." The "prophecy" of 1 Timothy 4:1–3 is not a real word of the Lord that comes into being in the author's own time but only a literary device to indicate that heresy did not come upon the church by surprise but was foreseen and "prophesied" by the earlier apostle.

Just as the Pastor's ideas of the relation of Christian prophecy and ordination seem to have been shaped by his reading of Acts 13:1–3 or memory of the tradition preserved there, so his view that earliest, heresy-free Christianity already prophesied the apostasy of succeeding generations seems to have been influenced by Acts 20:29–30 or its underlying tradition. Like Ephesians, the Pastorals have their own value as a witness to one way prophecy was understood in a later generation but give us little direct evidence for the nature of early Christian prophecy.

THE GOSPEL OF MARK

Mark seems reticent on the subject of prophets and prophecy. Although he quotes and alludes to their writings often, Mark specifically refers to Old Testament prophets only twice (1:2; 7:6; each time to Isaiah), plus two incidental references (6:15; 8:28). He refers once to the popular view that John the Baptist was a prophet (11:32) but never himself uses that term of him. Except for the implied self-identification in 6:4, the Markan Jesus never refers to himself as a prophet. Mark suggests that the populace sometimes understood Jesus as a prophet (6:15; 8:28; cf. 14:65) but that this was a mistake.

Mark's only reference to prophets in the time of the church labels them "false prophets" (13:22; cf. 13:6). They are the only opponents specifically placed in the post-Easter time of the church. If all the documents reflecting the beginnings of Christianity had been lost except for the Gospel of Mark, we would have no reason to think that prophets and prophecy played any positive role in the life of the church, except to pose a certain danger. Since we know otherwise from other sources, the picture given by Mark may indicate that Mark opposed or was suspicious of the prophetic phenomenon, and that he regarded Christian prophets who announced new sayings of the Lord as a problem for his church (see chapter 13 below).

THE GOSPEL OF MATTHEW

Matthew too seems to express reservation about charismatic claims since in addition to taking up Mark's warnings (24:11, 24), he transforms general elements of parenesis from the tradition into specific warnings against (false) prophets (7:15–23; cf. the parallels in Luke 6:43–46; 13:25–27). Since Matthew's interest in law, tradition, and rabbinic structure and authority has sometimes been thought to be incompatible with charismatic leadership, some scholars have concluded that Matthew considered the leadership of prophets who spoke directly in the name of the risen Lord to be contrary to the true nature of the church.

Yet it is clear that prophecy is a phenomenon well known in the Matthean church (hence the lack of specific information, which he can presuppose his readers already know) and that prophets are not to be rejected a priori and as such. Only false prophets are to be excluded, and that only on the basis of their "fruits," not because of their prophetic claims (7:15–16). Matthew's objection to "false prophets" is not to their prophetic claims per se but to their lawlessness (*anomia,* 7:23).

That prophets are a constituent element of the Matthean church is seen from the fact that in several instances, Matthew (or peculiarly Matthean tradition) has altered the tradition that came to him to make it apply more directly to the phenomenon of Christian prophecy. When Matthew 5:12 is compared to Luke 6:23, it is apparent that a general statement about ancient prophets has now, in Matthew's church, come to address Matthew's hearers as themselves standing in the prophetic succession. In 10:41, a logion peculiar to Matthew, dealing specifically with the reception of Christian prophets, concludes the missionary discourse. The Q logion in Matthew 23:34–36, paralleled in Luke 11:49–51, is in its Matthean form more clearly a reference to Christian prophets. Matthew has a large number of sayings in the form "sentences of holy law," which, as will be argued later, is characteristic of Christian prophets. While the claims of traveling prophets that come to Matthew's church from outside the community must be tested, prophets are sent forth from the community as its representatives.[6]

Eduard Schweizer has argued that, far from being skeptical about charismatic phenomena in the church, Matthew models his understanding of discipleship on the prophet.[7] Schweizer has shown convincingly that Christian prophecy is at home in the Matthean church. This accords with the reconstruction of the history of the Matthean church by Ulrich Luz, who sees the community behind the Gospel of Matthew as

---

6 Cf. Thomas Schmeller, *Brechungen. Urchristliche Wandercharismatiker im Prisma soziologisch orientierter Exegese,* 98–101.

7 "Observance of the Law and Charismatic Activity in Matthew."

having originally been founded by the prophets of the Q community (see chapter 12).[8]

Numerous students of Matthew have come to regard the Matthean church as including Christian prophets as a definite group within its leadership. Efforts to extract a precise description of Matthew's church order and the nomenclature used for it from his Gospel have thus far remained unconvincing, but it seems clear that prophets did play a distinct role in the leadership of Matthew's church, however this leadership was structured and named. Matthew was apparently able to embrace his whole community in the thrice-repeated "prophets" and "righteous" (10:41; 13:17; 23:29). His interest in this phrase is apparent in that the latter two instances are the result of Matthean modifications of his source in order to obtain this couplet, and in his alteration of one of the occurrences of "prophet" in 23:35 to "righteous" in order to complement the occurrence of "prophet" in 23:34 and thus obtain another prophet/righteous pair. As the Old Testament congregation was composed of prophets (leaders) and righteous (pious people, lay people), so Matthew sees his own church.

This does not, of course, mean that teachers played no role in Matthew's church. The contrary would be indicated by Matthew's "sages and scribes" in 23:34 and by the little self-portrait in 13:52—Matthew himself is such a teacher. The relations of such prophets and teachers in Matthew's church remain unclear, but they do not seem to have been in opposition. Teachers functioned in a church, the recognized leadership of which was characterized by the term "prophets."

While the exact nature of the church order of Matthew's community must remain an open question, the role of Christian prophets within this structure has been portrayed by the work of Alexander Sand in a manner that does most justice to the data.[9] Like Schweizer, Sand sees prophecy as *the* category in which Matthew interpreted discipleship to Jesus as such. But the Matthean community also knows a relatively small number of itinerant prophets, prophets who were not independent free-lancers but delegated missioners of the Matthean church. In addition, there was a larger group of congregational leaders in the church who were not itinerant but resident in the congregation, who recognized that discipleship to Jesus was to be practiced in prophetic terms. They performed prophetic functions in the community, including speaking in the name of the risen Lord. These are not sharply distinguished from the disciples in general,

---

8 *Das Evangelium nach Matthäus* 1:66.

9 "Propheten, Weise, und Schriftkundige in der Gemeinde des Matthäusevangeliums," in *Kirche im Werden. Studien zum Thema Amt und Gemeinde im Neuen Testament*, ed. Josef Hainz, 167–185; *Das Gesetz und die Propheten. Untersuchungen zur Theologie des Evangeliums nach Matthäus*, 168–177.

but they did form a recognizably distinct group. This is the picture of prophecy in the Matthean church that I accept. It would seem, therefore, that peculiarly Matthean statements about Christian prophets, and traditions representing the Matthean church, might be used in characterizing prophecy in Palestine—Syria in the last third of the first century.

To a lesser degree, and with less precision, Matthew's description of the disciples may be used to delineate the contours of Christian prophecy in his church, for Matthew emphasizes expressly that the disciples are prophets. Contrary to popular opinion, it is clear that Matthew has no interest in developing a picture of the Twelve as "apostles." He only uses the term once (10:2), in a tradition taken over from Mark. The verb *apostellō* ("send forth"—the root verb on which "apostle" is built) is no technical term in Matthew. Rather, *the Twelve are pictured as prophets* (5:10–12; 10:41; 13:17), the model of discipleship for those prophet-disciples whom the risen Jesus will send into the church (23:34). In four of the five major discourses, Matthew has described the disciples as prophets or compared them to the Old Testament prophets.

This obviously does not mean that all that is said about the disciples in Matthew may be transposed uncritically into a description of Christian prophets. But it does mean that when Matthew is thinking particularly of the prophetic ministry of the disciples, the redactional emphases of his description may be examined for their prophetic aspects. A particularly helpful instance is the discourse instructing the disciples concerning their mission in 10:1–42. Frank Beare and others have shown that Matthew conceives this scene in terms of the risen Lord sending forth his prophetic messengers.[10] Most commentators have contented themselves with referring to the Jewish juridical principle, "a person's representative is as that person." But the background of this discourse is not juridical but prophetic. The tasks with which the missioners are charged in 10:1 are the same as those that Matthew has already related to Christian prophets in 7:22. The discourse ends with a specific reference to Christian prophets, 10:41–42. The missioners are portrayed as preachers (v. 7) who on occasion are inspired by the Holy Spirit (vs. 19–20), who are charged with saying what the Lord reveals to them that they should proclaim (v. 26–27). These prophetic references at the beginning and end of the discourse, as well as the marks of prophetic speech within the discourse itself, indicate that Matthew here gathers up material that circulated in prophetic circles within the community and sets it forth as a manual of conduct for those Christian prophets and teachers on their missionary journeys in behalf of the church.

---

10 "The Mission of the Disciples and the Mission Charge: Matthew 10 and Parallels"; cf. Joachim Jeremias, *New Testament Theology,* 1:236–240.

On the other hand, one should be hesitant to use the elements peculiar to Matthew's description of *Jesus* as material for depicting early Christian prophets. Matthew seems to have no particular interest in portraying Jesus as a prophet. "Teacher" is the title that others use for a church office; Matthew reserves it exclusively for Jesus. Jesus calls himself "prophet" only once (13:57), in a traditional saying taken over from Mark, and is called prophet by others only in 16:14; 21:11, 46, all clearly misunderstandings of Jesus' true identity. There are no indications that Matthew was guided by the role Christian prophets played in his community as he shaped his own presentation of Jesus as the one "teacher" and "master" for the community (23:8–10).

There is only one exception to this. The final scene of the Gospel in which the disciples are commissioned is obviously a scene in which the risen and exalted Lord is portrayed as speaking. It is important to recognize that it is the exalted Lord who addresses his church here, not simply the resurrected Jesus who converses with his disciples shortly after the resurrection, as in 28:9–10. This is apparent both from the stance from which the address is given—"all authority in heaven and on earth has been given to me"—and from the fact that there is not, and cannot be, any later "ascension" of the Jesus who here speaks—"I am with you always, to the close of the age."

ACTS AND THE GOSPEL OF LUKE

Acts is our only New Testament document that purports to describe the early Christian prophets of the pre-70 Palestinian church. Agabus stands out most clearly (11:27–30; 21:1–14) as one who is not only called "prophet" by Luke but fits my functional definition of prophecy as well. Judas and Silas are prophets (15:32). Philip has four daughters who prophesy (21:9). Anonymous prophets proclaim their message by the Spirit, a term used interchangeably in such contexts with "Holy Spirit," "Spirit of the Lord," and "Spirit of Jesus," showing that it is the exalted Christ who is thought of as active in the prophetic event (16:6–7; 20:23; 21:4). A group of prophets and teachers at Antioch includes Barnabas and Paul (13:1–2). That Luke intends to include Barnabas among the prophets seems to be clear both from the grammar of this text and from 4:36, which Luke seems to understand as a reference to Barnabas's prophetic preaching. Paul also appears to be numbered among the prophets in 13:1–2, a fragment of earlier tradition taken over by Luke.[11] At the least, Paul is associated very closely with church prophets and is de-

---

11 For detailed arguments cf. Zimmermann, *Lehrer*, 123–135, and Gerd Luedemann, *Early Christianity According to the Traditions in Acts: A Commentary*, 147.

scribed by Luke as functioning as a prophet (9:3–6; 13:9–12; 16:6–9; 18:9–10; 22:6–21; 26:9–20; 27:23–24). In all, Acts refers to twelve specific individuals who prophesy, more than all the rest of Christian literature combined.[12]

In addition to this portrayal of particular individuals who manifest the prophetic gift, Luke understands that the Spirit has been poured out on the whole church, and this Spirit is pre-eminently the Spirit of prophecy (2:17–18, 38; 4:31; 6:10; 16:6–7). This means that, though Luke does recognize certain persons in the church who function consistently as prophets (whom he so designates), he does not draw a sharp line between prophets and nonprophets. Whoever in the church acts in the power of the Spirit is something of a prophet. This in turn means that even in those scenes where prophets are not specifically mentioned but where the Spirit is active in some extraordinary way the figures may be portrayed prophetically. Key examples would be 5:1–11 and 10:1–47, where Peter is portrayed as directed by the Spirit, for whom he serves as spokesman.

Luke knows of prophecy and tongues from his tradition, not from direct experience in his own church. This is seen, for example, in his lack of interest in distinguishing prophecy and tongues,[13] something that would have been very important in an actual situation where these phenomena were current (1 Corinthians 14!). Luke is dependent on church tradition for his knowledge of prophets. This does not mean, however, that a description of pre-70 Palestinian prophets can be read off the surface of the text of Acts. Luke adapts his traditions to his own interpretative tendencies. There are principally four of these.

1. Luke is interested in portraying the church as the continuation of the Old Testament people of God, which leads him to portray Christian prophets (and Jesus) as standing in the succession of Old Testament prophets and as resembling them. Agabus's binding himself with Paul's belt, for instance, is reminiscent of the symbolic acts performed by Isaiah, Ezekiel, and Jeremiah (Acts 21:10–14; cf. Isa. 20:2–6; Ezek. 4–5; Jer. 13:1–11). John the Baptist is introduced in Luke 3:1–3 with the same literary form used to introduce the books of Old Testament prophets (Isa. 1:1; Jer. 1:1–2; Ezek. 1:1–3; Hos. 1:1; Amos 1:1; Micah 1:1; Zeph. 1:1; Hag. 1:1; Zech. 1:1). In the speculations about Jesus' identity reported in Luke 9:8, 19, Luke each time adds "old" to the term "prophet" contained in his source. All this indicates a conscious intent on Luke's part to stylize his descriptions of prophets to conform to those of his Bible. Of course, it may well be that early Christian prophets did in fact resemble their Old Testament counterparts on several points. But since

---

12 Aune, *Prophecy,* 191.

13 Acts 2 applies the Joel prediction of latter-day prophets to tongues as Luke understands them; Acts 19 lumps prophecy and tongues together.

Luke seems to frame his language deliberately on Old Testament models, such elements in Luke's descriptions may sometimes be redactional rather than traditional. Decisions will have to be made from case to case.

2. Luke's portrayal of the prophets in Acts, including Paul, is uniformly noneschatological. Agabus's prediction of a famine that would cover the whole "inhabited earth" (Gr. *oikoumene*) was probably originally *the* famine that is often a part of the eschatological drama, but Luke has historicized it and reduced it to Judea. Similarly, Paul's oracles, which in his epistles are always eschatological, are in Acts this-worldly predictions of the historical future (20:22–23, 29–30; 27:22–23). Luke has a demonstrable tendency to historicize the eschatology of his sources (compare Mark 13 and Luke 21!); this tendency should be kept in mind when evaluating his portrayal of Christian prophets.

3. Luke chiefly values the prophetic phenomenon manifest in the early church for its evidential value rather than for the content of Christian prophetic oracles themselves. *That* persons in the early church prophesy is a proof that the eschatological gift of the Spirit is present in the church and that the church therefore is to be understood in continuity with the Old Testament people of God (2:14–18; 19:1–7). *What* the content of these "prophecies" is matters little to Luke. It may not be mentioned at all, as in 19:7, or need not be obeyed, as in 21:4. Luke's interest in prophecy does not extend to the careful preservation and handing on of prophetic oracles themselves. To the extent that this is present in Luke, it is incidental to Luke's purpose or represents an interest of the pre-Lukan tradition.

4. Although prophetic phenomena are frequent in Acts, Luke allows the prophets only a fringe role in the leadership of the church. So far as church structure and order are concerned, Luke tends to present the church as already developing in the direction of early Catholicism. He celebrates the presence of prophecy in the church as a supernatural validation of the church's claim to be the people of God but is hesitant to portray charismatics as playing too great a role in the actual policy-making decisions of the church. This role is filled primarily by "apostles and elders." In 13:1–3 prophets are explicitly involved in a major new departure in the history of the church, but no new policy is set there. Luke's own perspective is seen more typically in Acts 10, where the new policy vis-à-vis the Gentile mission comes by a revelation to Peter, in a scene filled with prophetic nuances. However, Peter is not called a prophet but an apostle, and his action is officially ratified by the other apostles and the Jerusalem church in chapter 11. Taken together, Acts 10 and 11 seem to be Luke's narrative portrayal of the event celebrated in Ephesians 3:5 (see above, "Ephesians: Prophets Remembered and Admired").

Acts 15:1–35 portrays a similar circumstance, in which prophets in the pre-Lukan tradition seem to have played a greater role in the decision-making process than is now apparent in the Lukan edition of the event. First, the problem is posed for which the will of God is sought. But instead of "inquiring" through a prophet, the standard phrase from Luke's Bible (compare 1 Sam. 9:9; 1 Kings 22:7; 2 Kings 3:11; 2 Chron. 18:6; Ezek. 14:7), the disputants go to Jerusalem to the "apostles and elders," a couplet used by Luke five times in this context to emphasize the role of the "official" leaders in the decision-making process (15:2, 4, 6, 22, 23). Judas and Silas, whom Luke designates as prophets (15:32), are "leading men among the brethren" (15:22), though they are portrayed by Luke as playing no role in the decision. They are entrusted with delivering the letter, which is called an "exhortation" (v. 31: *paraclēsis*), a word with prophetic overtones. The letter contains the phrase "it has seemed good to the Holy Spirit and to us" (v. 28), which corresponds to the typical process by which oracles were received by prophets and the testing function of the whole community by which they were validated. The interpretation of the Old Testament to apply to the present, another prophetic characteristic, also plays a role. The decision itself was arrived at on the basis of speeches by Peter, Paul, and Barnabas, all of whom are prophetic figures. But it is James, a nonprophet, to whom Luke assigns the role of declaring the verdict. Thus we have a scene permeated by prophetic phenomena, which is described by Luke in such a way as to give the prophets only a subsidiary role.

Luke has an obvious disdain for the Hellenistic type of pagan prophet, whom he refuses to dignify with the revered Old Testament term "prophet." He does not wish to portray the life of the church as penetrated by ecstatic types resembling pagan "prophets." Although he has a somewhat romantic appreciation of the prophetic ecstasy of the earliest church, seen for example in his adding "and they shall prophesy" to the Joel quotation in Acts 2:18, he no more wishes to promote it in the life of the church of his own generation than he wishes to perpetuate the earliest church's "communism" of 4:32–36. Luke is by no means antiprophetic, but he describes the role of prophets as operating within a firm structure controlled by apostles and elders. This interpretative tendency, like the others, must be kept in mind when using Acts to describe early Christian prophecy.

Not only Acts but also the Gospel of Luke manifests Luke's cautious appropriation of prophetic imagery. As in the other synoptic Gospels, the Lukan Jesus predicts the emergence of prophets in the church—though in the Lukan form prophets are complemented by apostles (11:49–51). Little help is to be gained, however, for the project of reconstructing the characteristics of early Palestinian Christian prophets from such incidental remarks about Christian prophets in Luke.

A more fertile field for our project may be found in the Lukan portrayal of Jesus, whom Luke intentionally pictures as a prophet. The image of the prophet had already been impressed on the traditional materials about Jesus prior to Luke. Indeed, it is very probable that the historical Jesus himself manifested prophetic characteristics. But Luke, and/or the peculiarly Lukan tradition ("L"), emphasizes the prophetic nature of Jesus' ministry. Jesus is made to represent himself self-consciously as a prophet, who compares himself with prophets of the Old Testament (13:33; 4:25–27). "Prophet" is a valid christological category for Luke, which is seen in the fact that Jesus is pictured in "L" materials as a prophet with no suggestion that this is an inadequate description or misunderstanding (7:16, 39; 24:19; cf. Acts 3:22–23). The description of the ministry of the risen Christ in 24:13–49 is especially relevant for our purpose, in that not only is the resurrected Lord called a prophet but the post-Easter speaking of the risen Lord is graphically portrayed. Although the older form of the story has been altered to express Lukan theology (e.g., the flesh-and-bone nature of the resurrection body, v. 40; and the pre-*ascension* setting), the older form, told in prophetic categories, still shines through.

Whence comes this predilection for portraying Jesus in prophetic garb? Some of it, at least, must be attributed to the influence of the Old Testament on Lukan theology. To the extent that this is the explanation, the Lukan portrait of Jesus would contain little of value for reconstructing the image of Christian prophets in earliest Christianity. But it is likely that Luke's image of prophecy was shaped not only by his reading of the Septuagint but also by the impression made on him or his tradition by prophets in the church. Jesus in Luke resembles not only his predecessors in the Old Testament but also his successors in the church. It is difficult to sort out which elements of this description may be attributed to the remembered prophetic ministry of Jesus, which to the church's casting of Jesus in the role of a prophet, and which to the Lukan view of prophecy, which has itself been influenced both by the Old Testament and by the phenomenon of prophecy in the church.

There is, however, another source in the Gospel of Luke that might be of great value for our reconstruction. The outburst of oracular hymnody that surrounds the birth of Jesus in the Lukan narrative is replete with prophetic materials. Elizabeth is filled with the Holy Spirit, which is identified as the Spirit that inspires prophecy, and with a loud cry—another mark of prophecy—she pronounces a prophetic utterance (1:41, 42–45). The Magnificat is spoken by one on whom the Holy Spirit has come (1:35) and who speaks as a Christian prophet. The Benedictus is called a prophecy, by one filled with the Holy Spirit (1:67–79). Simeon is one filled with the Spirit who receives divine revelations (2:25–26), so that 2:29–32, 34–35, should be regarded as prophetic utterance. No direct words of the prophet Anna are preserved, though her general characteristics as a prophet are clear. The words of the angel in 1:14–17 and 32–33 also have oracular-hymnic qualities, and, as we shall see in chapter 9, angels are a vehicle of Christian prophecy.

The complicated question of the sources and history of the tradition of the materials in Luke 1–2 may be left aside for our purposes. However the critical issues presented by these chapters may be resolved, it seems clear that (1) Luke is not here composing *ab ovo* but is rewriting a source or sources, (2) which come from pre-70 Jewish Christianity in at least one stage of their development; (3) these materials represent Elizabeth, Zechariah, Mary, Simeon, and Anna to be functioning as prophets; (4) the content of these oracles and conduct of the personages may be taken as representative of what some pre-70 Jewish Christian communities considered to be appropriate for prophets, the oracles perhaps being the very oracles of Christian prophets preserved and used in worship.

THE GOSPEL AND LETTERS OF JOHN

The Johannine literature never uses the word "prophet" for church figures but exclusively for the biblical prophets (1:23, 45; 6:45, 8:52–53; 12:38), for the expected eschatological prophet (1:21, 25; 6:14; 7:40, 52), and for Jesus (4:19, 44; 9:17). But to suppose too quickly that this means that the Gospel and Letters of John therefore have nothing to tell us about Christian prophecy would only be another instance of the mistake of limiting the prophetic phenomenon to the occurrence of a particular vocabulary. It was thus the keen insight of Ernst Käsemann to emphasize that John must be seen in the historical and theological context of Christian prophecy,[14] a conviction now shared by a number of students of the Johannine literature who believe that the Johannine community contained a significant group of Christian prophets among its leaders.[15]

The Gospel and Letters of John seem to have emerged at different points from the same "circle," "school," or tradition. In addition, there is some kind of connection between the Apocalypse and this Johannine tradition, even if only indirect. Since the Apocalypse was obviously written by a Christian prophet to churches familiar with the prophetic phenomenon, this means that the Johannine community was aware of prophets in its midst. The Letters too come from a circle that was familiar with Christian prophecy and was beginning to experience some manifestations of it as problematic, without denying its validity per se (1 John 2:20, 27; 4:1–3). In 1 John 4:1–3, prophecy as such is accepted as a given

---

14 *The Testament of Jesus,* 38.

15 E. g., B. H. Streeter, "John, Mystic and Prophet," chapter 13 of *The Four Gospels: A Study of Origins;* Hans Windisch, *The Spirit-Paraclete in the Fourth Gospel;* David Aune, *The Cultic Setting of Realized Eschatology;* D. Moody Smith, "John 16:1–15."

part of church life. "False" prophets are rejected not because of their prophetic claims but because of their heretical theology. And since the "we" of 1 John cannot be separated from the "we" of the Fourth Gospel, we would expect a priori that the Gospel would also originate from a circle in which the prophetic ministry was very much alive.

Christian prophets in John's community served as a model for the way in which the figures of both Jesus and the Paraclete are portrayed. Except for the biblical prophets of the past and the expected eschatological prophet, the appellation "prophet" is applied exclusively to Jesus in the Fourth Gospel (4:19, 44; 6:14; 7:40; 9:17). The Paraclete is Jesus' successor and plays the same role in the post-Easter church as had Jesus among the disciples, continuing the voice of Jesus in the Christian community (14:15–16, 25–26; 15:26; 16:7–15). The Paraclete is not merely the presence of the Holy Spirit in the heart of each Christian but represents a particular prophetic ministry of the Holy Spirit through the leadership of the Johannine community.[16] The Johannine understanding of the Spirit and prophecy is analogous to that of Paul, in that the Spirit is given to the community as a whole, and every Christian participates in the life of the Spirit and is potentially a prophet. There was no "order" or "office" of prophecy but nonetheless an identifiable group of leaders in and through whom the prophetic word was heard. The picture of Jesus in the Fourth Gospel is influenced by the presence of these prophetic figures in the Johannine community. The Jesus of the Fourth Gospel manifests particular prophetic traits, for example, his preaching is a "loud cry" (7:28, 37; 12:44; cf. Ignatius, *Philippians* 5.2; "Other Sources" below).[17]

The extensive Johannine discourses are to be explained not as the result of John's having christianized and historicized a pre-existing source but as the result of a long process of development in the preaching of the Johannine community, a process in which Christian prophets were active. During this process of development, no sharp line was drawn between sayings of the historical Jesus and post-Easter revelations, which is what one would expect from the description of the ministry of the Paraclete (John 14:25–26; 16:12–13). The self-understanding of Christian prophets is reflected in the discourses.

The author of the Fourth Gospel was himself something of a prophetic figure, that is, an inspired teacher[18] who handled the tradition he had received in prophetic style, allowing it to be the vehicle of the contin-

---

16 Cf. D. Moody Smith, "The Presentation of Jesus in the Fourth Gospel," 375.

17 This point is elaborated in detail in M. Eugene Boring, "The Influence of Christian Prophecy on the Johannine Portrayal of the Paraclete and Jesus."

18 The fallacy of regarding "prophet" and "teacher" as contrary or mutually exclusive categories has been thoroughly exposed by Riesner, *Jesus als Lehrer*, 276–297.

uing voice of Jesus. The author of the Fourth Gospel was a prophetic teacher who was concerned, as were other members of his school, that the message of the risen Jesus should remain bound to the event of the fleshly, historical Jesus. It is precisely for this reason that the evangelist does not set forth his message in letter form, as did Paul, nor in a collection of sayings of Jesus as did the Q community, and especially not in the form of revelation discourses of the exalted Lord as did the gnostics (and John of the Apocalypse), but in the narrative form of the Gospel.[19] Even though the exalted Christ and the historical Jesus blend into each other in John's portrayal, the earthly Jesus and his word are never simply replaced by the word of the exalted Christ, so that John does not sacrifice history to mythology. John is an author who has been influenced by Christian prophecy and functions in a somewhat prophetic mode himself but who already sees the problem involved in the typical prophetic form and presents an alternative based on extensive theological reflection. It is narrative that keeps prophecy from degenerating into oracle.[20]

The day when John could be characterized as a lone creative genius is now long past. John works creatively within a tradition, a tradition that is ultimately of Palestinian origin and places him in direct lineal descent from early Christian prophets. The Gospel and Letters of John may be used not only to describe the Christian prophetism of the time and place of the Fourth Evangelist himself, they may also be used, when critically balanced with other sources, to help reconstruct the contours of that Christian prophetism that was active nearer the source of the tradition that finds its deposit in the Johannine writings and other early Christian literature.

REVELATION

The Apocalypse is our most obvious, and most extensive, example of Christian prophecy among the sources relevant to our task. It is clear that the author claims to write prophecy (1:3; 19:20; 22:7, 10, 18–19). The repeated "prophecy of this book" represents a Greek epexegetical genitive, "the prophecy that this book is." It is also clear in 22:9 that the author designates himself as a prophet. The equation in 22:9 and 11:18 of "servant" and "prophet" would then make the most probable interpretation of the ambiguous "his servants the prophets" in 10:7 a reference that includes Christian prophets. This further means that "servant"

---

19 We will explore below the significance of this crucial move made by Mark and John (see chapters 13 and 16 below).

20 Cf. Paul Ricoeur, *Essays on Biblical Interpretation*, ed. Lewis Mudge (Philadelphia: Fortress Press, 1980), 76.

in 1:1 was probably understood by John to be the same as "prophet," so that the revelation was given "to his servant John," precisely "to his prophet John." Thus although it is correct that John never uses the word "prophet" explicitly of himself, this is incidental, for his claim to be a prophet is clear.

But even if the terminology were not present, Revelation would still be prophecy in terms of our functional definition. The book is throughout the address of the risen Lord to his church, delivered through an immediately inspired spokesperson. It is a misunderstanding of the nature of John's prophetic document to mark off the passages that have explicit prophetic formal characteristics and consider them alone to be prophecy.[21] Rather, the book *as a whole* is a "revelation of Jesus Christ," as the subjective genitive of 1:1 indicates. The revelatory chain God-Christ-angel-servant-(prophet) of 1:1 also indicates that God, the exalted Christ, and the revelatory angel are neither to be isolated from one another nor to be contrasted with each other but are elements of the same revelatory experience. This is seen, for example, in the series of quotations in 21:9, 15; 22:1, 6, 8, 9, 10, 12, which, if the strict logic of the series is followed, has the *angel* saying "Behold, I am coming soon," which is obviously to be taken as a word of the exalted Jesus. This is also seen in the structure of the book itself. From 6:1 on, the book unfolds as the seals of the sealed scroll are broken one by one. But this sealed book, which originates from the hand of God, is now in the hand of the exalted Jesus and is opened only by him. In this way, though the apocalyptic form of sealed scroll and interpreting angel is retained, it is subordinated to the understanding of revelation in Christian prophecy, in which the risen Lord speaks through the prophet.

It is to be remembered that our definition of prophecy is formal and functional, not material. This means that the categories "apocalyptic" and "prophecy" are not necessarily to be opposed to each other and particularly that the question of whether Revelation is "apocalyptic" or "prophecy" is misdirected. That apocalyptic materials can be incorporated in a Christian prophetic framework is clear from the above. That John specifically intends to break with apocalyptic, formally defined, and replace it with the direct address of the Lord who speaks in the present is clear from 22:10, where John's own "prophecy of this book" is marked off from all pseudonymous apocalyptic purportedly revealed to some ancient worthy. Revelation is thus a valuable example of one kind of early Christian prophecy.

The value of Revelation as a source for reconstructing early Christian

---

21 Contra Aune, *Prophecy* (275–287), who considers only 2:1–3:22, plus twenty-seven scattered verses, to be Christian prophecy.

prophecy is not exhausted by the fact that it is itself our most lengthy example of one kind of prophecy. Revelation also reflects the ideas and practice of John's church with regard to prophecy. For example, 10:8–11:13 pictures the eschatological prophet as he was understood in John's church, using traditional images that let us see their understanding of the essential features of the prophetic figure and ministry, and Revelation 2–3 lets us see not only John's oracles but something of the way the prophetic ministry was practiced and the response to it in the churches of Asia Minor. John was not the only prophet in the Asian churches he addresses (2:14, 20) although, as in the case of Paul, we get to see the other prophets only through his eyes.

In form Revelation is a letter directed to seven churches in Asia from the nearby island of Patmos, by one who had ministered in the area long enough to become a revered leader in this group of churches. Though written about 96 C.E.,[22] it is by no means the case that all its contents were created ex nihilo at that time. That the author is a Jewish Christian is apparent from the Old Testament and apocalyptic materials that form the substance of his writing and from his antipathy to those who claim to be Jews but are not (2:9; 3:9). Beyond this, that the author was originally a Palestinian Jewish Christian has been often and persuasively argued from the linguistic peculiarities of the book. Akira Satake has presented a detailed argument that not only John himself but elements of the churches of Asia Minor in which the seer was at home represent a transplanted Palestinian Christianity forced from Palestine at the time of the war of 66–70 C.E.[23] I find his argument basically convincing.

There are clear indications that many of the prophetic materials and ideas contained in the book originated earlier in a Palestinian setting. The careful analytical work of Müller has disclosed a tradition of specific prophetic forms used by John.[24] The substantial traditional elements in Revelation indicate that John stands in a tradition of Christian prophecy, a tradition originating in the life of the church in pre-70 Palestine. This means that in the Apocalypse we have not only an example of one kind of Christian prophetism in Asia Minor near the end of the century but also a source that can be judiciously used as a witness to pre-70 Palestinian Christian prophecy.

Since Revelation is our most direct source for early Christian prophecy, we might pause here and, leaving aside the complicated question of how typical John may be of those prophets we are seeking to reconstruct, simply list what we would be able to say about early Christian prophecy

---

22 The best recent discussion of Revelation's date is A. Y. Collins, *Crisis and Catharsis: The Power of the Apocalypse,* 54–83.

23 *Die Gemeindeordnung in der Johannesapokalypse.*

24 *Prophetie und Predigt,* 57–99, esp. 70, 77.

and prophets if Revelation were our only example. Each item on the list has been elaborated elsewhere,[25] and when relevant will be discussed later in its appropriate context.

1. Prophecy can assume written form.
2. Prophecy can be included as a constituent element of a letter.
3. Within this overall form, the prophet makes use of numerous formal elements that seem to be characteristic of prophetic speech.
4. Christian prophecy is eschatological-apocalyptic in orientation and content and can utilize much apocalyptic symbolism.
5. Christian prophecy is characterized by the rebuke of immorality and unfaithfulness and the call to repentance.
6. Christian prophecy is characterized by the pronouncement of (proleptic) eschatological judgment.
7. Christian prophecy is characterized by exhortations and encouragement to believers to remain faithful.
8. Christian prophecy makes use of tradition, including the Old Testament, traditional apocalyptic materials, previous oracles of Christian prophets, Christian writings that are not specifically prophetic, and traditional sayings of Jesus.
9. Christian prophecy can take up a traditional saying of Jesus and re-present it as the word of the exalted Lord (though this does not happen in Revelation to any great extent).
10. Christian prophecy can coin sayings of the risen Lord that could be taken into the tradition of Jesus' words and later considered a saying of the historical Jesus (though this is not the case with the sayings in the Apocalypse to any great extent).
11. The prophet is a figure who speaks with an assumed authority within the congregation and groups of congregations.
12. The Christian prophet exercises his or her function primarily in the setting of congregational worship.
13. The Christian prophet is the one through whom the risen Christ (and God and the Spirit—all these are identified with each other) comes to speech in the congregation.
14. The Christian prophet functions as interpreter of the events through which the church is living.
15. The Christian prophet functions by reinterpreting the Old Testament in the light of the Christ event.

---

25 These theses are elaborated and documented in M. Eugene Boring, "The Apocalypse as Christian Prophecy: A Discussion of the Issues Raised by the Book of Revelation for the Study of Early Christian Prophecy," in *SBL 1974 Seminar Papers* 2:43–62.

16. The Christian prophet is associated with miracles, signs, and other phenomena of the Spirit.
17. Prophets can be male (John, "Balaam," 2:14) or female ("Jezebel," 2:20).

THE *DIDACHE*

It is probable that the *Didache,* or one of its major sources, originated in the same general area as the Gospel of Matthew and is thus an independent witness to the prophetism of the church in the region of Syria. Although no consensus on its date has emerged, there is extensive agreement on the following position, which is adopted in this study: (1) The *Didache* is principally composed of two sources: the Two Ways in chapters 1–5 and the Manual of Church Order in chapters 6–15. (2) Each of these is itself composed of traditional material older than the source itself. (3) The Manual of Church Order (which contains all the explicit references to Christian prophecy) was originally of Syrian provenance. (4) The Manual is to be dated in the last third of the first century.

The Manual of Church Order comes from a Christian community that has resident prophets in its midst and must also deal with prophets who travel about. Prophets are highly honored, at least ostensibly, for they are to receive the esteem and first fruits formerly reserved for the high priest (13.3). A case is made for the importance of the more structured official ministry of bishops and deacons on the basis that they *"also* minister to you the ministry of the prophets and teachers" (15.2). The structured leadership seems to be on the ascent, gradually replacing charismatic leadership, but a case has to be made that this is in order. Yet prophets are not only highly esteemed, they also present problems for the community, particularly when they are traveling prophets wanting to settle down in the community. This is the reason for the intense interest of the author(s) in prophecy, an interest that causes the instructions on prophets to be elaborated far beyond what is said about "apostles" and "teachers."

These instructions do not seem to be all of a piece, indicating that they came into being from different hands over an extended period. For example, the prophet is considered to be above question when speaking "in the Spirit," so that to challenge him or her is the unforgivable sin (11.7), and yet some things that the prophet says are not to be tolerated even if said "in the Spirit" (11.12). The criterion of true prophecy is whether its teaching is according to the truth (11.1), but even that prophet who teaches according to the truth is a false prophet "if he does not practice what he teaches" (11.10). Such inconsistencies denote a developing *tradition* rather than composition by a single author. Some of the instructions regarding Christian prophets probably come from the editor of the Manual in the last decades of the first century. Others indicate earlier efforts of the same community to deal with the problem of true and false prophecy. We are justified, then, in taking *Didache* 10–15 as a source for Syrian Christian prophets of the late first century, which quite likely contains pre-70 material.

HERMAS

In the *Shepherd* of Hermas we have a Christian document, emanating from the Roman church in the first half of the second century, that claims both to describe the ministry of Christian prophets within the church (Mandate 11) and repeatedly represents itself as being the revelation of the Holy Spirit or Son of God to his church in the latter days (e.g., Vision 4. 1.3; Similitude 9. 1.1). As in the other sources described above, here too the author never refers to himself as a prophet, but this is incidental for our purposes, for if the self-description of the document is taken at face value the author precisely conforms to the functions of Christian prophecy in our definition.

If the "prophecy" of the author is regarded as only a literary device, we would have in the author's self-description an imaginative portrayal of the way the prophetic phenomenon was conceived to be by one not existentially involved in it. In view of the fact that prophecy is still a live phenomenon in the author's church, which he at least observes (Mandate 11), this would still be of some value. There are some marks of genuine prophetic self-consciousness, such as the revelation of a second chance of repentance in view of an impending persecution and the imminent return of the Lord (Vision 3. 1.9). But even if the author does have some personal prophetic experiences, for the most part his writing is a tedious, labored, uninspired, and uninspiring work, formally in the prophetic category but written by one for whom prophecy is already a traditional phenomenon that may be stereotyped.

The threads that connect Hermas with those early Christian prophets who are the subjects of this reconstruction are long and thin, if present at all. These connections are enhanced by the favored view today that Hermas belongs to Jewish Christianity. In Reiling's view, the Jewish-Christian elements in his writing are only a result of the Jewish-Christian tradition into which Hermas came at his conversion in Rome, where the church had a substantial Jewish-Christian element. It thus could be that images of prophecy and prophets of earlier Jewish Christianity had impressed themselves onto the tradition that came to Hermas and formed part of that understanding of prophecy that shaped both his own ministry and his response to other prophets of his time. At the most, however, we may expect to glean only a minimum of material for our purposes from

Hermas. In him, we hear the last faint echoes of the "old" prophecy. After him, references to prophecy in the church are oriented to the "new prophecy" of Montanism, either in affirmation or in repudiation—and in either case are too far removed from those early Christian prophets who might have influenced the Gospel tradition of Jesus' words to offer us anything for our reconstruction.

OTHER SOURCES

The above sources do not exhaust all the references to prophecy and "speaking in the name of the Lord" from early Christianity. The letters of Ignatius of Antioch, written about 110 C.E. as he was being taken to Rome for martyrdom, contain one (ambiguous) reference to Christian prophets (Ignatius, *Philippians* 5.2), and one instance in the same letter in which Ignatius seems to claim prophetic speech for himself: "I cried out while I was with you, I spoke with a great voice—with God's own voice—'Give heed to the bishop, and to the presbytery, and the deacons.' Some suspected me of saying this because I had previous knowledge of the division of some persons, . . . but the Spirit was preaching, and saying this, 'Do nothing without the bishop, keep your flesh as the temple of God, love unity, flee from divisions, be imitators of Jesus Christ, as he was also of the Father' " (Ignatius, *Philippians* 7.1–2). There seems to be authentic prophetic experience expressed in Ignatius's words but minimal content that is helpful for our project.

The *Odes of Solomon* are from the same general period and provenance as Ignatius. The words "prophet" or "prophecy" are not present. But like the hymns from Qumran, they frequently indicate that they are composed by divine inspiration and occasionally represent the deity, portrayed in the *Odes* as the risen Christ, as speaking through the mouth of the psalmist:

> Then I arose and am with them,
> And will speak through their mouths (42:6).

The hymnic form and function of the *Odes* makes them more difficult to use as a source for reconstructing what prophecy was like in the setting in which they were composed, yet they do clearly document the phenomenon of the risen Lord speaking in the first person through inspired prophets and associate this phenomenon with the worship life of the congregation.

The vast and varied literature of early Christianity contains other reports of post-Easter revelations of the risen Lord, but the sources discussed above provide the primary base from which any reconstruction of the nature of early Christian prophecy must proceed.

5

Prophecy Before the Gospels: How Can We Reconstruct Its Picture?

All of the sources just reviewed, in varying ways and to various degrees, reflect and refract the phenomena of early Christian prophecy. But no one of them contains, in such a way that it can be read off the surface, a portrayal of those early Christian prophets who were active in the early days of the formation of the Gospel tradition and whose oracles may be preserved within it. A workable method must make use of all the relevant information contained within these sources to reconstruct the features of a type or types of Christian prophecy that none of them directly attests. Although our sources are, relatively speaking, widely scattered in both time and place, the expectation that they might still yield a coherent picture of the prophetism of an earlier time and different place is not unrealistic because, as the previous discussion indicates, *several of these sources stand in that stream of tradition that emanated from Palestine* and flowed into the rest of the Hellenistic world and reflect this tradition in their representation of Christian prophecy.

In this regard our efforts to obtain a clearer picture of early Christian prophets is no different than our attempts to understand what the apostles of the early church were like. What Hans von Campenhausen has written of the apostles and early Jerusalem Christianity is equally relevant to the study of early Christian prophecy:

> We possess hardly one word which can, in its present form, be ascribed with certainty to their circle. . . . First and foremost, however, one thing is quite incontestable, namely that the primitive community was the point from which the whole succeeding development began. . . . Those who came after interpreted the tradition they received, and in so doing they naturally from the very first also transformed it, and in numerous ways placed it in a different light; but they did not invent it, and therefore their evidence concerning it can still be of use to us. . . . If we wish to recover the true circumstances in all their living, complex reality, we

must set aside the rigid formulas and concepts of a later age, and start by breaking down or at least teasing out the community into the individuals and groups which the records show to have been the leading elements within it.[1]

The following chapters will attempt to construct a characterization of early Christian prophecy that will bring into focus the profile of typical Christian prophets as they functioned in the churches of the Palestine-Syrian area in the first generation after Jesus' death. The characterization will be constructed as follows: the data regarding Christian prophecy contained in each of our sources will be projected carefully backward and in the direction of the earliest Christian community in Palestine, to the extent that this is possible. That is, the attempt will be made to determine the traditional picture of prophecy that has left its impression on each source, by allowing for the interpretative tendencies and situation of each author.

The second step will be to base our characterization on those features of Christian prophecy that are common to, or typical of, several traditional and/or general features of Christian prophets, providing us with a characterization logically, and frequently chronologically, prior to all our sources. In addition, some features that do not have multiple attestation but nevertheless seem to present some early or typical trait of Christian prophecy will be included.

This characterization must be more than an objective profile of the Christian prophet as an individual but should include the social and ecclesiastical context of Christian prophecy since by definition the prophet is not an isolated figure but operates within a community. Insights from a sociological perspective can be helpfully used when appropriate, but their utility is somewhat diminished by the nature of early Christianity as a varied subculture within the larger culture of the Hellenistic world. Due to the dramatic differences between prophecy in the culture at large and Christian prophecy, insights gained from the sociological study of the former are of limited validity in reconstructing the profile of early Christian prophecy.[2] No single sociological method can be rigidly applied. The general approach is similar to the classical approach of Max Weber, now experiencing a renaissance in modified and chastened form. Weber was concerned to construct "ideal types" by combining a number of diffused and discrete references to individual instances of the phenomenon and subjecting them to a concentrated point of view in order to form a more or less abstract ideal picture. He

---

1 *Ecclesiastical Authority and Spiritual Power in the Church of the First Three Centuries*, 12–14.
2 On both points, see Christopher Forbes (a student of E. A. Judge), "Prophecy and Inspired Speech in Early Christianity and Its Hellenistic Environment," esp. 289.

did not claim that this ideal picture is present in every or even any historical instance; it is a heuristic means of making sense of the phenomena.[3]

Since there is no choice but to use a combination of indirect sources, the characterization that results from this approach will of necessity be something of a composite, but it must be a critically constructed composite. The danger of drawing data from a variety of times and places to produce a conglomerate figure who in fact existed in none is recognized. This is indeed the danger of the classical approach of Max Weber, not altogether avoided in the recent work of Gerd Theissen. A flat-surface, timeless composite portrait resulting from a nonhistorical phenomenological approach is explicitly rejected.

The features characteristic of Christian prophecy may not be unique to prophets. To restrict the characterization to such features produces a minimal and distorted picture. The prophet may share some features with the apostle and the teacher, for example. It may sometimes be the case that the clustering of a number of features, none of which is of itself particularly prophetic in nature, is the characteristic prophetic feature. Also, a function shared by prophets and others may be performed by prophets in a characteristic manner, so that it is not the function itself but the way it is done that is prophetic. We shall see below that this is the case in the interpretation of scripture, for example.

We may not indiscriminately use materials from the whole Hellenistic world to construct a prophetism-in-general. A composite figure may legitimately be constructed, but historical distinctions must be maintained. This means that we may anticipate finding some variety in the kinds of prophetic figures that functioned within pre-70 Christianity. Prophecy was no more a monolith in the church than it was in Israel. But just as Amos, Hosea, Isaiah, and Micah, though quite different from each other, still form a recognizable entity, "the eighth-century prophets," which as a group is distinct both from Israelite prophecy of preceding and following centuries and from extra-Israelite prophecy, so it was with early Christian prophecy: although it embraces some variety, we may legitimately speak of a general category, "early (pre-70) Christian prophets," who are distinct both from non-Christian Hellenistic and Jewish prophets and from later Christian prophets, if the evidence seems to support such a reconstruction. It is this general typus that will be characterized in Part Two of this study.

It should be acknowledged in advance that there is no proof that the typus described corresponds point by point to pre-70 Christian prophets

---

3 Max Weber, "Die 'Objektivität' sozialwissenschaftlicher Erkenntnis" (1904) in J. Winckelmann, ed., *Soziologie—Weltgeschichtliche Analysen—Politik* (Stuttgart, 1960²) 235; cf. Schmeller, *Brechungen*, 26.

as they actually existed. To ask for that is to ask for what in the nature of the case is impossible. The method and results here proposed have their problems but are better than any of the alternatives, namely generalizations from one source, or radically hypothetical reconstructions extrapolated from Gospel sayings of Jesus supposed to come from Christian prophets, or despair about our ability to say anything at all about pre-70 non-Pauline Christianity. While like all historical reconstruction the results are not demonstrable, the reconstruction offered in the following chapters is less arbitrary than alternative approaches and is correctable in that it provides an itemized basis for continuing discussion of the phenomenon of early Christian prophecy. To the extent that this reconstruction is successful, it will have provided a valuable contribution to our understanding of early Christianity in and of itself and will provide the basis for a further exploration of the relation of prophets to the formation of the Gospel tradition and the Gospels themselves.

PART TWO

A PROFILE OF EARLY
CHRISTIAN PROPHECY

6

The Prophet as a Church Figure

THE EXTENT OF PROPHECY IN EARLY CHRISTIANITY

Early Christianity was a prophetic movement beginning with the prophets John and Jesus. After Easter prophets were widespread in the early church, not being limited to any one geographical area, sociological grouping, or stream of theological tradition. This is already apparent from the variety of settings of the sources discussed above that provide the evidence for our reconstruction. In addition, several of these explicitly indicate that prophecy was not an isolated phenomenon peculiar to only a few congregations. The seer of Revelation speaks generally of prophets as constituting an integral part of the worldwide church (11:18; 16:6; 18:24; 22:9). Paul supposes that there are prophets in the Roman church, though he has never been there (Rom. 12:6). Acts locates prophets in Jerusalem, Antioch, Caesarea, Tyre, and, with excusable exaggeration, "every city" in Greece, Macedonia, and Asia (13:1; 15:32; 20:23; 21:4, 10). Ephesians and the Pastorals look back upon a first-generation church that was generally characterized by the presence of prophets (Eph. 3:5; 4:11; 1 Tim. 1:18; 4:14). The presence of prophets is viewed as the normal situation by the *Didache* and Hermas. While in some cases the writer's perception of the whole church may be colored by his own church setting, the evidence is sufficient to indicate that in the early church prophets were neither rare, marginal, nor parochial.

THE PROPHET WITHIN THE CHURCH

Modern historical study of early Christian prophetism was given fresh impetus by the writings of Adolf Harnack at the end of the last century, who wrote under the spell of the then recently discovered *Didache*. Harnack himself first presented the *Didache* to the modern world in a Greek-German edition of the text with extensive introduction and commentary.[1] Harnack understood the *Didache* to portray a "two-fold ministry" in which apostles, prophets, and teachers (all charismatics) were a universal, itinerant ministry, and bishops and deacons were a settled, congregational ministry. Harnack's enthusiasm for the new discovery permitted him, not without violence, to read this schematization into the New Testament and all his sources, as is apparent in the following quotation:

> The *Didache* has finally brought us light [i.e., on the structure and leadership of the earliest church]. The precious information it gives us concerning the place of apostles, prophets, and teachers in the congregations provides suitable illumination for understanding passages such as 1 Cor. 12:28–29; Acts 11:27; 13:1–2; Eph. 2:20; 3:5; 4:11; Rev. 2:2; Matt. 10 par; Euseb *HE* 3.37 and many others.[2]

Quite apart from the methodological error of generalizing from one source, it is not at all as clear as Harnack supposed that the prophets represented by the *Didache* are of an exclusively wandering type. The first mention of prophets (10.7) occurs in the context of prescribed prayers for the cup, the loaf, and the meal, and simply says "but permit the prophets to give thanks as much as they wish," with no suggestion that such prophets are anything but local figures. The extended discussion of "apostles and prophets" in *Didache* 11 may be understood in terms of traveling prophets but need not be so, and certainly may not be the basis for interpreting ambiguous references in other sources as describing an itinerant prophetic ministry. Only "apostles" are clearly spoken of as coming to the congregation from without. "False prophets" is used of those "apostles" who are judged to be frauds, but this seems to be because "false prophet" is a general pejorative term that may be applied to a variety of types of fraudulent church leaders, not because the author of the *Didache* is making the equation "apostle" = "prophet." Nothing in this chapter explicitly refers to peripatetic prophets; everything said of apostles refers to their coming and going. Only at *Didache* 13.1 do we have a reference to a prophet coming into the community from outside, but here it is a matter of taking up residence among the congregation as a part of it and receiving payment from it, without any indication even here of a previous itinerant ministry. That there probably were wandering prophets is not excluded. But the evidence in these texts for making itinerancy of the essence of early Christian prophetism seems slender indeed.

---

1 *Die Lehre der zwölf Apostel nebst Untersuchungen zur ältesten Kirchenfassung und des Kirchenrechts.*
2 Ibid., 94.

This picture of the "wandering" prophet of the Syrian churches, based primarily on Harnack's interpretation of the *Didache* and reinforced by questionable analogies to the wandering Cynic preachers and "divine man" types, has had a continuing influence on the interpretation of Christian prophecy. Especially, the recent works of Gerd Theissen has popularized the figure of the "wandering charismatic" as the standard picture of the early Christian prophet.[3] The issue is an important one for the hypothesis explored here since it is difficult to imagine such prophets having had much influence on the developing tradition of the sayings of Jesus that led to our Gospels.

Before responding to the question of whether early Christian prophets were "wandering" or "settled," once again the question needs to be sharpened and definitions need to be clarified. Like other people, prophets may travel from place to place. A single prophet may travel on a circuit, visiting several congregations, without being an outsider to any of them, one of which may be "home base" where he or she would be considered a "resident" prophet. Itinerant prophets may or may not have such a home base, may or may not have abandoned home and family permanently, may or may not see themselves and be seen by the churches as free-lance outsiders. Thomas Schmeller's recent sociological studies[4] have shown that "wandering charismatics" is not a univocal term but that a variety of sociological types are included. Both he and Theissen argue that settled communities are presupposed as the counterpart for the "wandering charismatics," and the "home base" to which they are oriented. These groups transmitted sayings of Jesus that speak of abandoning home and family for Jesus' sake (e.g., Mark 10:29–30) but that does not prove that they had literally done so.

Sociological theory is careful not to make too direct a connection between the ideas handed on by a community and the community's own practice.[5] One cannot necessarily infer from the former to the latter. Theissen's view that sayings of Jesus that include a call for radical abandonment of home and family could only have been handed on by a homeless group on the fringe of society and church need not be accepted: Amos's words were preserved even by a community that never did quite succeed in establishing justice in the gate; Revelation was preserved by a church all the members of which did not become martyrs; and the thirteenth chapter of 1 Corinthians was preserved by a church that could

3 Gerd Theissen, *Sociology of Early Palestinian Christianity;* " 'Wanderradikalismus.' Literatursoziologische Aspekte der Überlieferung von Worten Jesu im Urchristentum"; *Studien zur Soziologie des Urchristentums.*

4 *Brechungen,* 50–116.

5 So also Klaus Berger, *Exegese des Neuen Testaments. Neue Wege vom Text zur Auslegung,* 240; Schmeller, *Brechungen,* 40.

hardly claim to have put it into practice. In advance of examining the evidence, it is historically and sociologically unjustified to picture prophetic types exclusively as "wanderers" outside the settled churches and only scribal types resident in them.

When our sources are approached without this prejudgment, another picture emerges. The prophet-author of Revelation writes to seven churches (1:4), which may well mean that he did not reside at one place but traveled from church to church. But he writes as a known insider who introduces himself simply as "John" and expects a hearing, not as a "wandering" stranger who does not belong within the churches he addresses. To be sure, he takes his stand with the exalted Lord over against the congregation he addresses, but this is because he is a *prophet,* not because he is an outsider to the local churches. On the contrary, the rich use of tradition and liturgical materials from the congregational worship found in Revelation presents John as one very much at home within the settled, ordered life of the Christian community, rather than as a traveling prophet who intrudes his oracles into a community to which he does not essentially belong. My point is not that there were no itinerant prophets, but that prophecy was an intra-community phenomenon, not an individualistic one.[6]

Paul, like John, is an example of a prophetic figure who, though he travels from place to place, is still to be seen as a constituent member within the church where he is located. Paul identifies with the congregations to which he ministers, takes his stance within them, is by no means a "wandering" itinerant who troubles the life of the "settled" churches. And Paul's understanding of the prophetic ministry is that it is a ministry of, and within, the church. God places prophets "in the church" (1 Cor. 12:28). Prophecy is repeatedly mentioned in the midst of a discussion of the corporate life of the church (Rom. 12:6; 1 Cor. 11:4–5; 12:-10; 14:1–39; 1 Thess. 5:20). Everything in the extended discussion in 1 Corinthians 14 indicates that the prophets in Corinth are resident members of the community, not wandering bearers of an individualistic charisma. Even so, there is a tension between Paul's understanding of prophecy and the understanding of "spirit" held by the Corinthians, in that theirs tends toward individualism while Paul rejects an individualistic anthropology in favor of the community, the new eschatological people of God, as the bearer of the Spirit. Here, Paul reflects the earlier Palestinian church, which grew out of a Judaism that, nurtured on the Old Testament promises, looked forward to a community of the Spirit.

---

6 James M. Robinson, "On Bridging the Gulf from Q to the Gospel of Thomas (Or Vice Versa)," in *Nag Hammadi, Gnosticism, and Early Christianity,* ed. Charles W. Hedrick and Robert Hodgson, Jr., 127–175, has given a correct nuance to my earlier extreme statements on this point.

Paul is here a witness to the idea of prophecy held by early Palestinian Christianity.

In Acts the fact that prophets are sometimes pictured as moving from place to place (11:27–28; 15:30–32; 21:10) has led some scholars to speak of prophets in Acts as "itinerant" rather than "settled." It should be observed, however, that Acts also represents the prophets as "settled" (13:1–2; 19:6; 21:4, 9). In 13:1–2, it is clear that resident prophets in the settled community are those who send out others. In 20:23 Paul and his company are pictured as traveling and receiving prophetic testimony from the (presumably "settled") prophets "in every city." In Acts the only figures specifically called prophets who are also represented as traveling are Judas, Silas, and Agabus (15:32; 11:27–28; 21:10). Judas and Silas are not itinerant individuals but are sent as delegates from one congregation to another and on missionary trips (15:32, 40). And even Agabus is not depicted as an extra-church individualist prophet but as one who is at home within the churches he visits, perhaps calling one of them, the Jerusalem congregation, his "home church." The prophetic phenomenon is located by Luke firmly within the Christian community.

Matthew also portrays Christian prophecy as an intra-church phenomenon. As in Acts prophets indeed travel (10:1–42). They are not to be characterized as itinerant, however, because they are sent out by the church in response to the prayers of the congregation (9:38). They are sent out not to intrude on "settled," noncharismatic congregations but to heal and preach to the unconverted. Thus Matthew 9:37–10:42 is a Matthean version of a scene like Acts 13:1–2. That there were prophets who came to the Matthean congregations from outside (7:15–23) is, of course, not disputed. But it is not clear that these were wandering, individualistic prophets; they could just as well be seen as the representatives of some other branch of Christianity with a "home base" elsewhere. In any case, Matthew regards them as false prophets, and they should not be regarded as characteristic of the Matthean community.

The authors of the Gospel and letters of John belong to a close-knit community within which the Spirit/Paraclete comes to expression as Christian prophecy. The false prophets who are opposed are not free-lancers but erstwhile members of John's own community and members of some opposing confessional community, as is indicated by 1 John 2:19; 4:1. If 2 John and 3 John come from the same community as the Gospel of John and 1 John, the traveling preachers to be rejected are not charismatic individualists but representatives of another confessional community; just as, conversely, the representatives of the elder's own community are rejected by the opposing communities (2 John 9–11; 3 John 7–10).

Our other sources confirm this view unanimously: Ephesians regards prophets as one of the ministries *within* the body or the very foundation of the structure of the church (4:11–12; 2:19–22). The author of the

Pastorals is doubly anxious to incorporate prophecy within the regular church life for it is either identified with that which is received at ordination (1 Tim. 4:14) or seen as fulfilled in the ministry of one who is regularly ordained (1 Tim. 1:18). Hermas stigmatizes as *false prophets* those who give private revelations to individuals in response to questions (i.e., who attempt to operate as prophets outside the congregation), while *prophets* speak *in the congregation* in response to prayers addressed to God. Christian prophets cannot manipulate their gift; it is not at their disposal but functions within the community as a part of its worship (Mandate 11. 1–21). All the above should indicate that the "wandering" aspect of early Christian prophecy has been exaggerated in the secondary literature on Christian prophecy.

In our working definition of Christian prophecy, we have emphasized that prophecy functions within the church. This does not mean that Christian prophecy had no message for, or influence upon, those outside the congregations. There is some evidence that outsiders are also addressed by the prophets' message, but there is no evidence that would modify either our working definition or our description above of prophets as essentially intra-church figures. Paul can picture a scene in which outsiders are addressed by prophetic preaching (1 Cor. 14:24–25) but this is because they are visiting within a Christian congregation. The Apocalypse pronounces judgment on the unbelieving outside world (e.g., the oracle against "Babylon" in 18:1–24), but this is only "overheard" by the world in a prophetic message prepared to be delivered in the congregation (1:3–4). Or, on the other hand, when "the world" seems to be addressed by the seer, as in 8:13, this is primarily an indirect message to the church to the extent that it has become like the unbelieving "world."

Similarly with the Paraclete, which is an intra-church ministry sent *not* to the world but to the believers, which functions in such a way that it brings judgment on the unbelieving world (John 16:7–11). The prophetic ministers in Acts (Paul, Barnabas, and Silas, but not Agabus) do address "the world" directly, as do the prophets among the missionaries in Matthew (10:40–41). In such cases, the prophet is directly engaged with the world, but this is because the prophet belongs to the church, and the church is engaged with the world. I am not contending that the prophet was any more isolated from the world than other Christians were, only that prophecy is basically an intra-church phenomenon, that when the prophet addresses the world he or she does this not independently but as a member of the church from within which he or she speaks. The prophet has no independent message directly to the world but stands within the Christian community that has a message to the world.

PROPHETS AS A DISTINCT GROUP
WITHIN THE CONGREGATION

In the Jewish community from which early Christianity sprang, the Holy Spirit was considered preeminently the Spirit of prophecy. The conviction of the early church, like that of Qumran, was that it was the eschatological community upon whom the eschatological gift of the Spirit had been poured out. The community as a whole, not just the select few, were the bearers of the Spirit. It is thus readily understandable that the idea could become diffused in the early church that all Christians were prophets, at least ideally or potentially.

John the Seer is a prophet; yet, as Eduard Schweizer points out, "precisely in his capacity of bearer of the Spirit he is only a brother and comrade of all the other church members (1:9)," and the testimony in which the whole church is engaged is the "spirit of prophecy" (19:10). This leads Schweizer to conclude that "the whole Church is understood in principle at least as a church of prophets,"[7] a conclusion that has been shared by several others.

This distinction is also blurred in Schweizer's discussion of the church in the background of the Gospel of Matthew. After arguing, correctly I believe, that Matthew and his church were not hostile to charismatic phenomena per se, Schweizer comments that: "In its preaching the church is a church of prophets."[8] Surely he intends to assert that prophets in the strict sense were active in Matthew's church and that in general the preaching of such a church would be characterized by a kind of authority associated with the community's belief in its possession of the Spirit, but not that every sermon preached in the community was by an immediately inspired prophet in the sense of our definition, or that every person in the community made such a prophetic claim for himself or herself. However, the phrase "in principle at least" and similar qualifiers are to be noted and underscored. The author of Revelation is obviously a prophet in a way that distinguishes him from most others in his church, as are the prophets described by Matthew. The situation in the Matthean community is best summarized by Alexander Sand,[9] who regards prophecy as *the* category that Matthew uses to present discipleship as such in terms of three concentric circles: (1) a small number of missionary prophets, who were the central core of (2) a larger number of resident prophets, who are not sharply distinguished, i.e., not in any "clergy/laity" sense, from (3) disciples in general in Matthew's church. Although it seems to me that the thrice repeated pair "prophets and righteous" (10:41; 13:17;

7 Eduard Schweizer, *Church Order in the New Testament*, 135.
8 Schweizer, "Observance of the Law and Charismatic Activity in Matthew," 226.
9 Sand, *Das Gesetz*, 168–177.

23:29) does suggest more distinction between prophets as such and other disciples than Sand's presentation indicates, I would agree that prophecy is not discontinuous with Christian life generally in the Matthean church.

This appears to be typical of our sources. Paul expects that anyone in the Corinthian church can prophesy by virtue of having been baptized into the body of Christ where the Spirit is common to all (1 Cor. 12:13; 14:1, 39), but he does not expect an affirmative answer to his question "are all prophets?" (12:29), as even the grammar attests (Paul's question begins with the Greek negative particle *me*, which introduces a question expecting a negative response: "All are not prophets, are they?"). Luke begins his story of the church by affirming programmatically that, unlike the experience in Israel, now the Spirit of prophecy has been poured out upon "all flesh," adding an emphatic "and they shall prophesy" to the citation from Joel (Acts 2:17–18). Yet as the story continues, it is apparent that only some are designated as prophets (11:27–28; 13:1–2; 15:32; 21:9–11).

So also in the Johannine church: The Paraclete-prophet is a manifestation of that Spirit in which all believers participate, yet not all members of the community perform the particular prophetic functions represented by the Paraclete. Hermas (Mandate 11) also seems to provide evidence for both a designated group of prophets within the congregation and the potential for any member of the congregation to be filled with the Spirit and begin to speak by inspiration. All our other sources evince a clear distinction between the prophets and the body of believers as a whole (Eph. 2:20; 3:5; 4:11–12; 1 Tim. 1:18; 4:14; *Didache* 11–13).

This dual perspective, in which the community as a whole has a prophetic self-understanding, although within the community only relatively few actually emerge as prophets, is also found at Qumran. The existence of such an understanding of prophecy in the environs within which early Christianity originated and the same understanding documented at several widely separated points in later first-century Christianity would indicate that this was also the case in earliest Christianity, which understood the Spirit (of prophecy) to be poured out on the community as a whole, not just on gifted individuals. Yet, when we speak of early Christian prophets, we are not talking about some amorphous entity vaguely diffused throughout the church. Although, as we have seen, early Christian prophets were not solitary individuals outside the churches, neither are they simply to be identified with the community as such. Without being an official "order," they are a recognizably distinct group within the early church who may be identified by characteristic features.

PROPHETIC UTTERANCE AS TESTED BY
THE COMMUNITY OF FAITH

That early Christian prophets were not independent figures over against the community is seen in the fact that their revelations were tested by the community, which also possessed the Spirit. A preliminary reading of our primary instance of Christian prophecy, the Apocalypse, seems to indicate that the prophets of John's church may have stood over against the community at large as the sole possessors of the Spirit. "Spirit" and "church" are repeatedly contrasted with each other (2:7, 11, 17, etc.), and the whole community seems to be divided into "Spirit" (prophets) and "Bride" (church) in 22:17. Further, the Revelation seems to be launched into the churches as a projectile to be obeyed without any indication that it is to be criticized and evaluated by the community.

No doubt something of the authentic prophetic consciousness comes to expression here. The prophetic mode was not to pose issues for discussion by the community but to deliver the unqualified word of the Lord. We should not expect the prophetic address itself to present us with a discussion of how the prophetic phenomenon was dealt with by the community. And yet even in Revelation there are some important clues in this regard. In addition to the common ground the seer shares with the church, which we have discussed above, it is to be noted that John begins and ends with an appeal to the hearer really to hear (1:3; 22:17). "He asserted that the truth of his message had been fully endorsed by the angel, the Spirit, and the Messiah. He appealed to every reader and every congregation to join in the circle of endorsement. Presumably this appeal succeeded; otherwise this book would doubtless have joined many other early Christian documents in oblivion."[10] This argument by Paul Minear is to be taken seriously: the book itself indicates that the author understood the churches he addressed to be fully capable of evaluating claims to Christian truth, including specifically the evaluation of prophetic claims, and that he expected them to do so (2:2, 6, 14, 15, 20).

Revelation does not discuss prophecy but presents us with an example of it. On the other hand, of all our sources, Paul is the most theologically reflective on this problem. He never introduces the subject of prophecy without including affirmations of the community's capability of, and responsibility for, the evaluation of claims to revelation.

1 Thessalonians 5:19–22

The earliest mention of prophecy in the New Testament is an apostolic admonition that it should not be despised. Paul finds himself in the situation of commending prophetic speech to those who are suspicious

---

10 *I Saw a New Earth,* 189.

of it. But while prophetic claims are not to be dismissed, neither are they to be uncritically accepted. The exhortations concerning the Spirit in verses 19–20 are joined to proverblike statements of verses 21–22 to form one unit. The congregation is not at the mercy of pneumatic claims for it possesses the Spirit, not only because it includes pneumatics in its midst but as a total community (4:8). Paul's original preaching to them in the power of the Spirit was complemented by their reception of the word by the same Spirit (1:5–6).

1 Corinthians 2:6–16

Christian prophecy and its role in the community is not limited to the key section, chapters 12–14, but is already in view here, expressed in the dual concern that the community does in fact receive revelations from beyond itself by the Spirit and that the community can and should evaluate such revelations by the Spirit resident in the community as a whole. Both these concerns are embodied in the pivotal verse 13, which Robert Funk paraphrases: "In so doing we are combining or comparing spiritual things with spiritual things, and thus discerning the spirits, i.e., engaging in substantive criticism. For the Spirit not only confers wisdom and spiritual gifts, but stands in critical judgment upon wisdom and spiritual gifts."[11]

1 Corinthians 12–14

The issue that has surfaced in the preceding texts becomes the object of a full-blown discussion in this key section of 1 Corinthians. In 12:3 the point is not only that in the basic Christian confession an "objective norm" of sorts is given by which the authenticity of inspired speech can be recognized but that the whole community that confesses "Jesus is Lord" is thereby authenticated as community of the Holy Spirit and is therefore capable of evaluating claims to pneumatic speech. In the light of the preceding, the gift of *diakrisis* (the ability to distinguish between spirits) in 12:10, closely associated with the gift of prophecy, should be understood as the Spirit-given gift to the community to evaluate the claims to revelation by the Spirit.[12]

This text should be seen in conjunction with 14:29, where "the others" are to exercise their critical judgment on what a prophet has said. Although it is not clear whether "the others" refers to the community as a whole or to the other prophets, it is clear that a prophetic declaration

---

11 *Language, Hermeneutic, and Word of God,* 293.

12 This standard interpretation has been challenged by Dautzenberg's lengthy monograph, *Urchristliche Prophetie,* in which he argues that *diakrisis* refers to the process of interpreting the Spirit-given oracles of the prophets. His argument has not been widely accepted and is effectively refuted by Müller, *Prophetie und Predigt,* 27–28; cf. David Hill, *New Testament Prophecy,* 133–134.

in the community is not to be simply received uncritically at face value but that others besides the receiver of the revelation are to exercise discriminating judgment in behalf of the community and that this discrimination is itself a charisma of the one Spirit that pervades the congregation as a whole.

Although Paul values prophecy as the highest charisma excepting only love, he also knows that even inspired speech claiming to be the very word of the Lord can be inflicted on a hapless community as the product of human arrogance. He thus writes in 13:9 (NRSV): "for we know only in part, and we prophesy only in part." "Direct revelation" is still historical, relative, to be tested. It still does not lift the prophet or apostle above the finite human condition. It is still a "treasure in earthen vessels, to show that the transcendent power belongs to God and not to us" (2 Cor. 4:7).

Romans 12:6

In a reflective mood, looking back on the stormy struggle with the Corinthians concerning pneumatic speech, Paul instructs the Romans that prophecy should be "according to the analogy of faith." This phrase can be understood and translated to refer either to the prophet's own subjective faith (*fides qua creditur,* the faith with which one believes) or the objective faith believed by the prophet and the community as a whole (*fides quae creditur,* the faith that is believed). The preceding discussion, and the corporate nature of the Christian life that is implicit throughout the context of this phrase, should confirm the insight of numerous recent interpreters that this text refers to the latter: the norm of prophetic speech is the content of the community's faith, presumably as expressed in its basic confessional statements. While this could never mean for Paul that there was an objective rule of faith that could be used to squelch the word of the Spirit—Paul's view of faith was too dynamic for that—it does mean that prophecy functions only within the corporate life of the community's faith, which forms the context for evaluating it.

Prophetic revelation functioned this way in Paul's own ministry. As a prophet, he was absolutely convinced that he had a revelation from the risen Lord (Gal. 1:11–12), yet if it did not correspond to the gospel that had been preached to the Galatians and received by them, it was to be rejected, even if preached by Paul himself or an angel from heaven (Gal. 1:8–9). The reference to the "angel" here is not an arbitrary rhetorical flourish but refers to the revelatory angel often a part of the prophetic experience (see chapter 9 below). Paul makes a journey to the Jerusalem church leaders, a journey that he believes he has been led by a divine revelation to make, to present the gospel to them, which he also believes is revealed from the risen Lord. He both believes that churchly confirmation of his revelation is necessary ("Lest somehow I should be running or had run in vain," 2:2) and has the prophet's confidence that his revelation is valid. This is also clearly seen in the closing words of Paul's discussion of Christian prophecy in 1 Corinthians 14:37–38!

Although only Paul gives a thorough discussion of this issue, our other sources indicate that prophetic revelation was dealt with in a similar or analogous way in the churches they represent. It is remarkable that, though Acts has a high view of prophetic revelation (13:1–3; 11:28–30; 16:6–10; cf. 3:22–23), revelation that is acknowledged to be from the Spirit can sometimes simply be ignored; at least it does not alter the decisions of the persons addressed (20:22–23; 21:4, 10–14). I am implying not that these scenes are precisely historical but that Luke's understanding of the prophetic phenomenon included both an affirmation of the revelation as having come from the Spirit and a judicious weighing of the message by the recipients; and that it was this combination of revelation-plus-response-by-the-community that was considered the revelatory event, and not the Spirit-inspired oracles alone. This is captured in one Lukan phrase in 15:28: "it has seemed good to the Holy Spirit *and to us."*

The issue of testing prophetic revelation is not directly discussed in the Fourth Gospel, but the way that instruction from the Paraclete is described does give criteria that the community may apply to purported revelations, in that it will bring to the church's remembrance the tradition of Jesus' words (14:26) and will bear witness to Jesus himself (15:26). The community addressed in 1 John itself has the Spirit (3:24; 4:13) and has no need for anyone (outside the community) to teach it because it itself has the "anointing" of the Spirit (2:27; cf. "for you yourselves have been taught by God," 1 Thess. 4:9). It is thus capable of discerning the validity of various claims to revelation by the Spirit, in part by means of the creedal confession that "Jesus Christ has come in the flesh" but also because it knows itself to be a Spirit-endowed community that confesses this faith (4:1–3; cf. 1 Cor. 12:1–3).

The Matthean community also acknowledges the continuing voice of its risen Lord, making himself known through Christian prophets, but knows that it must test such claims. In 7:15–20, Matthew himself seems to have taken up a traditional saying, "you will know them by their fruits" (v. 16), and applied it specifically to the problem of prophecy. Similarly in 7:21–23, *anomia* (lawlessness) is the community's criterion to sort out false claims to revelation. The *Didache,* which probably reflects the church in the same geographical area as Matthew as it struggles with the prophetic claims in its midst, is almost humorous in its effort both to respect the Spirit of prophecy (11.7: "Do not test or examine any prophet who is speaking in a spirit, 'for every sin shall be forgiven, but this sin shall not be forgiven' ") and to avoid being taken in by illegitimate claims to revelation by the application of rough and ready rules to distinguish true prophets from false (a prophet who orders a meal or asks for money while "inspired" is a false prophet, 11.8–12). Even in the early second-century Roman church, this same traditional manner of responding to inspired speech in the congregation was still practiced according to Hermas's Mandate 11.

Any community that accepts the reality of prophetic revelation must develop means of coming to terms with this claim and sorting out valid from invalid elements in its prophetic tradition. Early Christianity stood in a long tradition of claims to prophetic revelation, stretching from the earliest prophets of Israel to the prophets that arose in its midst. During this history, a number of criteria had emerged.[13] Yet, as the following list indicates, each criterion has inherent problems as well as conflicts with other criteria:

- The true prophet is validated by his or her ability to work miracles and signs (1 Kings 17–19). But false prophets also work miracles (Deut. 13:1–3; Matt. 7:21–23).
- The true prophet is validated by the accuracy of his or her predictions (Deut. 18:20–22; 1 Kings 22:28; Isa. 30:8–11). But, apart from the fact that the bulk of prophecy is not predictive anyway, the hearers must typically decide before this criterion could be helpful. Strictly applied, this criterion would exclude some canonical prophets (e.g., Amos 7:11 vs. 2 Kings 14:29; 2 Kings 22:20 vs. 23:29; Ezek. 26:7–14 vs. 29:17–20; Jonah 3:4 vs. 3:10; Jer. 22:30 vs. Matt. 1:12).
- The true prophet receives his or her message in a vision, while the message of false prophets comes through dreams (Jer. 23:16–18, 25–28, 32). Yet dreams are also evaluated positively by those who affirm prophetic revelation (Dan. 2: 4; 7:1; Matthew 1–2).
- The true prophet proclaims doom, the false prophet salvation (Jer. 23:17; 28:8–9; 1 Kings 22; Ezek. 13:10). This criterion too would exclude some canonical prophets such as 2 Isaiah. In any case, most prophecies contain a combination of the two.
- Fidelity to the covenant God and righteous conduct (not merely miracles) is the sign of the true prophet, while false prophets are immoral (Deut. 13:1–3; Matt. 7:15–20; *Didache* 11.8, 10). But what constitutes such fidelity and immorality is often a matter of interpretation.

---

13 For the Old Testament, cf. J. L. Crenshaw, *Prophetic Conflict*, 39–61, and the helpful summary in Aune, *Prophecy*, 87–88.

- True prophecy is in accord with the fundamental faith of the community as expressed in traditional creeds (Deut. 13:1–3; 1 Cor. 12:3; Rom. 12:6; 1 John 4:1–3; 2 John 7–9). Yet such creeds are not universal, and whether a particular claim to revelation is in accord with a particular creedal statement is always a matter of interpretation.
- True prophecy is oriented to the edification of the community, rather than being individualistic (1 Corinthians 14). But what builds up the community can be a disputed point.
- The true prophet will not order a meal for him- or herself in the Spirit, or ask for money for him- or herself, or want to stay more than three days (*Didache* 11.9; 12.2; Hermas, Mandate 11). Here the criteria are clear enough but of limited usefulness.
- One criterion is noticeably absent: "sincerity." It is assumed that all prophets believe their own revelation. The point of the peculiar story in 1 Kings 13 is apparently that each prophet must be true to the message he or she has received, even when it conflicts with other revelatory claims. Prophets may be deceived by the deity (1 Kings 22) or by themselves, but the term "false" in the phrase "false prophets" means that their message is false, not that they think of themselves as "false prophets." All the biblical prophets were thought of as "false prophets" by their opponents, and vice versa. Jeremiah himself had no criteria by which to measure true and false and agonized over the validity of his own message, while his prophetic opponents were self-assured (Jer. 20:7–18; 27:1–22). The prophets' sincerity does not help the community to adjudicate conflicting claims.

Since our sources, mostly literarily independent, all manifest essentially the same relationship between the congregation and its prophets, we may confidently assume that this relationship obtained also in that early stream of Palestinian-oriented Christian prophecy with which we are concerned. The prophetic charisma was widely honored; everywhere it was honored it was also judiciously criticized by a community that did not consider the prophets within it as the sole bearers of the Spirit. This aspect of prophetic ministry is important in considering whether or not Christian prophets might have contributed to the developing tradition of sayings of Jesus. While the process of evaluating the claims to speak the word of the risen Jesus should not be thought of in legal, official, systematic terms (boards did not meet after each "revelation" to decide on its validity), the evidence suggests that this process should be thought of as neither arbitrary nor haphazard.

The Christian prophet had neither the opportunity nor the authority to insert his or her own post-Easter revelations willy-nilly into the church's collection of sayings of Jesus.[14] The community itself was the arbiter of what was a saying of the Lord and what was not. The common denominator between the traditional sayings of Jesus and new prophetic sayings of the risen Lord was the community itself, the bearer of the tradition. This calls for a study of the relation of Christian prophecy to the tradition and the tradition process. But first we must examine the relation of prophets to worship, to determine if the worship life of the church might be the setting within the community in which prophecy and tradition have their vital interaction.

CHRISTIAN PROPHECY AND WORSHIP

The most substantial recent challenge to the view that Christian prophets influenced the developing Gospel tradition has been made by Rainer Riesner, who has well argued that for there to have been interchange between prophetic and traditional sayings of Jesus, the two types of sayings must have existed in a common setting.[15] It is quite true that if the sayings of Jesus had been transmitted only in a catechetical setting where rigidly formed materials were memorized verbatim and passed along without modification, while the oracles of Christian prophets were only ephemeral and inspirational outbursts spoken spontaneously into an unstructured setting, then it is not likely that sayings of Christian prophets would have influenced the developing tradition of Jesus' words.

Such a picture is exaggerated in the extreme. Riesner has made a good case, however, that the classical form critics too easily imagined the worship services of the community as the primary setting for the transmission of the word and that we should also think of catechetical settings separate from the worship gathering.[16] The distinction is well taken; classical form criticism did tend to generalize too uncritically. But Riesner's picture is too rigid. It is correct that there was more than one setting in early Christianity for the teaching and preaching of the word, but these settings were not as insulated from each other as he supposes. The distinction breaks down from both sides. On the one hand, the worship setting was not as unstructured and prophecy not as informal as he imagines, and, on the other hand, the instructional setting did not

---

14 James D. G. Dunn has rightly insisted on this point in "Prophetic 'I-Sayings.'" However, in responding to my argument that Mark 3:28–29 is the oracle of a Christian prophet, he arrives at the somewhat peculiar position that the saying must be from the historical Jesus since if it had not been in the tradition from the beginning it would not have passed the tests the early church applied to such sayings. His most recent discussion of this point is still wide of the mark ("Matthew 12:28/Luke 11:20—A Word of Jesus?" in Hulitt Gloer, ed., *Eschatology and the New Testament*, 36–37.

15 *Jesus als Lehrer*, 515 and passim.

16 Ibid., 57–58.

exclude the charismatic teacher and engagement with charismatic inter-pretations of and additions to Jesus sayings. Furthermore, the worship life of the congregation was itself a setting in which traditions were passed on and around.

Within the community of faith, prophecy was a function of the com-munity gathered for worship. "Early Christian prophecy was liturgical prophecy."[17] Prophecy functioned in a "public," communal setting rather than in a private, individual setting. This is vividly documented by the Apocalypse, which came as a revelation on the day when the congre-gation assembled for worship (1:10), indicating that even the enforced separation of the prophet from his church does not negate what must have been the usual circumstance, that the prophet received his revela-tion in association with the community's worship. The Apocalypse is written to be read in worship to the gathered congregation, in the ab-sence of the prophet himself (1:4). It begins with a greeting of grace and peace (1:4), closes with a benediction (22:21), and is permeated through-out with worship materials, of which 4:11; 5:9–13; 11:17–18; 12:10–12; 15:3–4; 19:1–5, 6–8 are only the more explicit examples, since the whole prophecy is conceived within a cultic framework that unites the heavenly and earthly cultic spheres.

All Paul's specific references to prophecy in 1 Corinthians are in-cluded in the extensive discussion of public worship that stretches from 11:2 through 14:39. Paul regards prophecy as occurring in worship, as a ministry performed before the gathered congregation, and only there. Presumably prophets might receive revelations at other times—though there is nothing in Paul that makes even this assumption necessary—but these revelations do not function as prophecy unless and until they are delivered to the community, for whose edification they are intended (14:3). A fundamental difference between tongues and prophecy for Paul is this difference between personal edification and the edification of the whole community (14:4). A prophecy must become the subject of the *diakrisis,* the critical examination of the wider community (12:10; 14:29). The close relationship between prayer and prophecy in 1 Thessalonians 5:19–20 and the possibility of the community's disdaining of prophetic utterance probably also indicate the worship setting of prophecy in Paul's thought. Paul speaks out of and in behalf of a tradition in which prophecy in the context of ordered worship is the rule (14:26–33, 40). In his thought, prophecy and structured worship are correlatives, not alterna-tives. In this as on other points, he reflects the tradition of early Pales-tinian prophecy over against the more spontaneous spiritual phenomena valued by the Corinthians.

---

17 Elisabeth Schüssler Fiorenza, *In Memory of Her: A Feminist Theological Reconstruction of Christian Origins,* 300.

The possibility of prophets giving private revelations to individuals outside the setting of the gathered congregation is utterly alien to Paul. The communal view of prophecy was maintained in the Pauline tradition that related pneumatic speech to the worship setting (Col. 3:16; Eph. 5:18–20; 1 Tim. 1:18; 4:14).

Prophets in Acts function in gatherings of the community that are sometimes specifically designated as worship settings (11:27–29; 13:1–3; 15:1–32; 19:1–7; probably 21:10–14); other references are not so clearly so (16:6–9; 20:23; 21:4). The prophetic figures of Luke 1–2 are all associated with a worship context, and their oracles have a liturgical ring. The speech material of the Fourth Gospel seems to have been handed on, continually re-formed, and used in the liturgy of a worshiping community. John's materials bear the marks of being grounded in worship as their setting in the church's life.[18] The Paraclete is not the individualistic teacher within the heart of every Christian but a functional ministry within the Johannine community.[19] It is clear that in the *Didache* the prophets are expected to lead in worship (10.7) and are seen as filling the role of "high priests" to the community (13.3), with nothing suggesting that prophets function outside the worship setting. This latter view is explicitly opposed in Hermas, who considers the context of worship by the holy community as the sine qua non of all legitimate prophecy (Mandate 11. 1–9), while false prophets avoid congregations (Mandate 11. 13). The prophets of the *Odes of Solomon* function in worship and generate materials used in the liturgy in the name of the risen Jesus (42.6). The "prophecy" of Ignatius occurs in the worship assembly of the congregation, where it serves to confirm church order (*Philadelphians* 7.1). When this almost unanimous evidence of the New Testament and early Christian literature is placed beside the fact that in Israel, Judaism, and paganism there was frequently a connection between prophecy and the cult, we may be justified in concluding that this was the case with early Christian prophets as well. This supposition is strengthened by an examination of the relation of prophecy to tradition.

CHRISTIAN PROPHECY AND TRADITION

The worship setting was typically not unstructured and without content but was a principal setting where the sacred tradition of the community was re-presented and communicated, passed on and around, reinterpreted in preaching and teaching for new situations, and re-experienced as the living voice of the church's Lord. The Jewish setting from which early

---

18 Cf. Oscar Cullmann, *Early Christian Worship*, 37–116.
19 Cf. Boring, "Johannine Portrayal of the Paraclete," 113–120.

Christianity derived already had this conception of worship. The Palestinian synagogue was heavily oriented toward the transmission and interpretation of tradition. The synagogue assemblies of Hellenistic Judaism are pictured by both Josephus and Philo as almost academic occasions, describing the synagogues as "teaching centers" and worship as "philosophizing" (*Jewish War* 2.119; *Antiquities* 18.11; *Life* 12; and *On the Special Laws* 2.61–62; *Life of Moses* 2.215–216; *On the Creation* 128; *On the Decalogue* 98, 100). In that Judaism from which Christianity sprang, the line between "school" and "worship" had grown thin.

The evidence is that in early Christianity as well, the worship life of the congregation was intensely engaged in the transmission and re-presentation of the Christian tradition. Since this is the setting where prophets were active, one should expect to find a close relationship between prophets and tradition. Yet a widespread stereotype of Christian prophecy pictures it as divorced from tradition. Some representative statements:

> All prophecy rests on revelation, 1 Cor. 14:30. The prophet does not declare what he has taken from tradition or what he has thought up himself.[20]
> This [early Palestinian Christian] prophecy spoke independently of the Scriptures and the developing tradition.[21]
> Preaching was oriented primarily to the word of God as handed on in the tradition, while prophetic speech breaks forth directly by the power of the Holy Spirit.[22]
> Since "prophecy," in contrast to "teaching," does not draw from tradition but rests on direct revelation, from the very beginning determining the legitimacy of a prophet was a matter of the greatest importance.[23]
> Prophets do not come in question as bearers of the tradition, since their task was not the preservation of material from the past, but addressing contemporary concerns in the name of the exalted Lord.[24]

This understanding of prophecy is a significant factor in the reluctance of some New Testament scholars to accept the relation of Christian prophets to the Gospel tradition. It is a misunderstanding.

The supposed separation of prophecy from tradition is not derived from the sources. Recent studies of Old Testament prophets have revealed how congenial the use of tradition is with the claim to speak directly for the Lord. To take but one example: as the careful commen-

---

20 Gerhard Friedrich, *"Prophētēs," TDNT* 6:853.
21 Leonhard Goppelt, *Apostolic and Post-Apostolic Times* (New York: Harper & Row, 1962), 45.
22 Bartholomäus Hennecken, *Verkündigung und Prophetie im 1. Thessalonicherbrief,* 113.
23 Joseph Schmidt, "Propheten (b) im NT," *Lexikon für Theologie und Kirche* 8:799.
24 Zimmermann, *Lehrer,* 34.

tary of Hans Walter Wolff reveals,[25] Joel was a prophet who operated in the context of the cult and its transmission of materials and was himself immersed in the transmission process, including taking up the words of older prophets and re-presenting them without directly quoting them, in a manner genuinely new—all of which, as we shall see, is similar to what early Christian prophets did.

In that Jewish apocalyptic which forms part of the background of early Christian prophecy, the seer typically understands himself or herself as standing in a long tradition and does in fact use traditional materials, even when communicating genuine visionary experiences. In the Judaism from which early Christianity was born, the prophets were not thought of as inspired innovators who brought radically new revelation but as strong links in the chain of tradition who only presented afresh what was already Israel's traditional lore. *Aboth* 1:2 shows that for Tannaitic Judaism the prophets stand in a line of tradition that they both hand on and expand: "Moses received the Law from Sinai and committed it to Joshua, and Joshua to the elders, and the elders to the Prophets; and the Prophets committed it to the men of the Great Synagogue." Thus Rabbi Hillel's saying preserved in *Aboth* 1:13: "He who adds not makes to cease." Expanding the tradition was understood as a necessary element in being faithful to it, and prophets were not considered to be outsiders to this process. It might be expected that Christian prophecy that originates from such a context will make no particular attempt to insulate itself from the church's tradition.

All the evidence that indicates that Christian prophecy typically functioned in the worship setting also serves to bring prophecy into proximity to the tradition, for the worship setting was a primary context where the tradition was handed on. This axiom of the classical form critics need not be pressed to mean that the sayings of Jesus were recited exclusively in the liturgy but only that the public gatherings of the community, of which worship was a part, formed the general setting in which the tradition was transmitted. Even the distinction between the worship setting and the school setting should not be firmly drawn; the school community was also a worship community, and vice versa. In general, tradition and Spirit should be seen as belonging together in early Christianity. But more than this general conclusion may be drawn: the evidence of our sources indicates that Christian prophets were not only active in the cultic setting in which the tradition of Jesus' words was transmitted but were sometimes involved in the process of transmission themselves.

It is a commonplace of research on the Apocalypse that the seer

---

25 Hans Walter Wolff, *Joel and Amos.* For this general phenomenon in the Hebrew prophets, see Mowinckel, *Prophecy and Tradition.*

expresses his revelatory experiences using materials that have in great part come to him from the church's tradition. First to be noted is the extensive amount of Old Testament materials of which he makes use, without ever expressly quoting a single passage. John's interpretative technique will be discussed later; here the significant point to be noted is that John's prophecy reveals that his mind is steeped in the traditional materials that were handed on and used in the church's worship and that there is no tension between the vertical dimension of "revelation" and the horizontal dimension of "tradition." The Old Testament materials are not cited as the historical evidence of a past authority but become the present address of the risen Lord. Every page of Revelation is replete with examples; an especially clear one is 18:1–8, where words and sayings from several Old Testament books are woven into oracles that are presented as voices from heaven to the seer. The prophetic charisma expresses itself through the appropriation and re-presentation of traditional materials. These materials also include (1) forms taken over from apostolic letters that have been read in the liturgy of the church (e.g., 1:4–5; 22:21), (2) the appropriation, modification, and re-presentation of oracles from earlier Christian prophets, which had been preserved and transmitted in the cult; and perhaps (3) material from non-Christian prophets (e.g., 11:1–13; 17:1–18).

Of central significance for our purpose, of course, is the fact that among the traditional materials that find expression in the seer's revelation from the heavenly Lord are reflections of sayings that were handed on in the church as sayings of the historical Jesus. The extent to which this was the case is disputed, but there are some clear examples that make it apparent that the seer does know sayings of Jesus that the Gospels place in the mouth of the pre-Easter Jesus (e.g., 3:5 = Luke 12:8 par.; 2:7 = Mark 4:9 par.). Especially when seen in the light of other evidence presented here, this phenomenon should prove that the two traditions—the sayings of the "historical" Jesus and the revelations from the "exalted" Jesus—were passed along in proximity to each other, the setting for both being the worship life of the congregation.

Though John has fewer sayings attributable to the historical Jesus than one might anticipate, there are enough to document the fact that sayings associated with the historical Jesus could become sayings of the risen Jesus. It is passing strange that this fact has sometimes been readily acknowledged by students who deny that the flow could go the other way, so that sayings of the exalted Lord were included in some circles with the sayings of the historical Jesus. Revelation was written after the Gospel form, in which sayings of Jesus were explicitly incorporated into a pre-Easter frame, had become common. As "Gospel" and "prophecy" became more fixed literary forms, the Christian message began to flow in channels that did tend to identify sayings of Jesus as "pre-" or "post-Easter" by virtue of the narrative framework of the literary form itself.

This was already happening by the end of the first century, which accounts for the relatively small number of sayings appropriate to the historical Jesus. A generation earlier the line between pre- and post-Easter sayings of Jesus was even less distinct, and the Christian prophecy of that era was even more related to the sayings of the pre-Easter Jesus.

Form criticism of the Pauline letter corpus has made it clear that Paul's letters contain an extensive amount of traditional material, including creeds, hymns, parenesis, and liturgical material, much of which derives from the worship life of the church. This traditional material includes "sayings of the Lord," among which may be quotations from and allusions to sayings of the earthly Jesus. As in the case of the Apocalypse, the extent of this is disputed, with some students finding hundreds of allusions to Gospel sayings of Jesus.[26] While allowing that Paul did not quote all the sayings he knew, this does not necessarily mean he knew a great many more. For reasons of methodological clarity, we will limit our discussion to those texts where Paul explicitly refers to "words of the Lord":

> 1 Corinthians 7:10: "I give charge, not I but the Lord. . . ."
> 1 Corinthians 7:12: "I say, not the Lord, . . ."
> 1 Corinthians 7:25: "I have no command of the Lord . . ."
> 1 Corinthians 9:14: "In the same way, the Lord commanded . . ."
> 1 Corinthians 11:23–26: "For I received from the Lord what I also delivered to you, . . ."
> 1 Corinthians 14:37: "what I am writing to you is a command of the Lord."
> 1 Thessalonians 4:15–17: "For this we declare to you by the word of the Lord, . . ."

It is immediately noticeable that all these references are from 1 Corinthians, which alone among Paul's letters contains a discussion of Christian prophecy, with the sole exception of 1 Thessalonians 4:15–17, which itself is Christian prophecy. This itself should suggest some relationship between Christian prophecy and the tradition of Jesus' words. There is no indication that the prophets at Corinth drew materials from the sayings tradition; their revelations seem to be entirely the spontaneous inspirations of the moment, received during worship without previous reflection (14:26–32). But the Corinthian idea of prophecy stands more in contrast than in parallel to Paul, being more spontaneous and ecstatic than his.

---

26 This spectrum is surveyed in Victor Furnish, *The Jesus-Paul Debate: From Baur to Bultmann.*

Over against the Corinthian enthusiasm, Paul places an understanding of prophecy that is closely related to the church's tradition. The understanding of prophecy held by Paul and Paul's own functioning as a Christian prophet includes not only the reception of words from the risen Lord but the taking up of sayings of Jesus from the tradition and re-presenting them, sometimes in modified and reinterpreted form, as from "the Lord," by which Paul means primarily the risen Lord.

This is obvious from the second remarkable aspect of the above list: "word of the Lord" for Paul includes sayings that could derive either from the historical or from the risen Jesus, with no attempt made to distinguish them. The sayings are consistently attributed to "the Lord." Although Paul uses the name "Jesus" 142 times, no saying is ever presented as a saying of Jesus. The subject from whom the sayings derive is designated as "the Lord" throughout, whether this is supposed to be the historical or the exalted Jesus. There is no set introductory formula for a saying from the historical Jesus to distinguish it from sayings of the risen Lord, e.g., nothing remotely resembling the "it is written" used for scripture citations.

We have already discussed the exaggerated importance sometimes attached to 1 Corinthians 7:10–13 in this regard (see chapter 1 above), but it may be further noted that 7:40b and 14:37 must be considered in any understanding of Paul's disclaimers in 7:12 and 7:25 pertaining to his having a command of the Lord. Paul's own apostolic-prophetic "opinion" (*gnōmē*, 7:25) is a result of the inspiration of the risen Lord who is the Spirit (Rom. 8:9–10, 2 Cor. 3:17); what the apostle-prophet writes is itself "command of the Lord" (1 Cor. 14:37). In the series of sayings introduced in 1 Corinthians 7–9, Paul does not distinguish traditional sayings of the historical Jesus from the inspired products of church prophets. Rather, what 1 Corinthians 7:12 and 25 tell us is that on these subjects Paul has no *traditional* saying of the Lord to appeal to, whether this be thought of as a saying of the historical Jesus or of the exalted Lord. Similarly in 1 Corinthians 11:24–26, Paul adds his own exhortation (v. 26) to the traditional saying of "the Lord," (vs. 24–25) without distinguishing what he says from what "the Lord" says. As in 7:10–13, both traditional material and contemporary expansion is offered under the one rubric, "word of the Lord."

From all this it is clear (1) that Paul does have a tradition (however small) of "sayings of the Lord." (2) This collection contains sayings of both the historical Jesus and the exalted Lord indiscriminately. (3) On occasion Paul must respond that he has no (pre- or post-Easter) saying of the Lord relevant to the situation at hand (this is the meaning of 7:25). (4) But Paul's own "opinion" (*gnōmē*) functions as an inspired "command of the Lord."

Paul's gospel is both tradition-receiving and tradition-creating. The way Paul handles the oracle of the risen Lord in 1 Thessalonians 4:15–17 shows that it was included in the tradition from which he drew; it was not created ad hoc. And his instruction that the oracle should be used to comfort the Christians of Thessalonica, as the letter becomes a part of their tradition (4:18; cf. 5:27), indicates that he expected the saying to continue to live in the church's tradition. Paul does not understand prophetic speech to be only a momentary inspiration, spoken into the air, to quickly disappear. Paul the prophet passes on a tradition of prophetic speech that he expects to continue to be passed on. It is no accident that Paul's discussion of charismatic speech in Corinth is prefaced by an appeal to a traditional creedal affirmation of the historical Jesus as decisive (12:3) and is immediately followed by a declaration of the gospel as expressed in the oldest traditional form (15:1–3). Prophecy and tradition are not only coordinates in Paul's ministry, they are inextricably interwoven with each other.

A different picture is given in Acts, where prophets are portrayed by Luke as having no particular relation to church tradition. Only Judas and Silas are incidentally engaged in passing along church decisions reached in Jerusalem (15:32; cf. v. 28). Agabus's revelations are particular disclosures of the future to an individual or congregation and are preserved in Acts in the same way that conversations are preserved, not because prophets are thought of as drawing from or creating church tradition. The prophets of Acts certainly have nothing to do with the transmission of Jesus' words. No doubt there were prophets such as Agabus is represented to be. But the uniform presentation of prophets in Acts as atraditional is to be attributed primarily to Luke's theology. It is a remarkable fact that no one in Acts, including apostles and teachers, is concerned to pass on the sayings of Jesus. In Luke's portrayal of the church in Acts, the church is not guided by citing the teaching of Jesus as a past authority. It is the risen Jesus who guides the church into new missionary paths by the Spirit. The sole reference to a saying of Jesus in all of Acts is 20:35—a saying not found in any of the Gospels.

In contrast, Luke takes great care to preserve, interpret, and transmit the teaching of Jesus in the first volume of his composition, without which Acts is incomplete. It is important for Luke's contemporary Christian readers to have the teachings of Jesus, as they are preserved at the proper history-of-salvation point in the "first book" (Acts 1:1), the Gospel of Luke. This allows Luke to present the story of the church in Acts without reference to the sayings of Jesus. It is not unexpected, then, that Luke's prophets in Acts are unrelated to the tradition of Jesus' own words.

On the other hand, the prophetic figures in Luke 1–2 do seem to be related to the tradition in that the oracles they deliver draw from traditional materials and then become church tradition, so that even in Luke-Acts there is still some reflection of the early prophets' relation to the tradition. The tradition underlying Luke's editing indicates that Christian prophets should therefore be seen as having formed a part of that group that Luke labels "ministers of the word" (Luke 1:2), which formed one of the links in the tradition from Jesus' day to Luke's.

The Paraclete-prophet of the Fourth Gospel functions both as bearer of tradition and medium of new revelation from the risen Lord (14:26; 16:12–13). The picture of Christian prophecy offered by the Johannine materials indicates a fusion of tradition and present revelation. The author of the Gospel himself functions as such a prophet, uniting in an inseparable bond the tradition from Jesus with the present address of the risen Jesus. Likewise the author of 1 John is an exponent of both tradition (1:1–3) and continuing revelation (2:26–27), so that relation to the tradition can even be used as a criterion of true and false prophecy (2:24; 4:1–3). In Johannine writings the tradition is made present by the charisma; the charisma is made valid by the tradition; a prophet who is not something of a traditionalist is a false prophet.

Reflecting on the decline of prophecy and the rise of wisdom teachers as authorities for the life of the community, a Jewish tradition declared: "From the day whereon the temple was laid waste, prophecy was taken from the prophets and given to the sages. Not everyone who opens 'Thus says the Lord' is a prophet, just as not everyone lacks prophetic gifts because he opens 'It is written' " (*Baba Bathra* 12a). The early church too could associate charismatic authority with the transmission of tradition. Tradition and prophecy interacted: prophecy kept tradition alive; tradition kept prophecy honest.

The significance of the above investigation for our particular project is threefold: (1) since prophets have a positive relation to the tradition, functioning in the setting of the life of the church in which the sayings of Jesus were transmitted and drawing materials from the tradition with which to express their revelations, it is not a priori unlikely that they also contributed to the tradition. (2) It is likely that the transmission process itself will sometimes bear the characteristic marks of Christian prophecy, so that the cluster of materials within which a saying is handed on or the particular shape of the context of a saying may be used as evidence that the saying has been created or shaped by Christian prophets. (3) Quite apart from the question of whether individual sayings were coined or re-formed in ways so characteristic of Christian prophecy that they may now be recognized as constituting a prophetic stratum within the tradition—a question that is to be explored in Part Three below—the prophets' relation to the tradition process may have influenced the tradition of Jesus' words taken as a whole.

Günther Bornkamm has made a very important point in this connection: the various renderings of Jesus' words in the tradition point to their prophetic use as the word of the living Lord to various situations.[27] To point to the tendency of popular, oral tradition to alter, adorn, and omit is not in itself an adequate explanation for the phenomena, though of course these laws of popular oral tradition also had their effect on the Gospel tradition. But the fact that the "there and then" of Jesus' word is taken up into the "here and now" of Jesus addressing the church is to be seen as one of the primary means of accounting for the variety of forms in which a saying of Jesus appears in the tradition.

What had once been a call to follow the earthly Jesus in a literal sense is now, after Easter, transformed into the call of the risen Lord to discipleship in a new situation. The radical message of the prophet Jesus of Nazareth to a relatively small number of Palestinian Jews in a particular situation is now made relevant and binding on all who believe in the Lord Jesus. "Following" has become identified with "believing," and the sayings of Jesus are adapted and expanded to convey the message of the risen Lord.

If this had regularly happened in the recitation of the sayings of Jesus in worship under the influence of the prophets who were present there, even noncharismatic interpreters of the tradition, such as Matthew and Luke, would have had a model for handling the Jesus tradition that could not be reduced to deductive logic, the laws of oral tradition, or midrashic interpretation, though all of these were factors. Because of the prophets' role in the tradition process, the tradition as a whole bears something of a prophetic character, whether or not we are able to isolate particular sayings that have been influenced by Christian prophets.

PROPHETS AND TEACHERS

The preceding discussion makes prophets appear more similar to early Christian teachers than is usually understood to be the case. The sharp line drawn by Harnack between "charisma" and "office" was exaggerated, but it still haunts the discussion.[28] We may in fact be surprised to note how alike prophets and teachers are in our sources.

In the first-century Jewish context from which early Christianity originated, "prophet" and "teacher" (or "scribe") were not mutually exclusive or even incompatible categories. They existed side by side in the same setting or in the same person. This corresponds to Israel's prophets, who gathered disciples about them, taught them their oracles which were then handed on in the prophetic circle, and modified and

---

27 *Jesus of Nazareth,* 17–21, 174.
28 Cf. Zimmermann, *Lehrer,* 50.

expanded by the disciples, who were prophets themselves. This view continued into first-century Judaism. Josephus explicitly names Elisha, follower and successor of Elijah, a *mathētēs* ("disciple," "student," *Antiquities* 8.354). Qumran's Teacher, who functions prophetically, is only one example of the way in which the offices of prophet and teacher had already merged in the thinking and life of first-century Judaism. Philo is another. And of course both Jesus and John the Baptist were prophets who were also teachers. Riesner's research concludes that *all* first-century Jewish groups considered prophecy and teaching to be related, complementary categories.[29]

Like the prophets, teachers are sometimes regarded as charismatics, who do not simply function on the basis of native gifts or acquired learning but are constituted as teachers by the Holy Spirit (1 Cor. 12:28; Rom. 12:7; Eph. 4:11; cf. 2 Tim. 1:11). Teaching is described as a charisma given by the Spirit in 1 John 2:26–27. That our sources are far from unanimous in this would suggest that teaching was not regularly seen as a charismatic function, but in some streams of early Christianity this was the case. All prophets were by definition charismatics, but "teacher" could be understood in a charismatic sense or not. But charisma per se did not distinguish prophets from teachers. The ministry of teaching was often understood not as mechanically transmitting a body of material but as interacting with a living tradition, modifying and expanding it to keep it relevant.

The Letter of James seems to be from a Christian teacher (cf. 3:1) who obviously knows and respects a tradition of the sayings of Jesus. But no effort is made to distinguish direct quotations of Jesus' words from hortatory additions of the teacher, other elements in the tradition not from Jesus, and James' own editorializing (cf. 5:12 = Matt. 5:34–37 as only one example of many). This suggests a style of dealing with the sayings of Jesus by Christian teachers in which "authentic" sayings of the historical Jesus were blended in Christian exhortation with the post-Easter products of the church's own teaching ministry.

So understood, the ministries of charismatic teachers and prophets fade into each other.[30] Heinz Schürmann has argued that early Christian teachers were distinguished from their Jewish counterparts by their claim to the Spirit and charisma. They were enough like the prophets to succeed and replace them in some Christian communities.[31]

Prophets and teachers are often closely associated in our sources.

---

29 *Jesus als Lehrer,* 297.
30 Cf. Floyd V. Filson, "The Christian Teacher in the First Century."
31 " '. . . und Lehrer': Die geistliche Eigenart des Lehrdienstes und sein Verhältnis zu anderen geistlichen Diensten im neutestamentlichen Zeitalter," in *Orientierungen am Neuen Testament. Exegetische Gesprächbeiträge,* 116–156.

This is the case in Paul (1 Cor. 12:28; Rom. 12:6–7) and his followers (Eph. 4:11), who place prophecy and teaching in the same series. Acts (13:1) and the *Didache* (12.1–2; 15.1–2) mention them together as forming a unit. Further, prophets are sometimes explicitly described as teaching (Rev. 2:20; *Didache* 11.10; John 14:26) so that the reception of prophecy results in "learning" or "instruction" (1 Cor. 14:19, 31). Whether Matthew identifies teachers with prophets or only associates them very closely is debated; in any case, he does not distinguish them sharply.

All the above discussion indicates that the picture of teachers who hand on the firmly guarded tradition of the sayings of Jesus in one context while charismatic prophets deliver their inspired, ephemeral revelations from the risen Jesus in another is based on fantasy. The horizontal, traditioning function of the church's ministry operated conjointly with the vertical, revelatory aspect. Prophets and tradents were partners engaged in a complementary and mutually enriching ministry of the word; prophet and tradent were sometimes the same person. This means that the tradition of Jesus' words was sometimes handed on by those who also received new revelations of the risen Lord, and that the tradition that came into our Gospels contains both kinds of sayings and their combinations.

I now come back to the important distinction between prophets and teachers. Prophets and teachers should not be simply identified without qualification. There were noncharismatic teachers as well as charismatic; only the charismatic, immediately inspired teachers were similar to Christian prophets. And not all charismatic teachers spoke first-person sayings in the name of the risen Lord. Their charismatic ministry of the word most often came in the form of parenesis, inspired interpretation of the scriptures similar to that of the Teacher of Righteousness at Qumran, or the revelation of Spirit-given "mysteries" that came in some other form than as sayings of the risen Jesus. But when an inspired teacher delivered his or her teaching by taking up a traditional saying of Jesus and representing it as the present word of the Lord, reinterpreted and modified to speak to the new situation, or when new instruction was given in the form of sayings of Jesus that had not previously been a part of the church's tradition, then the teacher was functioning as a prophet according to our definition and should be considered a prophet whether or not this term is used. Thus, for example, when Johnston and Müller prefer not to call the Paraclete a prophet but an "inspired teacher," the difference between their view and mine is mainly terminological, and the Paraclete, even as they describe him, represents the ministry of Christian prophecy.[32]

---

32 George Johnston, *The Spirit-Paraclete in the Fourth Gospel*, 128–135; Ulrich Müller, "Die Parakleten-Vorstellungen im Johannesevangelium," 77–78.

PROPHETS AS MALE AND FEMALE

The restriction of women's roles in the religious community has always been a matter of cultural mores. In the Judeo-Christian tradition, the Spirit has always transcended such culturally conditioned rules and expectations and has helped rewrite them. Through its charismatic leaders, the Spirit has guided the community into new paths that were not only without precedent or justification in the culture at large but also absent in the community's own theology, history, and tradition. The Spirit that inspires prophecy has always been egalitarian.

Women have thus been named among the prophets of Israel from the earliest times. The Bible names five: Miriam (Exod. 15:20), Deborah (Judg. 4:4), Huldah (2 Kings 22:14; 2 Chron. 34:22), Noadiah (Neh. 6:14), and the wife of Isaiah (Isa. 8:3). Hebrew tradition added four more, Sarah, Hannah, Abigail, and Esther (*b. T. Megillah* 14a).

Were there female prophets in that first-century Judaism from which early Christianity sprang? The role of women in first-century Judaism is not entirely clear, but one should not picture the first century situation only on the basis of the exclusion of women from leadership roles in the temple or the later synagogue's segregation of men and women. The synagogue was a somewhat egalitarian institution. There is no archaeological evidence for a separate section for women, nor does Luke 13: 10–13 suggest such. The actual social-religious status of women was apparently higher than portrayed in the later texts.[33] To be sure, women were discouraged from learning the Torah, but the provision for women to read the portion of the Sabbath lesson in the synagogue shows that there were some who could do so (*Tos. Megillah* 4 [3], 11; *b.T. Megillah* 23a). That women could occasionally assume leadership roles, at least in Hellenistic cities, is clear from an inscription from Smyrna (first century?): "The ruler of the Synagogue, Rufina, erected a tomb monument to her freemen and servants."[34] It seems that while first-century Judaism was hesitant to permit women to participate in *school* instruction, women were allowed to function as worship leaders.[35]

As in the later church, worship was often more charismatic and spontaneous than instructional settings. We know that women participated in the leadership of church worship. It was *charisma* that gave them authority, not the *tradition.* With the possible exception of the sect of the Therapeutae as described by Philo (*On the Contemplative Life* 83–87), no female prophets are documented in first-century Palestinian Judaism.

---

33 Cf. the data in Schüssler Fiorenza, *In Memory of Her*, 109; Bernadette Brooten, *Women Leaders in the Ancient Synagogue.*

34 Cited in Ulrich Müller, *Die Offenbarung des Johannes*, 105.

35 Riesner, *Jesus als Lehrer*, 104–105, 135.

There may have been women prophets in Judaism filtered out of our extant documents by the bias of our sources. In any case, it was expected in many circles that in the eschatological age, when the Spirit returned, both male and female prophets would reappear (Joel 2:28–29).

This is precisely what the early church claimed to have happened. The prophetic Spirit raised up women prophets as well as men. Paul not only speaks in general about the equality of women and men "in Christ" (Gal. 3:28), he specifically acknowledges that women prophesy in the congregational worship (1 Cor. 11:5) and urges all the congregation, not only men, to aspire to the gift of prophecy (1 Cor. 14:1, 5). The difficult 14:34, if from Paul at all (many take it as a later interpolation from the same post-Pauline stream expressed in 1 Tim. 2:11–15), must not be interpreted in a way that denies the presence of women prophets in the Pauline churches and Paul's acknowledgment of them. If from Paul, it is best understood as his prohibition of noncharismatic women from addressing the husbands of other women during the worship service— something that would have appeared extremely offensive in that culture—not Paul's effort to curb the charismatic leadership of the women prophets at Corinth.[36]

Likewise Acts not only cites the general affirmation that the time of fulfillment in which both men and women will prophesy has already dawned (2:16–18), women prophets are described as part of the church's leadership (21:9). The flurry of prophetic activity in Luke 1–2 includes both male (Zechariah, Simeon) and female (Mary, Anna) figures, which probably reflects prophetic phenomena in the church as perceived by Luke's tradition, rather than charismatic phenomena in first-century Judaism. There is no explicit reference to female Christian prophets in the Gospel tradition,[37] but the Matthean Jesus' addressing his disciples as prophets and his promise to send prophets in the post-Easter church are, in the light of other evidence, certainly to be understood inclusively (Matt. 5:12; 7:22; 10:41; 23:34).

Since 1980 we know from an inscription in Didymas of a *prophētis* (feminine, as in Rev. 2:20). The churches of Revelation were familiar with prophecy in general and specifically with female prophets not only from their Bible and Jewish religious tradition but from their own cultural context. Revelation knows of at least one female prophet, called "Jezebel" by John who considers her a false prophet—on the basis of her teaching, not because she is female (John's purported misogynism is based on a misunderstanding of Rev. 14:4; see chapter 7, "The 'Ascetic'

---

36 For an alternative reading, see Antoinette Clark Wire, "Prophecy and Women Prophets in Corinth," in *Gospel Origins and Christian Beginnings*.

37 Schüssler Fiorenza's designation of the woman who anointed Jesus (Mark 14:3–9) as a prophet is without foundation in the text (*In Memory of Her*, 153).

Lifestyle of the Prophets"). Since women played a role in the prophetic leadership of the church that influenced the Gospel tradition, modifying traditional sayings of Jesus and creating new ones (see Part Three), this means that some sayings of Jesus in the Gospels may represent the contribution of women prophets.

7

The Prophet as Religious Leader

Prophecy is a phenomenon of human religion as such. We have seen that prophecy is not unique to Israel or the church. As is the case with prayer and sacrifice, whatever may be distinctive about Israelite or Christian prophecy is not the existence of the phenomenon or idea as such but the way it functioned and was understood within the community of Israel or the church. As a religious community with developing institutions, early Christianity inevitably made use of and adapted itself to the categories of religious life already present. This does not necessarily mean it took them over wholesale. One way of gaining insight into the phenomena of prophecy in early Christianity is to look at Christian prophets in the categories that have been developed for studying religious movements in general, i.e., to look at it from the perspective of history-of-religions study.

THE PROPHET AS PNEUMATIC SPEAKER

Certain understandings of terms such as "inspired," "enthusiasm," and "ecstatic," when applied to Christian prophets, make it difficult to conceive of such figures uttering words that could be added by the community to its tradition of sayings of Jesus. Thus once again both a definition of terms and an investigation of our sources with these definitions in mind are needed before declarations concerning the possible "ecstatic" nature of early Christian prophecy can be meaningful.

I agree with Johannes Lindblom that all prophets function with the conviction that they receive direct revelations from the deity.[1] Such revelations are received in a psychic state that might, with Lindblom, be

---

1 *Gesichte und Offenbarungen. Vorstellungen von göttlichen Weisungen und übernatürlichen Erscheinungen im ältesten Christentum,* 164.

called, "the revelatory state," which embraces the entire spectrum between an ecstatic trance, in which consciousness and volition are lost, and
strong intuitive certainty, in which the prophet is in full possession of
both his or her reflective and volitional powers. "Ecstatic" and related
words should be reserved for the type of experience expressed in the
careful working definition of James Dunn:

> By "ecstasy" I mean here an unusually exalted state of feeling, a condi-
> tion of such total absorption or concentration that the individual be-
> comes oblivious to all attendant circumstances and other stimuli, an
> experience of intense rapture or a trance-like state in which normal
> faculties are suspended for a shorter or longer period and the subject
> sees visions or experiences "automatic speech," as in some forms of
> glossolalia.[2]

So defined, the revelatory experience, whether or not called "prophecy," was generally an ecstatic phenomenon in the Hellenistic world.
Firsthand experience of inspired speech had declined in the Hellenistic
world, and intellectuals such as Plutarch were inclined to discount it, but
in the popular imagination the prophet was literally a possessed person
whose powers had been taken over by the deity.

Lucan gives a typical description of this widespread understanding of
what happened to the seer/prophet in the moment of revelation: the
deity takes over the body of the seer and drives the human spirit out. One
loses consciousness, is "out of one's mind," reason is no longer present.
One is not responsible for what one says, cannot prevent oneself from
speaking, and cannot interpret what one has said (*Pharsalia* 5.161ff.).
Lucian's *Alexander the False Prophet* and Vergil's *Aeneid* (6.45–51) fill in the
picture by describing the violent physical phenomena that accompanied
the state in which oracles were both received and delivered: rolling eyes,
foaming mouth, pounding heart, gasping breath, all of which show that
the term *mania* was meant seriously.

It was once popular to draw a sharp contrast between the "sober"
experience of "Jewish" prophecy and the "ecstatic" experience of pagan
prophets. We now see that this line was drawn too sharply and sometimes
for apologetic reasons. The revelatory experience of the Old Testament
prophets was understood more and more in Hellenistic "ecstatic" terms.
Contrast the first-person account of Isaiah 6:1–13 with its later (second
century C.E.?) retelling in the *Ascension of Isaiah:*

> And while he [Isaiah] was speaking by the Holy Spirit in the hearing of
> all, he (suddenly) became silent and his consciousness was taken from
> him and he saw (no more) the men who were standing before him: his

---

2 Dunn, *Jesus and the Spirit,* 84.

eyes were open, but his mouth was silent and the consciousness in his body was taken from him; but his breath was still in him, for he saw a vision. . . . And the people who were standing around, with the exception of the circle of the prophets, did not think that the holy Isaiah had been taken up. And the vision which he saw was not of this world, but from the world which is hidden from all flesh. And after Isaiah had beheld this vision, he imparted it to Hezekiah, his son Jasub, and the remaining prophets . . . but the people did not hear for Micaiah and Jasub his son had caused them to go forth, when the knowledge of this world was taken from him and he became as a dead man (6.10ff.).[3]

The first writer known to us to develop a comprehensive syncretistic understanding of the prophetic experience is Philo of Alexandria, who explained biblical prophecy in terms of Hellenistic enthusiasm. He was the first to use "ecstasy" as a technical term, which he understood in its literal etymological sense. "Ecstasy" means "to stand outside (oneself)." Philo's understanding was that in the ecstatic experience the human mind *stands outside* in order that the divine spirit may enter. "The mind is evicted . . . mortal and immortal may not share the same home." "Ecstasy" is thus the corollary of "enthusiasm," which means literally "having a deity within." Ecstasy is the human vacating the premises to make room for the divine speech. Philo considers the authors of all Old Testament books to be prophets who receive their revelations in Dionysian ecstasy, so that, for example, the prophet of Deuteronomy 18:15–18 will only say what is given him but will not understand it. Lucan, Lucian, Vergil, and Philo only illustrate a point that could be documented many times over: the revelatory experience was generally considered to be an enthusiastic, ecstatic phenomenon in the Hellenistic world.

We are in a different world when we read the documents that represent early Christian prophecy. In regard to ecstatic experience, there is a clear contrast between the typical Hellenistic understanding of inspired speech and the type of prophecy manifest in our sources. Our primary example of first-century Christian prophecy, the Apocalypse, offers no descriptions whatsoever of the author's psychic state or extraordinary physiological or psychological phenomena during the reception of the revelations. The account of his being caught up into heaven in 4:1 is extremely restrained. The closing words of the book contain no description of the seer's transition back to the "normal" state. Everything is stated in a rather matter-of-fact manner with an amazing lack of interest in sensationalizing the phenomenon itself.

The revelatory state is not encouraged or manipulated by an external act. The initial entrance into the revelatory state and subsequent mo-

---

3 Quoted from C. Rowland, *The Open Heaven: A Study of Apocalyptic in Judaism and Early Christianity,* 230.

ments within it are described with the simple "in the Spirit" (1:10; 4:2; 17:3; 21:10). There is a conscious avoidance of the religious vocabulary of ecstasy that profane Greeks and syncretists such as Philo customarily use as synonymous expressions for "Spirit." In Revelation the state of being "in the Spirit" is an extraordinary state, the state in which things can be seen and heard that are not available to the natural human being, but I would hesitate to describe this state as an ecstatic experience because it is not involuntary but is expressed in terms of the author's own conscious intent, including the reflective use of traditional materials. There is an element of "ecstasy" in the reception of the revelation in that the seer does genuinely see visions and hear voices, but in the delivery of the message the seer is consciously reflective and intentional, not merely the vehicle for some supernatural power. Since the seer's writing is carefully composed and structured, consciously intentional and reflective, we may assume that had he not been separated from the congregation his oral delivery of his prophecy to the congregation would likewise have been conscious and intentional, though recognizably "inspired." In all of this he corresponds to the prophets of the Old Testament, whose heir he is.

Paul is obviously embroiled in a discussion with the Corinthians on the validity of ecstatic speech. The Corinthians prefer the more ecstatic gift of tongues, in which the speaker utters words incomprehensible to human beings (14:2), speaking mysteries in the Spirit (14:2), uttering speech that is not intelligible (14:9), in which the mind of the speaker is not engaged (14:14). They are critical of Paul because his speech is not sufficiently "spiritual," by which they mean ecstatic (2 Cor. 10:10).

Paul is tolerant of this manifestation of the Spirit in the congregation (1 Cor. 14:5, 18, 39) but exalts prophecy at the expense of glossolalia (14:1–3, 5, 18–19, 23–25, 39–40). Yet it is clear that by "prophecy" Paul intends something less ecstatic than the Corinthian view of prophecy. The Corinthians had associated glossolalia and prophecy, considering the latter only an inferior version of the former. They thought of glossolalia as the "language of angels" (1 Cor. 13:1, cf. *Testament of Job* 48–50). Paul not only inverts this valuation, he distinguishes them in kind, not simply in degree, and rejects the view that prophetic speech is validated by glossolalia.[4] He redefines prophecy in the act of commending it to them.

The crisis in the Corinthian understanding of charismatic speech that provoked all of 1 Corinthians 12–14 occurred when an ecstatic prophet, speaking intelligibly but under the compulsion of the supernatural power, proclaimed "a curse on Jesus" (12:3). This expression probably

---

4 Cf. Thomas W. Gillespie, "A Pattern of Prophetic Speech in 1 Corinthians," 80–85.

originated from an enthusiastic prophet within the "Christ party," a subgroup within the Corinthian congregation that claimed immediate revelation from the heavenly Spirit-Christ and disdained the earthly human being Jesus of Nazareth. Though a number of Corinthians were apparently sympathetic to this Christology, this radical statement delivered "in the Spirit" seemed to some to be going too far, and they questioned Paul about it.

Paul responded to their query by arguing that in their pre-Christian religious life they had also experienced ecstasy (12:2), so that ecstatic experience as such is no guarantee of truth. Claims to Spirit-inspired speech are to be measured by the confession of faith (12:3), by the community itself, which contains persons gifted by the Spirit with the ability to discriminate between competing claims to Spirit-endowed speech (12:10, 14:29), and by love (13:2). Such a stance shows that Paul does not regard prophecy as an ecstatic phenomenon in the Hellenistic sense, and that the Corinthians are inclined so to understand it.

This is borne out by Paul's descriptions of prophecy, which is a matter of speaking with the mind in contrast to "speaking into the air" (1 Cor. 14:9, 19). Paul takes the term generally used of inspired speech in the Hellenistic world *(mainesthai)* and uses it as a stinging rebuke (translated "you are mad" in 14:23) rather than a goal to be sought after, as it was in the Bacchic experience of the Dionysian cult. It can be no accident that neither here nor anywhere else in the literature of the early church is the customary vocabulary related to *mainesthai* used of the prophetic experience. Paul's discussion assumes prophecy to be a rather sober, understandable, meaningful language that leads to edification. There is no mention of trances, visions, or any kind of externally observable phenomena. The prophet, like the speaker in tongues, is in control of himself or herself and can be silent—though he or she may have to be reminded that this is the case (14:27–32).

Paul dissociates ecstatic experience from prophecy but not because he is unacquainted with the former. When pressed, he can document ecstatic experiences of his own (2 Cor. 12:1–5), but he does not call them prophecy; rather he contrasts such experiences with the kind of prophecy he commends. It was a rare experience, incommunicable, which he is reluctant to talk about and sees no edifying value in sharing with the church: different at every point from his understanding of prophecy.

This characterization consistently fits prophecy elsewhere in our sources as well. The Pauline School seems to have preserved Paul's own high estimate of prophecy as a gift of the Spirit, combined with a suspicion of ecstatic phenomena. The Fourth Evangelist conceives his own Gospel to be a product of the revelatory spirit and includes discourses developed under prophetic influence as sayings of Jesus. But in John there is nothing about the extraordinary nature of the Spirit's manifestations, ecstatic phenomena, or miraculous acts. Nothing in the Paraclete sayings suggests that speech given by the Spirit is characterized by enthusiastic frenzy; rather they indicate the opposite.

Hermas is careful to distinguish the true Christian prophet from the pagan *mantis:* the prophet is inspired by the Spirit but does not become mantic (Mandate 11.2–9). The *Didache* reveals a community in which the idea is alive that whatever a prophet does "in the Spirit" must be accepted because it is entirely the Spirit with which one is dealing and not the will of the prophet himself or herself. But though this understanding of prophecy is seductively present in the community represented by the *Didache,* it is altogether clear that it is rejected by the *Didache* itself. The community is indeed to recognize that it is dealing with more than mere human speech in the oracles of the prophet (10.7; 11.7, 11), but the Spirit-inspired prophet is also one who is to be held personally accountable for his or her speech since he or she is not simply the passive vehicle of the Spirit (11.8–12). In our terms, inspiration, but not ecstasy, is acknowledged as the authentic revelatory mode.

Luke-Acts is our most "Hellenistic" source on this point, in that it reports many dreams and visions as a common modus operandi of the Spirit's communication with the church and, alone of our sources, even uses the terminology of "ecstasy" in a positive sense in relation to inspired speech (Acts 10:10; 11:5; 22:17). But even Luke never describes the effects of such "ecstasy" in the Hellenistic terms of Lucian and Philo and never relates such "ecstatic" experiences to the prophets he describes.

We conclude that in our sources prophets are uniformly believed to be empowered by the Holy Spirit. Prophecy is never simply identified with the ordinary ministry of preaching, which is carried out in the context of the presence of the Spirit that is common to all Christians, but is always a special manifestation of the Spirit. Our sources never describe prophecy in ecstatic terms. Since this was also generally the case in that Judaism from which early Christianity sprang, it is almost a certainty that those early Christian prophets we are attempting to characterize were spokespersons for the risen Lord who understood themselves to be particularly inspired by the Holy Spirit to deliver their message and were accepted by the church as such. But they were not frenzied enthusiasts, and their charismatic claims complement, rather than contradict, their relation to the teaching ministry and the tradition that we have documented.

The pneumatic aspect of early Christian prophecy thus gives us no reason to be hesitant about the possibility of Christian prophets' influence on the developing Gospel tradition. Rather, it gives us a helpful identifying mark of prophetic material. In light of the above, we may expect some prophetic contributions to the Gospel tradition to be concerned with the Spirit, in particular with the idea that the Spirit gives to the church the capacity to speak with boldness.

THE PROPHET AND MIRACLES

"Spirit" is not to be understood in the idealistic or attitudinal sense but as a term denoting the divine *power* operative in those who possess it. Consequently, those who possess the Spirit not only speak by divine power but often also manifest other supernatural abilities. It is a truism of the history of religions that inspired speech rarely appears alone but is usually accompanied by other extraordinary powers, sometimes in the prophet personally, sometimes in his or her associates. Prophecy and miracles are correlates, both in the Hellenistic religious world and in Judaism. The expectation of signs and wonders, for example, was included in the Jewish expectation of the eschatological prophet.

In the Gospels Jesus is regarded as a prophet on the basis of his activity as a miracle-worker. It is probably the case that the prophets familiar to the seer of Revelation perform miracles, but the evidence for this is indirect: the prophets portrayed in 11:3–12 are endowed with miraculous power (11:5–6, 10), but it is difficult to penetrate the Old Testament imagery and apocalyptic symbolism with which the passage is laden to discern the specific traits of those prophets in John's church who were the occasion of this description. Certainly John knows that *false* prophets work miracles (13:11–15, with 16:13–14; 19:20; 20:10), but this does not mean that he rejects the miraculous element in prophetic ministry per se. They are false because of the content of their message, not because of their miracles, which John probably considered a typical feature of prophetic ministry.

In Paul's understanding this dialectic is sharply focused. He too believes that the one Spirit that inspires prophecy also gives the gift of miracles (1 Cor. 12:8–11, 28–30). He thinks of these gifts as ordinarily being distributed among the congregation in such wise that, if one has the gift of prophecy, he or she may not necessarily have the gift of working miracles, and vice versa. Still, the association between prophecy and miracles is present in Paul's understanding, and not only in that they are mentioned together in lists of charismatic gifts. Such lists are not intended to distinguish discrete gifts sharply from each other, as may be seen from comparing the various lists, but to illustrate the variety of energizings ("working," RSV of 1 Cor. 12:6) of the one Spirit. Paul is himself a prophet (1 Cor. 14:6) who works miracles (2 Cor. 12:12). My present purpose is not to develop Paul's theological critique of the claims that were made for the miraculous (1 Cor. 13:1; 2 Corinthians 10–13) but to note that, in spite of this critique, prophecy and miracles are closely related *even* in Paul.

Matthew, too, is unimpressed by miraculous phenomena per se and acknowledges that prophets who perform miracles are not thereby validated as true prophets (7:22–23). His polemic is not against associating miracles with prophecy, however, for the missionaries sent out by Matthew's community include prophets in their number, and such missionaries are commissioned not only to proclaim the word but to work miracles (10:1, 41). Luke 7:16 and 24:19 consider miracles, mighty deeds, even raising the dead, as marks of the true prophet, and not only the words he or she speaks. Although the portrayal of the Paraclete-prophet does not include miraculous gifts as part of the picture, the Fourth Gospel also knows a connection between miracles and prophets (6:14; 9:17). John's picture of the prophet Jesus may include miracles as a fundamental element not only because of the sources used by the evangelist but because miracles happen in the prophetic community.

In the *Didache* the connection between working miracles and speaking the word has been relaxed, and prophets appear mainly as ministers of the word, with miracles being assigned only to the eschatological deceiver (11.3–10; 16.4). The association of prophecy and miracles occurs often enough in our sources to suggest that early Christian prophets were frequently thought of in connection with miracles and functioned in a charismatic setting, where not only Spirit-empowered speech but also Spirit-empowered miracles were expected and experienced.

THE PROPHET'S SENSE OF CALL, AUTHORITY, AND MISSION

In the Hebrew-Jewish tradition from which early Christian prophecy sprang, the mark of the true prophet was that he or she had been "sent," while false prophets prophesied without this commission (e.g., Jer. 14:14–15; Neh. 6:12). Thus the repeated "the one who sent me" as the term for God used by the Johannine Jesus is a prophetic authorization formula, picturing Jesus as the true prophet. The prophet speaks with a sense of immediate authority resulting from his or her conviction that he or she has been personally commissioned by the deity to deliver a message to the people. This sense of mission is one of the primary distinguishing factors between mystics and prophets: the mystic seeks God in solitude and longs for undifferentiated union with the deity, while the prophet is persuaded that the deity has sought and commissioned him or her. Unlike the inspired mantics of Greek religion, who developed no sense of mission or claim to full personal authority because they tended to surrender their personality and consciousness to the deity, the biblical prophets of both Israel and the church emphasize the authority and purpose of the missioner, not his or her "union" with the sender.

This awareness of authority and mission is characteristic of all our sources. The author of the Apocalypse recounts his call and commission (1:9–19), identifies his word with the word of the Spirit and the risen Christ (2:7, etc.), places his writing on a par with the scriptures (1:3), contrasts his own immediate authority with that of the apocalyptists by writing in his own name (1:4) a book that is not to be sealed up (22:10, contrast, e.g., to Dan. 12:9) or tampered with under threat of divine retribution (22:18–19). Throughout his writing he neither pleads nor cajoles but announces and commands with a sense of unqualified authority. Revelation contains many pronouncements that only a prophet could make, such as the declaration in the name of the risen Christ in 3:4: "Yet you have still a few names in Sardis, people who have not soiled their garments; and they shall walk with me in white."

Paul's ranking of prophets as second only to apostles (1 Cor. 12:28) illustrates his own high valuation of prophetic authority, even higher than that of teachers. Although Paul designates his own authority as that of apostle rather than prophet, we have seen that there is every reason to consider Paul as a representative of early Christian prophecy. Paul's account of his call is expressed in terms borrowed from the prophets (Gal. 1:15 = Jer. 1:5; Isa. 49:1), as is his sense of compulsion in regard to his mission (1 Cor. 9:16 = Jer. 20:9) and his self-consciousness of mediating the divine authority in his own ministry (2 Cor. 10:8; 13:10 = Jer. 1:10). It is thus better to speak of Paul's "call" than his "conversion."

The immediate authority with which prophets act in Acts is illustrated by Agabus, especially in the introductory formula "thus says the Holy Spirit" (21:11). Prophetic speech is also reflected in the terminology used by Luke to describe those who spoke with the power of the Holy Spirit: Behind the "speak" and "address" of Acts 2:4, 14; 26:25 is the typical word for bold, inspired speech, *apophthengomai*, and "speak boldly" is the English translation of *parrēsia/parrēsiazomai* (Acts 9:27, 29; 13:46; 14:3; 18:26; 19:8; 26:26). The commissioning scene in Acts 13:1–2, in which prophets participate in designating and sending forth missionaries, shows that for Luke prophets were not marginal figures but acted with authority at critical moments in the church's life.

This latter term is a point of contact with the Gospel of John, which uses *parrēsia* as a characteristic term for Jesus' speech and action, an indication of his immediate authority in which the prophets of the Johannine community also participated (7:26; 10:24; 11:14; 16:25, 29; 18:20). The Fourth Gospel lays special emphasis on the "sending" of Jesus ("the One who sent me" or a variation thereof used twenty-seven times), whereby we may not only see the original prophetic authority of Jesus described but also an indirect reflection of the prophetic ministers of John's community since the Paraclete is repeatedly described as "sent" (14:26; 15:26; 16:7), as are the disciples (13:20; 20:21). The Johannine community knows a circle of prophets who claim a direct commission and authority from the risen Lord.

This is also the case in Matthew. The missionary speech in 10:1–41 represents the risen Christ as sending forth his missioners, including prophets, with his own authority (10:1, 40–41). Commentators often content themselves with referring to the Jewish juridical principle concerning the *shaliach,* "a person's representative is as the person," and see the chapter in terms of apostolic authority. The background is not juridical, however, but prophetic. This corresponds to the picture in 28:16–18, where the community knows that it is sent forth in mission with all the authority of the risen Christ, who speaks to it and is present within it. Likewise in the *Didache,* the prophets obviously claimed, and were accorded, great authority (10.7; 11.4–11; 13.3–6; 15.1–2).

Early Christian prophets, then, ought not to be thought of as pneumatic eccentrics who were regarded as curiosities within the life of the early church. Nor were they discussion leaders who posed items for consideration. As ministers of the word they spoke with an unqualified authority on subjects that could only be handled with hesitation by their uninspired brothers and sisters.[5] Being subject to the judgment of the community does not relativize the authoritative form of the prophet's speech, which is delivered with a sense of absolute authority. Consequently, the form and tone of such sayings would be very like the sayings of Jesus himself (Matt. 7:29), but by their authoritative form and tone they would sometimes be distinguishable from the sayings of Christian teachers and scribes who claimed no such inspiration and authority. This is doubly significant for our project, in that such sayings would the more readily be blended into the tradition of Jesus' sayings, on the one hand, and may the more readily be distinguished from nonprophetic additions to this tradition (scribal, redactional, midrashic, etc.), on the other.

THE SYMBOLIC ACTIONS OF
THE PROPHETS

The prophets of the Old Testament drew no sharp line between prophetic word and prophetic action, so that their "symbolic actions" were not merely illustrations or vivid portrayals of their message but were themselves prophetic words that, once enacted, set the process of ful-

---

5 This sense of authority appears in sharp profile when compared with some contemporary discussions of the modern phenomenon of "prophecy" as it occurs in charismatic Christian groups. One can hardly imagine Amos in Bethel or John on Patmos accepting such advice as given by Timothy Pain, who says that prophecies should not be prefixed with " 'Thus says the Lord,' or 'O my children'! It is much better, in humility . . . to prefix to the prophecy the words, 'I think the Lord is suggesting something like. . . .' " Cited in Grudem, *The Gift of Prophecy in the New Testament and Today,* 113.

fillment in motion (Jer. 13:1–11; 19:1–13; 27:1–28:14; Isa. 20:2–4; Ezekiel 4, 5, 12; Hosea 1, 3). There is some indication of a similar way of embodying their message among Christian prophets, but it is not always clear whether this is because early Christian prophets did in fact use symbolic actions, or whether our sources have described Christian prophets in Old Testament terms. In Revelation there is the additional complication of attempting to distinguish what is purely visionary apocalyptic imagery and what may have some counterpart in the ministry of the prophet-author himself and his fellow prophets in the Asian churches. Eating the scroll (10:8–11) and measuring the temple (11:1–2) probably belong only to the realm of vision, and the angel's throwing of the stone into the sea as a symbol of Babylon's fall (18:21) is probably a reflection of the prophetic symbol in Jeremiah 51:63–64. Nevertheless a Christian prophet whose thinking is so thoroughly permeated with such an understanding of the nature of prophecy probably engaged in such symbolic acts himself.

Likewise, while there is no explicit evidence that Paul or the prophets in his churches performed acts of prophetic symbolism, still one may ask how Paul "pronounced judgment in the name of the Lord Jesus" (1 Cor. 5:3–5) and how the Corinthian church, in which prophets were active, was to "deliver this man to Satan." If Acts 21:10–11 reflects a tradition that accurately portrays Agabus, and is not simply Luke's casting him into an Old Testament mold, then we have one clear example of such symbolic action by an early Christian prophet. The passage at least reveals that Luke or his tradition understood such prophets to have functioned in this way.

The shaking-off of the dust of the feet in Matthew 10:14, though a fairly common act to express the disavowal of fellowship, in the Matthean context has the connotation of a prophetic threat performed by missioners who include prophets in their number (10:41) and may indicate that church prophets known to Matthew performed such power-laden rituals. Even the baptism of John was probably a more symbolic act in the prophetic sense than sacrament in the church sense. The signs of Jesus in the Fourth Gospel are part of his revelatory, prophetic ministry: a symbolic presentation of his word, not miraculous proof of its truth. Though John himself strikes a profound theological note here, this understanding may have been partially shaped by the prophets of John's church who performed such symbolic embodiments of their word.

The *Didache*'s intriguing reference to a prophet who "enacts a worldly mystery of the Church" (11.11), who, if he or she is a "tried and true" prophet, is to be allowed to do such but is not to be imitated, probably refers to some bizarre symbolic acts or improprieties of worship. The "old" prophets, who are appealed to as precedents, could be Christian prophets of a previous generation, but more likely the strange acts of Old Testament prophets are invoked as justification of the behavior of contemporary ones. The evidence is slight and sketchy but taken together the above data may indicate that one characteristic trait of early Christian prophets was that they sometimes performed dramatic acts to communicate their message.

THE "ASCETIC" LIFE-STYLE OF
THE PROPHETS

As a person determined by the Spirit, the prophet rejects the cultural norms and lives a life in tension with the values and moral life of the culture of which he or she is a part. This is true to a greater or lesser extent of all members of the community called by the Spirit, but within this community of faith those who are self-consciously prophets seem to have lived in a particularly austere manner, rejecting involvement in family, occupation, and the accumulation of wealth. This is what I intend by "ascetic" and not some withdrawal from the world based on philosophical or theological dualism. There is no evidence for a hermitlike withdrawal from the world, and the evidence already presented regarding the involvement of the prophets in the life of the community shows that prophetic "asceticism" should not be understood in this way. We should rather think of a somewhat "ascetic" class living within the congregation but distinguished from their fellow Christians by their commitment to poverty and their rejection of family life, somewhat like a parish priest in the Roman Catholic Church, except that their "orders" are entirely a matter of the Spirit, and their authority is charismatic rather than institutional. This was the understanding of prophecy in the tradition from which early Christianity was born. Already in the Old Testament, the call to be a prophet was understood as a rupture with the normal social relations of the past (e.g., Amos 7:14–15). The dramatic social break represented by the call of Elisha (1 Kings 19:19–21) was understood to be paradigmatic. Jesus himself seems to have been influenced by this pattern, so that it is no surprise that, reinforced by the model of Jesus' own life, prophets in the later Christian community considered this variation a radical break with the social relations of the past, living a life without the usual commitments to home and family.

This general picture of the asceticism of early Christian prophets has been affirmed by a number of scholars, but it remains to fill in this picture with details and evidence from our sources. The seer on Patmos gives us no specific indication of his economic condition, but his appreciation of poverty and condemnation of wealth (2:9; 3:17; cf. 18:1–24) suggests his orientation clearly enough. Paul's view of himself as a prophet on this point is complicated by his self-understanding as an apostle. It is clear that as an apostle he claims the right to support from the churches, yet for his own reasons he has renounced this right and sometimes earns his own keep and sometimes accepts gifts from churches (1 Cor. 9:1–18; 2 Cor. 11:7–11; Phil. 4:10–17). How Paul's prophetic self-consciousness is involved in this is not clear; it is clear that Paul has abandoned the usual course of "making a living" and is sometimes in poverty as a result of his prophetic calling, and that this is something that distinguishes him from the general body of Christians and even from other "apostles."

Luke's focus on the poor in his Gospel (1–2; 4:18–19; 6:20–21; 12:13–21; 14:12–14; 16:19–31; 18:18–25; 19:8; 21:1–4) is somewhat modified in Acts, where with obvious relish he shows the church adding to its membership such persons as a Roman centurion, a business woman from Thyatira, "not a few of the leading women" of Thessalonica, and men and women "of high standing" in Berea (10:1–48; 16:14–15; 17:4, 12). Luke does not portray the church of Acts as such to be oriented toward the life of poverty. It is somewhat striking, then, to note that the prophet Barnabas is one who has sold (only some of?) his property (4:36), and that none of the prophets of Acts are described in the bourgeois terms Luke is so pleased to use of the church at large. The commitment to poverty of early Christian prophets may shine through Luke's tradition here, as it does in the Gospel.

The prophets of the *Didache* obviously are not engaged in normal occupations but are dependent on the congregations for support, even taking precedence over the poor: they are the poorest of the poor and more deserving of support because their poverty is not simply misfortune but is inherent in their prophetic vocation (11.8; 13.3–4).

In Hermas, only the *false* prophets receive fees for their oracles; the true prophet "makes himself the poorest of the poor" (Mandate 11.8). All of this corresponds to the general sociological description of the prophet as a religious typus, and to the general poverty characteristic of early Palestinian Christianity, and makes it quite likely that the typical early Christian prophet was characterized by the renunciation of wealth and worldly goods. The interest in fasting that is sometimes mentioned as a prophetic trait (Luke 2:36–37; Acts 13:1–2; Hermas, Visions 2.2.1; 3.1.2; 10.6; 14.23) is therefore probably not a part of the revelatory technique, since in any case the prophetic capacity was not thought to be subject to manipulation but was a part of their austere life-style.

Sexual abstinence also seems to have frequently been a prophetic commitment. Geza Vermes has assembled some interesting material documenting this view among the rabbis:

> According to the Talmud, Moses freely decided to terminate cohabitation with his wife after he received his call from God. He reasoned that

if the Israelites, to whom the Lord spoke only once and briefly, were ordered to abstain from women temporarily, he, being in continual dialogue with heaven, should remain chaste permanently.

One of the early rabbinic commentaries on Numbers treats the same theme from the woman's standpoint. Moses' sister, Miriam, noticing her sister-in-law's neglected appearance, asked her why she had ceased to look after herself. Zipporah answered, "Your brother does not care about the thing." (Siphre on Num. 12:1 [99]). The same passage of the document also notes that when it was announced that the two Israelite elders, Eldad and Medad, had started to prophesy, Miriam overheard Zipporah's muttered remark: woe to the wives of these men.[6]

Although this tradition comes from the second century C.E., Vermes is assured that it is also representative of rabbinic ideas contemporary with those prophets we are characterizing since Philo also makes use of it:

Moses cleansed himself of all the calls of mortal nature, food and drink and intercourse with women. This last he had disdained for many a day, almost from the time when, possessed by the Spirit, he entered on his work as a prophet, since he held it fitting to hold himself always in readiness to receive the oracular messages (*Life of Moses* 2.68–69).

It is well known that the Essenes, particularly at Qumran, also understood abstinence from sex to be an ingredient of the holy life belonging to the prophetic vocation. The presence of this understanding in such diverse streams of first-century Judaism makes the celibate life of the prophetic figures John the Baptist and Jesus easily understandable, even in a culture that placed a premium on early marriage, and suggests that Christian prophets emanating from such a context would understand their calling as a life of celibacy. It was prophetic eschatology, not a renunciation of the world itself as inherently evil, that formed the basis of this "ascetic" life-style.

Traces of this presumed trait of early Christian prophets remain in our sources. Revelation 14:1–5 exalts the celibate life, though John is no thoroughgoing ascetic. The prophetic "ideal" is reflected here, not a general theme of world renunciation, which is completely foreign to the Apocalypse. Luke associates virginity and the prophetic vocation very closely (Luke 1:26–55; 2:36–38; Acts 21:9). Paul understands that apostles and the brothers of the Lord have the right to marry, and as an apostle he has that right. However, he and the prophet Barnabas are not married (1 Cor. 9:5), which may reflect their prophetic ministry. Though Paul considers his own celibacy a charisma of the Spirit (1 Cor. 7:7), he does not make the connection with prophecy explicit. The successors of

---

6 *Jesus the Jew,* 100–101.

Paul, claiming the authority of prophetic revelation, *opposed* abstinence from marriage (1 Tim. 4:1–5), but this may be because Paul's earlier prophetic-eschatological idealization of the unmarried state (1 Cor. 7:25–40) was no longer understood eschatologically, but as a part of the general Gnostic rejection of the world.

The *Didache* makes no reference to spouses or families of the prophets, but this does not, of course, prove that they were celibate. There are some ambiguous texts in the *Didache* that fall into place, however, on the assumption derived from the other sources that prophets were typically unmarried. The criterion for distinguishing true prophets from false in 11.8, that the true prophet "has the behavior of the Lord," might well refer to a celibate state. The approved prophets who were to be permitted to manifest "the worldly mystery of the Church" in their lives, so long as they do not instruct others to do the same, may refer to the "spiritual marriage" of some prophets to their traveling companions. Such prophets may have interpreted the mystery of Ephesians 5:32 in this way, as well as appealing to the prophet Hosea (Hos. 3:1–3). In the light of the other evidence regarding the celibate expectations of Christian prophets, these two problematic texts seem best explained as dealing with prophets who attempted to avoid living strictly by this norm. Hermas' general aversion to sex and fascination with sexual matters, illustrated for example by his describing the holy spirits, the powers of the Son of God, as virgins (Similitude 9.13), is probably to be attributed not only to his personal psychology but to his understanding of the prophetic vocation. There is some significant evidence, then, that early Christian prophets typically were committed to poverty and sexual abstinence, and we may expect to find that sayings originating from, or shaped by, such prophets may sometimes manifest this commitment.

8

The Prophet as Hermeneut

The thesis of this chapter is that early Christian prophets functioned as interpreters of scripture in the light of contemporary events and as interpreters of events in the light of scripture. Scripture and event go together. The pairing of revelation-by-word and revelation-by-event is the unmistakable structural analogy that binds together the theology of the old covenant and its documents, on which early Christianity was founded, and the new, eschatological covenant, of which the early Christian prophets understood themselves to be ministers. We separate scripture and event only for purposes of clarity in discussion, with the understanding that each is interpreted only in the light of the other.

THE PROPHET AS INTERPRETER OF SCRIPTURE

The Judaism with which early Christianity shared a common Bible exhibited two, fundamentally different, hermeneutical stances toward scripture. While there were gradations and minglings of these two stances, for clarity I will describe them as polarities. The one, which may be designated "scribal-rabbinic," perceives the scripture to be an authoritative, objective, external collection of documents that contain deposits of God's eternal truth. These documents can and should be quoted, interpreted, and commented on by proper interpretative methods, a process that allows the word of scripture to illumine the interpreter's present. Scripture is by no means regarded as a dead letter in this view. It speaks the word of God to the present by being quoted and interpreted. Some New Testament authors, such as Matthew, use the scriptures within this hermeneutical framework with great effect (1:23; 2:6, 15, 18, 23; 4:15–16; 8:17; 12:18–21; 13:35; 21:5; 27:9–10). This approach distinguishes clearly between the word of scripture and the word of the interpreter, between "text" and "sermon," between the historical "then" of scripture

138

and the hermeneutical "now" of proclamation. The scripture is an external object that is interpreted by means of an external method, a method that may be articulated and examined by others. One's interpretation may be evaluated as to its methodological correctness by more-or-less objective criteria.

The other hermeneutical stance may be called "pneumatic-apocalyptic," in which scripture is taken up into the present word of the interpreter and becomes indistinguishable from it. The text is not quoted but internalized and re-presented as the word of the interpreter himself or herself, that is, as the word of the Spirit spoken by the prophet. Text and interpretation are fused; the "then" of scripture and its addressees is collapsed into the "now" of the interpreter and congregation. There is no objectifiable method that the interpreter may present to his or her hearers for consideration, to justify the correctness of the interpretation offered. Rather, the interpreter seems to have meditated on scripture as illuminated by the history of his or her own time until the text spoke its own word to the present, which was perceived as a word of revelation and delivered with the authority of one who is not a secondary interpreter of a text but an immediately inspired spokesperson through whom the text finds a new voice.

Such pneumatic-intuitive exegesis of texts began in Israel soon after the exile and is exemplified in Joel, who is thoroughly versed in the ancient prophecies but, instead of quoting them, bodies forth his interpretation of their current word as his own inspired word of the Lord, as can be seen in a careful comparison of the text of Joel and the canonical prophets prior to him. In Daniel, this development is already full blown, so that we see a prophet who self-consciously functions as an inspired interpreter of the old scriptures for a new day (9:1–24). This self-understanding is characteristic of all Jewish apocalyptic that regarded itself as prophetic. Jewish prophets who derived their oracles from inspired exegesis of scripture persisted throughout the first century, as 4 Ezra and the Zealot prophecies described by Josephus make clear. Qumran offers the most illuminating example, for there the Teacher is definitely a prophet who speaks "revelation" directly "from the mouth of God" (1QpHab 2.2–3) but is just as clearly an exegete whose "revelation" is "interpretation" of the prophetic texts (the Hebrew word for "revelation" [*galah*] is here used interchangeably with the word for "interpretation" [*pesher*]).

There were rabbis who understood the prophetic experience of revelation in terms of the hermeneutical interplay of words of scripture in the reflective imagination: "Rabbi Johann said, 'If one rises early and a scriptural verse comes to mind, this is a small prophecy" (*b. Berakoth* 55b, 57b). Rabbis who believed that prophecy had ceased still believed in the heavenly voice of the Bath Qol, which was believed to express its heavenly message in the phrases of scripture. Even a rabbi such as Akiba, who normally made no claims to inspiration, could, in the light of the advent of Simeon bar Kosiba, declare that the "star . . . out of Jacob" of Numbers 24:17 had now arrived. This is analogous to those early Christian prophets who reinterpreted the scriptures in the light of their faith that the Messiah had come in Jesus of Nazareth. Even the great majority of rabbis whose handling of the scripture was noncharismatic and who were personally far removed from prophetic experience nonetheless understood the prophets to be interpreters of scripture: the Old Prophets had been such, and the Eschatological Prophet, when he arrived, would function as an interpreter of scripture. Not only was the identification of prophecy and inspired exegesis at home in several streams of Palestinian Judaism, but Philo and Josephus show that this view was shared by Hellenistic Jews as well.

Fascher has collected evidence that suggests that prophets in the pagan world sometimes delivered their oracles in conjunction with the interpretation of written documents.[1] As an example he cites a passage from Aristophanes (*Birds* 960ff.) in which an oracle giver *(chrēsmologos)* operates by means of a collection of the sayings purported to be from Bakis. He reads them forth and gives their interpretation, which apply mostly to the oracle giver himself and his personal advantage. As the possessor of these older predictions, he calls himself a prophet and would apparently claim that their interpretation, like his other oracles, is given by divine wisdom. It may be that Fascher has here pressed his argument too far, but he has at least shown that in the Hellenistic world it was not unheard of that one who claims to give divine revelations and calls himself a prophet also operates as an interpreter of ancient written prophetic texts that he interprets to apply to his own situation. The similarity of some Christian prophets to this model is striking.[2]

All of this evidence is introduced not because it proves anything about the character of early Christian prophecy, for it does not; this must be done on the basis of the Christian sources themselves. But since some contemporary readers still tend to think of inspired prophets as speaking on the basis of spontaneous emotional outpourings—a typus quite common in the Hellenistic world, as we have seen—it is helpful to know that in the Hellenistic world, and especially in that Judaism from which early Christian prophecy sprang, "prophet" and "interpreter of the scripture" were very congenial concepts.

---

1 Fascher, *PROPHĒTĒS*, 25–26.

2 My thanks to Christopher Forbes, "Prophecy and Inspired Speech," 278, who corrected my earlier misreading of Fascher's data. As argued above, it still seems to me (contra Forbes) that Fascher's argument supports the case for prophetic exegesis. In any case, Forbes's leaving the Revelation of John out of account in his discussion of New Testament prophecy tends to distort his own conclusion on this point.

When we turn to the early Christian sources and inquire concerning the nature of scripture interpretation present in them, we are touching an area that is of fundamental importance in the development of New Testament theology. C. H. Dodd has shown that while New Testament theology has substantial Hellenistic elements, its substructure is built upon the Old Testament and the conviction that what is written there is now being fulfilled in the ministry of Jesus and the life of the church.[3] This fundamental point has recently been elaborated.[4] Likewise, Heinz Schürmann declares that "the mother of all theology is the exposition of Scripture."[5] Their thesis is that whoever explained the scriptures to the early church was the real architect of New Testament theology.

The church's understanding of itself as the true and ultimate people of God, its christological understanding of the essentially nonmessianic life of Jesus (measured by traditional messianic expectations), and its understanding of Jesus' death as a redemptive act that led to Christ's glory and exaltation were all derived from its new understanding of the scripture—assuming, of course, that something happened to evoke this reinterpretation. The event was interpreted by scripture, just as the scripture was interpreted by event. Since the basic creative interpretation had already been done by the time of Paul, who presupposes it as familiar, Dodd correctly argues that we must look in the period prior to Paul. And though Dodd acknowledges that there may have been some anonymous creative thinkers between Jesus and Paul, he prefers to accept the witness of the New Testament itself (Luke 24) that "it was Jesus Christ Himself who first directed the minds of His followers to certain parts of the Scriptures as those in which they might find illumination upon the meaning of His mission and destiny."[6]

It may be granted to Dodd that Jesus himself may have given the original impetus toward a fresh understanding of the Old Testament in view of the dramatic events of his own ministry. All the evidence that indicates that Jesus saw the End as rapidly approaching would carry with it as its corollary that he saw the promises of the scriptures as being in the process of fulfillment. Apocalyptic is by nature an interpreter of prophecy. But to whatever extent this interpretative process was begun by Jesus, it was greatly extended and elaborated in the earliest church, as is seen from the fact that most of the *testimonia,* those collections of Old Testament texts seen to be in the process of fulfillment, reflect a post-Easter perspective.

---

3 *According to the Scriptures: The Sub-Structure of New Testament Theology.*

4 Dodd's classic study has been followed and supplemented by, e.g., Barnabas Lindars, *New Testament Apologetic,* and more recently by Donald Juel, *Messianic Exegesis: Christological Interpretation of the Old Testament in Early Christianity,* who provides a thorough bibliography.

5 ". . . und Lehrer," 125

6 *According to the Scriptures,* 110.

How did this creative rereading of scripture come about? Studies such as Juel's *Messianic Exegesis* are helpful in that they set the process of early Christian interpretation in its Jewish context, and in laying bare the lines of the logic that led from one text and idea to another, showing it was not a random process that occurred as the language of scripture was reinterpreted to apply to Jesus.[7] But such studies tend to leave the issue too much in the abstract—if the pre-Easter Jesus did not do this job of theological reconstruction himself, who did, and by what authority? The question has hardly been asked since Dodd.

When we ask who in the earliest Christian community might have been responsible for this inspired, authoritative interpretation of the scriptures as the vehicle for expressing the ultimacy of the events surrounding Jesus (Jesus as the eschatological savior figure; the church as the eschatological community), one group comes readily to mind in view of our previous discussions: early Christian prophets. Evidence will be presented for the view that church prophets did indeed serve as the inspired, intuitive interpreters of the scripture for the earliest church and are thus key figures in the formation of New Testament theology.

If this hypothesis can be substantiated, we have an important insight into the problem of how to bridge the historical and theological gap between the teaching of Jesus and the theology of the early church. One of the fundamental issues of New Testament theology is how the proclaimer became the proclaimed. Jesus of Nazareth did not preach himself; the core of his message was the (soon) coming of the kingdom of God, the expectation of which already transformed the present. The church did not merely continue Jesus' message but in the light of the crucifixion and resurrection proclaimed Jesus himself as the saving act of God. How did early Christianity bridge this gap between proclaimer and proclaimed?

The Christian prophets of which we are speaking played a key role in this transition. They would both take up the traditional message of Jesus, re-presenting it as the word of the exalted Lord, and affirm the redemptive eschatological significance of the person of Jesus himself, uniting both in a proclamation given in Jesus' own name. Jesus the self-proclaimed (by post-Easter Christian prophets who interpret the Jesus event via scripture) emerges as a middle term between Jesus the proclaimer (of the Kingdom of God during his pre-Easter ministry) and Jesus the proclaimed (in the post-Easter *kerygma* of the church). The continuing voice of Jesus in the mode of Christian prophecy represents both continuity with the historical Jesus and the discontinuity represented by the crucifixion, resurrection, and birth of the church in the power of the

---

7 *Messianic Exegesis*, 103, 113, 130, 141.

Spirit. The new insights into the meaning of Jesus' life and death given by the prophetic Spirit came in conjunction with interpretation of the scripture.[8] We have struck on a significant point. We must now inquire what evidence there is in our sources for relating Christian prophets to the interpretation of scripture.

I turn first to Revelation. The twenty-fifth edition of the Nestle-Aland Greek text follows the practice of previous editions in printing in bold type every direct quotation and clear allusion to the Old Testament texts. In Revelation, 499 such usages of Old Testament materials are found, an average of 11.3 per page. The Westcott-Hort text, which used a similar procedure, had approximately the same number of allusions. It is clear that the Apocalypse is saturated with words and phrases from the Old Testament. The sheer amount of Old Testament material shows that in the case of the Apocalypse, Christian prophecy functions primarily by interpretation of the scriptures. Heinrich Kraft hardly overstates the matter when he asserts that for every statement in the Apocalypse the seer has a scripture source, which he reinterprets and sets forth afresh in the light of the Christ-event.[9]

The manner in which John does this is important and may be compared to the way in which Old Testament allusions and quotations are handled in the third edition of *The Greek New Testament* of the United Bible Societies. The editorial policy of this edition is to call to the reader's attention, by printing in bold type, "only those passages which are clearly quotations from the Old Testament, . . . eliminating references to words and phrases which are only allusions or literary echoes."[10] The result is that in all the twenty-two chapters of Revelation, not a single Old Testament reference is indicated, either by bold type or in the "Index of Quotations." This is correct procedure in terms of the edition's editorial policy, however misleading it may be regarding John's use of the Old Testament, for in fact the prophet-interpreter never once formally cites an Old Testament passage. To have done so would have bifurcated the inner unity between his own prophetic word and the prophetic word of his texts. The prophet no longer experienced the inspired texts as a *past* voice of the Lord that was to be "applied" to the *present* experience of the congregation. The texts became the vehicle for communicating the pre-

---

8 Cf. Howard Teeple, "The Origin of the Son of Man Christology"; William O. Walker, Jr., "The Origin of the Son of Man Concept as Applied to Jesus"; Norman Perrin, *A Modern Pilgrimage in New Testament Christology*, 5, 10–22, 36, 55–59; Hendrikus Boers, "Where Christology Is Real"; Lindars, *New Testament Apologetic;* Juel, *Messianic Exegesis.*

9 Heinrich Kraft, *Die Offenbarung des Johannes,* 112.

10 Kurt Aland et al., eds., *The Greek New Testament* (New York: American Bible Society, 1975[3]), ix. The current 26th edition of the Nestle-Aland text has attempted to adopt a mediating approach in Revelation but without success. The phenomenon calls for the either/or approach of Nestle[25] and *The Greek New Testament.*

sent word of the risen Lord. They are thus not quoted but re-presented in new forms and combinations so that neither the past/present distinction nor the subject/object distinction between text and interpreter is maintained.

The way the scriptures are used in Revelation points to a community intensively occupied with scripture, which suggests in turn that there were definite persons in the community charged with its interpretation. John was one such person, and apparently in a role of leadership, but the extent to which familiarity with scripture and the prophetic mode of handling it is presupposed makes it unlikely that he was the only such interpreter in the community. We may postulate a group of prophetic interpreters to whom the community looked for guidance in interpreting the scripture.

No identifiable revelations from the Christian prophets at Corinth have been preserved, but there is nothing specific in Paul's (not altogether objective) reports of Corinthian prophecy to indicate that interpretation of scripture played a role in it—though that is possibly reflected in the "interpretations" presented in the congregational assembly in 1 Corinthians 14:26. Probably prophecy at Corinth was too enthusiastic to be related closely to exegesis of the scriptures.

It is when we turn to Paul himself as a prophet that the connection between prophecy and exegesis is first suggested by the Pauline materials. As a prophet, Paul functioned as an interpreter of the scriptures to the church for the last times. He interprets the Old Testament in the light of the contemporary eschatological events, and these events in the light of the Old Testament, as for example his treatment of Adam in Romans 5 and 1 Corinthians 15, his treatment of Abraham in Galatians 3–4, his treatment of the exodus events in 1 Corinthians 10, and the plethora of Old Testament interpretation in his history-of-salvation exposition of Romans 9–11 make clear. The Old Testament sayings and narratives were not written for their own sake but for the "encouragement" of Christian believers (Rom. 15:4), an "encouragement" of which Christian prophets are also the agent (1 Cor. 14:3). He reinterprets the Old Testament as "types," not, however, as "types" of soul events as does Philo, but as foreshadowing the Last Times, which he believes now to have dawned.

The interpretation of scripture in the eschatological times is not left to human logic and inference but is accomplished by the eschatological gift of the Spirit. There is no doubt that Paul considered his own interpretations to have been given him by the Spirit. It is the Lord who is the Spirit who gives to Paul that freedom to see the Christian events already revealed in the Old Testament, which are veiled to the Jews precisely because they do not have this Lord-who-is-the-Spirit (1 Cor. 2:6–16; 2 Cor. 3:15–17). That Paul's own oracles sometimes came to him and were formulated in conjunction with his exegesis of scripture is to be seen from the quotations related to them in Romans 11:25–27 and 1 Corinthians 15:51–55. Further, the use of "search" *(eraunō)* of the Spirit who gives revelations (1 Cor. 2:10) in this prophetic passage corresponds to the "search" *(darash,* "interpret") of rabbinic exegesis (cf. John 5:39) and points to the connection here posited between Christian prophecy and the interpretation of scripture.

Luke's descriptions of those he specifically designates as prophets give no indications that prophets function as interpreters of scripture, unless Agabus's prediction of famine (Acts 11:28) may be taken as originally an eschatological oracle derived from a reinterpretation of Old Testament prophecies. The incidental references to inspired speech in the Gospel and Acts paint quite another picture. The prophetic figures of Luke 1–2 deliver oracles that, like the Apocalypse, contain many Old Testament allusions, indicating that they were derived from charismatic interpretation of scripture, the Magnificat and Benedictus being almost entirely composed of Old Testament phrases. The "prophecy" of Acts 2 is replete with Old Testament interpretation from an eschatological perspective, applying the promises of the End of the ages to the events of Jesus' life, death, and resurrection. The issue in Acts 15 is resolved prophetically by an interpretation of the Old Testament that declares its fulfillment in contemporary events.

Luke 24:13–32 portrays the whole process by which the risen Lord gave to the church its new understanding of the scripture in one scene filled with motifs from Christian prophecy: Jesus is called a prophet (24:19); the travelers are reproved for not believing the prophets (24:25), *all* of whom are emphasized (24:27); the scene is a cultic one in which there is table fellowship, blessing, breaking, and distribution of bread (24:30); the "burning" of their hearts as he opened to them the scriptures perhaps reflects the response to fervent charismatic preaching. Luke knew that the church did not receive its new understanding of the scriptures in one day, just as he knew that the church did not perceive the risen Lord sending it on a mission to all nations on the first Easter Sunday (24:47; cf. Acts 1–15). Each of these was the result of a gradual process of prophetic insight in the early church, as depicted in Acts. Yet Luke also knew that the church's new insight into the scriptures did not come about by a deductive process, nor by the application of an objective method to the text, but was the direct gift of the risen Lord. Christian prophets who speak in the name of the risen Jesus as they interpret the scriptures to the church are portrayed in Luke 24:13–35.

The Fourth Gospel quotes the Old Testament explicitly relatively few times but, like the Apocalypse, prefers to weave Old Testament allusions into the structure of its presentation without formal quotation. Interpretation of scripture is a charismatic function in the community of the

Fourth Gospel, for the Paraclete-prophet has the interpretation of scripture as one of his functions. The postresurrection gift of the Spirit is related both to the remembrance of Jesus' words and the understanding of scripture in 2:22 and 12:16 (cf. 2:17; 7:39; 14:26; 20:9). When the Paraclete is described as having the prophetic gift of predicting the future (16:13), this too should be related to scriptural exegesis, since prediction among early Christian prophets was not the prediction of mundane historical events, but eschatological predictions on the basis of charismatic interpretation of scripture—as the examples of Revelation and Paul make clear.

In Hermas revelation takes place through a study of the scriptures: "The understanding of the scriptures was revealed to me" (Vision 2.2.1). The matter is less clear in the *Didache,* but here too the prophet's teaching function probably includes the exposition of scripture in view of the way the author-editor himself understands "teaching" to combine sayings of Jesus, Old Testament commandments, and church teaching. As in *1 Clement* 22, the Old Testament is quoted in the *Didache* as the word of the Lord (Jesus). This is seen throughout the opening chapters of the *Didache,* particularly in the "Two Ways" section, chapters 1–5. In 14.3 the Lord who speaks there (in the Old Testament) is probably intended to be the Lord Jesus, in view of the fact that of the other seventeen instances of "Lord" in the *Didache,* sixteen probably refer to Jesus, the only exception being the "Lord" in the prayer of 10.5, which could also, of course, refer to Jesus. For the *Didache,* the Lord who speaks in the scripture and the Lord who speaks through Christian prophets is one and the same.

The evidence of our sources, seen against the Jewish background from which early Christian prophecy developed, gives us ample reason for believing that the earliest Christian prophets frequently spoke the word of the risen Lord as a result of their inspired interpretation of the scripture. The eschatological mood of earliest Christianity both required and produced more than a scholastic exposition of the sacred text. The Spirit had been poured out to reveal that the Old Testament promises were now in the process of realization. The Spirit, which was the common possession of all members of the community, opened it up to the reception of new interpretations. The Spirit's gift of prophetic insight was focused in relatively few inspired spokespersons, i.e., prophets, in whose hands scripture became a living book, speaking directly of and to the present. The prophets handled the text with a new freedom, even reshaping it to fit more clearly the fulfillment that they saw happening before them, just as did the charismatic interpreters of Qumran. Speaking from the Old Testament text in a way that was no longer bound to its words means that reflection on the scriptures may have influenced the formation of New Testament texts in such a way that this influence is no longer to be documented simply by explicit quotation or direct allusion to an

Old Testament text. No claim is made that prophetic speech was universally related to scripture, even in that free sense described here. And there were certainly authoritative interpreters of scripture in the early church who were not prophets. But the evidence indicates that it was indeed frequently the case that prophets functioned by charismatic interpretation of scripture, and this feature may be used as one identifying mark in the quest for prophetic oracles now imbedded in the Gospel tradition as sayings of Jesus.

THE PROPHET AS INTERPRETER
OF EVENTS

"The Old Testament is a history book."[11] With this terse manifesto Gerhard von Rad affirms that even the prophets of the Old Testament should not be regarded as purveyors of inspired information from heaven but interpreters of the meaning of the historical events in which they and their hearers found themselves. The prophet in Israel did not begin with a personal experience of revelation, as though prophecy were an episode in the life of an individual, but with an event that shaped the life of both prophet and people and bound them together. The prophets of the Old Testament are typically interpreters of the historical deeds of Yahweh, who does nothing without revealing the divine "secret" to God's "servants the prophets" (Amos 3:7). Amos declared Yahweh's judgment on the historical acts of nations, including his own, and this on the basis not of an ahistorical, individualistic, mystical experience but on a claim of divinely given insight into the meaning of contemporary history: the illusory prosperity occasioned by the advance of Assyria was temporary for Assyria would soon bring destruction to Israel. Isaiah had a similar hermeneutical function in relation to the same historical crisis for Judah, Jeremiah to the advance of Nebuchadnezzar, 2 Isaiah to the rise of Cyrus with its accompanying events, Joel to the locust plague, Haggai to the drought, Daniel to the persecution by Antiochus IV. And Moses is considered the prophet par excellence (Deut. 18:15–18; Hos. 12:13) not because he goes into trances and delivers revelations from the heavenly world but because he reveals that the event at the Red Sea was not simply good fortune but the saving act of God. The prophet is that figure in the community who is enabled, by the Spirit, to recognize the otherwise mute, surd-like events of history as acts of God, to interpret their meaning, and to proclaim them to the community. The prophet is hermeneut not only of the tradition (and/or scripture) but of the event in which God

---

11 "Typological Interpretation of the Old Testament," in *Essays in Old Testament Hermeneutics,* ed. Klaus Westermann (Richmond: John Knox Press, 1963), 25.

also speaks but which is mute or unintelligible until interpreted and given voice by the prophet.

The revelatory *Gestalt* typical of the Old Testament consists of three interdependent elements: event, interpretation by a prophetic figure, and reception by the community. The revelatory event is not self-contained within the prophet, but he or she is the essential mediator if the event is to be revelatory to the community. In itself, the event is opaque, or, at the most, ambiguous; the event needs to be given voice and interpretation by the prophet before God's word is heard in it. But neither is the word of the prophet a purely vertical word from heaven directed at the point of individual human life; the prophetic word always operates by engagement with the horizontal line of that history which forms the essential context, and often the content, of the prophet's message.

The prophet's insight into the meaning of events as God's act is not a rationalistic process but an intuitive, pneumatic, "ecstatic" one. "Ecstatic" is not used here in the history-of-religions sense, for early Christian prophets were not ecstatic in that sense, but in the sense used by Paul Tillich for that noninferential kind of insight into the divine reality of things that can be called "revelation."[12] There is a nondeductive gap between history seen in ordinary secular terms and history seen as the arena of God's redemptive act, between event as such and revelation. Although the revelation is there in the event, it remains hidden until seen and interpreted by the prophet. This prophetic "seeing" is not a matter of the prophet being a more astute observer of the historical scene than his or her contemporaries, but a charismatic illumination of the event as the revelation of God, a revelatory insight quite beyond the power of, and sometimes contrary to the will of, the prophet.

The prophet's interpretation of the event becomes revelation when it is heard and acknowledged as such within the community. This can happen only as a confession of faith on the part of the community, which acknowledges both event and interpretation interdependently as the Word of God. Such is the Old Testament understanding of prophecy. Its connection of prophecy to history represents a prophetic type sui generis in the ancient world. There were many shamans, prophets, soothsayers, and diviners in the ancient Near East, as later in the Hellenistic world, but only in Israel does prophecy represent the claim that the deity has addressed the prophet for the purpose of conveying a message to others—a message that interprets history in its totality as the arena in which the deity's covenantal purpose for humanity is worked out, a revelatory word that draws history and previous revelatory moments into a unity.

---

12 Paul Tillich, *Systematic Theology* (Chicago: University of Chicago Press, 1951), 1:111–118.

This style of prophecy, which functioned by interpreting current events as part of the eschatological redemptive plan, extended into first-century Judaism. Not only is this evidenced at Qumran (e.g., the Habakkuk Commentary), but the prophets described by Josephus were also of this sort. Though he attempts to describe the outbreak of prophecy just prior to the outbreak of the war in c.e. 66 as simply the enthusiasm of revolutionary fanatics, his descriptions reveal that such men as Jesus ben Ananias, the Egyptian prophet, and the prophet who gathered six thousand men in the temple court during the last battle for Jerusalem were apocalyptic prophets who saw in the war's events the beginning of the final act of the drama of salvation (*Jewish War* 2.261–266; 6.285–300). Since early Christian prophets typically modeled themselves more on the pattern of Old Testament prophets than on pagan prophets in the Hellenistic world, we might anticipate that the revelatory *Gestalt* of event/prophet/community would characterize prophets in the early church as it had in Israel and Judaism. This anticipation is confirmed by an examination of our sources.

The Apocalypse was born out of a historical crisis in the life of the church, a threat of imperial persecution that had already claimed one victim, Antipas of Pergamum, a "test case" who had already been executed (2:13). In such a situation, the absurd meaninglessness of the events that seemed imminent was more of a threat to the faith than the events themselves. With prophetic insight, John sees that the threatening persecution, the historical reality in which he and his church must live out their lives, is not a meaningless tragedy but the last act in the drama of God's redemptive history.[13] It is to "his servants the prophets" that the "mystery of God" has been revealed (10:7), which means that the prophets are those who, by the Spirit, recognize and proclaim the contemporary events to be integral to God's saving act. John is less inclined to cosmological speculation and more closely related to history than the typical Jewish apocalypse, although he expresses his prophetic insight in traditional apocalyptic imagery. Not only the major sociopolitical events of the time are given a prophetic-eschatological interpretation, the religious events of the community's own life are interpreted in prophetic perspective. As Adela Yarbro Collins has pointed out, in John's prophetic interpretation of contemporary events as the scene of God's eschatological act, "an archetype is used to give meaning to a present event. . . . The nameless man who had a following at Pergamum is no longer a fellow Christian who holds opinions and teaches practices that must be evalu-

---

13 As Elisabeth Schüssler Fiorenza has succinctly commented, Revelation shows no interest in speculative long-range prediction, for "John's primary concern is to give a prophetic interpretation of the present situation of the Christian community" (*The Book of Revelation: Justice and Judgment*, 49).

ated on their merits. Suddenly he is Balaam, who led Israel into idolatry and harlotry."[14]

John has a prophetic word to say because of his interpretation of the historical event that confronts him, and he is able to do this not only from the resources of scripture and the apocalyptic tradition in which he is immersed but fundamentally because of his and his predecessor-prophets' interpretation of the historical event of Jesus Christ. The prophet's call for the churches of Asia to "conquer," i.e., witness faithfully even to the point of martyrdom but without violent resistance to the imperial power (2:7, 11, etc.; 2:10), is based on the christological insight that in the face of the same imperial power Jesus "conquered," i.e., surrendered his life (1:17–18; 3:21; 5:5–6, etc.).

The prophet continues to reinterpret the meaning of the event of Jesus of Nazareth to his contemporaries, even in new categories. The book as a whole is a fresh "revelation of Jesus Christ" both in the sense that Jesus is the speaking subject in revelation (subjective genitive) but also in the sense that the document offers a new interpretation of the meaning of the event of Jesus Christ (objective genitive). This is particularly so in the christological affirmations that begin each of the seven letters, in which the risen Lord identifies himself by means of christological affirmations that are particularly relevant to the crisis of the Asian churches as they faced impending persecution. For example, Jesus calls himself "the faithful and true witness" (3:14), a title that had hitherto never been used of Jesus but was particularly meaningful in the situation of a "confessing church." Here is illustrated the creative role of Christian prophets in the formation of Christology. This is apparently the significance of the author's own key statement concerning the prophetic role in 19:10: "the testimony of Jesus is the spirit of prophecy." This genitive is properly regarded by Charles and others as an objective genitive, as in the first part of the verse, and means that in John's view the very essence of Christian prophecy is testimony to Jesus. But the view that this is a subjective genitive also fits very well both the context and John's other instances of the phrase "testimony of Jesus" in 1:2, 9, and 12:17. Like the similar phrase in 1:1, the genitive construction here seems to have both subjective and objective aspects and may have been chosen to express the unique aspect of Christian prophecy in which the risen Christ is both subject and object, both proclaimer and proclaimed.

The event of Jesus of Nazareth thus becomes the touchstone of authentic prophecy, as in 1 Corinthians 12:3, 1 John 4:1–3, and Romans 12:6, so that prophecy is not freed by the Spirit to declare just any content but is bound to the event of Jesus of Nazareth, which it *interprets* and does

---

14 *Crisis and Catharsis,* 147.

not simply *repeat*. Christian prophets go beyond what the historical Jesus actually said and did, but it is testimony to *this* event that makes them Christian prophets. "Fundamentally the exalted earthly Lord cannot make himself present in the word that denies his history."[15]

So also in the Fourth Gospel: the risen Christ is the interpreter of the event of Jesus' life and death as Christ speaks through the Paraclete. When the Johannine Jesus promises with reference to the Paraclete: "he will bear witness to me" (15:26), this is analogous to the "testimony of Jesus" affirmed to be the essence of prophecy in Revelation 19:10—to declare the saving significance of Jesus, to reveal the act of God in him. Despite the Johannine account's retrojection of the exalted Christ's glory and the church's faith into the preresurrection ministry of Jesus, there are unmistakable signs that the prophet-evangelist knows that during Jesus' lifetime even his close disciples did not recognize the significance of his person and work (1:10–11; 2:17, 22; 7:5, 39; 12:16; 13:7; 14:20, 29; 16:12, 20–26; and the Paraclete passages 14:16–17, 26; 15:26; 16:7–11, 13–14). In the author's view, it was after the resurrection, in conjunction with a fresh understanding of scripture given by the Spirit, that Jesus was recognized and declared to be the saving figure. It should be noted that the only occurrence of the verb "prophesy" in the Fourth Gospel (11:51) reveals the form that prophecy takes for John, namely the divinely given interpretation of the meaning of the life and death of Jesus and not merely prediction—though here expressed with deep Johannine irony.

When we turn to the data preserved in Paul's letters, we find nothing to indicate that the prophecy of the Corinthian enthusiasts was related to historical events, except as they were influenced by Paul's own views of prophecy. Rather, prophecy at Corinth seems to have been a spontaneous occurrence in worship, not particularly related to events of the past, present, or future. But when Paul encounters the charismatic speech of the Corinthians, his efforts to mold it into forms that he considers to be authentic prophecy indicate that Paul stands in that traditional stream of Christian prophecy that related prophecy to the interpretation of events. Beginning with the Corinthians where they were, enthralled with the mysterious goings-on that were occurring in their worship, the thrust of Paul's discussion is that prophecy, as the most valuable charismatic gift, belongs to that person who can translate the numinous events happening in their midst into meaningful, edifying language (1 Cor. 14:1–5, 26–29). The prophet has insight into the meaning of the act as God's act and declares this meaning to the community in intelligible language.

For Paul, interpretation is thus seen to be of the essence of Christian

---

15 Thomas W. Gillespie, "Prophecy and Tongues: The Concept of Christian Prophecy in the Pauline Theology," 197, on 1 Cor. 12:3.

prophecy. It has, in fact, not been sufficiently noticed that Paul seems simply to equate the gifts of interpretation and prophecy. Thus 14:5: "The one who prophesies is greater than the one who speaks in tongues, *unless that person interprets* what he or she says in tongues, so that the church may be edified" (my trans.). The RSV and NRSV translate the underlined phrase "unless someone interprets." But there is no "someone" (not even in the variant readings, all of which indicate that it is the tongue-speaker himself or herself who interprets), and 14:13 clearly indicates that it is the speaker-in-tongues himself or herself whom Paul desires to be the interpreter. The KJV, ASV, NEB, REB, Moffatt, Goodspeed, J. B. Phillips, and Jerusalem Bible all translate the Greek better by identifying the speaker-in-tongues him- or herself as the one who interprets. Verse 5 indicates that if the one speaking in tongues *interprets* his or her own speech, he or she is of equal value to the congregation as the prophet. It should be noted that Paul designates the content of the tongue-speech as "mysteries" (14:2). Thus the "interpretation" of "mysteries" is considered by Paul to be the same as "prophecy." Although Paul's understanding of the "spiritual gifts" is not so mechanical that it can be represented mathematically (the gifts have overlapping functions and are not always to be sharply defined from each other), something of Paul's thought on this point is captured by the following equations:

> The Spirit ➡ *tongues* = "mysteries"
> "Mysteries" + "interpretation" = "edification."

But:

> The Spirit ➡ *prophecy* = "edification,"
> Therefore: "Prophecy" = "mysteries" + "interpretation,"
> Which means that *prophecy* also = "tongues" + "interpretation."

Prophecy is a two-stage process, involving the reception of the revelation "mystery" and the translation of it into edifying language before it is spoken forth to the congregation. Tongues are inferior to prophecy precisely because the "mysteries" are received and then *expressed* without being "translated" or interpreted into intelligible language. The tongue-speaker gives vocalization but not conceptualization to the "mysteries" he or she has received, in which the person's "spirit," but not his or her "mind," is active (14:14–19).

In the prophetic oracles contained in Paul's letters, some of which may be revelations to Paul himself, the element of revelatory interpretation of the "mystery" is also prominent. This "mystery" is the eschatological plan of God, which is already being worked out in contemporary events. This understanding is integral to the prophetic stream of tradition emanating from the Old Testament and especially from Daniel, where the prophets are those who understand the "mystery" (Aramaic *raz*), of the saving plan of God, which is already in operation. Thus the oracle of Romans 11:25–27 is called a "mystery," which refers not to an esoteric secret but to the eschatological significance revealed to the prophet of a historical event in the redemptive plan of God.

Paul here speaks as a pneumatic who has special prophetic insight into God's historical saving process. The connection with a historical event, the general rejection of the gospel by Israel, is to be noted here. The event does not mean what it seems to mean on the surface; its true eschatological meaning is perceived only by the prophet. Here it is seen that prophecy does not speak from a vacuum but is bound to history; it interprets events, revealing their salvation-historical significance. In 1 Corinthians 15:51–52, the event that the revealed mystery interprets is the resurrection of Jesus. In 1 Corinthians 2:6–16, the prophetic Spirit gives the interpretation of the event of Jesus' crucifixion, thus making it a revelation. The bare event is ambiguous; it is the Spirit that reveals that it is from God and that leads to proclamation in words given by the Spirit (2:12). This is a portrayal of the prophetic function.

Paul's view is continued in Ephesians, where the author regards the inclusion of the Gentiles in the church as the mystery revealed in the Spirit to apostles and prophets. This event, which was understood to be a part of the eschatological redemptive plan of God (Isa. 2:2–4; 19:24–25) is identified with a present event in the developing mission of the church. This identification of contemporary historical events with the eschatological redemptive events is remembered to be the work of the first-generation figures of prophetic insight, the apostles and prophets (Eph. 2:20; 3:5). Here, as in Acts 10 and 15, which also have prophetic overtones, an accurate memory of the earlier function of Christian prophets is preserved. So also in Acts 2, the interpretation of scripture is interwoven with the interpretation of the life, death, and resurrection of Jesus as God's decisive saving act. It is specifically emphasized that the hermeneutic of scripture-plus-event is "prophecy" (2:17, with the addition of an extra "and they shall prophesy" to the Old Testament text in 2:18). The prophetic figures of Luke 1–2 recognize and proclaim the salvific character of events that to the natural eye are absolutely ordinary (1:43, 68–69, 77; 2:29–32, 38).

This does not mean that everyone who writes theologically understood history, such as Luke himself does in Acts, is thereby a prophet. Luke's is a secondary, consciously reflective theological interpretation of a history that early Christian prophets had already taught the church to see as theologically significant. The initial insight must be charismatic, which can then be theologized by others. Luke here stands in the same relation to the events he records as do Ephesians and the Pastorals to Paul.

The prophets of the early church, like their Old Testament counterparts, do not spin their messages out of the air, nor from their "experiences," but begin with a given: concrete events that have happened and are happening. The content of the prophets' messages was not a *creatio ex nihilo* but a fusion of interpretation of event and interpretation of scripture.

THE PROPHET AS INTERPRETER OF
THE SAYINGS OF JESUS

We have seen that the prophet stands within the stream of tradition handed on by the church, that this tradition included the sayings of Jesus, and that prophets functioned in conjunction with this tradition, both influencing it and being influenced by it. We have seen that some of our sources contain evidence that words of Jesus were taken up by Christian prophets and re-presented as sayings of the risen Jesus. This would suggest that Christian prophets also functioned as interpreters of the sayings of Jesus within the church, elaborating and modifying traditional sayings to express the word of the risen Lord more clearly to the present situation. We have seen that a number of students have come to this general conclusion, though it is rarely supported in particular cases with evidence. There were others besides prophets in the community who elaborated the traditional sayings of Jesus. The thirteen types of alterations of the parables during the period of oral transmission that Jeremias has documented,[16] for example, and the redactional activity of the evangelists, show that there were a variety of interpretative ways of making the tradition more relevant to the present without any claim to be speaking prophetically for the risen Lord. In Part Three of this study we will examine the evidence that indicates that Christian prophets did in fact sometimes take up a traditional saying of Jesus, modify and elaborate it in characteristic ways (prophetic "peshering"), and re-present it as a word of the risen Lord. In such sayings, there will be no sharp line between pre-Easter words of Jesus and words of the risen Lord through the prophet. We must not come to the Gospel sayings of Jesus with the a priori view that the sayings of Christian prophets therein, if there be such, will necessarily be totally new creations. The prophet may have served as hermeneut not only of the scriptures and the times but of the sayings of Jesus as well.

---

16 *The Parables of Jesus,* 23–114.

9

The Prophet as Spokesperson
for the Risen Jesus

The preceding discussion has presented evidence for the view that sayings of Christian prophets may be included in the Gospels as sayings of Jesus. If one attempts to identify particular sayings that have been created or modified by Christian prophets, characteristic identifying marks are needed. In addition to those already suggested in the general discussion, the following formal and material characteristics of early Christian prophetic speech may be identified.

FORMAL CHARACTERISTICS OF
PROPHETIC SPEECH

The Formal Nature of Prophetic Speech
The rediscovery of the formal and often poetic nature of the prophetic speech of Israel's prophets is one of the achievements in which modern biblical scholarship can take justifiable pride. It is now recognized that the initial revelatory experience was expressed and elaborated in the prophet's own words, and that traditional, somewhat stereotyped forms were available for this. The Old Testament would teach us that formal structure, even a degree of formal rigidity, need not be incompatible with genuine prophetic inspiration.

This can be said even more strongly for prophetic speech in the Hellenistic world where elegant poetic form was considered a hallmark of inspiration. Wandering prophets normally spoke in hexameter verse. It was considered unusual when the Pythia at Delphi spoke in prose rather than in meter. At Claros the prophet responded in verse to what-

ever question the inquirers had, or an oracle singer would put the revelation into metrical form and sing it to the inquirer.[1]

The close association between particular forms and prophetic speech
is seen in the fact that sometimes the term "prophet" was not used for
the one who received the oracle but was reserved for the speaker who put
the oracle in "proper form." There was in fact a striking uniformity of
style, based on the "canonical" style of Homer, somewhat analogous to
later Christian prophets adopting a biblical style and vocabulary to indicate that their speech was inspired. Martin Hengel describes the prophecy of a Syrian soldier, Buplagus, who arose from the dead and
prophesied—in hexameters—the vengeance of Zeus against Rome, and
the oracle of a severed head that spoke—in verse—the message of Apollo
against Rome.[2]

Josephus's discussions of biblical prophecy show that when he wrote
as a Jew for Hellenistic readers, he presented prophecy as a matter of
poetic form. In *Antiquities* 4.303 he refers to the "prophecy" of Moses in
Deuteronomy 32 as composed in meter, namely the hexameter common
in Greek prophecy, though the Hebrew text of Deuteronomy 32 was in
fact written in Semitic poetic style and no known Greek translation is in
hexameters. Josephus makes this comment to indicate to his Greek readership that Moses spoke in the "standard" poetic form supposed to be
characteristic of prophecy.[3]

That contemporary Jewish prophecy was typically expressed in mem-
orable, rhythmic forms is seen from Josephus's report (*Jewish War* 6.5.3)
of the constantly repeated oracle of the Jewish prophet Jesus ben Ananias
during the war of 66–70, which has a strikingly neat form, even in the
English translation of Josephus's Greek, itself a translation of the original
Aramaic. The oracle has two strophes of three stichs each:

> A voice from the east
> A voice from the west
> A voice from the four winds
> A voice against Jerusalem and the temple
> A voice against the bridegroom and the bride
> A voice against all the people

New Testament prophecy also manifests formal regularities. A considerable portion of the Apocalypse is presented as formally structured

---

1 See Aune, *Prophecy*, 30–31, 50–51, who gives other examples. Emphasis on the forms
of prophetic speech in the Hellenistic world is one of the major strengths of Aune's work.

2 *Judaism and Hellenism: Studies of Their Encounter in Palestine During the Early Hellenistic
Period,* 1:186.

3 Aune, *Prophecy,* 362.

units. Not only the hymns and other poetic passages, which are printed as poetry by the RSV and NRSV, but briefer oracles such as 3:5b, 10; 13:10; 16:6; 22:12, 18–19, also exhibit recognizable formal patterns. Such translations as Heinrich Kraft's and Paul Minear's[4] print the entire text in rhythmical, structured units. Kraft even argues that it is occasionally possible to explain the seer's choice of words and constructions on purely rhythmical grounds.[5] They have perhaps pressed a valid point too far but are still closer to the linguistic form of the Apocalypse than those who regard it as primarily straight prose. Incidentally, this formal characteristic serves to relate Revelation more closely to prophecy than to apocalyptic, which in contrast to prophecy is typically prose.

The oracular material of Luke (1:14–17, 32–33, 35, 46b–55, 68–79; 2:29–32, 34–35) is in strophic, metrical form, as is also the case to some extent in the Johannine discourses. W. H. Raney claimed to have "restored" the Johannine discourses to their "original" metrical arrangement.[6] The attempt has not been widely accepted, but that it is made at all shows the Johannine discourses do have formal regularities reminiscent of prophetic speech. Both the oracular material in Luke 1–2 and the Johannine discourses seem to have been influenced by Christian prophets.

It is less often noticed that Paul's prophetic oracles manifest formal structures, as is seen for example in 1 Corinthians 15:51–52:

> Lo! I tell you a mystery.
> We shall not all sleep,
> But we shall all be changed,
>   in a moment,
>   in the twinkling of an eye,
>   at the last trumpet.
> For the trumpet will sound,
>   And the dead will be raised imperishable,
>   And we shall be changed.

Formal and structural regularity are apparent even in English translation. This is all the more apparent in Greek, which has rhyme as well as rhythm. The word order of the second line has been changed, placing the negative particle *ou* ("not") after the word for "all," which it normally would precede, in order to achieve a neater parallelism.

Romans 11:25–26 also manifests a schematization, one strophe of three members, past/present/future, in which the emphatic verb comes last in each line. The following translation, though awkward in English, preserves the formal neatness of the Greek:

4 Minear, *New Earth*, 300–365; Kraft, *Offenbarung*, passim.
5 Ibid., 193, 194, passim.
6 *The Relation of the Fourth Gospel to the Christian Cultus.*

> A hardening upon part of Israel has come
> Until the full number of the Gentiles enter
> And so all Israel will be saved.

It has been argued that this tripartite form is a specific indicator of prophetic speech.[7]

Käsemann finds still other formalized oracles in Paul: 1 Corinthians 3:17; 14:38; 16:22; 2 Corinthians 9:6; Romans 2:12; Galatians 1:9, and the most recent studies of Roetzel and especially Müller find even more.[8] The studies of Müller and Dautzenberg have shown that the roots of these prophetic formulae are found in the apocalyptic literature,[9] which reveals that it was the circles behind the production of such literature that kept alive Old Testament prophetic forms; these were then borrowed by early Palestinian Christian prophets, whence Paul himself derived them.

All of the preceding is to provide some support for the general thesis that when we speak of "sayings of Christian prophets" we do not have in mind formless emotional outpourings or short staccato ejaculatory utterances, but sayings formed according to intentional patterns, sometimes of considerable length. We may now ask what particular formal characteristics may inhere in the oracles of early Christian prophets.

Speaking for the Risen Lord in
the First Person

Celsus gives an interesting description of the Christian prophets he encountered in the second century (cited in Origen, *Contra Celsum* 7.9):

> There are many who, although of no name, with the greatest facility and on the slightest occasion, whether within or without temples, assume the motions and gestures of inspired persons; while others do it in cities or among armies, for the purpose of attracting attention and exciting surprise. These are accustomed to say, each for himself, "I am God"; "I am the son of God" [*pais theou*, also "servant of God"]; or, "I am the Divine Spirit"; "I have come because the world is perishing, and you, O men, are perishing for your iniquities. But I wish to save you, and you shall see me returning again with heavenly power. Blessed is he who now does me homage. On all the rest I will send eternal fire, both on cities and on countries. And those who know not the punishments which await them will grieve in vain; while those who are faithful to me I will preserve eternally."

---

7 W. C. van Unnik, "A Formula Describing Prophecy."

8 Käsemann, *New Testament Questions*, 66–81; Müller, *Prophetie und Predigt*, 140–233; Calvin Roetzel, "The Judgment Form in Paul's Letters."

9 Müller, *Prophetie und Predigt*, 132–133, 215–216; Dautzenberg, *Urchristliche Prophetie*, 43–121.

The prophets described are not the churchly figures we have discovered in earliest Christianity but independent street-corner prophets whose prophecy has degenerated considerably from its earlier form. Yet characteristic features remain: the eschatological orientation, the pronouncement of blessing and curse (see below, "Blessing and Curse/Woe"), the claim to inspired, but intelligible, speech. But one important point is misunderstood by Celsus: the prophet is claiming nothing personally, but the exalted language used ("I am the son [or "servant"] of God" etc.) is the prophetic mode of discourse by which the prophet speaks for the deity in the first person, either with or without the messenger formula. The fact that the prophet says "You shall see me returning again with heavenly power" shows that he or she is not speaking personally but in the person of the heavenly Lord who speaks *through* the prophet.

Here we hit upon a striking feature of prophecy in the Hellenistic world. Like the prophets in the ancient middle East and in the tradition of Hebrew prophecy, the prophet considered himself or herself the messenger of the deity, who spoke through him or her in the first person. This was a common, but not exclusive, form of prophetic speech. According to David Aune,

> Oracles which originated from the great oracle centers at Delphi, Dodona, Claros, Didyma, Siwah, and many lesser centers scattered throughout the Greek world were regarded as utterances of the gods who presided there. Oracles attributed to the Sibyls and Bakides, legendary or not, were formulated as the speech of the prophetesses and the prophets who uttered them, and not as the speech of the inspiring divinity.[10]

Hellenistic prophets thus spoke both for the deity in the first person and in their own person. In the former mode, "I am" and "I have come" were spoken in the name and person of the god.[11] Despite the general typology mentioned above, the same prophet or oracle center could utilize both forms. Of the more than six hundred oracles attributed to Apollo, all but sixteen are in the first person. At Delphi, the god spoke through the Pythia almost always in the first person, never in the third. First-person speech for the deity was thus a common, but not exclusive, form of inspired speech in the environment of early Christianity.

As indicated in the quotation from Celsus above, later Christian prophets utilized this form. When Montanus says "I am the Father and the Son and the Paraclete," and "Neither angel, nor ambassador, but I,

---

10 Aune, *Prophecy*, 55.
11 Ibid., 71–72 gives examples.

the Lord God the Father," it is a matter of prophetic speech form, not personal arrogance or delusion. Of the sixteen oracles from Montanus considered authentic by Kurt Aland, five speak for God in the first person.[12]

Moving closer in time to the early Christian prophets, we find that the *Odes of Solomon* manifest this characteristic in a way particularly relevant for the relationship of Christian prophets to the Gospel tradition. In Ode 42 for example, we have sayings of the risen Jesus, who speaks in the first person through the mouth of the inspired singer. This must have been a not-uncommon phenomenon in the time of the poet, according to the ode itself: "For I live and am resurrected, am with them and speak through their mouth" (*Odes of Solomon* 42.6). Such revelations of the deity spoken in the first person were quite common in the syncretistic Hellenistic religions of the first century.

This prophetic mode of discourse appears in a significant way in some of our sources for early Christian prophecy. Its absence from others is also significant. The prophet of Revelation does not hesitate to speak in the person of the risen Lord. The formula "I Jesus" (22:16) concludes a prophetic document that contains no less than sixty "I-sayings." The prophet can take material from the Old Testament, re-form it, and present it as a first-person saying of the risen Jesus (e.g., 21:6; cf. Isa. 55:1). The repeated use of the I form is a recovery of the prophetic style of direct address by the deity, which had declined in apocalyptic in favor of third-person discourse. Acts 13:2 is direct evidence that the first-person form of prophetic speech was familiar in the Lukan tradition. The prophets pictured by Luke in the Antioch church spoke through the Holy Spirit for the risen Jesus in the first person: "Set apart *for me* Barnabas and Saul for the work to which *I* have called them." Indirect evidence corresponding to this is found in the "I am" of the risen Jesus in 9:5; 22:8; 26:15. The "this is" of 8:10 probably corresponds to the revelatory "I am" of the false prophet Simon, showing that "I am" was the customary form of prophetic speech. The formula with which Agabus begins his prophecy, "Thus says the Holy Spirit" (= the Lord, Acts 21:11) may accurately represent one of the forms of Christian prophetic speech or may be another example of Luke's casting church prophets in the same role as Old Testament prophets, for the LXX regularly renders "Thus says the Lord" with the Greek expression used by Agabus.

This prophetic "I am" is also a dominant feature of the discourses of the Fourth Gospel. This is to be expected, in view of the identification of (the risen) Jesus and the Paraclete-prophet who will not speak "on his own authority" (16:13). The many "I-sayings" of the Fourth Gospel

---

12 Ibid., 314–315.

should not be accounted for as simply literary fiction, the retrojection into the mouth of the historical Jesus of traditional christological statements about Jesus that he could not have said. They are rather to be seen as prophetic utterance in which the risen Lord speaks through the prophet in the first person. The repeated "this is" with a christological predicate is the confessional response of the community to such prophetic declarations.

Hermas speaks only occasionally with the "I" of the risen Christ (e.g., Vision 3.9.10). His normal mode is to report on visionary conversations with a Sybil-like woman, an angelic young man, and the shepherd-angel of repentance.

The absence of the first-person form in the prophetic passages in Paul's letters is significant. He can hardly have been unaware of it since it is so frequent in the Old Testament and in Jewish and Hellenistic prophecy. This form is in fact congenial to his understanding (1 Cor. 13:3). It was probably the danger of being misunderstood as a Hellenistic prophet from within whom the god spoke that caused Paul to avoid this form. Celsus could not have misunderstood Paul and prophecy in the Pauline style as a claim to deity. In 1 Corinthians 15:51, for example, the "I" is clearly not that of the risen Jesus but the prophet's own "I." Like other early Christian prophets, Paul understood his prophetic speaking to be "in Christ's stead," commissioned by the risen Christ. But the prophetic oracles he transmitted are spoken with the ego of the prophet, not in the first-person form of "I-sayings" spoken with the ego of the risen Christ. This may have been too readily understood as a kind of Hellenistic mystical union with the deity, which Paul wished to avoid.

Paul's own substitute for the prophetic messenger-formula seems to have been formulae such as "in the name of Christ" (the Lord, etc.); "by the word of the Lord"; "this is the . . ." (1 Thess. 4:2, 15; 2 Thess. 3:6, 12; 1 Cor. 1:10; 5:4; 9:14; 14:37), which both declared his message to be directly from the risen Lord and distinguished the person of the message-bearer from that of the message-giver. Other early Christian prophets also made use of these forms, especially "in the name of the Lord" (Matt. 7:22; Mark 13:6 par.; John 14:26; Acts 9:27, 29). Mark 13:6 par. and John 14:26 make it clear that "I-sayings" and speaking "in the name of" the risen Lord are the same genre of (prophetic) speech.

The result is clear. *One* of the forms of speech used by early Christian prophets was the first-person speech of the risen Lord, including the revelatory "I am." But this was not the only style appropriate to the prophetic self-consciousness, and Christian prophecy may not be identified with the first-person form alone. Both types of sayings could later have been included within the pre-Easter framework as sayings of Jesus.

"Sentences of Holy Law"/"Eschatological Correlative"

The form "sentence of holy law" is a statement marked by a legal style, eschatological fervor, and the pairing of lex talionis and chiasmus, as found, for example, in 1 Corinthians 3:17 and 14:38. Due to the influence of Ernst Käsemann, this form and the related "eschatological correlative" have been widely accepted as indicators of Christian prophetic speech.[13] This view has also been severely criticized, especially by Klaus Berger,[14] who has shown that the form is more closely related to the wisdom tradition than to the combination legal-apocalyptic genre posited by Käsemann. But Berger did not sufficiently consider the fact that both the forms and content of the wisdom[15] tradition were used by prophets,[15] so that "wisdom" and "prophecy" are not necessarily alternatives. Though the "sentences of holy law" are expressed according to wisdom forms, the content of such sayings is often of an eschatological nature not characteristic of the teaching of a sage. The form "sentences of holy law" seems to have survived the discussion and is to be regarded as one indication of prophetic speech.

As defined by Käsemann, this prophetic form functions by confronting the hearers with a pronouncement that anticipates the judgment of the Last Day, where they hear the legal verdict of the eschatological judge. Legal utterances presented in the power of the Spirit also correspond in general to this form. In our sources, then, we are seeking not only precise examples of the eschatological lex talionis chiastic form but also indications of this function of the form, even where formal precision is less exact.

Both the form and function of "sentences of holy law" are in fact found in our primary example of Christian prophecy, the Apocalypse. Revelation does not simply predict the imminent coming of the Last Day but brings the hearers before the eschatological judge as they hear the prophecy. "Pure" examples of the form are found, such as 22:18–19, which is in the chiastic ABB_1A_1 form, with the same verb in the protasis and apodosis, the protasis being introduced by "if anyone" *(ean tis)* and the aorist subjunctive, the apodosis having the future indicative, the whole being eschatological in tone and legal in form. Other more-or-less pure examples of the form are found in 3:5, 10; 11:18; 13:10; 16:5–6; 22:11.

---

13 *New Testament Questions,* 66–137; for the eschatological correlative, see Richard Edwards, "The Eschatological Correlative as a *Gattung* in the New Testament," *ZNW* 60 (1969): 9–20.

14 "Zu den sogenannten Sätze heiligen Rechts"; "Die sogenannten 'Sätze heiligen Rechts': Ihre Funktion und Sitz im Leben." For a critique of Edwards, see Daryl Schmidt, "The LXX *Gattung* 'Prophetic Correlative,' " *JBL* 96 (1977): 517–522.

15 See "Wisdom Motifs," below.

Paul's writings manifest the general function of prophetic speech of bringing the hearer before the eschatological judge (e.g., 1 Cor. 5:3–5; Rom. 11:31, where the troublesome "now" should be explained in terms of anticipatory prophetic eschatology). Specific instances of the form also occur in Paul, some in explicitly prophetic contexts (Rom. 2:12; 1 Cor. 3:17; 14:38; 16:22; 2 Cor. 9:6; Gal. 1:9).

Likewise in the Fourth Gospel, the Spirit-Paraclete will convict the world by declaring the things to come as already operative; the final judgment is anticipated in the conviction of the world by the Paraclete (16:8), and the post-Easter Jesus does in fact speak in the chiastic form related to "sentences of holy law" (20:23). So also the prophetic Ignatius uses this form surprisingly often—nineteen examples are counted by David Aune.[16]

These converging lines of evidence are significant but not over-whelming. They suggest that "sentences of holy law" and related forms were indeed used by Christian prophets, that there is much prophetic speech not in this form and that the form was not used exclusively by Christian prophets. Further, the form occurs only rarely in its "pure" state. The conclusion must be that the form is somewhat characteristic of prophetic speech but is not unique to Christian prophets, that prophetic speech may occur in other recognizable forms and that no saying in the Gospel tradition may be attributed to a Christian prophet on the basis of this form alone.

Initial "Amen I say to you"

The Hebrew word "amen" (usually translated "truly" in the RSV) normally appeared as the confirming response to the words of another, meaning "certainly," or as the affirmative response at the conclusion of a blessing or benediction. When Jesus of Nazareth *began* some solemn sayings with the Hebrew word "amen," he apparently introduced a new usage of this word. A number of scholars, of whom Joachim Jeremias may be taken as representative, have argued that this peculiar linguistic form was introduced by Jesus himself, and that it is a characteristic mark of the very voice of the historical Jesus.[17] Claims for pre-Christian and para-Christian instances of the form turn out to be unconvincing.[18] The form is an indication of Jesus' prophetic self-consciousness, a signal that what follows represents revelation spoken with a claim to divine authority, corresponding to "Thus says the Lord" in the Hebrew prophets.

---

16 Aune, *Prophecy*, 295.

17 *New Testament Theology*, 1:35–38.

18 Jeremias responded to these claims with persuasive arguments in "Zum nicht-responsorischen Amen," 122–123. Cf. most recently Sato, *Q und Prophetie*, 239–247, who generally supports Jeremias and my argument above.

Such sayings are then communicated to the hearers with the complementary form "I say to you," which always follows "amen" in the Gospels. The "I say to you" formula, with or without the preceding "amen," was used as an authoritative formula by prophetic figures, but not exclusively by them, in paganism and Judaism contemporary with early Christianity.[19] Early Christian prophets also used this formula (e.g., Rev. 2:4; 1 Thess. 4:15; 1 Cor. 15:51; Hermas, Vision 3.9.7; Mandate 12.6.1; Similitudes 9.23.5; 9.28.7). Jesus seems to have adopted the Aramaic equivalent of the "I say to you" formula, which had already acquired the overtones of prophetic authority. Jesus then added the initial "amen" as his own "trademark," i.e., his own characteristic symbol of speaking by divine authority.

As Jeremias already saw, this situation of receiving revelation and delivering it to the community with formulae that claim revelatory authority is appropriate not only to the situation of the life of Jesus but also to the setting in the post-Easter church. "Christian prophets . . . spoke in the name of the exalted Lord and with his words."[20] Thus though "amen" is a mark of the peculiar speech of Jesus himself, it is not confined exclusively to sayings of the historical Jesus, and of itself is no guarantee of the authenticity of any particular saying. It is also appropriate on the lips of a Christian bearer of revelation.

Our sources suggest some use of this form by Christian prophets. Outside the Gospels, the word "amen" is found more frequently in Revelation than in any other New Testament document. There are, however, no clear instances in Revelation of a saying beginning with the formula "amen, I say to you." This should not cause us to leap to the conclusion that all the instances of "amen" in Revelation are of the usual responsorial kind. Some of these (1:6, 7; 5:14; 22:21) may represent the usual nonprophetic liturgical usage, and even those that precede the statement to which they are attached may in fact be a response to the preceding affirmations of praise (7:12; 19:4). Even so, it should not be overlooked that twice the "amen" is the prophet's response to revelation he receives (1:7; 22:20), and that the voices to which the "amen" respond are in every case heavenly voices. This suggests that the frequent occurrence of "amen" in Revelation is analogous to the prophetic usage posited by Jeremias and an indication of some connection between "amen" sayings and prophetic speech. Furthermore, the manner in which "yes" and "amen" are equated in 1:7 suggests that the "yes" in 14:13; 16:7, and 22:7 is analogous to the introductory "amen." The pronouncement beginning with "yes" (= "amen") in 14:13 is in fact an excellent example of this prophetic form.

---

19 Aune, *Prophecy,* 164, who gives illustrations and documentation.
20 Joachim Jeremias, *The Prayers of Jesus,* 34.

Victor Hasler's redaction-critical study of "amen" in the Gospel tradition,[21] including those places where "amen" is obviously a secondary addition, indicates that in the church "amen, I say to you" was used as an authority-formula to describe a word of the exalted Lord. Hasler also contends that the fact that a discussion of "amen" sayings emerges precisely in the discussion of Christian prophecy in 1 Corinthians 14:16 is a positive link between the two. The repeated use of the formula in the Fourth Gospel's speech material, where it has been doubled for liturgical solemnity, is another point of contact between the formula and Christian prophecy. Obviously some occurrences of "amen" are only due to prosaic imitation in the development of the tradition, as a comparison of Matthew with Mark will immediately make clear, so that by no means is every occurrence of "amen" a guarantee that, if not Jesus, then a Christian prophet is the speaker. But the converging lines of evidence do seem to point to a time when "amen, I say to you" was an indication of prophetic speech.

Blessing and Curse/Woe

In the New Testament the unconditional pronouncement of blessing and curse is almost entirely limited to the Gospel sayings of Jesus and to those who claim to speak by the inspiration of the risen Lord: Paul and the prophet John of Revelation. That the great majority of cases in which blessing and cursing are attributed to charismatic types, especially the high incidence found in Revelation, would suggest that this is one of the forms of prophetic speech. This impression is strengthened when one examines the passages separately; for many of them proceed from an awareness of God that goes beyond the realm of warning or exhortation and becomes the type of unconditional pronouncement, in which the word effects what it proclaims. This kind of performative language can be uttered only by one conscious of great authority and would be appropriate to Christian prophets who spoke in the Spirit with charismatic authority.

The woe form distinctive of Hebrew prophecy was preserved in some apocalyptic circles such as those behind the *1 Enoch* literature (cf., e.g., *1 Enoch* 100.7–9). That the unconditional pronouncement of woe continued to be a part of early Jewish prophecy is illustrated by the oracle of Jesus ben Ananias as reported in Josephus (see above, "The Formal Nature of Prophetic Speech").

The prophet-author of the Apocalypse, indeed with full awareness of what he is doing, makes use of the blessing and curse form as a vehicle

---

21 *Amen. Redaktionsgeschichtliche Untersuchung zur Einführungsformel der Herrenworte "Wahrlich ich sage euch."*

of his prophetic message. He delivers exactly seven blessings (1:3; 14:13; 16:15; 19:9; 20:6; 22:7, 14), which resemble their Gospel counterparts in that blessings are pronounced on the poor, crying, persecuted congregations of Asia. He likewise presents exactly seven sentences announcing woes, containing a total of precisely fourteen occurrences of the word "woe" (*ouai:* 8:13; 9:12; 11:14; 12:12; 18:10, 16, 19). All these blessings and curses give anticipatory voice to the eschatological blessing and curse.

Some themes of the beatitudes in the Gospels also come to expression in Revelation's beatitudes. This has sometimes been explained as the seer's speech having been influenced by the Gospels or the Gospel tradition (cf. the alleged parallels between Rev. 21:6–7 and Matt. 5:3–12). But examination reveals that traditional words of Jesus are neither quoted nor alluded to. Rather, it is the case that the themes of the Gospel beatitudes are there (eschatological blessing for the hungering, thirsting, crying). This would argue that such pronouncements have their *Sitz im Leben* in the speech of Christian prophets but not necessarily that John here has a traditional saying of Jesus in mind.

Unless it is hinted at in 1 Corinthians 14:23–25, there is no trace of the prophetic blessing/curse form in the speech of the Corinthian prophets. The ejaculatory curse of 1 Corinthians 12:3 is doubtless to be associated with the kind of ecstasy opposed by Paul, rather than the prophecy that he encourages, but it may be a gnosticizing version of the prophetic curse form. The blessing and curse form is not explicitly present in Paul's own prophetic speech. The one instance of his pronouncement of blessing (Rom. 14:22) is probably to be taken at the more prosaic "conversational" level rather than as a pronouncement of eschatological prophecy. It may be that Paul deliberately avoided such terminology, which was perhaps being abused by his gnosticizing opponents. More likely, the absence of explicit blessing/curse formulae is simply accidental and related to the epistolary form and function, rather than a result of intentional disavowal of the form, since Paul does pronounce eschatological judgments, occasionally using explicit anathema (1 Cor. 5:3–5; 16:22; Gal. 1:8–9). The curse form of Galatians 1:9 is likely a reflection of a prophetic curse pronounced in the liturgy, as is probably also the case in Revelation.[22]

The speech of those figures in Acts explicitly named prophets by Luke does not contain the blessing/curse formulae, but the function of such forms may still be traced in the pronouncements of the prophetic figures in Acts 5:9 and 13:10–11. The speeches of Luke 1–2 relate the pronouncement of blessing to inspired prophetic speech (1:42, 45, 67–

---

22 Cf. Müller, *Prophetie und Predigt,* 201.

68). When the above is taken with the fact that Old Testament prophecy and Jewish prophecy contemporary with early Christian prophecy also used blessing and curse forms, we may conclude that this was one of the characteristic forms of early Christian prophetic speech.

Characteristic Prophetic Vocabulary

Without making the absurd claim that any of the following words were used exclusively by Christian prophets, it is nonetheless possible to compile a list of words used frequently or in a characteristic prophetic sense in the extant texts from early Christian prophets. As our clearest and most extensive example of early Christian prophecy, Revelation supplies most of these, though Hermas and the prophetic oracles in Paul also form the basis for the list.[23]

> *amēn,* "amen" ("truly")
> *apokalypsis,* "revelation"
> *doulos,* "servant"
> *eidon, ēkousa,* "I saw," "I heard"
> *sēmainein,* "signify," "deliver a message in signs"
> *ha dei genesthai,* "what must take place"
> *idou,* "look," "behold"
> *krazō,* "I cry out"[24]
> *limos,* "famine"
> *logos, logos tou theou,* "word," "word of God"
> *makarios,* "blessed"
> *martys, martyria, martyreō,* "witness," "testimony," "testify"
> *mysterion,* "mystery"
> *oida,* "I know"
> *ouai,* "woe"
> *parakaleō, paraklēsis, paraklētos,* "I appeal to/urge you," "exhortation," "Paraclete"
> *pneuma, en pneumati,* "spirit," "in the spirit"
> *prophētēs, prophēteuō, prophēteia,* "prophet," "I prophesy," "prophecy"
> *tade legei,* "thus says . . ." or "the words of . . ."

---

23 For an elaboration of the items from Revelation, see my article "The Apocalypse as Christian Prophecy," 44–48.

24 Cf. Heinrich Schlier, *Der Brief an die Galater,* 198, and the usage in the Fourth Gospel, as well as Gal. 4:6, Rom. 8:15, *1 Enoch* 71:11, Ignatius, *Philadelphians* 7.

MATERIAL CHARACTERISTICS OF EARLY CHRISTIAN PROPHETIC SPEECH

Eschatological Parenesis

Eschatological-Apocalyptic Content

It was widely accepted in first-century Judaism that the Spirit (= the Spirit of prophecy) was essentially the eschatological gift, so that when prophets reappeared, this itself would be a sign of the dawning End. Any talk of prophecy was by definition eschatological. This view was the common denominator of both those circles that affirmed the presence of the prophetic Spirit (e.g., Qumran) and those that denied it (many streams of rabbinic tradition). Thus Jewish prophecy of this period has a consistently eschatological content.

This is seen, for example, in the declarations of the Teacher of Righteousness, who interprets the scriptures as directly describing the things happening to the (present) last generation, (1QpHab 7.1–2; cf. 2.7). The contemporary understanding of prophecy is also seen in the apocalyptic promises of those prophets described by Josephus, who proclaimed the imminent deliverance of God in the very days that the Romans were destroying the city and the temple. He considers them "suborned by the tyrants to delude the people, by bidding them await help from God, in order that desertions might be checked" (*Jewish War* 6.285–286). It is far more likely that these were apocalyptic prophets who saw in the Roman devastation the death-throes of the old age and the sure prelude to the new (cf. 2.258–259, 261–262; 6.312). The portents he enumerates were taken as signs of *hope* by the populace: a starlike sword stood over the city; a comet appeared for a full year; a cow brought to sacrifice gave birth to a lamb in the temple court (6.30). Josephus sees these as signs of political, this-worldly doom. But the populace, at the instigation of the prophets, understood these as apocalyptic signs, as the throes of nature immediately preceding the advent of the victorious End Time, as in 2 Esdras 5:9–13.

Within this milieu, where prophecy was by definition eschatological, early Christianity arose. It was a confirmation of the church's conviction that the Last Times had dawned that prophets emerged within it. One of the primary presuppositions for the Apocalypse is that the author and his hearer/readers are living in the Last Days of history, that the eschatological events described will take place soon (1:1, 3; 2:16, 25; 3:11, 20; 6:11; 10:6–7; 11:2; 12:6, 12; 17:10; 22:6, 7, 10, 12, 20). This fundamental orientation of the prophet should not be suppressed in the interests of supposedly making the book more relevant for later readers. The guilt of all preceding generations is summed up in the last generation (18:24). The imperial power presently persecuting the saints is a combination of all the evil empires predicted in previous apocalyptic writings (13:1–2; compare Dan. 7:1–18). In accordance with traditional prophetic understanding, the church exists as the eschatological community which alone can hear the prophetic word, the holy remnant of the End Time, when even the traditional people of God have apostatized.

The prophetic oracles included in Paul's letters are uniformly of an eschatological nature (1 Thess. 4:15–17; 1 Cor. 15:51–52; Rom. 11:25–27). Käsemann's insight regarding Paul's affirmations in 1 Corinthians, originally somewhat startling, has become almost commonplace: Paul was an advocate of the old apocalyptic Palestinian tradition in opposition to the excessive "realized eschatology" of the Corinthian enthusiasts.[25] In this respect, Paul becomes almost a direct witness to the eschatological nature of early Palestinian Christian prophecy. The eschatological orientation of prophecy is fundamental to Paul, not a quirk of his response to a local situation at Corinth. Also at Thessalonica, exaggerated eschatological enthusiasm, based on Paul's original prophetic preaching, had led to excesses among local prophets, resulting in a disdaining of all prophecy, which Paul found necessary to correct (1 Thess. 4:15–17; 5:19–20).

The older eschatology shines through Luke's consistently noneschatological descriptions of Christian prophets. In Acts 11:27–30 Agabus was probably more eschatological than Luke's depiction reveals. In Luke's text, Agabus is the predictor of a this-worldly historical famine, which in fact occurred a short time later. But there are indications that the tradition that came to Luke reported Agabus's prophecy as more eschatological. The word translated by the RSV as "foretold" *(sēmainō)* indicates not that straightforward, unambiguous speech such as Luke represents it to be (by regarding the predicted famine to be a mundane historical disaster), but that mysterious, prophetic speech such as is used by the Pythia at Delphi and is used specifically in Rev. 1:1 to refer to eschatological events. Likewise, the words "would be" *(mellō)*, "great famine" *(limos megalē)*, and "all the world" *(holē oikoumenē)* represent traditional apocalyptic expressions and betray the original eschatological nature of Agabus's oracle. In accord with his practice elsewhere, Luke has made earliest Christianity appear more congenial to his own time by de-emphasizing its eschatological dimension. But the tradition he hands on was eschatological. Thus all the oracles of the prophetic figures of Luke 1–2 strike the eschatological note. In 1:76–79 particularly, the prophet is the forerunner of the eschatological epiphany of God.

With the exception of the Pastorals and the *Didache,* which give only minimal indications of their understanding of the *content* of Christian prophecy, all our remaining sources testify to the eschatological nature

---

25 *New Testament Questions of Today,* 125–130.

of Christian prophecy. The Paraclete of the Fourth Gospel declares eschatological data: "judgment," "glory," "the things to come." Since the
Fourth Evangelist himself has only a modest interest in futuristic eschatology, this characterization of the proclamation of the Paraclete un-
derscores the fact that for the Fourth Evangelist too, prophecy and
eschatology were coordinates. Ephesians, like Acts, indicates in an indirect and unconscious way that Christian prophets declared the eschatological time to be breaking in, when they point out that it was by prophets
that the inclusion of the Gentiles (a part of the eschatological drama) was
revealed to be the will of God. Hermas announces the last chance to
repent in relation to the impending second coming of the Lord (Visions
2.2.5; 3.8.9).

On the basis of the above evidence, we may anticipate that oracles of
early Christian prophets in the Gospel tradition, if there are such, will
manifest an eschatological orientation and frequently contain specific
items of eschatological content. Among these we might expect to find a
particular interest in the "Spirit" (identified in Judaism specifically as the
Spirit of prophecy and not expected to reappear until the eschaton) and
the terminology of "mystery" (thought of as the eschatological plan of
God for history revealed through the prophets). In addition to such
specific terms, there are eschatological themes particularly related to the
ministry of Christian prophets.

"Upbuilding and Encouragement
and Consolation" (1 Cor. 14:3)

The eschatology of the early Christian prophets was not formulated for
its own sake but as the foundation for, and in inseparable union with,
parenesis, the instruction given church members for living Christian
lives. The church was not edified by sharing speculative apocalyptic information about the future but by the call to a certain way of life that was
the outcome of the eschatological vision of the prophets. In this, early
Christian prophecy was more akin to Old Testament prophecy than to
apocalyptic. This contrast should not be drawn too sharply, however, for
the Jewish apocalyptic tradition that formed part of the context for the
emergence of early Christian prophecy was itself more concerned with
ethical exhortation than is sometimes taken to be the case.

Our sources indicate that the eschatology of the prophets functioned
not as curiosity-satisfying speculation but as pastoral edification. The
"Book" of Revelation is, despite its saturation with apocalyptic imagery,
a pastoral letter offering encouragement and instruction to Christians
seeking the will of God for their lives during a particular crisis. The letter
is intended to inform Christians of the real situation in which they find
themselves, a perspective gained only by divine revelation, and thus to

reveal the kind of life called for, while at the same time inspiring strength and courage to act. This is the meaning of prophetic parenesis.

When Paul sums up the content of prophecy as "upbuilding and encouragement and consolation," he clearly indicates the hortatory and parenetic goal of prophetic speech (1 Cor. 14:3; cf. 14:31). It would appear that the word "encouragement" (Greek *paraklēsis*) in particular has a prophetic, eschatological overtone in Paul, for he concludes the prophetic saying of 1 Thessalonians 4:15–18 with "therefore encourage [RSV "comfort"] one another with those words" and, in a passage replete with prophetic references, encourages the Thessalonians with the exhortation "therefore encourage one another and build one another up" (1 Thess. 5:11). Similarly, Paul's own prophetic oracles are for the purpose of building up the Christian life of his churches, as is seen from the parenetic notes that express the implications of the oracles in 1 Corinthians 15:51–52 (v. 58) and Romans 11:25–27 (v. 25).

Luke represents the prophet Simeon as waiting for the "consolation" *(paraklēsis)* of Israel, which he recognizes and proclaims to be present in the advent of Jesus (Luke 2:25). In this text the prophetic "encouragement" is the heartening, edifying word that the hopes of the community are presently being fulfilled, along with the assurance that those yet to be fulfilled will certainly come to fulfillment. Luke (mis-)understands "Barnabas" to be a nickname given him because of his facility at prophetic preaching, i.e., "son of encouragement," a Hebrew idiom for "a person characterized by encouragement" (Acts 4:36). This indicates that Luke understood a close relationship, if not identity, between "prophecy" and "encouragement," understood almost in a technical sense. We have seen that Luke's description of the Apostolic Council reflects prophetic phenomena, and that the decree, which is called an "exhortation" (Greek *paraklēsis;* elsewhere = "encouragement"), is delivered by prophets who further "exhort" (= "encourage," *parakaleō*) the people (Acts 15:31–32). Here, the prophetic "exhortation" functions for the edification of the community because, as in Revelation, it is the concrete word of God addressed to a particular problem for the present moment.

The Fourth Gospel does not use the verb "encourage" or the noun "encouragement," but the prophet-author chooses "Paraclete" ("encourager," from the same Greek root) as the appropriate term to designate the ministry of Christian prophets in his community. The announcement of the fulfillment of the messianic hopes, which constituted a basic element in Christian prophetic speech (cf. Luke 2:25 above), is one of the overtones of the term "Paraclete." The parenetic aspect of Christian prophecy is also seen later in Hermas, who uses apocalyptic form and style but whose purpose is parenetic throughout. It would appear, therefore, that eschatological parenesis in general, with "encouragement" terminology in particular, is sufficiently evidenced in our sources to indicate that it was a traditional prophetic element characteristic of earlier Christian prophets.

Persecution and Suffering

The motif that the true prophet must suffer, and that he or she proclaims suffering as the lot of the faithful, is also an aspect of the eschatological message of the prophet. In the Old Testament some prophets suffer as an integral part of their prophetic vocation—Ezekiel and Jeremiah come immediately to mind—but suffering is not characteristic of prophetism as such. On the contrary, in some circles the prophet was pictured as quite beyond the realm of ordinary human suffering by virtue of his divinely given miracle working capability, as in the Elijah-Elisha cycle of stories. But with Jeremiah as the beginning point, there developed in later Jewish literature the firm idea that the true prophet must suffer as a badge of his or her authenticity. Isaiah, for example, who strides through the pages of the Old Testament rather triumphalistically, is pictured as the suffering martyr in the literature of the first century C.E. (*Martyrdom of Isaiah* 5:1; cf. Acts 7:52; Heb. 11:32–38). When this tendency combined in Christian prophecy with the apocalyptic view that terrible sufferings must come to the faithful as a prelude to the End, the Christian prophetic tradition became marked with many references to persecution and suffering.

It is understandable that Christian prophets were in fact persecuted. Their claim to have the eschatological Spirit sounded like both heresy and blasphemy in the ears of those whose theology denied that it was possible for the Spirit to be present; yet the prophets were in possession of, or sometimes appeared to be possessed by, *some* "spirit." Thus there inevitably arose the counterclaim among the Jewish opponents of early Christianity that the speaking of those who claimed to possess the eschatological Spirit was in fact the raging of those possessed by demons (cf. 1 Cor. 14:23; John 7:20; 8:48, 52; 10:20–21).

In the understanding of the prophet-author of Revelation, the true prophet is the one who in word and deed lets the meaning of Jesus' suffering and death become manifest as the saving act of God in Jesus, which is the point of orientation for the Christian's own manner of life. John writes as one who has himself suffered the official rejection and persecution of the state (1:9), and his message to the church abounds in references to present and anticipated sufferings (2:9–10, 13, 22; 3:10; 6:9; 7:14; 12:11–17; 13:7; 16:6; 17:6; 18:24; 20:4). The repeated promise to "the conquerors" (2:7, 11, 17, 26; 3:5, 12, 21), when seen in the light of 5:5–6, obviously refers to those believers who have been faithful in the face of persecution even to the point of death (cf. 2:10; 12:11). In particular, the prophets are singled out as being the objects of persecution and victims of suffering (10:8–11; 11:1–8 [cf. v. 10]; 16:6; 18:24).

In a manner that is closer to the prophet of Revelation than is usually recognized, Paul also understands his present time as the dawn of the Last Days, which must include persecution and suffering for the saints, so that his prophetic message too is characterized by references to suffering, a motif that is also continued in the Pauline school (1 Thess. 3:3b–4; 1 Cor. 7:25–31; cf. Col. 1:24; 2 Thess. 1:4–7; 2 Tim. 3:12).

It may be that in 1 Thessalonians 2:14–15 we have an explicit reference to the Jewish persecution of precisely those early Palestinian Christian prophets whom we are attempting to characterize. This passage is frequently regarded as a post-Pauline interpolation, and, when it is considered Pauline, the prophets referred to are usually considered to be Old Testament prophets. However, in view of the unusual word order (Jesus—prophets—Paul), the context in which Paul is speaking of recent events in Palestine, and the several allusions to Christian prophets among the Thessalonians (1:6; 4:8, 9, 15–18; 5:11, 19–20), the possibility must be kept open that Paul is here referring to Jewish persecution of those earliest Christian prophets who identified Jesus with the Son of Man. Such a persecution also seems to be reflected in other New Testament data (Acts 6:8–8:3; Matt. 23:34; John 16:2). The passage does seem to stand out from its context, as those who consider it a post-Pauline interpolation point out. But the explanation for the several non-Pauline features that appear in this text may be that Paul takes over a preformed piece of tradition, which reflects the judgment speech form characteristic of early Christian prophets.[26]

When Luke is describing some prophetic figure *qua* prophet, such as Agabus, there is no suggestion that rejection and suffering are inherent in the prophetic vocation. Agabus, in fact, is a rather commanding figure. But this may be due more to the minor role that the theology of the cross plays in Luke's own theology, particularly his reluctance to portray those endowed in a special measure with the Spirit as *thereby* designated for suffering. However, some of those incidentally identified as prophets (Paul, Barnabas, Silas, Acts 12:1–2; 15:32) do suffer repeated rejection and persecution as a characteristic mark of their ministry (Acts 12–14; 16–28). And the ministry of Jesus is portrayed in prophetic terms that make one point clear: *no prophet is acceptable,* period.[27]

The early Christian prophetic conception of God's messengers as persecuted and suffering sheep rests on Jeremiah 11:18–19, then on

---

26 See Müller, *Prophetie und Predigt,* 177.

27 Cf. Waldemar Schmeichel, "Christian Prophecy in Lukan Thought: Luke 4:16–30 as a Point of Departure," in *SBL 1976 Seminar Papers,* 294–301.

Isaiah 53. So in Matthew 7:15, the self-understanding of early Christian prophets is represented: the true prophet is sheeplike rather than wolf-like, oppressed rather than oppressor. This is also the meaning of Matthew's (or his tradition's) allegorizing addition to the Parable of the Great Supper, in which the messengers from the king (= the prophets, including Christian prophets) are abused and killed. The peculiarly Matthean elements in 23:29–36 also suggest that in the Matthean church the prophet was known to be a rejected, persecuted figure. The prophetic revelation of Ignatius, who probably ministered in the same setting as Matthew, is likewise from a figure who assumes martyrdom is an integral part of his vocation.

The rejection and persecution of the true prophets is only the penultimate reality, however. With prophetic insight, the prophets announce that in the eschaton those who are rejected now will be accepted, and those who are considered blessed now will learn that they are rejected. This note of the *eschatological reversal* of roles is sounded by both the author of Revelation and Paul, who see it as already occurring in the rejection of the Jews and acceptance of the Gentiles (Rev. 2:9; Rom. 11:25), and by the oracles in the Lukan birth narratives, which celebrate the rejection of the rich and the acceptance of the poor (Luke 1:52–53). We might anticipate that this theme too would surface in Christian prophetic sayings in the Gospel tradition.

Rebuke of Immorality and Announcement of Judgment

Reinhold Niebuhr was thinking primarily of the prophets of Israel when he declared that the essence of all prophetism is the note of "against-ness"—the prophet speaks against the people in the name of the people's own God.[28] Yet this description fits the prophets of earliest Christianity as well, for their eschatological orientation came to expression in yet another form: the rebuke of immorality and the pronouncement of judgment on sinners within and without the community. The Apocalypse is throughout a prophetic rebuke of immorality and unfaithfulness and a pronouncement of judgment upon those who do not repent (e.g., 2:23; 3:10; 13:10; 16:6; 22:12, 18–19). This is not a moralizing rebuke from a self-righteous stance; the seer does this as the spokesman for the eschatological judge who is already making himself present in the prophetic word.

In this the author of the Fourth Gospel stands close to the Apocalypse, for he emphasizes that a primary function of the Paraclete is to

---

28 Reinhold Niebuhr, *The Nature and Destiny of Man* (New York: Charles Scribner's Sons, 1941–43), 2:28.

"convict" the unbelievers, and the basis for it is the eschatological judgment pronounced on "the ruler of this world" (16:8–11). The identical word "convict" *(elegchein)* used of Christian prophets in 1 Corinthians 14:24 should be noted. The legal connotation of "Paraclete" is important here, for the agent represented by this term functions as a prosecuting attorney, rather than counsel for the defense, as the agent of the heavenly court who presses the case against the unbelieving world before the eschatological judge. By realizing the future eschatological judgment, the Paraclete reproves or exposes the unbelieving world.

Paul's discussion of prophecy at Corinth does not directly state that rebuke and pronouncement of judgment are prophetic functions, but this is implied in 1 Corinthians 14:24–25. The hearers of the prophet's message respond as they do because they are addressed as those who already stand before the court of the eschatological judge, whose sentence they hear in the prophet's announcement. In the case of Paul himself, the living Christ who speaks through him will execute powerful judgment against the Corinthian sinners (1 Cor. 5:3–5; 2 Cor. 13:2–3). When the secondary literature on Paul also portrays him as one who pronounces judgment (Acts 13:11; 28:25–28; 1 Tim. 1:20), it is pointing to a prophetic characteristic of Paul. So also the prophetic oracles of Luke 1–2 contain the element of eschatological judgment (1:51–53; 2:34–35). Although Hermas is something of a pale literary reflection of his prophetic predecessors, both in Israel and the church, he does preserve this element of rebuking and judging immorality. In sum, the prophets appear to have been not moralizers but those who rebuked the sins of the eschatological community in the name of the judge who would shortly appear.

Revelation of People's Hearts

Another characteristic of early Christian prophecy evidenced in our sources that seems to be an aspect of its eschatological nature is that extraordinary revelation of people's hearts described, for example, by Paul in 1 Corinthians 14:25. In the presence of prophetic preaching in the congregation, people's inner thoughts are exposed, and they are driven to confess that God is truly present. This has sometimes been called "clairvoyance," one of the primary characteristics of Hellenistic prophets that is practically absent from descriptions of Jewish prophets. In addition to 1 Corinthians 14:25, several references in our sources indicate that knowing the secrets of the human heart is a mark of the prophet (Mark 14:65 par.; Luke 2:35; 7:39; John 2:24–25; 4:19; 6:64; 13:11, 21; 16:19; Rev. 2:23; 3:1, 8, 15; Ignatius, *Philadelphians* 7.1–2). It may be that some Christian prophets simply shared this characteristic with other "divine man" *(theios anēr)* types or that the tradition process had imposed this common Hellenistic prophetic trait onto the image of the Christian prophet and that "clairvoyance" is the proper designation for this phenomenon. But a better explanation may be found in terms of the eschatological nature of early Christian prophetic preaching, so that such references as 1 Corinthians 14:25 are to be explained not by "thought reading," but by the kind of direct address in which the prophet, speaking in the person of the eschatological judge, brings the hearer proleptically before the judgment (cf. 1 Cor. 4:5). As will happen on the Last Day, so already in the prophetic encounter, the heart's hidden secrets are revealed and confessed.

In particular, it is the Son of man who will know the hearts at the Last Judgment, and it is especially the voice of the Risen One who speaks as Son of man that is heard in the prophet's word, as we shall see. Since the christological designation "Son of man" was peculiar to only a few streams of early Christian tradition, the term itself is only rarely testified to by our sources. Paul uses the phrase not at all; Revelation uses it only minimally and tangentially. Yet there is some contact between "Son of man" terminology and Christian prophecy. All the Gospels have been influenced by Christian prophets, and all the Gospels refer to Jesus as the Son of man. Acts 7 is a prophetic scene in which Stephen has a vision— and in this vision the risen Jesus appears as the Son of man. When the Christian prophets pronounce judgment in the name of the exalted Christ, they are exercising the function of the eschatological Son of man.

Concern for False Prophets

Wherever the phenomenon of prophecy appears, the problem of distinguishing true from false prophets also emerges. Thus it is no surprise that the early church speaks of "false prophets" as well as "prophets." The use of false-prophet vocabulary was encouraged by two other developments antecedent to the rise of prophecy in the church.

First, since the time of the translation of the LXX, which used "false prophet" for the prophets who opposed the canonical prophets, "false prophet" had become a term of abuse for one's theological opponents. This represented a claim that the content of the teaching that was opposed was false, without necessarily indicating that the opponents made claims to prophetic inspiration. The operative element in the phrase "false prophet" was "false," not "prophet." We thus find "false prophet" used as a polemical insult, as a synonym for "false teacher" (2 Peter 2:1; *Didache* 11.3–6).

Secondly, a common feature of the apocalyptic drama was the multiplication of false prophets just before the End, part of the furniture of apocalyptic. This meant that an apocalyptically oriented community, such as early Christianity, would find talk of false prophecy to be a given part of its theological resources. Some references to false prophets in our literature may be simply a reflection of this apocalyptic milieu (e.g., *Didache* 16.3).

As in the Old Testament (Jer. 14:13–16; 23:9–32; 29:8–9; Ezek. 13:1–16; 1 Kings 22:5–28; cf. Zech. 12:2–6), those in the early church who themselves claim the gift of prophecy, or who are most sympathetic to the prophetic ministry of the church, are those who are most sensitive to the prophetic claims of others and most able to resist them. Deuteronomy 13 and 18 and *Didache* 11–13 illustrate the difficulty the noncharismatic community had in dealing with prophetic claims. The prophet-author of Revelation is concerned with false prophets not merely as a traditional element of apocalyptic theology but because he is met by counterclaims in his own churches from prophets who present a different message from his own (2:20; cf. 2:14, 15). It is quite likely that the False Prophet of 16:13; 19:20, and 22:10 represents not only the pagan priesthood promoting emperor worship in Asia (cf. 13:11–18), but also, or even primarily, the church prophets who encouraged sacrifice to the emperor by announcing this as the will of the exalted Lord.

Likewise Matthew, who values the prophetic ministry very highly, is also concerned to point out the danger of false prophets within the church (7:15–23), as is the *Didache* (11.8–12), the Johannine community (1 John 4:1–3) and Hermas (Mandate 11). Paul does not use the term "false prophet" but as a charismatic himself is very concerned that the congregation which experiences inspired speech recognizes that the claim to inspiration taken by itself is not sufficient to distinguish authentic from false prophecy (1 Cor. 2:6–16; 12:1–11; 14:1–39; 2 Corinthians 10–13). Of our major sources, only Luke–Acts is unconcerned with the problem of false prophecy within the church, but this is readily explained by Luke's reluctance to describe *any* internal problems between Paul and his mission churches.

Historical Prediction

All the material characteristics of prophetic speech so far considered have been aspects of the eschatological nature of early Christian prophecy. Were the prophets also predictors of historical, this-worldly events, as distinct from the events associated with the End? In the popular mind, this kind of prediction is so clearly associated with "prophecy" as to be practically identical with it. In the Hellenistic world, this kind of mundane predictive power was an integral part of the prophet's role, and to a lesser degree, this was also the case in first-century Jewish prophecy.

The support in our sources for the view that Christian prophets predicted the historical future is extremely slight. The author of Revelation does not predict the future in the normal sense of this expression because in this sense the future did not exist for him. The series of catastrophes that he announces are not predictions of events *in* history but those which form the end *of* history. Even the predicted persecution that he announces as about to fall upon the churches is in his view an aspect of the eschatological events, not a purely historical event.

So also Paul never uses "prophesy" to mean "predict," nor is there any indication that forecasting historical events was a part of Corinthian prophecy. Paul's "predictions" (e.g., 1 Thess. 3:4) were an element of his eschatology, as we have seen. It is primarily from Acts that the picture of the Christian prophet as predictor comes (11:27–28; 20:23, 29–30; 21: 10–11; 27:10, 23–26), but this is due to Luke's modeling of church prophets on the pattern of Old Testament prophets, whom he understands to have been primarily predictors (1:16–20; 2:16, 25, 30–31; 3:18, 21, 24; 4:25; 8:35; 10:43; 11:27–28; 13:27, 33–41, 47; 15:15).

The evidence of predictive prophecy in John may be more significant, in that he names prediction of the future as one of the Paraclete-prophet's functions (16:13). This might be a clue to the role some Christian prophets played in John's church, whose ministry is portrayed in the description of the Paraclete, although the prophet-author himself is not at all interested in the prediction of historical events. This might also account for the emphasis on Jesus' ability to announce events before they happen (13:19; 14:29; 16:4; 18:4, 32; 19:28). Also in 1 Timothy 4:1–3, prophecy is remembered as the gift of predicting the mundane future, "in later times" probably being intentionally set over against the more eschatological "last days."

Concrete Directions for Church Life

The prophet appears in several of our sources as that figure who is empowered by the Spirit to declare to the community what it must do in situations for which the tradition provided ambiguous guidance or none at all, or when the church's life had outgrown its tradition. The Apocalypse is such a prophetic word to a specific problem: how should the church respond to the cultural pressures that promoted the idolization of the state, including the specific issue of worship of the emperor as a divine being?[29] The book as a whole gives one clear answer to this burning question, not by a direct appeal to tradition (Mark 12:17 is conspicuous by its absence) but by direct revelation, in which elements of the old tradition are taken up and recast as a new message from the exalted Lord. In the course of this prophetic response to the primary issue, answers to other problems of church life are also revealed: the

---

29 See my commentary, *Revelation: A Bible Commentary for Teaching and Preaching,* 13–26 for a discussion of the religiopolitical crisis faced by Revelation's readers and their perplexing options in facing it.

"Nicolaitans" are a heretical sect and are to be rejected (2:6, 15); food sacrificed to idols is not to be eaten by faithful Christians (2:14, 20).

Like John, Hermas also writes to deliver the prophetically revealed answer to a major issue of church life: is repentance for postbaptismal sin possible? But en route Hermas too responds with prophetic decisions regarding other concrete questions within the church: does a husband sin if he continues to live with an adulterous wife (Mandate 4.1.4–6)? If one's spouse dies, does the surviving partner sin if he or she remarries (Mandate 4.4.1–4)? Just as Paul had also done, questions of marriage and divorce are dealt with not rabbinically but charismatically. Thus not only the somewhat "Haggadic" disclosures of the eschatological future, but also the "Halakhic" regulations of church order and Christian life formed part of the substance of the prophetic message. Ignatius's "Do nothing without the bishop" (*Philadelphians* 7.2) was offered by him not as sage advice but as prophetic revelation. Law and prophecy in a charismatic community are not so far apart as one might suppose.

The author of the Fourth Gospel apparently knew that prophets in his church dealt pastorally with problems of church life by giving prophetic answers to particular problems since he pictures the Paraclete as one who will "teach all things" (14:26) and "guide . . . into all the truth" (16:13). The author is aware that it is the function of the prophet to address disputed theological questions, especially those that affect practical church life (4:19–20).

In Acts 10 and 15, as in Ephesians 2:20 and 3:5, the prophets are the primary figures in the church's making the momentous decision to extend the gospel to the Gentiles. Here a question faced the church for which the tradition had no answer, an unsatisfactory answer, or contradictory answers. Only a charismatic leap around and beyond the tradition or charismatic insight into the tradition's current meaning, a fresh revelation of the will of God for the present moment in the church's life, would have sufficed to guide the church, and this is apparently what occurred. This great new insight *did not come only as a vague spiritual osmosis* but by the leadership of those prophets who claimed to have a word from the risen Lord that transcended all previous tradition.

Not only major theological issues but sometimes the day-to-day life of the church appears as directed by the Spirit through the prophets. In Acts 13:1–3 and 1 Timothy 1:18 and 4:14, Christian prophets designate certain persons for specific service in the church, and repeatedly in Acts directions that affect the mission of the church are given by Spirit-inspired spokespersons or by revelatory experiences of the prophetic figures in their dreams (8:26, 29; 16:6, 9; 18:9–10; 21:4; 22:17–21).

That this is not merely the legend-building thrust of the tradition nor Luke's romantic editorializing (though some of the latter is present) is confirmed by Paul's own reference to his call, which he describes in prophetic terms (Gal. 1:12–17), and by Paul's claim to have gone to the Jerusalem conference "by revelation" (Gal. 2:2). This latter reference shows clearly that as a Christian prophet Paul believed that his life was directed, at crucial points, for the sake of the church, by a revelation that was not merely a private experience but the Spirit's directing an individual for the purpose of facilitating the church's mission. Paul himself typically settles practical questions of church life (e.g., divorce, eating meat sacrificed to idols, glossolalia during worship) not on the basis of personal prophetic revelation but by an appeal to a "word of the Lord" or by his apostolic authority (1 Cor. 7:10–40; 8:1–11:1; 14:1–39). But too much should not be made of this—the line between traditional words of the Lord and words of the heavenly Lord is a thin one for Paul, as is the line between apostle and prophet. Paul too, as a Christian prophet, speaks to the practical problems of church life.

Since we know that rendering decisions on disputed issues of religious life was also understood to be a function of the prophet within Palestinian Judaism (e.g., 1 Macc. 4:41–46; 14:25–49; John 4:19–20), we may assume that this characteristic, as documented in Christian sources, was also an aspect of the ministry of early Christian prophets. In fact, if prophets continued to play such a role after the church had developed official structures, it is even more likely that this was the case in the earliest days of the church.

Revelatory Spirit and Angel

In Revelation, the prophetic state is described as being "in the Spirit" (1:10; 4:2; 17:3; 21:10), the prophetic mode of discourse is called "spiritual" (RSV: "allegorical," see Rev. 11:8), and "Spirit" is frequently used in other expressions as the vehicle of revelation or the power at work in the revelatory event (2:7, 11, 17, 29; 3:6, 13, 22; 14:13; 19:10; 22:6, 17; probably also 1:4; 3:1; 4:5; 5:6). Since apocalyptic thought in general includes revelation by angels as a common element, it is not unexpected to find many references to angels in Revelation as well. But it is striking that some of the Apocalypse's references to angels are not simply a part of the idiosyncratic language of apocalyptic but are found in a group of statements closely parallel to statements about the revelatory Spirit. To "in the Spirit" corresponds "by sending his angel" (1:1); to "spiritually" (RSV: "allegorically") corresponds "a man's measure, that is, an angel's" (21:17); and to the series of statements where the Spirit is the vehicle of revelation, there is an equally long list in which the angel performs this function (5:2, 11; 7:2, 11–12; 10:1–11; 14:6, 8, 9, 15, 18; 17:1, 7; 18:2, 21; 19:17; 22:6, 16). In some of these, the Spirit and the angel are identified (17:1–3; 22:6). We see that the Spirit and angels are associated very closely in Revelation, that the prophetic ministry is associated closely with both, and that this has left its mark on the vocabulary of the prophet's message.

Acts associates the Spirit with the revelatory experiences of prophets, so that the utterances of prophets contain references of the Spirit (2:33; 11:28; 13:2; 15:28; 16:6, 7; 20:23; 21:4, 11). Acts also associates angels with such revelatory experiences, sometimes using "angel" and "spirit" interchangeably (Acts 8:26–29; 10:3–19; 23:8–9; 27:23). The prophetic scenes of Luke 1–2 alternate between revelation by an angel (1:8–22, 26–38) and by the Spirit (1:41, 47, 67; 2:25–27). Luke-Acts is thus a witness to the use of Spirit/angel terminology as an indication of Christian prophecy. This is also clearly the case in Hermas throughout, especially in Mandate 11. In all of this there is nothing unique to Christian prophecy, for in several streams of heterodox Judaism the revelatory angel and revelatory Spirit were identified or closely associated (*2 Apocalypse of Baruch* 55:3; 1QM 13:10–11; *Testament of Judah* 20:5; *Jubilees* 1:25; 15:31–32; *1 Enoch* 15:4–6; *2 Enoch* 16:7; *Martyrdom of Isaiah* 1:7–8 and passim).

There are two items of negative evidence from the New Testament that are important for this discussion. Paul often speaks of revelation as coming to prophets by the Spirit (1 Thess. 5:19; 1 Cor. 2:9–16; 12:4–11; 14:1, 31–32, 37; cf. 1 Cor. 11:10, which refers to angels in a context discussing prophecy), but he hardly ever has a good word to say about angels and never refers to angels as the vehicle of prophetic revelation. He does indicate clearly that others in the early church had this understanding, of which he himself is suspicious (Gal. 1:8; 1 Cor. 13:1; 2 Cor. 11:14).

So also the Fourth Gospel replaces the traditional angel in the revelatory event with the Paraclete, which is clearly defined as the Spirit. The Paraclete figure had probably previously been understood as an angel figure, which John is subtly demythologizing.[30] This shows that some in John's tradition and community had associated angels with prophetic speech, as had also been the case in Paul's.

I am not suggesting that all the references to angels in first-century Jewish and Christian literature should be related to the prophetic experience, nor is there any reason to explore here the various ways that angelology functioned theologically in the many streams of early Judaism and Christianity. Rather, I am calling attention to the striking way in which angel/Spirit terminology appears in our sources for early Christian prophecy and suggesting that in the Gospel tradition an interest in the Spirit and/or angels as the media of revelation may be a mark of prophetic speech.

---

30 Cf. Boring, "Johannine Portrayal of the Paraclete," 114–117.

Wisdom Motifs

The profile of the prophet is sometimes made to stand out the more clearly by contrasting it with that of the sage. Sato, for instance, lists a number of points of contrast between the Old Testament wisdom tradition and prophecy.[31]

1. Unlike prophecy, wisdom is founded not on a transcendent revelation but on a perception of the immanent order of creation derived from human experience.
2. Thus a sage is not "called" but "educated."
3. In the Old Testament wisdom tradition, God never speaks in the first person.
4. Since the given order of the world is the presupposition of wisdom, it can hardly generate a radical reversal of inherited traditions and accepted norms, as often happens in prophecy.
5. Old Testament wisdom presupposes no concrete situation of specific addresses but is addressed to the general and universal. Thus reference to the history of Israel is lacking, except in late examples such as Sirach.
6. Symbolic actions are lacking.
7. Eschatology is lacking; the present is not qualified by the absolute or in-breaking future.
8. Wisdom has its own tradition and does not draw from the prophetic tradition.

As Sato recognizes, this stereotyped picture of wisdom and prophecy flowing in two unrelated channels is based on Old Testament models and is not accurate when thinking about the relation of wisdom and prophecy in the first century. Even in Old Testament times, prophecy was much more open to wisdom influence and materials than vice versa. It is now a commonplace of Old Testament studies that the prophets and wise men of Israel are not simply to be contrasted with each other, but that Israel's prophets utilized themes, materials, and forms from the wisdom tradition in the expression of their prophetic message. Particularly after the exile, wisdom, which had formerly sometimes been little more than common sense honed by community experience, assumed more and more the role of the divine call to humanity. This role had formerly been held primarily by prophecy, and this development brought wisdom and prophecy even closer together. Although von Rad has overstated the case in declaring that apocalyptic is not prophecy at all but is to be classified under the

---

31 Sato, *Q und Prophetie,* 106–107.

heading of "wisdom,"[32] it is true that in Jewish prophecy and apocalyptic, the categories of prophecy and wisdom had collapsed into each other. Prophets could use wisdom materials; sages had difficulty using the prophetic gestalt of revelation, but still claimed to fill the slot once occupied by prophecy. A wide spectrum of the literature of early Judaism shows that not only did sages sometimes feel themselves to be the heirs and successors of the prophets, writing with a consciousness of divine commission, but prophets were seen to be envoys of Wisdom. Many examples could be given: Wisdom of Solomon 1:6–7; 7:27; 9:17; Sirach 24:30–34; 39:1–6; 2 Esdras 14:1–48; *1 Enoch* 37:1–5; 42:1–2; 49:3; 63:2; 82:1b–3; 84:3; 92:1; *Baba Bathra* 12a; 1QH 2:4–5; 11QPs^a 1–4. In *1 Enoch* for example, wisdom is the major category *within* which prophetic revelations are conceived; Enoch can speak readily of "visions of wisdom" (37:1). Wisdom is not merely the accumulated insight of human experience but is revealed from heaven (42:1–2). It thus should come as no surprise that our sources for early Christian prophecy indicate that prophecy in the early church manifests some wisdom features.

The Apocalypse has the same wisdom heritage as apocalyptic in general. In particular may be noted the "conquering" sayings in chapters 2–3, which are a borrowing of wisdom formulae. For Paul, too, wisdom and prophecy are correlative modes of discourse that blend into each other, as can be seen from the train of thought in 1 Corinthians 1:18–2:16, where Paul's use of "wisdom," in distinction to that of the Corinthians, is oriented toward prophecy/apocalyptic, rather than to Gnosticism. This Pauline affinity between wisdom and prophecy is preserved also in Ephesians, though in a somewhat more gnosticizing way, as is illustrated, e.g., by the combination of "wisdom" (Sophia) and "knowledge" (logos) in 1:17. Similarly, the Logos (RSV: "word") concept lying behind the Johannine prologue has points of contact with both the Jewish wisdom speculations and the prophetic understanding of the Johannine community. When we remember that in the wisdom tradition the heavenly, preexistent Wisdom came upon selected recipients and made them "friends of God and prophets" (Wisd. Sol. 7:27), we probably have a clue as to how the Johannine community understood John 15:15b: "I have called you friends, for all that I have heard from my father I have made known to you." The disciples of the envoy of heaven are "friends," i.e., "prophets." Not only does this sapiential context reveal the presence of prophecy in the Johannine community more clearly, it alerts us to look for wisdom motifs in the products of Christian prophecy.

---

32 Gerhard von Rad, *Old Testament Theology* (New York: Harper & Row, 1965), 2:36–37, 72–73.

Numerous scholars have pointed out the presence of wisdom forms and materials in the tradition of Jesus' sayings in the Gospels. This is certainly to be related to the probability that Jesus himself was a figure who combined sapiential and prophetic characteristics, and to the probability that Christian prophets after Easter continued to make use of wisdom forms. Thus "wisdom" and "prophecy" are not alternatives when discussing either Jesus or the early Christian prophets. Certain kinds of wisdom formulae may even be an indication of prophetic speech.

10

Summary

Without claiming that every early Christian prophet embodies all the features discussed above, I can now assemble a list of characteristics that, with more or less certainty from case to case, may be considered typical of early Christian prophets. Prophets were not uncommon figures but were widespread in early Christianity. The prophets functioned as a distinct group within the community but as an integral part of it, within the worship life of the congregation in close proximity to the teachers and the tradition process. Both men and women received the prophetic gift.

Although the prophet was respected as a pneumatic whose words were permeated with a sense of call, authority, and mission, the community knew that the true prophet was not possessed but retained responsibility for what he or she said, and that his or her words were not to be automatically accepted but to be tested by the community. The prophet frequently was associated with miracles and other pneumatic phenomena of the charismatic community. Like the Old Testament prophets, Christian prophets might engage in symbolic acts and exhibit a peculiar lifestyle frequently marked by poverty and asceticism. The prophet did not fashion oracles *ab ovo* but functioned as an inspired interpreter of the community's history, of the scriptures, and of traditional sayings of Jesus.

Prophetic speech was not chaotic but might be characterized by particular forms: "I am" and first-person address in the name of the risen Lord, "sentences of holy law" and related forms, initial "amen," the pronouncement of blessing and curse, and a characteristic vocabulary.

Prophecy also was characterized by particular items of content. Since the rebirth of prophecy in the church was itself an eschatological phenomenon, the prophet's message had a dominant eschatological orientation, which was expressed from time to time in apocalyptic content, eschatological *paraclēsis*, rebuke of immorality and pronouncement of proleptic judgment of the Last Day, references to persecution and suffering, the revelation of the secrets of people's hearts, and a concern for false prophets. The prophet's message might involve historical prediction and give concrete directions addressed to ambiguous or controversial issues in church life. Wisdom motifs and an interest in the modes of revelation (angels, Spirit) might appear in the prophet's sayings.

PART THREE

PROPHETIC SAYINGS
OF THE RISEN JESUS
IN THE GOSPELS

11

A Note on Method

The preceding discussion has argued for the general probability that Christian prophets were the kind of figures who might have affected the developing Gospel tradition in a variety of ways, including the proclamation of new sayings of Jesus, and that the tradition developed in such a manner as to be open to such prophetic influences. But whether the particular contributions of Christian prophets to the Gospels can be identified with any degree of probability is another question. Some scholars consider it likely that the Gospels do contain prophetic sayings of the risen Jesus, but are skeptical about the possibility of identifying them.[1] I remain convinced that it is possible to identify the prophetic sayings in the Gospel, often with a considerable degree of probability. In the following pages I will identify and briefly discuss the particular sayings in the Gospels that seem to have been created or significantly modified by Christian prophets. In a few cases, I will present the kind of detailed evidence on which these conclusions rest.

My procedure will be as follows. I will first examine each saying of Jesus in the Gospels and formulate a preliminary list of candidates for possible prophetic origin. To be included in this list, sayings must meet two criteria: First, they must be able to be seen as having existed independently of a narrative context, even if they are now contained in narratives. This includes even apophthegmata ("pronouncement stories"), sayings that are now integrated into narrative units but may have been inserted into them or even have generated them.[2] Secondly, they must be considered to be secondary, i.e., church products (at least in their present form),

---

1 E.g., Hill, *New Testament Prophecy,* 182, and cf. Aune, *Prophecy,* 194, 245. Aune's skepticism does not extend to the issue of identifying prophetic sayings in other documents such as the letters of Paul, 248–261.

2 Cf. Bultmann, *Synoptic Tradition,* 11–12, 21, 47.

rather than words of the historical Jesus, on other grounds than their similarity to Christian prophecy. It should be explicitly noted that there were other means of expansion of the tradition besides the prophetic, e.g., scribal, and that the formula "not from Jesus, therefore from a Christian prophet" is to be rejected. Since Jesus was himself something of a charismatic figure, who is frequently portrayed in the Gospels as a prophet, sayings cannot be declared secondary only on the basis that they bear certain marks of prophecy. Authentic sayings are also likely to manifest prophetic traits. The questions of authenticity and of prophetic origin should be kept separate and the latter introduced only after a judgment has been given on the former.

This procedure will result in a list of secondary sayings, each of which could have circulated as an independent logion. Some of such sayings—and only such—could be the products of Christian prophets. Whether or not that was likely must be decided from case to case. Each such saying will be compared with the profile of early Christian prophets formulated thus far in this book. Sayings that have significant points of contact with the characteristics of Christian prophecy may be considered to be prophetic sayings with some degree of probability.

Each of these steps is a detailed and somewhat tedious process. To elaborate the process and give the detailed evidence for each saying in the Gospels would make a very long book. In the following, I will give detailed evidence for only the first such saying examined, the Q beatitudes (Luke 6:20b–23/Matt. 5:3–12) so that the reader may see how the method works. For other sayings identified as prophetic, only a minimum of evidence and argument will be given, or none at all, so that space may be given to presenting the significance of interpreting the sayings as prophetic. Readers interested in the detailed evidence for each saying may consult my earlier monograph, which concentrated on evidence and argument for the prophetic origin of each saying identified.[3]

It will become apparent that the typical either/or manner of posing the question: "Is this saying from the historical Jesus or from an early Christian prophet?" is too simple an approach and that the question needs to be refined, since Christian prophets may have influenced the developing Gospel tradition at more than one point, in more than one way, including reshaping sayings that originated from the historical Jesus.

---

3 M. Eugene Boring, *Sayings of the Risen Jesus: Christian Prophecy in the Synoptic Tradition.*

12

Prophetic Sayings of the
Risen Jesus in Q

We now turn to an examination of the streams of tradition in which the sayings of Jesus were handed on and the documents in which the deposit of these traditions was preserved. The oldest of these is the hypothetical common source for Jesus' sayings used by Matthew and Luke, dubbed "Q" as the abbreviation for *Quelle* ("source") by the nineteenth-century German scholars who first identified it.

Research on Q has experienced a renaissance of late.[1] Previously important as a factor in the Synoptic problem or in studies of the historical Jesus, more recent studies have concentrated on a socio-historical approach to Q, attempting to infer something about the nature and history of the "Q community" from the reconstructed history of the hypothetical document. This means moving from Matthew and Luke to the hypothetical document, then from the reconstructed final form of the document to its prior forms and layers, then making inferences about the history of the community from this reconstructed history of the document. All these moves are hypothetical and become increasingly speculative. Yet they are necessary in historical reconstruction and offer our only view into some aspects of early Christianity.

Although at some point(s) in its history the Q materials were written into a document or series of documents, we should not regard Q simplistically as a static, flat-surface entity. The Q materials and the Q community had a history, a trajectory, of expansion and modification. Sato has

---

1 Cf., e.g., the technical study of John S. Kloppenborg, *The Formation of Q: Trajectories in Ancient Wisdom Collections,* and Ivan Havener, *Q: The Sayings of Jesus,* for a readable nontechnical introduction with a reconstruction of Q by Athanasius Polag. The growing edge of Q studies is represented by the International Q Project of the Society of Biblical Literature, directed by James M. Robinson. The results of Robinson's and the Seminar's work will be published in two volumes of the Hermeneia series from Fortress Press.

recently argued that the physical form of Q was that of an "expandable notebook."[2] While it is unlikely that this was literally the case, he has rightly pointed to the nature of Q as a series of expanding "editions." There are earlier and later sayings in Q. The International Q Project, directed by James M. Robinson, is currently attempting to identify the layering and history of Q and the Q community. How convincingly this can be done remains to be seen. The following discussion assumes that some sayings in Q reflect earliest Palestinian Christianity and that some sayings reflect later phases of the community's history but that there was an identifiable community with a continuous history within which the Q traditions were transmitted and shaped, and to some extent created.

My procedure will be to take the hypothesis that Christian prophecy existed in the early Palestinian-Syrian church as I have reconstructed it in the preceding pages and to proceed through the Q materials saying by saying, in the Lukan order, comparing each saying with our profile of Christian prophecy. Those sayings will be discussed that seem to have significant points of contact with Christian prophecy and seem to be illuminated by being considered in the light of the hypothesis here explored. An effort will be made to come to a decision as to whether the saying originated as Christian prophecy (or was affected by Christian prophets in some other way) or the apparent points of contact are only coincidental. The results of such an investigation are as follows.

Q 6:20b–23: PROPHETIC PRONOUNCEMENTS OF ENCOURAGEMENT

Q originally contained four beatitudes, those in Luke 6:20b–23, paralleled in Matthew 5:3, 4, 6, 11–12 (= Q 6:20b–23[3]). The additional beatitudes in Matthew 5:5, 7–10, are additions to Q in the Matthean stream of tradition (Q[Mt]) or from Matthew himself, and will be discussed later. That they are not documented in the earliest reconstructable source does not necessarily mean that they are secondary.

As a sample of how the method of identifying prophetic sayings works, I will discuss in some detail the questions of whether the Q form of the Beatitudes derives from Jesus or the early church, and whether there is reason for attributing the saying that appears to come from the post-Easter Christian community to a Christian prophet.

No one except the most extreme uncritical fundamentalist attributes every word of the Gospels just as we have them to the historical Jesus. All acknowledge that the church interpreted, modified, and augmented

---

2 Sato, *Q und Prophetie,* 62–65.
3 As a result of the International Seminar on Q, directed by James M. Robinson, it has become conventional to designate Q texts by their Lukan chapter and verse locations.

the tradition in the course of transmission. Historical-critical scholars have developed a set of criteria for sorting out materials that may be attributed to Jesus and those that derive from the church. The following list represents something of a consensus in critical method.[4]

1. *Attestation in multiple sources*—sayings appearing independently in more than one source are more likely authentic than those that do not.

2. *Attestation in multiple forms*—sayings that appear in multiple literary forms (parable, miracle story, pronouncement story, etc.) are more original than those that do not.

3. *The linguistic criterion*—assumes that since Jesus spoke Aramaic, the closer a Gospel saying is to the style and idiom of Aramaic, the more likely it is to be original.

4. *The environmental criterion*—assumes that sayings couched in terms of Jesus' own environment (the domestic, social, political, economic, agricultural, and religious milieu of early first-century Palestine) cannot be the creation of the later Hellenistic church.

5. *Tendencies of the developing tradition*—It has been argued that, generally speaking, as the tradition was handed on, it (a) became longer, (b) became more detailed, (c) tended to reduce the incidence of Semitisms, (d) tended to shift from indirect to direct discourse, and (e) tended to conflate various versions.

6. *Dissimilarity*—Material that stands in contrast to both Judaism and Christianity is more likely from Jesus than material that does not.

7. *Modification*—When it can be perceived that the tradition has been modified, e.g., in the variety of sayings on divorce, the more radical form is usually the earlier form.

8. *Coherence*—Once a "critically assured" minimum has been obtained, other sayings that are congruent with it are more likely original than those that are not.

9. *Plausible tradition history*—If a plausible genealogy of the various forms of a saying can be reconstructed, it is only the earliest form that could be from the historical Jesus. But such a descriptive genealogy is also an argument that the earliest form is indeed that.

10. *Hermeneutical potential*—This approach looks at the various forms of a saying and asks what the earliest form must have been in order to generate the others.

---

4 Cf. Joachim Jeremias, "Characteristics of the *ipsissima vox Jesu*," in *The Prayers of Jesus*, 108–115; William O. Walker, Jr., "The Quest for the Historical Jesus: A Discussion of Methodology"; D. G. A. Calvert, "An Examination of the Criteria for Distinguishing the Authentic Words of Jesus"; Dieter Lührmann, "Die Frage nach Kriterien für ursprüngliche Jesusworte. Eine Problemskizze" in *Jésus aux origines de la christologie*, ed. J. Dupont, 59–72; Dennis Polkow, "Method and Criteria for Historical Jesus Research," in *SBL 1987 Seminar Papers*, 336–355; M. Eugene Boring, "The Historical-Critical Method's 'Criteria of Authenticity': The Beatitudes in Q and Thomas as a Test Case."

Practically everyone agrees that there are objections to each of the above criteria taken by itself, that in practice some criteria tend to cancel out others, that they must be applied in concert and not mechanically. To illustrate the method, I shall in this one instance look at the Q beatitudes in the light of each of the criteria.

1. Multiple Sources

The beatitudes of Q 6:20b–23 are found or reflected in Matthew/Luke (= Q), the *Gospel of Thomas,* log. 54 and 68–69; Polycarp, *Philippians* 2.3; 1 Peter 3:14 and 4:14.

Q

The four beatitudes in Q 6:20b–23 are found as a cluster only in Q: B1 = "poor"; B2 = "hungry"; B3 = "crying"; B4 = "reviled." The following reconstruction enjoys substantial agreement among recent Q scholars:

> Blessed are the poor,
>> for theirs is the kingdom of God.
> Blessed are those who hunger,
>> for they shall be filled.
> Blessed are those who weep,
>> for they shall be comforted.
> Blessed are you when people hate you
>> and exclude you and revile you
>> and utter evil against you
>> on account of the Son of man.
> Rejoice and be glad
>> for your reward is great in heaven:
>> for this is the way they customarily treated the prophets.

The Gospel of Thomas

B1, B2, and two versions of B4 (taking "reviled" and "persecuted" as functional equivalents for the moment) are found in the *Gospel of Thomas* in this order:

> *Gospel of Thomas* 54 = B1: "Jesus said: 'Blessed are the poor, for yours is the kingdom of heaven.' "
> *Gospel of Thomas* 68 = B4: "Jesus said: 'Blessed are you when you are hated and persecuted; and no place will be found where you have {not} been persecuted.' "
> *Gospel of Thomas* 69a = B4: "Jesus said: 'Blessed are those who have been persecuted in their hearts; for these are those who have known the Father in truth.' "

> *Gospel of Thomas* 69b = B2 "Jesus said: 'Blessed are they who are hungry, that the belly of him who desires may be satisfied.' "

It is not clear whether or not this is an independent witness: in the *Gospel of Thomas* the different order and clustering argue for independence from both Matthew and Luke, but the thrice-repeated "persecuted" is found only in the redactional Matthew 5:10–11: the expression "kingdom of heaven" (*Gos. Thom.* 54) seems to reflect the Matthean idiom; and the second-person plural in *Gospel of Thomas* 54 seems to reflect Luke rather than Q.

Polycarp, *Philippians 2.3*

Polycarp cites as a dominical saying a beatitude that contains elements found separately in two of the Q beatitudes, B1 and B4: "*Blessed are the poor,* and they who are persecuted for righteousness' sake, *for* theirs *is the Kingdom of God.*" Underlining represents verbatim agreements with Matthew; italics represents verbatim agreements with Luke. This version thus seems to be based on the Gospels of both Matthew and Luke, and therefore offers no independent witness to our sayings.

1 Peter 3:14

"But even if you do suffer for righteousness' sake, you will be blessed." It is difficult to say whether or not this reflects independent tradition, or is a reflection of Matthew 5:10. Beatitude B4 does seem to be reflected in 1 Peter 4:14: "If you are reproached for the name of Christ, you are blessed, because the spirit of glory and of God rests upon you." It is not cited as a word of the Lord, but is thoroughly integrated into the author's own parenesis. There seems to be no literary dependence on any of our other texts, but there are enough similarities despite the difference of form (dominical saying/church parenesis) to justify the conclusion that we have here an independent reflection of pre-Gospel tradition.

We thus may have four independent witnesses to this cluster of sayings: Q, *Gospel of Thomas*, Polycarp, and 1 Peter:

B1	Q	GT	Pol.	
B2	Q	GT		
B3	Q			
B4	Q	GT2x	Pol.	1 Peter

If the *Gospel of Thomas* and Polycarp are dependent on the canonical tradition, we have:

B1	Q			
B2	Q			
B3	Q			
B4	Q			1 Peter

In either case, the fourth beatitude is the best attested by this criterion. In the first instance, the fourth is much better attested, with the third the least supported by this criterion.

2. Multiple Forms

Although B1–3, blessings on the poor/hungry/crying, are not concerned with three different groups but with three aspects of one group (as in Isaiah 61:1–3 with which there is a connection), we may examine each motif separately as it appears in other forms in the Jesus tradition besides beatitudes.

Using Bultmann's form-critical categories and rubrics, we note that Jesus' declarations affirming the "poor" are found in the wisdom logia/exhortations (Luke 14:12–14), in prophetic sayings (Matt. 11:5–6/Luke 7:22–23), and in parables of reversal (Luke 14:15–24, 16:19–31). The combination of affirmation of the poor and the expectation of eschatological reversal occurs in more than one form in the Jesus tradition and tends to support the authenticity of B1.

Jesus' concern for the hungry expressed in B2 is also found in miracle stories (Mark 6:30–44 par., 8:1–10 par.), in apothegms/conflict and didactic stories (Mark 2:23–28, par.), and in parables (Matt. 25:31–46; cf. Luke 14:15–24 above). Thus this criterion tends to support B2 as authentic.

There is some reflection of Jesus' concern for the crying (B3) in other forms of the tradition: Q^{Mt}'s "mourn" does not occur elsewhere in the Gospels where it supports this view of Jesus, but Q^{Lk}'s "weep" does occur in other forms of the tradition: miracle stories in Mark 5:38 and Luke 7:13, and in a didactic story in Luke 7:38, but these are tangential connections.

Being reviled/excluded/hated because of loyalty to Jesus (B4) is only weakly attested in other forms of the tradition. Except for such Johannine sayings as 15:18–19 and stories such as 9:1–34, which obviously reflect a Christian situation rather than the life of Jesus, only the prophetic-apocalyptic saying Mark 13:13 (= Matt. 10:22 and 24:9; Luke 21:17) speaks of being hated for Jesus' sake, and it too is generally considered a post-Easter product. "Utter evil against" and "exclude" do not occur at all in this sense elsewhere in the synoptic tradition.

The correspondence between B1–3 and other forms of the authentic Jesus tradition extends beyond details of vocabulary and theme to the underlying structure of eschatological reversal. Thus this criterion strongly supports the authenticity of B1 and B2, B3 a bit less strongly, and B4 not at all.

3. The Linguistic Criterion

"Blessed" is not a peculiarly biblical or Christian word nor are pronouncements in the form "Blessed are the ——" peculiar to the biblical tradition. But the passive in B2 and B3 is a Semitic circumlocution for God's act that is characteristic of Jesus. Wellhausen[5] explained the variations between Luke 6:22 and Matthew 5:11 as different translations of a single Aramaic original. With the possible exception of the "divine passive" in B2–3, the linguistic criterion seems to offer little for or against the authenticity of these sayings.

4. The Environmental Criterion

Beatitudes as such were not unknown in the Judaism of Jesus' day, though they were not common. Although Strack-Billerbeck devote thirty-four pages to points of contact between Matthew 5:3–12 and rabbinica, there are few if any real parallels cited. Likewise the "parallels" frequently cited in the Apocrypha and apocalyptic literature (e.g., Tobit 13:14–15; *1 Enoch* 81:4; 82:4; 99:10–15; 103:5; *2 Baruch* 10:6–7)[6] are only tangential points of contact, not parallels. The pronouncement of blessing on the poor, hungry, and crying as such sets the beatitudes apart from contemporary Judaism. Thus the effort to relate the beatitudes to their Jewish environment produces an impression of dissimilarity—see criterion 6f below.

Do these sayings have marks that relate them to an early Christian setting? To what extent does the description of the life world of the earliest form of the text we can recover, that of the Q community, overlap with the life world of the pre-Easter Jesus and his disciples? This is a particularly difficult question since both life worlds must necessarily be the hypothetical reconstructions of scholars. The life world of the Q

---

5 *Einleitung in die drei ersten Evangelien,* 79–80.

6 E.g., Robert A. Guelich, *The Sermon on the Mount: A Foundation for Understanding,* 64; Klaus Koch, *The Growth of the Biblical Tradition: The Form-Critical Method* (New York: Charles Scribner's Sons, 1969), 7; and Walter Grundmann, *Das Evangelium nach Lucas,* THNT (Berlin: Evangelische Verlagsanstalt, 1972), 141.

community is described by Howard Clark Kee[7] as characterized by devotion to a charismatic leader whose mighty works are a sign of the overcoming of the powers of evil and a summons to repentance, by a redefinition of the family in terms of discipleship to Jesus, by an abandonment of all earthly securities of home, family, and job in order to join with him in announcing the coming of the kingdom of God, by an eschatological orientation that contrasts the alienation from the ordinary present world and the marginality of existence "now" with the reversal of fortunes in the impending new age. To what extent this characterization overlaps the life world of Jesus himself is an aspect of that circularity which inevitably characterizes all research into the life and message of Jesus.

The situation is somewhat different with B4, however. Here, it is not a particular socio-religious class as such that is pronounced blessed, but those who endure hatred, insult, and ostracization (or excommunication) because of their confession of Jesus as the Son of man.[8] What does this mean? It is not a matter of general objections to the Q community's continuing advocacy of the teaching of Jesus, but their confession that the "Son of man" is Jesus. In Q, "Son of man" is the primary term of christological confession, indeed practically the only one (see below "Christian Prophecy in the Q Community: A Summary"). The Q community confesses that the earthly Jesus has been exalted to heaven where he is identified with the "Son of man" who is to come in eschatological glory as the judge of the Final Day. The Q community is persecuted for this confession. This presupposes the environment of early Christianity rather than that of Jesus, and argues for the secondary origin of B4.

If "who were before you" at the end of the Matthean version of B4 was in Q, it would clearly point to the time of the church in which new prophets had arisen. But even if this phrase were not in the Q form, as assumed in the reconstruction above, it only makes explicit what was already implied in the Q form: the hearers stand in the succession of the prophets, which was a belief of the earliest church but not of Jesus.

---

7 *Christian Origins in Sociological Perspective,* 135–137.

8 Those who arrange Q into layers uniformly assign 6:20b–23 to the earliest "wisdom" layer. On these presuppositions, "Son of man" (1) must be omitted from Q in favor of Matthew's "me" (so Heinz Schürmann, "Beobachtungen zum Menschensohn-Titel in der Redequelle," in *Jesus und der Menschensohn: Für Anton Vögtle,* ed. R. Pesch and R. Schnackenburg, 124–147), (2) understood generically (so Robinson, "The Q Trajectory: Between John and Matthew via Jesus,") or (3) considered a later interpolation into an early saying (so John Kloppenborg, "Blessing and Marginality: The 'Persecution Beatitude' in Q, Thomas, and Early Christianity," 46, 49; cf. Robinson, "Q Trajectory," 19 "apocalyptic flickers or interpolations"). But any of these options seems to force the evidence in favor of the theory of an original noneschatological Q devoid of apocalyptic "Son of man" sayings referring to Jesus.

5. Tendencies of the
Developing Tradition

This criterion is more helpful in determining the oldest extant form than in deciding the question of authenticity. Consideration of these tendencies has already been used in reconstructing the Q form above. The tendency toward conflation is probably seen in Polycarp, *Philippians* 2.3. Unless our texts were generated as words of Jesus from beatitudes in Christian parenesis, 1 Peter 4:14 would represent a reverse example of the usual tendency for indirect speech to become direct. The lack of direct speech there cannot be taken as an indication of an early or original form of B4, though, as indicated earlier, it may be evidence for the independent existence of the beatitude in Matthew 5:10.

The tendency of the tradition to form clusters is then seen in both Q and *Thomas*. That B1–4 were not "originally" together is clear from comparing Q and *Thomas*. This observation will become important in the discussion of the history of the tradition below.

6. Dissimilarity

Since being persecuted for Jesus/the Son of man's sake argues for a Christian origin rather than for an authentic saying of Jesus, this criterion argues against the authenticity of B4. How this criterion is used becomes quite crucial in assessing the authenticity of B1–3. Bultmann, the purported inventor of this criterion, found that these three beatitudes survive the test, presumably because they exhibit that "contrast between Jewish morality and piety and the distinctive eschatological temper which characterized the preaching of Jesus; and . . . on the other hand we find no specifically Christian features."[9] On the first page of his explication of the teaching of Jesus, Bultmann thus refers to these three sayings as key expressions of Jesus' teaching.[10] Bultmann applied this criterion to the beatitudes with regard to their content. At least from the time of Johannes Weiss and Albert Schweitzer, one factor in the presumed content of Jesus' teaching has played an important role in formulating the "criteria of authenticity," namely the eschatological factor.

James M. Robinson's earlier work has shown that Jesus' distinctive understanding of existence caused him to structure his sayings in a characteristic way. Since Jesus' message "consists basically in a pronouncement to the present in view of the imminent eschatological future,"[11] a particular structure emerged in Jesus' language to express this.

It is precisely this polarity in the message of Jesus that can be detected

---

9 *Synoptic Tradition*, 205.

10 Bultmann, *Jesus and the Word*, 27. See also *Theology of the New Testament* 1:6.

11 "The Formal Structure of Jesus' Message" in *Current Issues in New Testament Interpretation*, ed. Wm. Klassen and Graydon F. Snyder, 97.

as a structuring tendency in the individual logia. "One gradually catches sight of a structure in terms of two members. . . . The first member, the pronouncement to the present, is related primarily to 'the present evil aeon'; the second member, the allusion to the near future, looks to the 'aeon to come.' "[12]

Some of Bultmann's students, such as Hans Conzelmann,[13] have followed him in claiming the first three Q beatitudes for Jesus. Other members of the Bultmann school, on the basis of the same criterion, have considered all the beatitudes to be from the church rather than from Jesus. Käsemann is the chief example.[14] He finds the near expectation of the coming Kingdom to be distinct from Judaism, but the "distinctive eschatological temper" that Bultmann still found to mark Jesus off from the church Käsemann attributed to earliest Christianity, especially to Christian prophets, in contrast to Jesus, who in Käsemann's view had no apocalyptic view himself.

But even if Jesus did proclaim an eschatological message within which B1–3 would have been appropriate, the fact that the earliest church had a similar message makes it difficult to use this criterion as an argument for their authenticity. For example, both Norman Perrin and Siegfried Schulz attribute all the beatitudes to Christian prophets.[15] A rigid application of the "dissimilarity criterion" that denies to Jesus everything which *can* be attributed to Judaism or the church is problematical, as is a use that excludes only what *must* be attributed to Judaism or the church. If one operates on Perrin's basis, that whoever affirms that these sayings are from Jesus should be able to argue that they probably do not come from Judaism or the church (on other bases than the criterion of dissimilarity itself), then it is not clear whether this criterion supports the authenticity of B1–3. But by this criterion, B4 is more similar to the church's teaching than it is to that of Jesus.

7. Modification

The modifications in Matthew in the direction of changing the announcement of eschatological reversal toward a list of virtues to be encouraged argues for the radicality of the Q form reconstructed above. *Gospel of Thomas* 54 preserves the radicality of B1, and *Gospel of Thomas* 68 seems to preserve the radicality of the pronouncement upon those who are persecuted (no "without cause" or "for righteousness' sake" is added).

---

12 Ibid.

13 *An Outline of the Theology of the New Testament*, 111.

14 "The Beginnings of Christian Theology," 100.

15 Perrin never refers to the beatitudes throughout his book *Rediscovering the Teaching of Jesus*. Schulz attributes them explicitly to Christian prophets in *Q: Die Spruchquelle der Evangelisten*.

But *Thomas* 69a seems to internalize the pronouncement and diminish its radicality. *Thomas* 69b may or may not preserve the radicality of B2, depending on its meaning. Even Luke seems to have modified the original third-person pronouncement into a second-person direct address, which has a limiting effect and reduces its universal absoluteness.

All this indicates that the Q form above is probably the earliest obtainable form, the radicality of which caused it to be modified in the later tradition. While this makes it appropriate to the radical Jesus, it is also appropriate to an early Christian prophet. Which is the more appropriate depends on how one assesses other evidence. This is as far as this criterion can take us.

8. Coherence

B1–3 cohere with each other and with other genuine sayings of Jesus as reconstructed by other criteria (e.g., the beatitude in Luke 10:23/Matt. 13:16). B4 is an extension of this into the Christian situation and is coherent with sayings of the early church on this same theme. This criterion thus supports the authenticity of B1–3 and opposes B4.

9. Plausible Tradition History

If Q is earlier than *Thomas,* B1–4 was already a cluster in our earliest source. Since "poor," "hungry," and "crying" can readily be understood as aspects of the self-understanding of one group of Ebionim in first-century Palestinian Judaism, and since the connection with Isaiah 61:1–3 suggests that B1–3 are not separate pronouncements regarding three different groups but represent three aspects of one group, it is easy to regard these three beatitudes as an original unity. These three sayings seemed to have formed a unit in the pre-Q tradition and also in the preaching of Jesus.

But B4 stands apart from B1–3 in several respects that indicate it was added to them later. The differences are striking: The first three have alliteration, all beginning with the letter *pi* in Greek, while the fourth does not. The first three are terse, while the fourth saying is longer than the first three put together. The first three pronounce blessing on particular persons as such, while the fourth refers to persons in a particular situation. The first three promise eschatological reversal of present conditions, while the fourth simply promises heavenly reward. The first three address those whose condition is inherently distressing, while the fourth speaks to those who are in difficulty only because of their relation to the Son of man. Adjectives and active participles describe the blessed in the first three beatitudes, while "when" clauses and "passive" finite verbs (= active verbs of which the hearers are the objects, not the subjects) are used in the fourth. The subordinate clause that states the basis for the pronouncement begins with a different Greek word *(hoti)* in the first

three, than in the fourth *(gar),* though both are translated "for" in the
RSV. If, as is argued here, the first three beatitudes were originally in the
third person, another important difference is seen in the second-person
formulation of B4. The evidence is overwhelming that B4 had a different
origin than B1–3 and was joined to them later in the tradition process.
While not arguing conclusively for the authenticity of B1–3, this criterion
is a very strong argument against the originality of B4 in its Q form as
reconstructed above.

10. Hermeneutical Potential

The tradition contains a large number of beatitudes attributed to Jesus,
dispersed throughout canonical and noncanonical witnesses (Mark is
conspicuously absent—see below). This is not unexpected since beatitudes were a traditional form. But the Jesus tradition contains a mixture
of "conventional" blessings and those that pronounce ultimate blessing
on completely unexpected groups. There are blessings that are eschatologically radical which clearly do not come from Jesus but from Christian
prophets (see Rev. 14:13). But what is the source of this stream of the
Jesus tradition? It could be that the earliest, eschatologically radical beatitudes in the tradition, i.e., B1–3 in Q, derive from Christian prophets who
created them in continuity with Jesus' own radical affirmation of the poor,
hungry, and crying. If one uses the criterion of dissimilarity in the exclusive sense, one might well come to this conclusion, as does Käsemann.
But if B1–3 had been spoken by Jesus, they, coupled with the person of
Jesus, contain the hermeneutical potential to account for the plethora of
divergent beatitudes in the tradition. I would regard the Jesus represented in B1–3 to be sufficient cause for the generation of later beatitudes
in the church such as B4.

It is possible to arrange the results of the preceding discussion into
a semblance of objectivity. The beatitudes in Q 6:20b–23 are supported
by the various criteria as follows. [# = support; #! = strong support;
? = weak support; (—) = opposition]

Criterion	1	2	3	4	5	6	7	8	9	10
B1	#	#		?			#	#	?	#
B2	#	#	?	?			#	#	?	#
B3		?	?	?			#	#	?	#
B4	#!			(—)		(—)	#	(—)	(—)	

Such neat charts can give a false impression of objective evidence. They should be a curb on arbitrary subjectivity. But subjectivity remains. In any case, witnesses and criteria should be weighed as well as counted, and assigning relative weight has considerable subjective elements. Sorting out the Jesus tradition is not an unhistorical task, but the line between historian and artist is difficult to draw.

After working through the criteria, and working the beatitudes through the criteria, it seems that the first three Q beatitudes may be assigned to Jesus with some measure of confidence, and the fourth Q beatitude to the post-Easter church with an even greater degree of confidence.

Jesus of Nazareth did not say Q 6:22–23. Is there evidence to suggest that the saying was later spoken in his name by a Christian prophet? The following features of the saying match up with the profile of Christian prophets developed earlier in this book:

1. The saying speaks for *Jesus* in the first person, rather than being a general beatitude that could have been spoken by anyone and then attributed to Jesus (such as Luke 14:15). This beatitude makes sense only if it was originally conceived as coming from the mouth of Jesus; for the distress of those who are blessed is incurred precisely because of their commitment to the speaker, whether this be expressed as the "for my sake" of the Matthean form or, as is more likely, the Lukan "on account of the Son of man."

2. The saying is formally a pronouncement of blessing, which, as we have seen, is a characteristic prophetic form.

3. Such pronouncements originate either from wisdom settings or eschatological ones from a prophetic context.[16] In the New Testament period, beatitudes were rarely found in rabbinical teaching, and then without eschatological grounding. In the Q saying, however, the basis of this pronouncement is obviously not practical wisdom but prophetic revelation. The saying is typical of Q in general, which is not to be seen as a collection of proverblike catechetical materials for the moral instruction of the early church but as a setting-forth of a radical understanding of life, and a call to such a life, that can only be understood as *revelatory*. Such forms of speech are at home in Jesus' own mouth, and in the mouths of Christ's inspired post-Easter spokespersons, but are not particularly appropriate to teachers and noncharismatic transmitters of tradition.

4. The setting in the life of the church where such a saying would be most at home is the worship of the gathered community. "The declaring of well-being as a word of power and not simply as an observation leads

---

16 Cf. Koch, *The Growth of the Biblical Tradition,* 7.

to the *cultic* use of the form . . . within a well-defined *community.*"[17]
Beardsley's observation about beatitudes in general is especially appropriate as an indication of the prophetic origin of this beatitude, which
cannot have been invented simply as a wise saw for general exhortation.
The saying, rather, has the tone of a proclamation in the worship of the
gathered, persecuted community, where Christian prophets announced
the divinely given word of encouragement.

5. This speaking "upbuilding and encouragement and consolation"
in the name of the risen Lord is another specific mark of Christian prophets (1 Cor. 14:3).

6. The saying represents a prophetic hermeneutic, interpreting
events that are happening to the community, the scriptures, and perhaps
a traditional saying of Jesus. The events being experienced by the persecuted community are interpreted as part and parcel of salvation history:
thus it has always been with God's prophets, in whose succession the
persecuted community now stands.

7. While there is no allusion to particular Old Testament texts, the
saving history witnessed to by scripture as a whole is interpreted as the
context for understanding the community's own suffering.

8. The saying may have existed as an independent saying, but even
so it was generated as an interpretation of and in continuity with the
beatitudes pronounced by the historical Jesus that were in circulation in
the Q community. This saying functions to interpret and make relevant
the traditional saying of Jesus in Q 6:20b–21.

9. In this case, the saying is thoroughly eschatological, contrasting
the now of the community's persecution with the way it shall be in the
time of receiving the eschatological heavenly reward.

Each of these nine features are characteristic of Christian prophets
as they are profiled in the reconstruction in Part Two above. Taken
together, they are sufficient to suggest that the saying derives from a
community in which Christian prophets were active and is in fact the
product of Christian prophecy.

There are two additional features of the saying that also point in this
direction, but it is not certain that they were in the Q form of the saying.

10. First, the hearers seem to be addressed as members of a community that numbers prophets in its midst, but this is made explicit only in
the Matthean form, which contains the clarifying words "who were before
you" at the end. If these words were in the Q form of the saying, which
was probably *not* the case, there would be no doubt that the saying comes
from a community with a prophetic self-consciousness. But even without

---

17 William Beardsley, *Literary Criticism of the New Testament* (Philadelphia: Fortress
Press, 1970), 37.

these words, the saying expresses a relationship with the prophets of Israel and a sense of being their successors that is typical of the Q community. This does not mean that every member of the community is addressed as a prophet, but that the pronouncement of blessing originally applied particularly to the prophetic messengers of the community, who were persecuted for propagating the message that Jesus was the Son of man in the synagogues of Palestine-Syria and who were rejected just as were the earlier messengers to Israel, the prophets.

11. A final prophetic feature of this saying is its reference to the Son of man, if indeed "Son of man" belonged to the Q form. Although this is a disputed point, the recent study of Q has revealed a strong tendency to regard Luke's "on account of the Son of man" as original and Matthew's "for my sake" as secondary on the basis that Luke never adds the title to his Markan source, and Matthew does tend to substitute "I" for "Son of man" in Markan passages. I shall argue below that "Son of man" is a mark of earliest Christian prophetic speech, which strengthens the arguments both that the Q version of the saying did contain "Son of man" and that this helps confirm the saying as coming from a Christian prophet. In the early Palestinian church, confession of Jesus as the Son of man, that is, identifying Jesus with the imminently expected judge of the world, was a more radical statement, and a more important one, than is indicated by our New Testament documents, all of which are from the late Greek-speaking church. But "Son of man" is certainly the major christological title found in Q, and perhaps the only such title. Confessing Jesus as "Son of man" was both fundamental to the community's confession of Jesus and the cause of its persecution. We shall see that there is a close relation between the identification of Jesus as Son of man and Christian prophecy (cf. "Christian Prophecy in the Q Community" and chapter 17 below).

The saying Luke 6:22–23/Matthew 5:11–12, then, should be seen as having originated as the pronouncement of an early Christian prophet, addressed to missionary preachers of the Q community, who were told to anticipate persecution and rejection because of their identification of Jesus and the exalted Son of man on behalf of whom they preached in the Palestinian-Syrian synagogues. The saying was accepted by the Q community as a saying of the exalted Son of man and transmitted by it within its stock of Jesus sayings. When these were arranged into longer complexes, and finally into a written document, this saying was combined with the three beatitudes spoken by the historical Jesus, as the opening words to the Great Sermon of Luke 6:20–49. The persecuted and threatened community heard the familiar words of Jesus from the tradition as the word of the exalted Lord, who now addressed their particular situation with a pronouncement of hope and promise. The line between sayings of the pre-Easter Jesus and those of the exalted Son of man, if it ever existed at all in the Q community, was blurred; the community was addressed by the same Lord in the whole series of pronouncements. And later on, when the whole series of sayings was incorporated within a pre-Easter framework, this saying too was incorporated within that stock of sayings in the Gospels that picture the historical Jesus as saying words that now also address the church as the Risen Lord.

Q 10:2-16: A PROPHETIC MISSION CHARGE

In Q this missionary address is not located in the ministry of Jesus, that is, it was given neither to the Twelve nor to the Seventy(-two) at the time of their being sent out by Jesus, for these historicizing frameworks for the speech belong to the redactional work of Matthew and Luke respectively. What we have is a group of sayings that have been combined by the Q community into one more-or-less unified address on the nature of the disciples' preaching mission, their conduct and equipment for it, and their response to their anticipated reception or rejection. Analysis indicates that the mission charge was composed from individual sayings that circulated independently, some of which may go back to the historical Jesus. Of those sayings that were formulated in the Q community, some were originally spoken by Christian prophets. In the Q community, the whole was heard as the address of the risen Lord who sends out workers into the eschatological harvest (10:2), in a scene reminiscent of Acts 13:1-2.

The harvest was a common symbol for the eschatological judgment in both Jewish and Christian apocalyptic (Isa. 27:12; Joel 3:13; 2 Esdras 4:28-32; 9:17-21; 2 Baruch 70:2; Rev. 14:15-16; Matt. 3:12 par.; 13:24-30). The Lord of the harvest sending out laborers into the harvest is thus an eschatological scene. The work of gathering in, "harvesting," people either for salvation or damnation was not simply a human, historical work but was part of the eschatological events, sometimes attributed to the angels who accompany the Son of man at the parousia (Matt. 13:41; 24:31). "Workers" *(ergatas)* was a church word used of Christian missioners (2 Cor. 11:13; Phil. 3:2; 1 Tim. 5:18; 2 Tim. 2:15). In this saying the risen Jesus instructs the disciples to pray for God to send human beings as workers into the harvest work, participating in the eschatological work shared by angels. The strong verb "cast out" *(ekballō,* the same word used in exorcisms) indicates urgency almost to the point of violence. As in Matthew 10:23 (also a prophetic saying; see below), it is not the extent of the mission field that is the question but the shortness of the time before the end that compels the believer to pray for God to send out workers quickly, before it is too late.

"Behold, I send you out as sheep/lambs in the midst of wolves" (10:3) seems to have been an independent saying that was taken up into the Q discourse at this point. Formally, the saying is a prophetic saying. Both the "behold" *(idou)* and the "I send you out" *(apostellō hymas)* fit the speech forms known to be characteristic of Christian prophets. The emphatic "I" *(egō)*, unnecessary for Greek style and therefore probably dropped from the saying by Luke, represents the intense consciousness of the prophet who speaks authoritatively with the ego of the risen Christ, "I" being relatively rare in the Gospel words of Jesus.

The saying also bears the imprint of motifs of Christian prophetic thought. The reference to sheep among the wolves refers to the situation of the church (the true Israel) among the wolflike Gentiles (whose place is now taken by the persecuting Jews). Thus the Jewish people, who traditionally saw themselves as sheep among the Gentile nations of the world *(Ps. Sol.* 8:28; *2 Esdras* 5:18; *Tanchuma Toledoth* 32b; *1 Enoch* 89:55), are here declared to be no better than Gentiles themselves. A prophetic pronouncement of judgment upon "this generation" is implicit here, just as it was in the preaching of John the Baptist, whose prophetic message of repentance and call to baptism placed the Jews in the situation normally accorded to Gentiles (Q 3:3, 7–8). The saying also implies a thoroughly eschatological orientation, not only in the expected persecutions, which are a mark of the End Time and of prophetic speech, but in that the generation to which the missioners are sent is seen to be radically evil, the purported people of God having become themselves the persecuting wolves. As at Qumran, this evil generation is assumed to be the last.

The saying in 10:4 was originally in Q simply a series of prohibitions of purse, knapsack, sandals, and staff for traveling missioners. Several features of Christian prophecy inhere in the saying. The radical series of prohibitions presupposes an intensely eschatological view of the mission. The missioners *can* "travel light," without even the minimal equipment usually carried by the wandering Cynic-Stoic preachers, because they are freed from the normal cares of providing for themselves and the future by the near approach of the Kingdom. And the missioners *must* not be hindered in their journey by the usual traveler's gear, not even taking time for the usual courtesies of exchanging greetings on the road, because of the eschatological urgency of their message.

The word of the prophets was a radical word, announcing the absolute will of God. The radicality of these mission instructions was noticed by the earliest evangelists or their tradition, each of which came to terms with them in his own way: Mark by modifying them to be less radical, permitting sandals and the staff that Q had forbidden (Mark 6:8–9); Matthew by inserting the consoling word about receiving provisions from people along the way into the list of prohibitions (Matt. 10:10b, removed from its later context in Q), and Luke by indicating that these rigorous demands were only for the special period of Jesus' life but are rescinded for the post-Easter period of the church's mission (Luke 22:35–38). But

the radicality remains and is best seen as an expression of the eschatological faith of the early Christian prophets for whom the End was already
dawning, and as analogous to the radical symbolic actions of Israel's
prophets, in whose tradition the Q prophets self-consciously stood. To
go barefoot on an extended mission without even the simplest means of
provision or protection was a "sign" that accompanied the missioners'
verbal message and gave credibility to it.

An important dimension of the prophetic message of the Q community was its preaching of peace. Palestine-Syria in the middle of the first
century was a tinderbox building up to the explosion of 66–73. The Q
messengers continued Jesus' message of peace and nonresistance. In a
context where militaristic parties flourished that finally resulted in the
Zealot revolution of 66–73, such preaching would invite persecution.[18]
The rejection suffered by the Q community was not only for its religious
convictions understood in narrow doctrinal and ritual ways; the continuing Jesus movement was a "peace movement" as well as a religious
community. It may well be, as Iris Bosold has argued, that the Q messengers refused to give the customary greeting shalom/peace because its
conventional use had emptied it of religious and political meaning (cf.
10:4b).[19] This makes all the more pointed the use of the peace formula
when it is pronounced upon a household (10:5). Those who respond to
the Q messengers are called "sons of peace," which in the Semitic idiom
means a person for whom peace is appropriate, or even "member of the
peace movement." The overtones of the eschatological peace preached
by the Q prophets is inherent in the formula, but the political dimensions
are not absent. The Q community preached as its first command "love
your enemies" (6:27) and told stories in which Roman soldiers came off
looking better than anyone in Israel (7:1–9). Such preaching would not
have endeared them to their patriotic and militaristic neighbors. Here is
a prophetic, eschatological community thoroughly embroiled in the political struggle of its day. Its apocalypticism did not cause it to withdraw into
other-worldliness. The eschatological vision of peace provided a theological framework for concrete political action and courage to withstand the
prevailing stream.

The sayings in 10:9–11 too are permeated with early Christian eschatology. The nearness of the Kingdom explicitly proclaimed in 10:9,
11, as the substance of the missioners' message, the urgency implicit in
the directions in 10:10–11, the reference to "that day" (Luke 10:12) or
"day of judgment" (Matt. 10:15) as the validating horizon within which

---

18 This interpretation of Q has been argued especially by Paul Hoffmann, *Studien zur
Theologie der Logienquelle.*

19 Iris Bosold, *Pacifismus und prophetische Provokation: Das Grussverbot Lk 10, 4b und sein
historischer Kontext.*

the declaration is made, the pronouncement of blessing and curse that already anticipates and makes present the pronouncement of the final judge—all indicate that the speaker is imbued with the message of the early Christian prophets. The rejection anticipated for God's messengers (10:6, 10–12) is also a part of the eschatological scenario for the prophets of the last generation.

Miracles accompany the charismatic word (10:9) and further relate this passage to Christian prophecy. The dramatic act of shaking the dust of unreceptive cities from the feet of the missioners is reminiscent of the symbolic acts of the Old Testament prophets and resembles the description of the dramatic symbolism of the Christian prophet Agabus (Acts 21:10–11). This is more than the customary shaking of the dust off the feet when the Palestinian Jew returned to the sacred land, to prohibit the holy land from being profaned with soil from pagan countries. Here, the customary ritual has become a sign against the cities of Israel itself. As in 10:3, in this eschatological reversal of roles Israel is assigned the role usually reserved for Gentiles because all evil has been summed up in this "last generation." Thus not only the symbolic act but the judgmental message embodied in it is of prophetic character.

The woes pronounced on the Galilean cities of Bethsaida, Chorazin, and Capernaum (10:13–15) have often been considered to be of prophetic origin. That they are independent of their present contexts is clear from their different settings in Matthew and Luke and the inappropriateness of pronouncements against Galilean cities delivered as part of a commissioning address to the disciples. And that they did not originate in the lifetime of Jesus is indicated by the facts that they look back on the ministry of Jesus as a whole and regard miracle as a sufficient basis for faith. Furthermore, they refer to two cities that seem to have played no role in the life of Jesus as we otherwise know it.

The sayings correspond to the profile of prophetic speech both formally and materially. The antithetic parallelism and pronouncement of woe are properly regarded as prophetic forms; the "I say to you" of Matthew, if original, is also prophetic. The oracle announces in advance the verdict of the judge of the Last Day, which functions as an implicit call to repentance, in the manner of the Christian prophets. The emphatic positive valuation of miracles, the allusive use of Old Testament words to express the message of the present (Isa. 14:13), and the eschatological reversal of roles, in which an oracle directed against the king of Babylon is now directed against Israel are all characteristics of Christian prophecy. It thus seems that these words originated in an early Christian prophetic group whose mission to these Galilean towns had been rebuffed.

Since their offer of salvation to these towns was seen as part of the eschatological event itself, and since this offer had been rejected, the prophets respond with the pronouncement of eschatological doom, spoken from the mouth of the final judge through these prophets. Just as the pronouncements of blessing are not exhortations but contain an implied imperative, so the pronouncements of woe do not have the form of appeals to repent but still *function* as such; they are not simply vindictive responses of wounded pride but stand in the tradition of Old Testament prophetic preaching in this regard (e.g., Amos 6:1–8).

The mission charge exhibits other formal indications of prophetic speech such as the "Amen, I say to you" formula of 10:12, but even more than the detailed particulars of prophetic speech, the form of the whole argues for the prophetic origin of these sayings: the speaker speaks for God/Jesus/Spirit, so that to accept the words of the speaker is to be encountered directly by the powerful word of God, and to reject the words of the speaker is to reject God/Jesus/Spirit. The self-consciousness of the concluding word in 10:16 is the same as in Luke Q 12:10 (= Mark 3:28–29), which is also of prophetic origin. Although there may have been a pre-Easter original form in which Jesus asserted that to hear him was to hear God, which would have been an authentic expression of Jesus' own prophetic self-consciousness, the present form, in which Jesus himself is the primary sender, is properly regarded as a post-Easter (re-?) formulation of the church.

The speaker is the risen Jesus, who has the definitive place in the revelatory "chain of command" second only to God (cf. Rev. 1:1–2). Even as the exalted one, Jesus is still the "sent one," who now sends forth his own missioners to speak his word. The speaker is to declare the message in the first person with the "I" of the exalted Lord, not reporting what Jesus once said but speaking the word of the Lord in the first person in the present, so that the hearer is addressed by the risen Jesus, who speaks on behalf of God. The latter part of the saying, in which Jesus is the "sent one" from God, must be understood in prophetic terms, and this is also the case in the first part of the saying, in which Jesus now stands in the place of the ultimate sending deity, sending forth his own prophets.

This community does indeed look back to Jesus, who was once sent by the Father, and forward to the return of Jesus as the Son of man. But the present is not a time of passive waiting. Jesus continues to speak to the community in the words of Christian prophets, who preserve the traditional words of Jesus and continue to declare them as the contemporary word of the Lord. Thus even the elements of this speech that may have had a pre-Easter or nonprophetic post-Easter origin are now heard as the present word of the exalted Lord who continues to send out messengers. Some of these messengers may themselves have been prophets but not necessarily all of them. The mission is seen from a prophetic point of view, but this is because the speaker is a prophet. In view of the frequent assertion that early Christian prophets were "wandering," it should be noted here that it is those who are addressed who "wander," not necessarily the prophet-speaker of this mission charge.

Q 10:21–22: THE RISEN LORD AS REVEALER

The original form of Luke 10:21 is here taken to be an authentic saying of Jesus. Luke 10:22 is a post-Easter expansion of this original saying of Jesus made by a Christian prophet. The secondary nature of the saying is readily apparent: Jesus speaks of himself absolutely and uniquely as the "Son," a manifestly post-Easter Christology. He claims to possess a knowledge of God that others may possess only by his mediation. The saying itself is a different form from the saying to which it is joined (10:21 is a thanksgiving prayer, addressed to God; 10:22 is a revelatory declaration addressed to human beings). The union of the two sayings is secondary but not arbitrary; nor is it a matter simply of association by catchwords ("revealed," v. 21 and "reveal," v. 22). The second saying presupposes the first and is something of an interpretation of it, representing it in a different light.

The prophetic self-consciousness is manifest in the way the saying presupposes a revelatory "chain" as in Revelation 1:1–3. The Father gives the revelation to the Son, who is the exclusive mediator of revelation to the community. The understanding of the "Son" in this passage is not the content of the revelation but the presupposition of it, that is, the Son is a constituent part of the revelatory configuration presupposed by Christian prophets. The "Spirit" or "angel" was also sometimes inserted as a link in this revelatory chain, as in Revelation 1:1–3 and Matthew 28:18–20, neither of which should be explained in terms of trinitarian speculation but in terms of the prophetic context from which they emerged. The mutual and exclusive knowledge of the "Father" and the "Son" should thus no longer be explained as related to Hellenistic mysticism or the adaptation of a Jewish proverb. The saying is better understood as Christian prophecy. The wisdom motifs inherent in the saying, where the role of wisdom (Sophia) as the mediator of revelation is played by the exalted divine figure (not the earthly Jesus), are also an indication of the prophetic character of this saying; for Christian prophecy, like apocalyptic generally, included a significant admixture of wisdom motifs and materials.

Several recent interpreters of Q are agreed that the saying claims to reveal the eschatological significance of the events that have recently transpired and are presently transpiring in the Q community: the advent and exaltation of Jesus, the sending of the Q missioners (some of whom were prophets, the reappearance of prophecy being understood eschatologically). Here as elsewhere prophecy functions as interpreter of events.

This is the meaning to the Q community of the mysterious "these things" of verse 21. This salvation-historical, eschatological kind of insight into the meaning of history (rather than gnostic or mystic "knowledge") is what is meant by the key verb ("know"). The combined sayings have become a veritable manifesto of Christian prophecy, affirming that revelation continues as the risen Jesus (understood in terms of both the Son of man and the wisdom traditions) interprets through his messengers the meaning of the history they are experiencing and have experienced. The worship setting that the saying presupposes is appropriate to Christian prophecy as seen in our reconstruction.

The often-noticed similarities of 10:21–22 to the Johannine sayings of Jesus and to 1 Corinthians 2:6–16 should be explained not in terms of a common gnosticizing or Hellenistic-mystical approach but in terms of their common denominator, Christian prophecy. The clearest formal parallel in the literature of the first century is found in our prime example of Christian prophecy (Rev. 11:17–18). It is thus no surprise that Luke recognizes the prophetic nature of the saying, introducing it with the same phrases ("Holy Spirit," "rejoiced") with which he introduces prophetic speech in 1:14–15, 47.

Q 10:23–24: A BLESSING ON THOSE WHO RECEIVE ESCHATOLOGICAL REVELATION

This isolated saying, placed by Matthew and Luke independently in their respective contexts, has been regarded as an authentic saying of Jesus by even the most skeptical critics. Yet the saying, brief as it is, does exhibit several features of Christian prophecy: the form of a pronouncement of blessing, the "[amen], I say to you" formula, the eschatological reversal in which the last generation obtains the privileges of the people of God from which the traditional chosen people are excluded. These features are also appropriate to the prophet Jesus, and there is no good evidence for denying the saying to him. It is better to see this as a traditional saying now re-presented as a saying of the exalted Lord in the Q community. In the context of the Q community, the new things "seen" and "heard" would not be only the eschatological realities in general, which are seen to be breaking into the present in the working of miracles and gift of the Spirit, but would refer to the new revelations in particular, which the Q prophets "see" and "hear." Here is another example of how a pre-Easter saying of Jesus would be heard in the early Christian prophetic community as a saying of the exalted Lord addressing the post-Easter situation.

Q 11:14–23: THE CHARGE OF COLLUSION
WITH BEELZEBUL

This complex of Q sayings, some of which may go back to the historical Jesus, has no sayings that can be directly linked with Christian prophets, but the situation here reflected was likely typical of the situation in which Christian prophets frequently found themselves. Their speaking and acting was obviously in the power of *some* spirit. Their opponents explained the phenomena as the working of demonic spirits. Christian prophets claimed that the eschatological Holy Spirit had come upon them. Thus the prophetic saying concerning blasphemy against the Spirit (Q 12:10 below) was appropriately later inserted into this context by Mark or the pre-Markan tradition (cf. Mark 3:22–29) and is an additional pointer that the complex in Q 11:14–23 was shaped in a prophetic context.

Q 11:29–32: THE SIGN OF JONAH

The original form of 11:29a, the absolute refusal to give a validating sign, and the twin sayings of 11:31–32 are independent logia that derive from Jesus himself. The saying regarding the sign of Jonah that binds the two units together is widely accepted as a secondary development and is best understood as the saying of a Christian prophet. The two original sayings of Jesus (Luke 11:29a par., and 11:31–32 par.), now fused into a single sayings unit by the prophetic addition of 11:29b–30, were then re-presented as in toto the word of the exalted Son of man to the situation of the Q community.

Q 11:39–52: AGAINST THE PHARISEES

The historical Jesus spoke against some forms of Pharisaic piety, so that some of his words may underlie, or be contained in, the series of Q oracles against the Pharisees. But the present forms of the discourse as it appears in both Matthew and Luke, and as it appeared in Q, represent a group that has marked itself off (or been marked off) completely from Pharisaic Judaism as such, against which it launches indiscriminate broadsides. This was not the situation for Jesus and his disciples but was the case for some streams of early Christianity. The present forms of this speech derive from one such stream, the Q community.

The present settings of this discourse are altogether the work of the evangelists. Matthew (23:1–39) has combined these oracles with materials from his own tradition and inserted them into the life-of-Jesus framework provided by Jesus' warnings against the scribes in Mark 12:38–40. Less happily, Luke has incorporated the woes into the table talk at the house of a Pharisee, apparently in Samaria (cf. 9:52; 17:11). In Q the speech appeared entirely without a narrative framework, as a series of seven woes followed by an oracle of doom. The original order of these woes in Q has been jumbled in the tradition and by the editing of both Matthew and Luke, and can no longer be recovered. It appears, however, that Matthew has preserved the general pattern of Q, which consisted of seven woes, with the climactic seventh woe concerning the treatment of prophets having been elaborated by further prophetic material, an oracle of doom. The Lukan form of two groups of three woes, separated by a little dialogue, with the initial woe rewritten as a transitional piece, can then be seen as his effort to accommodate an inappropriate series of oracles to a dinner party setting.

The more clearly the Q form of the speech becomes visible, the more closely it is seen to be related to early Christian prophets. The woe form itself is a prophetic form, and the sevenfold pronouncement of woe is characteristic of the Christian prophecy of the Apocalypse.

The series of oracles throughout presupposes this eschatological orientation of early Christian prophecy. The threat against "this [last] generation" (vs. 50, 51) with which the series ends makes explicit the eschatological tone of the whole. The prophetic-eschatological perspective from which the woes are spoken is manifest in the sharpening of the demands of the Torah as in 11:39–40, for the near advent of the eschaton brings with it both the demand to keep the total intent of the law and the ability to do so, since this-worldly considerations no longer count. The criticisms of Pharisaic piety here found are thus analogous to those of the Zealots and Qumran covenanters, both of which were eschatological communities with prophets in their ranks. The latter-day prophetic revelation has made it clear to the community that the eschatological reversal of roles has occurred: the Pharisees, claiming to be the leaders of pseudo-Israel, are in fact the false leaders of Israel. It is rather the rejected and persecuted Q community that is the eschatological Israel, whose prophets pronounce judgments upon purported Israel, very much as the prophet of Revelation condemns those who "say they are Jews and are not" (Rev. 2:9; 3:9). No attempt is made at converting the Pharisees; it is eschatologically "too late" for that, as the proleptic verdict of condemnation of the judge of the Last Day is already pronounced by the risen Lord's prophetic spokespersons. Such pronouncements could have been made only by those convinced of their charismatic authorization to speak for the Lord himself. That the supposed guardians of the purity of Israel are themselves hidden contaminators of Israel's purity, corrupting the unsuspecting, is not the carping grumbling of those who resent the Pharisaic piety or are repelled by it, but the pronouncement of those who claim a divinely given ability to see beneath the surface of things, to interpret the present as it really is. The basis for such authoritative speaking is most likely the revelation claimed by the prophetic band in the Q community.

The prophetic nature of this series of woes becomes explicit in the climactic pronouncement, which deals with the relation of the Pharisees to prophets. Just as the final beatitude (Luke 6:22 par.), which deals with prophets, is the most extensive, so also here. As in the beatitudes, the conviction of the Q community that true prophets must suffer comes to expression here. The Pharisees attempt to disavow the deeds of their ancestors, who killed the prophets of Israel, by building memorial tombs for them, but in fact they show that they are no better than their fathers; for they honor only the prophets of the past and, like their fathers, reject the prophets of the present (11:47–48). Here is the expression of a continuing conflict between the Pharisaic leaders of the Palestinian synagogues and the prophets of the Q community. This is echoed in the declaration of 11:52 par.: a dispute has been raging concerning who has the authority to open the Kingdom to people. The Pharisees claim this authority of the "keys" by insisting on keeping the Law, oral and written. The Christian prophets claim this authority of the "keys" by proclaiming Jesus as the coming Son of man, the keeping of whose word will be the criterion of acceptance on the Last Day. The prophets were without political and religious power and received the worst of this conflict, interpreting their rejection in terms of that persecution which is always the mark of the true prophet.

In this regard, what are we to make of the unique formula that introduces this saying, "Therefore also the wisdom of God said" (v. 49)? This introduction has sometimes been taken to mean that the saying was taken from a lost wisdom book from which Jesus is pictured as quoting by Q. The theory that a wisdom book is here quoted has not, however, found general support. We do not seem to have a general theologoumenon that is here taken up by either Jesus or the prophets, but a saying the content of which suggests it first came into being among Christian prophets. This might lead us to ask whether the difficult introductory formula itself is an expression of the prophetic form of speech. Lührmann has observed that "the wisdom of God said" is reminiscent of the prophetic formula "thus says the Lord."[20] The analogy with this formula would also explain the presence of the aorist "said" in the midst of the present-tense address. As an alternative possibility to the view that a Christian prophet here mediates the word of the risen Jesus by quoting a lost wisdom-apocalypse, serious consideration should be given to the view that the Q prophet is here speaking directly for the risen Jesus, who is identified with

---

20 *Die Redaktion der Logienquelle,* 46. Cf. also Müller, *Prophetie und Predigt,* 177.

preexistent Wisdom. Suggs has shown convincingly that the Q community did not identify the *earthly* Jesus as the incarnation of Wisdom but saw Jesus as a messenger of Wisdom.[21] The earthly Jesus was one of a series of Wisdom's messengers, preceded by the Hebrew prophets and by John the Baptist, and followed by the Q prophets themselves. Jesus was thus not the last messenger, chronologically speaking, but he was the decisive messenger.

The exalted Jesus is also interpreted by the Q community in terms of the figure of Wisdom. The Q community used both the figure of the Son of man and the figure of Wisdom to interpret the exaltation of Jesus, but here the Wisdom image dominates. What is implied in other Q sayings (e.g., 10:22) becomes explicit here: the exalted Jesus is the preexistent Wisdom of God (cf. 1 Cor. 1:30), who foresaw the sweep of history in which she/he would send her/his prophets, who would be rejected in all generations, including this present final one. "Wisdom of God" functions in the same role in the revelatory chain characteristic of prophetic thinking as "Son" (of God) in 10:22 (cf. Rev. 1:1–3) and the Paraclete in the Fourth Gospel.

The revelatory event expressed in this oracle would then be as follows: at the climax of the series of woes, the Christian prophet delivers to the community the revelation of the ancient decrees of heavenly Wisdom, now identified with the exalted Jesus, which decreed the sending of prophets throughout the generations until their repeated rejection resulted in the culmination of guilt in the final generation, which has now arrived. Not only does this interpretation of the exalted Jesus in terms of personified Wisdom mesh with the other wisdom motifs sprinkled throughout the woe pronouncements, the saying is somewhat related to apocalyptic modes of thought in that both have a kind of retrojection into the past of a speaker who "predicts" what has actually already occurred in the author's present. Apocalyptic and wisdom are fused in this saying, which, as we have seen, is characteristic of Christian prophecy.

Q 12:2–12: EXHORTATION TO FEARLESS CONFESSION

This section of Q is a complex unit with a complicated history in the tradition that can be recovered only partially. There were at least five originally independent units: verses 2–3, 4–7, 8–9, 10, 11–12, some of which may themselves be composite. Within the Q community these sayings seem to have been fused into one speech complex. Apart from the prophetic characteristics of the individual sayings to be examined

---

21 *Wisdom, Christology, and Law in Matthew's Gospel.*

below, the sayings cluster as a whole is permeated with the themes of near-expectation of the End, persecution by Jewish opponents, and the Christian's conduct in this eschatological situation—all of which are appropriate to Christian prophets. It is not unexpected that this group of sayings has been regarded en bloc and in each of its parts as sayings of the risen Jesus through church prophets. The extent to which this general impression is true can only be tested in the examination of the individual sayings.

Q 12:2–3: Revelation of Hidden Secrets

This pair of sayings represents a prophetic transformation of a secular proverb: "Don't tell secrets at all unless you want them to become public." Prophecy turns the insight of secular wisdom into its opposite. Eschatologically, it is demanded to do just what otherwise would be avoided. The neatly structured form is in fact appropriate to a prophetic figure, as are the themes of the eschatological reversal and the revelation of the secrets of human hearts. However, there is nothing that clearly points to a post-Easter setting, nor is there sufficient evidence to compel a Christian prophetic origin for the sayings, so in their original form they may have been part of the authentic teaching of Jesus. As taken up by the Q community in conjunction with the other prophetic words of this sayings cluster, however, the sayings would be a word of prophetic assurance ("upbuilding and encouragement and consolation," 1 Cor. 14:3) to the Q community that the hardly noticed beginnings of its proclamation will be revealed to the whole of Israel and the world because God himself will bring it about (divine passives "be revealed, be made known").

Q 12:4–7: Fear God, Not Human Beings

Among the several points of contact with early Christian prophecy is Jesus addressing his disciples as "friends," which might have the prophetic overtones that this world had in the Johannine community (John 15:14–15). It is the risen Jesus identified with heavenly Wisdom who addresses his prophetic servants as friends, just as divine Wisdom makes her followers "friends of God and prophets" (Wisd. Sol. 7:27). The encouragement to fearless confession has a near parallel in the prophetic promise of Revelation 2:10. The words concerning God's care for sparrows and numbering the hairs of our heads represent prophetic exhortation with the motifs of persecution and eschatological judgment in the background, not a romanticist view of nature. The words are prophetic declarations, but it is not clear whether they originated with the prophet Jesus of Nazareth or among his prophetic followers in the church. Some of the characteristics of church prophets may have been impressed on the sayings secondarily in the course of the tradition process. Even if the sayings, or some elements from them, derive from Jesus himself, these words would be heard in the Q community as the address of the exalted Jesus to the current situation of the threatened Q community.

Q 12:8–9: The Ultimate Consequences of Confessing and Denying the Son of Man

This saying also seems to make a fundamental distinction between the Jesus who speaks and the Son of man who is to come, a distinction that the post-Easter church would not have originated. Thus some of the most skeptical scholars have regarded this as an authentic saying of Jesus, and others have regarded a more primitive form of the saying as probably deriving from Jesus. It seems clear that if Jesus had not made declarations that distinguished between himself and the coming Son of man, this distinction would not have originated in the church after Easter. There must have been stereotyped Son of man sayings that made this distinction circulating in the church, which the church did not create. The pre-Easter Jesus did apparently assert that the coming Son of man would vindicate those who were committed to him and his ministry. But such a view of the teaching of the historical Jesus is no guarantee that any particular saying is an authentic saying, nor is the evident antiquity and Aramaic background. In the case of this saying, the situation presupposed, in which the issue is confessing and denying Jesus, centered on the person of Jesus, indicates a church formulation. The disciples' situation of having to decide whether to confess or deny Jesus, in such a way that the verdict they would hear in the Last Judgment depended on their decision, is a situation that simply did not arise prior to the early Christian church's conflicts with Judaism in Palestine.

Considered by itself, the saying has a certain oracular quality appropriate to Christian prophets. Analysis of the saying reveals several points of contact with our profile of Christian prophecy. As we shall see, the promulgation of Son of man sayings in the name of the risen Jesus was the work of Christian prophets. But particularly the way in which "Son of man" functions in this saying suggests a prophetic background: the Son of man is an advocate before the heavenly court,[22] as well as functioning as judge. The indications of prophetic speech in this logion would seem to be confirmed by the presence of a very similar saying in the Apocalypse (3:5). Even if the prophet-author of Revelation has taken up a saying from the Gospel tradition and re-presented it as a saying of the exalted Lord, it is significant that it was *this* saying, so in accord with Christian prophecy, that he chose.

---

22 On the role of the Paraclete in the Fourth Gospel and its relation to Christian prophecy, see chapter 4 above.

As is the case with the other Son of man sayings in Q, the Son of man in this saying is the exalted Son of man who will shortly come as judge. But the "I" that speaks is also that of the exalted Jesus as he speaks through the prophets. For the community that created this saying, there was no history-of-salvation distinction between the "I" of the speaker and the Son of man. To confess faith in the risen Jesus who speaks through his prophets is to be acknowledged by the Son of man when he comes.

Q 12:10: The Ultimate Consequences
of Confessing and Denying
the Son of Man

The saying is extant in several variations (Mark 3:28–29; Luke 12:10; Matt. 12:31, 32; *Didache* 11.7, *Gospel of Thomas* 44; *Gospel of Bartholomew* 5.2), but these are all variations of the two basic forms, the Markan form and the Q form. Of these, the Markan form is the more primitive.[23] The saying is an originally independent oracle that rests uncomfortably in all its present contexts. It exalts the Spirit in a way completely uncharacteristic of the historical Jesus. References to the Spirit are amazingly scarce in the Gospel tradition and practically absent from the tradition of Jesus' words. Mark 3:29/Luke 12:10/Matthew 12:32 is the only saying in the Synoptic Gospels in which Jesus refers to himself as the bearer of the Spirit. The earliest church, on the other hand, knew itself possessed of the Holy Spirit with which Jesus was identified as the risen Lord.

The limitation of forgiveness pronounced so arbitrarily also makes the saying difficult to regard as authentic. Not only does the logion limit the divine forgiveness—in itself very inappropriate to Jesus, for whom the pronouncement of judgment rather than the limitation of forgiveness would seem more fitting—but the limitation is imposed for dogmatic reasons, that is, it is pronounced against those who are guilty of theological, and not just moral, error. The saying is easily intelligible as the answer to a charge that was raised against the early Christian community in its Jewish environment, a charge that not only denied that the power impelling the Christian movement was from God but described it in some way blasphemous to the Christian community: that it was from Satan or some such. The saying reflects the consciousness of the failure of the Q community's mission to the Jews and pronounces prophetic judgment on those who had rejected this mission. A prophetic group, claiming by its very existence to have the Spirit, has run foul of those Jews who held that the Spirit (of prophecy) ceased with Ezra or Malachi. They have provoked their derision and have themselves been provoked to utter, in the name of the exalted Lord, just the rejoinder found in this saying.

---

23 I have traced the trajectory of this saying in "The Unforgivable Sin Logion Mark 3:28–29/Matt. 12:31–32/Luke 12:10: Formal Analysis and History of the Tradition."

A part of this earliest pre-Markan saying may go back to Jesus himself: the initial declaration, staggering in its radicality, that all sins shall be forgiven to people, however much they may blaspheme. It is not difficult to imagine Jesus making such an announcement since several independent streams of tradition clearly portray him as announcing forgiveness even to those considered blasphemous by the pious (Mark 2:5–10; Matt. 11:19/Luke 7:35; John 7:53–8:11; Luke 7:47–49; 15:1–32). This unconditional declaration of universal forgiveness might be a pre-Easter kernel that was taken up by an early Christian prophet and expanded into the following chiastic form, which is the ancestor of both the Markan and Q forms of the saying:

> All things shall be forgiven to the sons of men
> However much they blaspheme
> Whoever may blaspheme against the Holy Spirit
> Has no forgiveness but is guilty of eternal sin.

Recognizing that the saying originated as the oracle of a Christian prophet clarifies an exegetical problem that has long burdened commentators. The reason the sinner has no forgiveness forever but is guilty of "eternal sin" is not that he or she has committed a sin that is beyond the scope of God's forgiveness or has entered into a state in which repentance, and therefore forgiveness, is impossible. Rather, the ultimate character of the sin derives from the fact that the judgment is pronounced in an ultimate situation from which there is no appeal. Christian prophets proleptically pronounce the verdict of the eschatological Judge in the Last Day. In this respect the prophetic logion is like the pronouncement in Revelation 22:11, "Let the evildoer still do evil, and the filthy still be filthy, and the righteous still do right, and the holy still be holy." There too it is not a matter of the sinner having entered into a state in which he or she can do no other, but the affirmation is surrounded by the words "the time is near" and "behold, I am coming soon," thus it is a matter of prophetic eschatology.

This prophetic saying was taken up by the Q community and re-formed to speak to its situation. Since the Q form of the saying is also in the form of a sentence of holy law, preserving the eschatological fervor of the original saying while modifying the form from ABB^1A^1 to ABA^1B^1, and since the saying has now become a Son of man saying, this reformulation was probably done by a prophet of the Q community, who takes up this traditional prophetic saying and re-presents it as the relevant word of the exalted Lord for the present moment. If the saying was still in circulation in Aramaic, the Q prophet may have understood the *bar nasha* of the first line—rendered "to the sons of men" in the oldest Greek form—as "according to the Son of man."

A particular problem is in view as the Q prophet deals with this text:

that some have "spoken against the Son of man." The Q prophet wishes to declare that this is a forgivable offense—only speaking against the Holy Spirit is unforgivable. The second half of the saying has lost its cutting edge and has now become a theologoumenon, from which conclusions may now be drawn. The prophet's conclusion, the new "sentence of holy law" that he is promulgating in the name of the risen Lord, is found in the reformulated first half of the saying, which now receives the emphasis: speaking against the Son of man *can* be forgiven.

The popular understanding of this emphasis has been that in the Q community a kind of history-of-salvation consciousness has developed that presupposes two periods: the pre-Easter incognito lowliness of the Son of man and the post-Easter period of the Spirit. The "speaking against the Son of man" is thus often supposed to refer to those who rejected the ministry of the pre-Easter Jesus and who, this logion declares, can now be forgiven.

An alternative understanding has been that the saying is a ruling on those Christians who, under duress from non-Christian Jews, have (temporarily) renounced their faith in the Son of man: they can in fact be forgiven. Since "Son of man" in Q rarely if ever refers to the lowly historical Jesus but usually refers to the apocalyptic, exalted, and coming Son of man, this latter interpretation is preferable to the former one.

But an even better interpretation has been proposed by Richard Edwards, who correctly perceives that the saying is entirely an eschatological statement, not looking back at the past history of Jesus but forward to the imminent coming of the Son of man and outward to the mission, the eschatological harvest.[24] In the mission of the Q community to the Jewish population of Palestine-Syria, forgiveness is announced not only to those who rejected the earthly Jesus but even to those who have reviled Jesus, the exalted Son of man who is soon to come as judge. But those who reject this last offer of forgiveness mediated through the Spirit-inspired Q prophets and revile them and it—for such there is no forgiveness, ever. The presupposition of the prophetic origin and reinterpretation of the saying thus seems to offer the most satisfactory explanation at every point in its trajectory. I have given detailed evidence elsewhere that the saying is from a Christian prophet.[25]

Q 12:11–12: Speaking by the Power of the Spirit

This too is an originally independent saying that has found its way into the pre-Markan apocalypse (Mark 13:11), at which point Luke uses it

---

24 "Christian Prophecy and the Q Tradition," in *SBL 1976 Seminar Papers*.
25 "How May We Recognize Oracles of Christian Prophets in the Synoptic Tradition? Mark 3:28–29 as a Test Case"; *Sayings of the Risen Jesus*, 159–164.

again in modified form (21:14–15). The Johannine community seems to have recoined it as one of the Paraclete-prophet sayings in John 14:26. The Johannine context is especially revealing, for it is precisely the Paraclete function that is emphasized in the saying as it circulated in the Q community. The saying in the Q community seems to have been the promise of the risen Lord through a Christian prophet that the prophetic charism, which was usually only associated with certain persons in the community and functioned primarily in worship, would come upon any member of the community who needed it in the hour of trial.

In conclusion, the speech complex in Q 12:2–12 has some sayings that probably originated as Christian prophecy, perhaps with a minimum of pre-Easter words of Jesus as their core (12:8–9, 10, 11–12), which were combined by the Q community with other sayings of Jesus from the tradition (12:1–3, 4–7), some of which may have originated with the historical Jesus. But these sayings from the tradition were taken up, re-presented, and sometimes reformulated in the forms of Christian prophetic speech as the message of the exalted Lord to the present of the Q community, in immediate and undifferentiated union with sayings from Christian prophets. Rather than sayings of the risen Jesus being placed in the mouth of the historical Jesus by the Q community, it appears in this section that the tendency was the other way: traditional, even pre-Easter sayings of Jesus are claimed for the risen Lord.

Q 12:22–34: PROPHETIC WISDOM

This extensive section seems to be a redactional unit in Q. It has generally been regarded as wisdom material, containing some authentic sayings of Jesus, but recently Schulz has argued that the whole is "clearly a prophetic speech of admonition."[26] He bases this judgment on the prophetic introductory formulae "Therefore I say to you" (12:22), "who among you" (12:25), and "But I say to you" (12:27), supposing that in Q there was also an "I say to you" formula in verse 33, and on the eschatological presupposition of the whole unit, of which the poverty motif in verses 33–34 is a part. While it is true enough that prophecy did take up wisdom materials, eschatologize them, and incorporate them into its oracles, this is no ground for labeling all the wisdom materials in the Gospel tradition as prophetic without further evidence. In this case, the evidence seems to be insufficient. The traditional critical view is here better. We should continue to regard this material as traditional wisdom teaching, some of which goes back to Jesus himself. But the value of Schulz's argument is that he does enable us to hear these sayings with the ears of the Q

---

26 Schulz, *Q: Die Spruchquelle*, 153; cf. 143–145.

community: the risen Lord speaks words of assurance and command to this eschatological community that is attempting to put into practice the radical life of trust in its situation over against its Jewish environment. Schulz is correct that it is eschatological radicalism (not nature mysticism, interim ethic, or the romanticizing of poverty) that comes to expression here. The prophetic introductory formulae were probably added to the traditional sayings by the Q prophets as they re-presented the tradition as the word of the risen Lord. But there is no indication that we have material of prophetic *origin* in these sayings.

Q 12:51–56: CONFESSION OF JESUS
CAUSES DIVISION

Of this Q section, only verses 52–53 are possibly secondary. They are often so regarded on the basis of their representing a common apocalyptic topos and reflecting the situation of the post-Easter Palestinian church. There are a few indications that the expansion of the original saying of Jesus was made by a Christian prophet but hardly enough evidence to make a firm decision regarding the prophetic origin of verses 52–56. It seems to be clear, however, that in the Q community, this entire complex of verses, 51–56, was proclaimed and heard as the present address of the exalted Son of man to his distressed community. Even the difficult verse 56, though ambiguous in Jesus' situation, is clear in the Q community. The persecution of the Q community and the radical events happening in it (persecution, division of families) are the signs of the times. To understand them eschatologically, as the Q community did with the interpretation of its prophets, is to experience them as signs of hope and salvation; to be blind to them is to receive judgment.

Q 12:57–59: PREPARE FOR THE COMING JUDGMENT

There is nothing here to call into question the traditional view that the original saying was from Jesus. The sage advice not to go to court with a hopeless case has been transmuted by the eschatology presupposed into a warning to come to terms with the accuser before the imminent Last Day, but this eschatology is as appropriate to Jesus' situation as it is to that of the Q community. Also, the prophetic formula "(amen) I say to you" could derive from the original saying in Jesus' ministry. But even if from the pre-Easter Jesus, the saying would be heard in the Q community in the light of *its* expectation of the near End, as a word of the exalted Jesus speaking directly to its situation. Also, the "(amen) I say to you" could be the secondary addition of a prophet to the original saying, but there is no way to determine this in a saying that itself originated from Jesus. Here we have an excellent example of a probably authentic saying of the pre-Easter Jesus that was prophetically re-presented in the Q community as the word of the exalted Lord. Such sayings illustrate the fluidity between prophetic and nonprophetic sayings. Even such nonprophetic and undoubtedly authentic sayings as the Parables of the Mustard Seed and the Leaven (Luke 13:18–21 par.) could be proclaimed and heard in the Q community as the direct expression of its own theology, as Schulz's instructive discussion has shown.

Q 13:23–30: WHAT WILL COUNT IN THE LAST JUDGMENT

The unit in its present form contains three independent sayings, each of which has been assigned to Christian prophecy by various scholars. The best candidate for prophetic origin is the saying in 13:28–29. Käsemann and Zeller have labeled the saying as Christian prophecy, and Schulz has supported their assertions with some evidence:[27] the "I say to you" formula, the proleptic eschatology inherent to the saying, and its radicality, which calls for some charismatic authority as the presupposition of its emergence, since no ordinary teacher or apocalyptist would presume to utter it. Yet even this saying manifests no compelling evidence of a post-Easter origin, and since it has no reference to the person of Jesus, it may well be authentic. I fail to find convincing evidence that any of the sayings in this group originated as oracles of Christian prophets, but the considerations of the scholars mentioned above, especially Schulz, show how traditional materials did tend to take on prophetic features in the Q community and how fluid the line was in this community between traditional sayings of Jesus and the contemporary address of the risen Lord.

Q 13:34–35: THE LAMENT OVER JERUSALEM

The speaker in this saying must be regarded as a transcendent being who, by sending prophets through the generations, has attempted without success to bring Jerusalem within the true people of God—for this is the meaning of the allusion to bringing Jerusalem "under her wings." In this saying, the historical Jesus is one of the prophets sent by the transcendent Wisdom, not the sender of them, so it is fruitless to attempt to find a setting for it in the life of Jesus. The post-Easter, churchly origin of the saying is clear.

The saying belongs generally to the class of prophetic judgment pronouncements. Steck, who does not affirm the Christian prophetic

---

27 Käsemann, *New Testament Questions,* 100; Dieter Zeller, "Das Logion Mt. 8.11f/Luke 13:28f und das Motif der 'Völkerwallfahrt' "; Schulz, *Q: Die Spruchquelle,* 327–328.

origin of the saying, lists seven formally prophetic traits that place this saying in the tradition of the Old Testament prophets:[28] introductory "behold" or "lo" (*idou; hinneh*), the combination reproach/threat, the repeated naming of the addressees, the characteristic naming of the addressees with participles describing their rebellious conduct, the contrast motif, the metaphorical comparison, and the repetition of the introductory formula near the end of the oracle. Of these, "behold" and "I say to you" are particularly associated with Christian prophets. Formally, the saying is a prophetic oracle.

Themes associated with, or even peculiar to, the Christian prophets permeate the saying. The characteristic eschatology of Christian prophetism provides the presupposition of the declaration: the hearers are addressed as the last generation, in whom guilt is summed up, and who are set over against the prophetic speaker as "this generation," even though this expression is not used. The eschatological judgment is already spoken and is already effective: "Your house is forsaken [by God]." As in other prophetic sayings, the sentence of the judge of the Last Day is proleptically present.

Whether this is a hopeless sentence or one that still holds open the door of repentance depends in part on how one understands the concluding "Blessed is the one who comes in the name of the Lord." This has traditionally been understood in relation to the return of Jesus as the Son of man, so that the meaning is supposed to be "You will not see me [the earthly Jesus] until, at the eschaton, you will say: 'Blessed is the one who comes in the name of the Lord'—but then it will be too late." This is the natural explanation if in fact what we have here is a bit of wisdom tradition artificially placed in the mouth of the pre-Easter Jesus by the church. In favor of it would be the formula "the one who comes" (RSV "he who comes"; cf. "the Coming One" as messianic title, Q 7:20; cf. 3:16), which was certainly used of the Messiah. At the level of the final redaction of Q, "the one who comes in the name of the Lord" may have been understood as Jesus when he returns in glory, since "the coming one" does refer to Jesus elsewhere in Q.

But there are problems with seeing "the one who comes in the name of the Lord" as a christological reference in the original oracle of 13:34–35. There is no evidence that Psalm 118:26 was understood messianically in first-century Judaism. Indeed, the "one who comes in the name of the Lord" is the worshiper who comes to the temple, who is pronounced blessed for having done so by the priests. The phrase "in the name of the Lord" may in fact have been understood adverbially in connection with "blessed," as argued by McNeile, with the resultant meaning: "Blessing

---

28 O. H. Steck, *Israel und das gewaltsame Geschick der Propheten*, 57–58.

in the name of the Lord is pronounced upon the one coming [to the temple to worship]."[29] The messianic use of the phrase is first broached in Mark 11:9 and then made explicit by the addition of "king" in Luke 19:38 and John 12:13. Even if it could be assumed that the one coming in the name of the Lord is the Messiah at the eschaton, it has never been clear why unbelieving Jews should be told that they will someday greet the returning Jesus with this new messianic acclamation.

Perhaps exegesis has too quickly taken "the coming one" as the clue that has led to a messianic understanding of the statement, which is in fact a misunderstanding. It may rather be the case that the significant element is the phrase "in the name of the Lord," which may be readily understood in terms of Christian prophecy.[30] The saying would then have meant in the prophetic Q community: "You who reject the exalted Lord who now speaks to you through his prophets, will never 'see' [= be accepted by, experience the blessed presence of] me until and unless you say: 'Blessed is the prophetic messenger of the risen Lord.' " (In this interpretation, "Lord" refers to Jesus. Otherwise, if spoken with the *egō* of the earthly Jesus, "Lord" means "God.") As in Hermas and Revelation, the prophet offers the exalted Lord's last chance for repentance.

The saying is often regarded as an item from the wisdom tradition simply attributed to the earthly Jesus in a literary manner. Yet, we have seen repeatedly that "wisdom" and "prophecy" are not alternatives. Ronald A. Piper's recent study of wisdom in Q emphasizes the sapiential character of the Q materials but still points out that in the development of the Q tradition sayings of prophetic origin could be incorporated into a later wisdom speech, and wisdom aphorisms could be joined to a prophetic speech.[31] There was a profound interest in the transcendent figure of Wisdom in the prophetic Q community, an interest fed by the community's concern for prophecy and its own prophetic self-understanding. The community adopted the view that it was the transcendent figure of Wisdom who had sent prophets to Israel through the generations, with John, Jesus, and the prophets of the Q community itself climaxing the series. Seen in terms of the series of prophets, the historical Jesus was simply one of the series, though the decisive one. The Q community did not identify the earthly Jesus as the incarnation of Wisdom.[32] But the community conceived the exaltation of Jesus after his death not only in terms of identification with the coming Son of man but

29 *The Gospel According to St. Matthew*, 296.
30 "In the name of the Lord" is used explicitly of Christian prophets in Mark 13:6, par. and Matthew 7:22, with which may be compared John 5:43; 10:25; 14:26; Acts 3:6; 4:10, 17, 18, 30; 5:28, 40; 1 Corinthians 1:10; 5:4; 2 Thessalonians 3:6.
31 *Wisdom in the Q Tradition: The Aphoristic Teaching of Jesus*, 60, 137–142.
32 Cf. Suggs, *Wisdom, Christology, and Law*.

also (in a manner not neatly worked out conceptually) in terms of an identification with the transcendent Wisdom who had inspired all the prophets and who now speaks through the Q prophets. The earthly Jesus had once spoken of the coming Son of man. And it was Wisdom who once spoke through the Jesus of history. It is the exalted Jesus, now identified with transcendent Wisdom (and the coming Son of man), who speaks through the Q prophets.

This seems to me to be the most satisfactory way of regarding the saying under discussion: it is both the voice of Wisdom and the voice of the exalted Jesus speaking through a prophet in the Q community. Although the Jewish community rejected Wisdom in rejecting the historical Jesus, they are now given a second and final chance to accept him/her, as he/she addresses them in the prophecy of the Q community. This pattern of thinking corresponds exactly to the way the Q community conceived the relation of the ministry of the historical Jesus and the Son of man: the one who is now identified as Son of man was rejected when he appeared on earth, but he now offers through his prophets absolutely the last chance of forgiveness (Luke 12:10).

Q 16:17: A PROPHETIC RESPONSE TO A DISPUTED QUESTION

This saying, which circulated as an independent unit, is an absolute declaration of the validity of even the smallest bit of the Law until the eschaton, and hence presupposes the debates about the Law in early Christianity. There are some significant indications of prophetic speech, including its chiastic form and the declaration that something will not happen "until" *(heōs)* some eschatological event happens. Further, the apocalyptic orientation of the saying should be taken seriously. "Until everything happens"/"until heaven and earth pass away" is not a folk-expression for "for ever" but is meant the way Christian prophets intended it: the end of history when the Son of man returns. We have here, then, a response that was given to an early church question: "since the Kingdom has already started to come in the ministry of Jesus and his post-Easter followers, is the Law abolished, as some of our traditions say will happen at the eschaton?" The reply is given in an authoritative, legal-sounding declaration: "For the time being, the Law remains totally in effect; it will not pass away until the end of history, which will occur shortly when the Son of man returns." Here, Christian prophecy settles a disputed issue as it responds to a burning question in the post-Easter community.

Q 17:23–35: THE DAY OF THE SON OF MAN

With the editorial framework and insertions removed, we have a speech that, though composed of originally independent sayings, has been secondarily arranged into a somewhat unified declaration on the coming of the Son of man (17:23–24, 37, 26–35). The prophetic message declares that the advent of the Son of man will be not a local but a universal event that cannot be hidden. The Son of man will arrive without warning, but there will be no doubt that the eschaton has come—it will not be an esoteric event. The speech calls for unreserved commitment to the eschatological future that will vindicate the lives of the members of the Q community, who now seem to be rejected by God in the eyes of their Jewish opponents (17:31–33). The speech concludes with the picture of the separation that will occur at the unexpected arrival of the Son of man (17:34–35).

The speech is almost universally regarded as secondarily composed of originally disparate elements, with considerable variation existing in the evaluations of how many, if any, of these elements derive from the pre-Easter Jesus. Taken as a whole, however, the speech is unquestionably a secondary composition of someone in the early church although it may contain some authentic words of Jesus. I use the word "composition" advisedly here, because the speech is far from a haphazard conglomeration of individual sayings. Although the originally independent elements are still apparent, the speech is now a unified whole. It has no historical framework, nor any reference to the historical Jesus. As a whole, it belongs to the genre of "prophetic and apocalyptic" sayings, as Bultmann recognized. It has one main thrust, to which all else is subordinated: the Son of man will certainly arrive as the judge of the Last Day; he will make an ultimate separation between those whom he accepts and those whom he rejects, so that it is this eschatological future that is to be the orientation point of all of life in the present, for it is worth any sacrifice. One gains and loses life in reference to this and nothing else (17:33).

There is no apocalyptic calculating of the times in this speech. Even 17:31 is not, as commonly interpreted, a fragment of apocalyptic advice about when to flee to avoid the terrors of the eschaton—the "flight" motif is not present in the Q version and is mistakenly read into it from the Markan apocalypse. Rather, like verse 33, verse 31 is a warning not to be attached to earthly things; even in the last moment one can, like Lot's wife, forfeit participation in eschatological salvation by turning toward material possessions. The present poverty and other-worldly orientation of the Q community must be maintained until the very end in order to obtain salvation. This kind of eschatology, which functions as parenesis, is appropriate to Christian prophets and suggests that it was a prophet of the Q community who compiled this speech. The use of traditional sayings, some of which may derive from the historical Jesus, is no argument against prophetic origin. Comparison with the characteristics of Christian prophecy reveals only a minimum of specific evidence of prophetic origin. The most that we should say is that someone in the Q community, influenced by the prophetic eschatology of the community, combined traditional sayings of Jesus into a unified eschatological speech that would have been heard as the contemporary word of the exalted Lord urging the community to be prepared for the sudden coming of the Son of man, and that he or she incorporated a few of the forms of prophetic speech that were current in the community. The speech could well be the work of the final redactor of Q who is influenced by the prophetic forms and phenomena in the community.

Q 22:28–30: THE DISCIPLES' ROLE IN ESCHATOLOGICAL JUDGMENT

The eschatological discourse and thus the Q document itself concluded with an oracular promise that may be reconstructed as follows. Its original chiastic form is still apparent.

Amen I say to you,
A you who have followed me
B in the new age,
B when the Son of man will sit on his glorious throne
A you also will sit upon thrones judging the twelve tribes of Israel.

The logion describes what will happen at the eschaton. The Son of man is portrayed as not only "coming" or "appearing" at the End but as sitting on his throne, apparently for the purpose of judging, as in Matthew 25:31–46. The saying also pictures the eschatological reconstitution of the twelve tribes of Israel. In the typical apocalyptic scenario, this eschatological regathering of all Israel is thought of as a blessing, but here the twelve tribes are judged by the Son of man—a fate usually reserved for the Gentiles. Those who now believe in Jesus as the Son of man will share his function of judging the twelve tribes of Israel. This "judging" is sometimes understood, in the Semitic sense of *shaphat*, "judge," to mean "rule," with the result that the disciples are promised the ruling seats within the blessed eschatological Israel. But the Greek word for "judge," *krinō*, does not mean "govern," except in semitizing Greek such as the LXX where *krinō* translates *shaphat*. The New Testament nowhere else adopts this usage. The familiar apocalyptic picture of the saints participating in the judgment of the world (*1 Enoch* 108:12; 61:8; 62:2; 69:27; 45:3; 1 Cor. 6:2; cf. Rev. 20:4, 11) suggests that judgment in the critical, condemnatory sense is intended.

The oracle thus affirms the reversal of eschatological expectations: all Israel will in fact be regathered at the eschaton—for judgment. The saying thus presupposes a historical setting in which "all Israel" can be juxtaposed to the followers of Jesus, a setting in which blanket condemnation can be pronounced upon Israel, presumably for its consistent rejection of the prophets of past and present, as in Q 11:49–51. Here we have another Q saying that reflects the failed mission of the Q messengers to Israel. They are promised by the word of the exalted Son of man that they will participate with him in meting out judgment to all Israel for its rejection of the prophets, culminating in the rejection of this last generation of Israel of the prophetic messengers of the Q community.

The Apocalypse also declares that the believers who are presently persecuted will share the judgment throne of the returning Lord (3:21 and cf. 20:4), as does Paul (1 Cor. 6:2). Thus the only two other references similar to the saying under consideration are from Christian prophetic figures, one of them being in the form of a declaration of the risen Lord through prophetic speech. The saying functions within the congregation of suffering eschatological saints as a word of consolation ("encouragement and upbuilding and consolation," 1 Cor. 14:3) by picturing the reversal of roles that will take place at the near eschaton. The elaboration of apocalyptic detail then functions not speculatively but as parenesis. In all these features the saying corresponds to the Christian prophecy of the Apocalypse. In the Q community, which had attempted to prepare Israel for the imminent encounter with Jesus the Son of man and had been rebuffed, "judged," and persecuted, some anonymous prophet, on the basis of an inspired interpretation of Daniel 7, announced the consoling word of the exalted Lord: contrary to present surface appearances, it is you, the suffering disciples, who will be the judges of those who now reject you, in the great renewal of the world that is about to take place.

CHRISTIAN PROPHECY IN THE Q COMMUNITY:
A SUMMARY

Analysis indicates that, with varying degrees of probability, we can designate a considerable number of sayings in the Q tradition that originated as the oracles of Christian prophets:

6:22–23	10:3	10:4
10:5–12	10:13–15	10:16
10:21–22	11:29b–30	11:39–52
12:8–9	12:10	12:11–12
13:34–35	16:17	22:28–30

This represents 22 percent of the words in Q.

An additional impressive number of sayings have been identified, which, while probably not originally created by Christian prophets, do bear the marks of the reformulation and/or re-presentation by Christian prophets of traditional material that originated from the historical Jesus and nonprophetic sources in and outside the church:

6:20b–21	10:2(–16)	10:23–24
11:14–23	11:29a, 31–32	12:2–3, 4–7
12:2–7	12:22–34	12:51–56
12:57–59	13:23–30	17:23–35.

This represents an additional 26 percent of the words in Q, making a total of 49 percent of Q that has been created or affected by Christian prophets.

There are also numerous prophetic touches to the nonprophetic forms within the Q tradition, such as the "I say to you" concluding formula to the parables in Luke 14:24; 15:7, and 19:26. There is a considerable amount of other material in Q, not discussed in the above, such as 6:27–49, which, though probably from Jesus and nonprophetic sources in the church, could readily have been heard in the Q community not as the remembered voice of the historical Jesus but as the word of the exalted Son of man.

Although it was not a criterion for identifying them, it is striking how many of the prophetic sayings are Son of man sayings. Of the ten Son of man sayings in Q, seven are in those influenced by Christian prophets, with five of the seven in the sayings generated by prophets themselves. There seems to be a correlation between Christian prophecy and Son of man sayings that will be of significance in the discussion to follow.

The mass of prophetic sayings and prophetic influence in Q does not mean that the Q sayings were entirely transformed into the prophetic mode. As sayings circulated singly or in clusters, there was a tendency for them to create a historicizing frame for themselves, whether this was some brief introductory formula, such as "and he said to them," or a miniature narrative of which the saying was the point and generating core. The Q community never severed the exalted Son of man from the figure of its recent historical past, Jesus of Nazareth, and thus felt no compelling need to purge the tradition of all historicizing elements. The document began with the appearance of John the Baptist, probably told of Jesus' baptism, and related the temptation of Jesus in the wilderness, none of which were transformed into present-tense messages from the risen Lord. A very few apothegmlike sayings such as Luke 7:9b and 10:21–22 are preserved with their historicizing framework. But this is not the central thrust of the Q material. The sayings are not those that were once said by a rabbi of a past generation; their validity does not rest on the authority of a past figure. To picture Q as intending simply to preserve the teaching of a historical figure is to miss the point.

The work of James M. Robinson has made popular the phrase "Words of the Wise" *(logoi sophōn)* as a designation for the genre of Q.[33] While it is true that Q has many points of contact with the wisdom tradition in both form and content, Q is in no sense a "Christian Book of Proverbs."[34] Over against those who claim to live by traditional wisdom, the Q community knows itself to live by revelation (Q 10:21–22). The manner of address of wisdom materials is that of a "timeless truth," which speaks to the hearer because of its inherent validity although it may be incidentally attached to a figure of the past: Solomon, Ahikar, Sirach. We have seen that Q does contain expressions of what was once gnomic wisdom, just as it contains teachings appropriate to a rabbi, but, as proclaimed and heard in the Q community, these tend to be transformed into the prophetic address of the exalted Jesus who is not only a figure of the (recent!) past, but is now identified with the transcendent figure of Wisdom and is imminently expected to return as the Son of man and judge of the world. There are thus two tendencies present in the Q materials: (1) the historicizing tendency, represented by the introductory formula "and he said to them" *(kai eipen autois)*, which places wisdom and prophetic sayings into a past-narrative setting and opens up the way to regard them as sayings of the pre-Easter Jesus; and (2) the contemporizing tendency, represented by the prophetic "I say to you" *(legō hymin)*, which takes prophetic sayings in the first person and sayings that have already been historicized and re-presents them as contemporary address.

This is not to minimize the presence and importance of the considerable wisdom tradition found in Q, but it is often wisdom in the prophetic mode. More than one mode of address is still present in Q, representing the literary remains of struggles to perceive Jesus as rabbi or teacher of wisdom as well as exalted Lord, but the fundamental orientation of the Q sayings as they came to Matthew and Luke is neither the timeless mode of wisdom nor the traditional mode of rabbinica but the present/future mode of prophecy. Thus *logia sophias,* "oracles of (transcendent) Wisdom" might be a more appropriate label for Q.

In addition to the analysis of particular sayings, there are some general features of the Q complex of materials that relate it to Christian prophecy. The form of the "book" itself is prophetic, beginning with the

---

33 James M. Robinson, " *'LOGOI SOPHŌN':* On the Gattung of Q," in *Trajectories Through Early Christianity,* 71–113.

34 The phrase is from Vincent Taylor, *The Formation of the Gospel Tradition,* who rejects it as a characterization of Q, but the view has reemerged in the current proclivity to see Q as a wisdom document.

baptism and temptation stories analogous to a prophetic "call" in which the Spirit (of prophecy) is received, and continuing with a collection of oracles and a minimum of narrative, somewhat like Jeremiah.

The view that prophets are persecuted seems to be an overarching concern of the document, not just of individual pericopae, so that the whole document can be described as a "Persecution Code" formulated by prophets and teachers. Similarly, the perspective of the Q materials on miracles corresponds to that of the prophets. Jesus and his post-Easter followers work miracles but not by virtue of their divine "essence," as the pre-Markan miracle stories tended to portray Jesus (Mark 3:10; 5:25ff.; 6:56). Rather, Jesus (and his disciples in the Q community) perform as (prophetic) agents of *God*, who alone works miracles, in carrying out their mission of eschatological proclamation. As in the prophetic books, the center of gravity is on the proclamation itself. The manner of using the Old Testament is also more closely related to the prophetic use of scripture than to other styles of interpretation. Although there are many allusions to scripture, in which the present proclamation is couched in images and phrases from scripture, exactly as in Revelation, there is only one direct quotation in the whole of Q (7:27). In conjunction with this charismatic-eschatological interpretation of scripture, the Q community knew itself to be charismatically enabled to interpret the events through which it had lived and was living as the eschatological act of God. It had the revealed mystery of the meaning of the appearance of John and Jesus and the meaning of the struggles of its own time. This is the prophetic self-consciousness.

This view has recently been thoroughly elaborated and documented by Mikagu Sato, who argues that Q belongs to the genre of prophetic books.[35] Sato begins with the prophetic books of the Old Testament and follows the tradition forward; I have begun with the early Christian documents and worked backward. Our results are approximately the same: Q is a prophetic document from a prophetic community.

The historical Jesus was indispensable for the theological understanding of the Q community. He had been the decisive prophetic messenger of transcendent Wisdom and had been exalted to become the Son of man. His words, and a few of his deeds, had formed the original nucleus of the Q materials. But the prophetic understanding of the Q community tended more and more to focus on the post-Easter exalted Jesus. What Jesus of Nazareth had said became dissolved in what the post-Easter Jesus said through his prophets. If these two categories of material were ever distinguished, they had ceased to be by the time of the redaction of the Q materials. While the dissolution of the word of the

---

35 *Q und Prophetie*, esp. 69–95.

historical Jesus into the word of the heavenly Jesus had not yet occurred in Q, the center of gravity had shifted, so that Q was moving in the direction of a collection of "sayings of the living Jesus" such as the *Gospel of Thomas.*

13

Prophetic Sayings of the Risen Jesus in Mark

If one examines the sayings of Jesus in Mark with the same criteria used above for Q, which Markan sayings emerge as having been created or influenced by Christian prophets?

MARK 8:38, 13:26: SON OF MAN SAYINGS

The preceding analysis of the Q materials indicates that Christian prophets were a primary source for the promulgation of Son of man sayings in the name of the risen Jesus. We may first examine this category of sayings in Mark to determine whether any of them appear to be of prophetic origin.[1] The results are surprising. Mark contains fourteen instances of "Son of man" in thirteen sayings: 2:10, 28; 8:31, 38; 9:9, 12, 31; 10:33–34, 45; 13:26; 14:21 (twice), 41, 62. Of these, only two seem to be the products of Christian prophets: 8:38, Mark's rewriting of a traditional saying identified as prophetic in Q (12:8–9) and 13:26, in the "Little Apocalypse" identified as Christian prophecy below.

Our analysis seems to uncover a peculiar fact: although there was a close relation between Christian prophets and Son of man sayings in earliest Christianity and in Q, Mark's larger number of Son of man sayings exhibit only a minimum of contact with Christian prophecy.

---

1 The reader is again reminded that only the results of the investigation are given here. For detailed evidence and argument, see my *Sayings of the Risen Jesus: Christian Prophecy in the Synoptic Tradition.*

MARK 3:28–29: THE UNFORGIVABLE
SIN SAYING

We have seen above, in the discussion of the Q form of this saying, that it was probably originally formulated as an oracle of a Christian prophet, the more primitive form of which is preserved in Mark.

MARK 6:8–11: THE MISSIONARY COMMISSION

Here Mark has sayings similar to, and partly identical with, the Q Missionary Address (Q 10:2–16). It is difficult to say whether this is excerpted from Q or represents independent tradition, just as it is difficult to be sure whether the historicizing framework is first supplied by Mark, or was already traditional. In any case, Mark here includes a brief collection of sayings that, as we have already seen, derive from, and have been formed by, Christian prophecy.

MARK 9:1: THE IMMINENCE OF THE PAROUSIA

This saying seems to reflect a concern over the delay of the parousia and offers an encouraging word to a post-Easter community in which some members have already died, reaffirming that the parousia will come after all. Some (even if not all) will live to see it. The saying functions in the same manner as the prophetic declarations of 1 Corinthians 15:51 and 1 Thessalonians 4:15–17, offering revelatory consolation to the community that is distressed by the delay of the parousia.

MARK 13:5–31: THE MARKAN "APOCALYPSE"

This is the most extensive and significant unit in Mark related to Christian prophecy and calls for an extended discussion. The proposal first made by Timothy Colani in 1864, that Mark 13 contains an independent apocalypse by an unknown Jewish-Christian author, was widely adopted by the end of the century and was still considered by many to be "assured results" of Gospel criticism as late as 1954.[2] Suggestions that the author of this "apocalypse" was a Christian prophet were accompanied by efforts to identify the occasion of its promulgation, with the Caligula crisis of 40 and the war of 66–70 being the chief candidates.

Recently, however, the "Little Apocalypse" theory has fallen on hard times. On the one hand, there are efforts to argue that the discourse

---

2 G. R. Beasley-Murray, *Jesus and the Future: An Examination of the Criticism of the Eschatological Discourse, Mark 13, with Special Reference to the Little Apocalypse Theory,* traces the history of the theory from Colani to the mid-twentieth century.

should be regarded as mainly a redactional composition of Mark. On the other hand, recent studies have appeared arguing that Mark incorporates a pre-Markan apocalypse.[3] Study of Mark 13 may be regarded as at something of an impasse. The time is ripe for a reconsideration of the question from the point of view of the hypothesis being proposed in this study.

Even though the discourse may contain some elements from the pre-Easter Jesus, someone in the church is the author of the present form of the discourse. On the other hand, the redactional activity of Mark need not be denied. If Mark did incorporate a "Little Apocalypse" into his eschatological discourse, it has been at least semidigested and integrated with Mark's other sources, partially rewritten in Mark's own style and formed into a speech complex that now bears something of a Markan stamp throughout. We may now ask whether the theory of a pre-Markan apocalyptic document can be reasserted and strengthened by seeing it as Christian prophecy. Since verses 1–4 are a Markan introduction, verses 32–37 are an obvious appendix, and verse 31 forms a proper conclusion, I shall consider 13:5–31 as the unit to be examined.

1. The most obvious prophetic feature of Mark 13 is its claim to reveal the events of the End Time and of the eschatological future. The general eschatological themes found in this passage are, of course, present throughout broad streams of early Christianity and were shared by many who did not function as prophets. Mark 13 has striking points of resemblance to the explicit revelations about the eschatological future that occur as the oracles of Christian prophets (e.g., 1 Thess. 4:15–17; 1 Cor. 15:51–52), its closest parallel being that one clear example of Christian prophecy, the book of Revelation. The label "Little Apocalypse" is well chosen.

2. A related feature that distinguishes Mark 13 from Jewish apocalyptic and associates it with Christian prophecy is its hortatory character. Nineteen imperatives are found in the discourse, fifteen of them within the unit we are considering, verses 5–31. This parenesis is not tacked on to an "apocalyptic fly-sheet" but comprises the fundamental structure of the discourse itself. The structure of eschatologically motivated parenesis already characterized the pre-Markan unit. The difference from Jewish apocalyptic on this point is clear and has often been documented. Again, the only real parallels to the hortatory apocalyptic of Mark 13 are found in Christian prophecy, above all in Revelation.

3. Christian prophets could speak directly to their hearers/readers, using second-person imperatives, because they spoke with the ego of the

---

3 Rudolf Pesch, *Naherwartung. Tradition und Redaktion in Mk 13;* Egon Brandenburger, *Markus 13 und die Apokalyptik.*

risen Christ, not pseudonymously in the name of some ancient figure. If Mark 13 is regarded as Christian prophecy, this must not be called pseudonymity, for it is precisely here that there is another characteristic feature in which Jewish apocalypse and Christian prophecy differ. Not only does Mark 13 not appeal to some ancient worthy such as Enoch, Noah, or Elijah, it does not appeal to *Jesus* in the sense of claiming the authorship of a figure of the past. What we have here is not the literary phenomenon of placing words in Jesus' mouth "back there," in a way that bifurcated Jesus' word and the hearer's present. The difference between Christian prophecy and Jewish apocalypse in this regard is more than a difference in the length of time that elapsed between the writing and its purported author, though that difference too is significant. It is a difference in nature. If Mark 13 contains Christian prophecy, this was never conceived as the words of Jesus spoken in the past—even the recent past—and handed down to the Christian situation but was heard from the first as the message of the contemporary Christ. On the other hand, no writer of Jewish apocalypse considered himself to be the "mouthpiece of the exalted Enoch" or any such. As we shall see below, the prophetic address inherent in the pre-Markan apocalypse is not at all negated by the fact that Mark has placed the discourse within the pre-Easter narrative framework.

The consciousness of speaking with the "I" *(egō)* of the exalted Christ is present throughout the discourse, especially in the forms of the first-person pronoun found in verses 6, 9, 13, 23, 30, and 31. The author is acquainted with the revelatory formulae "I am" *(egō eimi)* and "in my name" used by Christian prophets but does not use them himself because they have been appropriated by his opponents. The "I am" of 13:6 is not a claim to be the returned Jesus Christ but is the prophetic formula by which the Christian prophets opposed by the author authenticated their oracles and is itself an indication that the discourse derives from a situation where the phenomenon of Christian prophecy was very much alive.

4. This concern with false prophets is very important to the author of the discourse. He or she begins with it (v. 5b–6) and comes back to it in verses 21–22. The deceivers against whom the author warns his or her readers have been understood to be Jewish messianic pretenders, false Christian teachers, those claiming to be the returned Jesus himself, or a group of gnosticlike pneumatic "divine men" *(theioi andres)*. There are difficulties with all these explanations, a primary one being that the persons named will both speak "in my name" and will characteristically say "I am." But both phrases are comprehensible in terms of Christian prophecy (and only there, I think), for only Christian prophets speak both in the name of Jesus ("in my name" = with and under Jesus' authority) and in Jesus' person (saying "I am"). This is an important exegetical point: the phenomenon of Christian prophecy clarifies the meaning of the

problematic verse 6. But it is also a point for regarding the discourse as the product of Christian prophecy, for, as we have seen, it is characteristically the prophets themselves who raise the cry against "false" prophets.

5. There are numerous points at which phrases from the Old Testament, especially Daniel, have been woven into the eschatological discourse. Yet there are no explicit quotations as such; the Old Testament material is re-presented as an integral part of the present address of the prophet's speech, exactly as in Revelation. We have seen that this style of interpretation is characteristic of Christian prophets. The eschatological discourse, or its core, can readily be seen as having come into being as a charismatic interpretation of scripture predicting the eschatological future as the basis for hortatory admonitions. One need not posit an "apocalyptic fragment" that was "supplemented" with Christian exhortations.

6. In 13:11 we find a text that circulated independently, which I have already argued was the product of Christian prophecy (see chapter 12 above). Its presence in this discourse is, of course, another point of contact with prophetic circles. It should also be noticed here that the saying expresses a "prophetic" understanding of the way the Spirit functions. This saying conceives of the Spirit not as a general gift "immanent" in the church but as the occasional gift to particular persons in times of crisis, a charisma that confers supernatural speech abilities. This is not the typical understanding of the Spirit in early Christianity, but it would have been very appropriate among Christian prophets. This promise of the risen Christ of pneumatic speech in crisis situations was also transmitted in the prophetic circles of the Johannine community, where it was generalized and made the subject of theological reflection, to emerge as the Paraclete-doctrine of the Fourth Gospel.

7. The note to "the reader" in verse 14, "let the reader understand," has been understood in the sense that the private reader is to attend to the veiled meaning of the document in hand. But the only parallel in early Christian literature to the absolute "the reader" is found in Christian prophecy, Revelation 1:3, which refers to the lector who reads aloud in public worship a prophetic document written for that purpose. Ordinarily the prophets would deliver their own oracles in the setting of the worship service, but in the case of Revelation the message concerned a present crisis of history that involved many churches, so the revelation was committed to writing and provision made for it to be read by others to the congregations gathered for worship. The numerous second-person plural imperatives suggest this as the setting for the delivery of the "Little Apocalypse," as does the expression "let the reader understand" and the other points of contact with Revelation discussed below.

8. The document originates from a setting in which persecution was the expected lot of both author and hearers, the theme appearing in verses 8, 9–13 and 14–19. These sufferings bear the dual aspect of the

eschatological sufferings that the faithful must undergo as the prelude to the End and the suffering that is the lot of the true prophet, both of which are characteristic prophetic themes. Related to this is the pronouncement of eschatological blessing for those who endure, so that 13:13b finds its closest parallels in the promises of Revelation 2:7, 10, 11, 17, 26–27; 3:5, 10, 12, 21.

9. There are points of contact between Mark 13 and the forms associated with Christian prophets: the first-person speech for the risen Lord, the reflection of "I am" as a prophetic formula, the plethora of parenetic second-person plural imperatives, the abundance of prophetic-eschatological vocabulary such as "this generation," the announcement of "woe" (13:17), and the "amen, I say to you" formula in verse 30, which comes in the final, grounding position as it does in several of the prophetic speeches in Q. The discourse as a whole has a rhythmical formal structure as well. Although this is variously reconstructed (the uncertainties as to the precise form being due in part to materials taken over by the prophet that were not completely digested and in part to Markan rewriting), it is clear that the discourse as a whole was not a formless jumble, nor the characteristic prose of Jewish apocalyptic, but reflects the formally structured speech of Christian prophecy.

10. To what situation was this oracle directed? We have seen that prophecy and interpretation of event are closely related, so that the indications that we are dealing with Christian prophetic speech already discussed would lead us to expect that the discourse was the interpretation of the meaning of some event. The discourse itself clearly indicates that it is not free-wheeling speculation about the End but is related to a particular crisis (verses 6, 7–8, 9, 11–13, 14, 19, 24). But which?

Colani's original suggestion was that the prophecy is to be seen in relation to the imminent fall of Jerusalem, probably identical to the "oracle" that Eusebius says commanded the Jerusalem Christians to flee (Hist. Ecc. 3.5). It seems more likely that this was the time for the writing of Mark, who already considered the "Little Apocalypse" a traditional speech from Jesus. It must therefore have been written some time before the war of 66–70. An excellent setting for this prophecy is provided in the threat of Caligula to place his image in the temple in Jerusalem in the year 39–40, a threat that would certainly have been carried out but for his death. The hypothesis of Christian prophecy makes it all the more understandable that in the year of crisis 40 c.e. a church prophet might declare the word of the risen Lord to give eschatological meaning to this situation, precisely as in Revelation.

11. I shall conclude this discussion by summarizing the numerous parallels between Mark 13 and Revelation that illustrate that the Markan discourse is more like our one clear example of Christian prophecy than anything else in early Christian literature:

13:5–8—The same four woes, in the same order, are found in Revelation 6.

13:5—The warning against false prophets who will deceive *(planaō)* the faithful if possible; compare Revelation 2:20; 13:14; 19:20.

13:7—The prediction of wars as part of the prelude to the End. Of the thirteen occurrences of "war" outside Mark 13 and its synoptic parallels, nine are in Revelation, always in an eschatological context.

13:7—The expression "what must take place" *(dei genesthai)* is found in the New Testament only here and in Revelation 1:1; 4:1; and 22:6.

13:7—*telos* as the expression for the eschatological End (Rev. 2:26; 21:6; 22:13).

13:7–8—As in Revelation, these terrors are only signs of the beginning of the End, not of the End itself.

13:9—The suffering of the prophetic community is "for testimony/ witness" *(eis martyrion);* compare Revelation 6:9; 11:7; 12:11, 17; 19:10.

13:10—Unless this verse is entirely redactional, which may well be the case, the preaching of the gospel to all the world may not have been, in the original prophetic oracle, an exhortation to the hearers to evangelism but the apocalyptic event described also in Revelation 14:6 (but nowhere else in the New Testament).

13:11–13—The general situation of being persecuted "for the sake of my name" corresponds to the general situation of Revelation and verbally to 2:3, 13.

13:13—"Steadfast endurance" *(hypomonē)* as *the* Christian virtue under persecution; compare Revelation 1:9; 2:2, etc.

13:13—Salvation promised to the one who holds fast until the end; compare Revelation 2:10c.

13:14—The interpretation of the present historical crisis as full of eschatological meaning corresponds to the raison d'être of Revelation. Both documents use the terminology of "abomination," which with one exception (Luke 16:15) is used in the New Testament only in Mark 13 and its synoptic parallels and three times in Revelation (Rev. 17:4, 5; 21:27).

13:14—The expression "the reader" is used only in Mark 13, par., and in Revelation in the New Testament, having the same function in each instance.

13:14—"Let them flee to the mountains"; compare Revelation 6:15–16; 12:6.

13:17—"Woe." Revelation has fourteen announcements of woe in seven passages. Revelation 8:13 has the same grammatical construction as the Mark passage.

13:19—The great "tribulation" is also a part of the eschatological drama in Revelation 1:9; 2:9, 10, 22, and especially 7:14.

13:20—In the Markan apocalypse, God himself is not *bound* by the apocalyptic scheme (as in, e.g., 2 Esdras) but is sovereign over it and can change his mind, as in the dynamic understanding of God's relation to history in the prophets of both Israel and the church, illustrated in Revelation 2:5, 16, 22.

13:21–22—Both the Markan apocalypse and Revelation respond to false prophets for whom earthly "signs" are validating credentials; cf. 13:14–15; 16:14; 19:20. For both Revelation and the Markan apocalypse, the only sign to be expected is the sign from heaven at the End.

13:24–27—Both the Markan apocalypse and Revelation have the same general scheme of historical troubles, final tribulation, cosmic dissolution, and then the coming of the Son of man on the clouds.

13:30—For the writers of both the Markan apocalypse and Revelation, their generation is the last; the End will come soon (cf. Rev. 1:1, 3; 2:16, 25; 3:11, 20; 6:11; 10:6–7; 11:2; 12:6, 12; 17:10; 22:6, 7, 10, 12, 20).

It thus seems clear that the "Little Apocalypse" was most likely written by an early Christian prophet. I would accept in general the thesis of Rudolf Pesch, that an eschatological Christian prophetic document that was having an influential circulation in Mark's church was included by him partly in order to neutralize the false theology and inflammatory effects it was causing in the hands of those Mark considered false prophets.[4] Because of this special circumstance, Mark included an extensive product of Christian prophecy, which he otherwise would not have done. Even so, I consider Pesch's 1968 conclusion, that this was an old, traditional prophetic oracle, dating from the 39–40 Caligula crisis and made *au courant* by the 66–70 crisis, to be more probable than his later view[5] that the oracle was first promulgated at that time. Mark himself probably considered it authentic tradition from the pre-Easter Jesus.

MARK, CHRISTIAN PROPHECY, AND THE
ORIGIN OF THE GOSPEL FORM

The study of the sayings of the risen Jesus in Q and Mark respectively has revealed an important difference that is fundamental to understanding

---

4 See *Naherwartung,* chs. 5–6
5 *Das Markusevangelium.*

the relation of Christian prophecy to the canonical Gospels. Whereas Q contains a considerable number of prophetic sayings, is tending to be understood as a whole as sayings of the risen Jesus, and by its nature is open to continued expansion by the addition of new revelatory sayings, Mark contains only a few prophetic sayings, which are no longer represented as sayings of the risen Jesus, but are entirely contained within the historicizing pre-Easter narrative framework, closing the door to further prophetic expansion. Apart from the "Little Apocalypse," only 6 percent of the sayings material in Mark is from prophets, contrasted with almost half of Q that was either created or influenced by them.

Why is it that Mark contains only five sayings, plus the eschatological discourse, that may be attributed to Christian prophets? This question is related to the problem of why there is such a dearth of sayings material in Mark at all. Mark not only has far fewer sayings of Jesus in his Gospel than either Matthew or Luke, proportionately he devotes only about half as much of his Gospel to sayings as do the other Synoptic authors. It thus might be assumed that Mark has few prophetic sayings as a result of including only a few of *any* kind of sayings. The hypothesis being proposed here is that precisely the opposite relation obtains: the paucity of sayings in Mark is to be explained on the basis of Mark's view of the prophetic sayings.

The problem is magnified when one considers that Mark seems to be interested in Jesus as a *teacher*. "Teacher" *(didaskalos)* is by far the most common "title" given to Jesus by others in the Gospel and is used by Jesus of himself (14:14). "Teach" and "teaching" are used with reference to Jesus more than they are in either Matthew or Luke, despite Mark's smaller size. Likewise, Mark has an interest in the sayings of Jesus, as is seen not only by his including seventy-nine of them but also by his repeatedly including such statements as 8:32 "and with boldness he was speaking the word" (RSV "he said this plainly"; cf. also 2:2; 4:14ff., 33). These considerations would lead one to expect more sayings of Jesus to be included in Mark and only make their paucity more noticeable and in need of an explanation.

Within the framework of the two-source theory, this problem has usually been expressed by the question: "Did Mark know Q?" with numerous scholars standing on each side of this debate. The dilemma is clear: If Mark did not know Q, then how can we account for the several places where he seems not only to overlap Q and Q-like materials but to be excerpting from them (e.g., 6:7–13)? If he did know Q, then how can we account for his using so little of it and for his selection? The chief argument, in fact, in favor of the theory that Mark did *not* know Q has been that he would surely have included more of it had he known it.

The variety of explanations for the paucity of sayings in Mark may be categorized and summarized as follows: (1) Mark *presupposes* the existence of Q or a Q-like collection as a factor in his situation to be reckoned with; (2) Mark *historicizes* his material, relating it to the story of the pre-Easter Jesus; (3) Mark *selects* his material to correspond to his emphasis on the cross-resurrection kerygma; (4) Mark *opposes* some kind of Christianity represented by the Q materials. The advocates of these theories each had an aspect of the truth. Yet as they expounded them, their theories were conflicting alternatives. I propose a unifying theory that affirms the valid insights of them all, in terms of Christian prophecy. My hypothesis may be briefly stated: *Mark has so few sayings of Jesus because he is suspicious of Christian prophecy as it is present in his community and expressed in the sayings tradition. He creates a new narrative form to mediate the continuing voice of Jesus intended as an alternative.*

We have seen that Q contained substantial prophetic materials and was coming to be regarded as altogether "sayings of the risen Jesus." It was not a rabbinic Q against which Mark was reacting but a prophetic Q. This prophetic aspect of Mark's opponents is an interpretative key to Mark's Gospel that should be followed up. It is of the utmost importance to note that the *only opponents* of the church specifically named in the Gospel itself are called "false Christs and false prophets" (13:22). The troublesome "false Christs" may be best understood if the "and" is regarded as epexegetical. One category of opponents is described, who speak as Christ ("I am," 13:6), who call themselves "prophets" and are so called by others, and whose trademark is that they come "in my name" (13:6), as do the prophets of Matthew 7:22. The "in my name" is a revelatory, but not messianic, claim, meaning that the claimants come in the authority of Jesus' name, as the prophets did, but not claiming to be the messiah or the already-returned Jesus. Mark's opponents are intra-church prophetic figures, not extrachurch messianic claimants.

There seems to be an antiprophet motif in Mark. It comes to expression, for instance, in the fact that, except for the proverb in 6:4, Jesus is only twice called "prophet" in Mark 6:15 and 8:28, and in each case this is clearly to be taken as a misunderstanding. While Matthew and Luke modify these passages to indicate only that Jesus is none of the Old Testament prophets who has risen, Mark alone denies categorically that Jesus is "one of the prophets," period. Mark seems to be an opponent of prophecy as it is expressed in his environment. The most probable reason for Mark's hesitating use of the Q material is to be found in his suspicion of the genre that it represents: the post-Easter revelations of the risen Lord.

Mark is indeed a spokesperson for the risen Lord, and he mediates the address of the risen Lord to the community, but he is not an "immediately inspired" prophet of the same religious type as his predecessors and opponents. In the Gospel of Mark, it is the risen Lord who addresses the hearer/reader's own present, not merely a historical figure whose words are reported and repeated. But the message of the risen Lord is now bound to, and contained within, the tradition of Jesus of Nazareth as this is contained within a narrative presented entirely in a pre-Easter framework. In short, one important factor in Mark's creation of the Gospel form was his response to the challenge of Christian prophecy in his time by *developing an alternative form to mediate the continuing voice of Jesus to the church.*

Mark does not oppose the view that the risen Lord still speaks—he is an exponent of this view. What he opposes is the view that the risen Lord comes to speech in the collections of sayings such as Q that were so open to being considered the post-Easter address of the exalted Lord, an address no longer grounded in history. Such collections were not only composed of material much of which did in fact come into being after Easter, they were open to this interpretation in toto and to continued growth and expansion by the risen Lord.

To counteract this tendency, Mark took a step at once paradoxical and radical: he presented the message of the living Lord in a narrative form in which the post-Easter Jesus, in the narrative story line, says nothing. His message is confined entirely to the pre-Easter framework of the Gospel form that Mark devised for this purpose. There is an intentional dialectic here. It is no accident that Mark ends at 16:8 with the announcement that Jesus is risen but without his having appeared. To tell an appearance story is to have the risen Lord speak in an undialectical way and to open the door to a flood of post-Easter revelations of which Mark is very critical. Mark believes that the voice of Jesus continues to be heard in the new Gospel form he has created, but he is absolutely unwilling to tell the story in such a way that the risen Lord continues to speak in the story line after Easter.

This dialectic may also be helpful in understanding Mark's view of the presence and absence of Jesus with the church. Of late numerous scholars have pointed to the absence of Jesus from the resurrection to the parousia as an important Markan theme. The argument is well supported by evidence from the empty tomb and Lord's Supper pericopae. But there seems to be another, equally important emphasis in Mark that portrays the Jesus of the Gospel as present, dealing with his disciples in Mark's own day. The story of 6:45–52, for example, pictures the disciples alone in the boat in the midst of the sea, in great trouble, "being tormented" (rsv: "distressed in rowing"), a picture in which the Markan church could see itself reflected. It is impossible that Jesus can come to them; yet he comes, even though they disbelieve and misunderstand. He makes himself known with his revelatory, prophetic "I am" (rsv: "It is I"). Although the absence of Jesus is "a presiding feature in the Markan gospel," still "the gospel (itself) functions in such a way as to extend Jesus into the Markan present."[6] Jesus is not present physically, nor in terms of resurrection appearances, nor mystically, nor sacramentally. And *he is not only absent, he is silent.* He does not speak directly, as Christian prophets deliver new post-Easter revelations in his name, nor is the word of the post-Easter Jesus mediated by prophetic sayings collections such as Q. Mark avoids Q and has few Q type sayings for this very reason. But neither is Jesus absolutely absent or mute. He is present and speaks in the new literary form, the Markan Gospel.

Mark speaks with the voice of the risen Jesus, but at the same time wishes to curb the uncontrolled increase of prophetic revelations. He composes his narrative in such a way that the reader is confronted by the living Lord, but the structure of the narrative does not allow new revelations. The Gospel narrative is so constructed to contain Christian prophecy, in both senses of the word "contain." In this respect he is like Paul, who is a prophet himself, yet is opposed to the wild enthusiasm that strays too far from the tradition, and asserts his own writing as of prophetic authority (1 Cor. 14:37–38), thereby putting a restraint on others. When Mark and his contemporary Paul put pen to paper, we already have the nucleus of "Gospel and Epistle": the New Testament canon.

------

6 Both quotations are from Werner Kelber, *The Passion in Mark,* 164, and *The Kingdom in Mark,* 5. A Markan dialectic is involved here.

14

Prophetic Sayings of the Risen Jesus in Matthew

In an earlier section I have dealt with the general relationship of Matthew to the Christian prophets in his church (see chapter 4 above). I now wish to discuss the sayings of Christian prophets peculiar to Matthew's Gospel (those he takes over from Q and Mark having already been discussed) and to investigate Matthew's own stance vis-á-vis sayings of the risen Jesus.

MATTHEW 28:18b–20: THE COMMISSION

This commissioning speech of the risen Jesus is the most obvious place to begin, for as it is a post-Easter saying of the risen Lord in the first person, the possibility of prophetic origin is immediately suggested. But did the saying originate as the oracle of a Christian prophet in the strict sense, or is it a literary composition of Matthew or one of his predecessors, or some combination of the two?

The present form of the passage represents considerable redactional activity on Matthew's part, containing some of his favorite expressions ("in heaven and on earth," "therefore," "make disciples," "teaching"). Analysis reveals, however, that Matthew is not composing from whole cloth but is rewriting a traditional commissioning saying.[1] When this saying is compared to the profile of Christian prophecy, several common features are apparent.

1. In addition to the obvious overall form as a post-Easter saying of the risen Lord delivered in the first person, there are other features of form and vocabulary that relate the saying to Christian prophets. The saying is neatly composed of three elements: a declaration of authority,

---

1 Cf. Benjamin J. Hubbard, *The Matthean Redaction of a Primitive Apostolic Commissioning: An Exegesis of Matt. 28:16–20.*

a commissioning charge, and a promise of the abiding presence of Jesus. This schema corresponds to the Old Testament schema in which Yahweh commissioned prophets (Ezek. 1:1–3:15; Isaiah 6; Jer. 1:1–10; cf. Isa. 49:1–6), except that here Jesus plays the role of Yahweh, precisely as in Christian prophecy. This form is paralleled in the only firsthand report of the call of a Christian prophet in the New Testament, Revelation 1:12–20: declaration of authority (1:17b–18), commissioning (1:19), promise of presence (1:20, taken with 1:13, is a declaration that the risen Christ is present in the churches in Asia). In addition, the "therefore" *(oun)* of verse 19 is a characteristic prophetic word (though it is also characteristic of Matthew), and the "I am with you" is reminiscent of the prophetic "I am" not only in form but also in function.

2. Related to this is the prophetic "chain of command" from God the Father through the risen Jesus and his prophet to the church and the world, which we have found in Revelation and the Fourth Gospel, as well as in the Q prophetic logion Luke 10:22/Matthew 11:27. The saying in Matthew 28:18b–20 is conceived in terms of that pattern, which corresponds to Christian prophecy.

3. The emphatic note of authority with which a pronouncement on a disputed point (the carrying of the gospel to Gentiles) is made is appropriate to Christian prophets.

4. It has long been a commonplace of exegesis that the text is composed as a kind of midrash on Daniel 7:14. The parallels are clear:

Daniel	*Matthew*
and to him was given	was given to me
authority	all authority
and all nations	all nations
of the earth by their	
races and all glory	
serving him	in heaven and on earth

Yet scripture is not directly quoted in the promise/fulfillment scheme characteristic of Matthew himself but is allusively peshered and represented as the word of the exalted Jesus, as in Revelation and Christian prophecy generally.

5. This relation to Daniel 7:14 involves an implicit claim to be the exalted Son of man. The speaker knows that he or she speaks with the authority of the heavenly Son of man. We have seen that this self-consciousness was characteristic of Christian prophets.

6. The reference to the End of the age represents the eschatological perspective that was characteristic of Christian prophecy, though the saying itself is not aflame with near-expectation of the eschaton. But there

seems to be another kind of polemic that comes to expression in this declaration that the risen Jesus who speaks in the logion will be with the church until the End of the age: the prophetic gift is not to pass away but is to last as long as the church does.

7. Thoroughly prophetic is the way in which the word of the Lord is given to bring the church the message appropriate to its post-Easter situation and to resolve a disputed issue (the validity of the mission to Gentiles). The prophetic speaker knows that the pre-Easter Jesus did not carry on a mission to Gentiles nor command his disciples to do so. Yet the prophet believes that it is the will of the exalted Lord, who is present in the mission of the church, to carry out a universal mission and expresses this not in the form of his or her own exegetical theological reasoning but as a revelation of the risen Lord. We have seen above that there is considerable evidence that the Christian prophets played a major role in the broadening out of the church's mission to include Gentiles; here we seem to have one of their oracles that played a part in this important transition in the history of the church.

MATTHEW 5:3–12: BEATITUDES

We have seen that the Q form of the beatitudes contains both original pronouncements of Jesus and an expansion from Christian prophets. As the beatitudes appear in Matthew, they have been expanded by the peculiarly Matthean tradition and/or by Matthew himself. The additions bear the marks of prophetic origin and reshaping. For instance, the addition of "who were before you" in the concluding line makes it explicit that the hearers are themselves considered prophets. The beatitudes, already formed by Christian prophets in Q, are even more prophetic in their Matthean form, which strongly suggests the influence of the Christian prophets of the Matthean community. This phenomenon is typical of other Matthean sayings.

MATTHEW 5:18: VALIDITY OF THE LAW

In the Matthean stream of tradition this prophetic saying from Q (cf. chapter 12 above) is assimilated even more closely to typical prophetic forms.

MATTHEW 5:19: REWARDS AND PUNISHMENTS

This saying certainly comes from the post-Easter church, has the form of a "sentence of holy law," and may come from a Christian prophet. The evidence is not clear, however, and it may also be a scribal addition.

MATTHEW 6:14–15: FORGIVENESS

Here too we have a saying reformulated (cf. Mark 11:25) in the Matthean tradition into a "sentence of holy law," but it is not clear whether it comes from a prophet or was rewritten by Matthew in the prophetic style.

MATTHEW 7:2: JUDGMENT

As in 6:14–15, a nonprophetic saying circulating in the Matthean church has been tautened and recast in a form resembling the sayings of Christian prophets, but this is no proof that this was done by a Christian prophet.

MATTHEW 7:15–23: FALSE PROPHETS

In this section, sayings from the Q tradition are taken up and rewritten to bring out more clearly their reference to the threat of false prophets. Verses 20–23 may be the oracle of a Christian prophet.

MATTHEW 10:5b–42: THE MISSIONARY COMMISSION

In this extensive composition, Matthew takes the Q commissioning speech, which had already been created and formulated by Christian prophets, and elaborates it with material drawn partly from Mark but mostly from his own sources. As the materials from Q and elsewhere developed in the Matthean community and in Matthew's own hands, their prophetic character becomes even more pronounced, partly by the addition of oracles formulated by Christian prophets in the Matthean stream of tradition (10:5b–6, 17–22, 23), partly by editorial changes made by Matthew and his predecessors under the influence of Christian prophets.

The saying in 10:23 is particularly noteworthy as an example of a saying of a Christian prophet added to the tradition. While it is notoriously difficult to fit this saying into the pre-Easter ministry of Jesus, a most appropriate Sitz im Leben for the origin of such a saying would be a "commissioning service" in which the church sends forth its missioners, as in Acts 13:1–3. In the Acts scene, not only are Christian prophets among the missioners but the prophetic voice is heard among those who send their missioners forth, as someone speaking by the power of the Spirit gives instructions for the mission. So also in this case. Matthew 10:23 can be readily understood as the pronouncement of a Christian prophet made in the Spirit during a worship service in which missioners are commissioned and instructed for their task.

The saying fits the function of Christian prophecy of supplying a word of the risen Lord to settle an ambiguous situation for which there was no clear or satisfactory dominical saying in the tradition. There was a clear tradition that the Christian missionary should stand firm in the face of opposition. Some of this tradition was from sayings of Jesus and some was from Christian prophets, as Revelation, for example, shows. But what if standing fast in the face of persecution endangers the mission with which the missionaries have been charged by the risen Lord himself? Should the missionaries stand fast, even at the risk of their lives (and of the mission), or flee? The latter course seemed not only to accept defeat but to concede that the mission itself was illegitimate, since the true prophet does not retreat at the threat of suffering. It appears that it was to just such a situation that the oracle of 10:23 was directed. *Belief in the Spirit could legitimize breaks with the tradition.* Flight in the face of persecution was not cowardice or strategy but obedience to the exalted Lord, authorized by a word from his prophet.

The saying represents the eschatological-apocalyptic paraclesis typical of Christian prophets. However Matthew himself may have understood the saying, the reference to the coming of the Son of man that is the motivating power for the paraclesis was originally a fervently eschatological declaration. The coming of the Son of man can be understood as the parousia at the (near) End of history, but other explanations were at least possible for Matthew: a meeting of Jesus and the Twelve during the course of their mission, Jesus' death and/or resurrection, the crisis of the Jewish war 66–70. Such explanations may help a later generation—Matthew's or ours—to make acceptable sense of a saying that in its obvious meaning has become an embarrassment. But no one who wanted to speak of a rendezvous between Jesus and the Twelve, or the resurrection, or the Jewish war, would choose to express any one of these meanings in the form in which Matthew 10:23 now stands. The original meaning of this oracle must refer to the parousia at the End of history. The inner logic of the saying is this: "When you are persecuted, the heavenly Lord authorizes you to flee to another town. This is not cowardice but is made necessary by the shortness of the time before the eschaton and by the missionary imperative. Do not remain in an inhospitable town, because you will not have completed the assigned task of preaching in every city in Israel before the End." It is on the basis of their claimed insight into the eschatological saving plan of God that the Christian prophets offer their word of command for the present situation. The command is not arbitrary, nor based on its authority as an inspired oracle alone, nor is the eschatological content simply speculative. Eschatological insight functions pastorally; pastoral "advice" is more than that, it is command grounded in a revealed eschatological mystery, as in Paul. The Apocalypse is similar in form and function, though the resulting command is different.

Thus we see that at almost every point the selection and editing of the missionary discourse to the disciples in Matthew 10 shows the influence of Christian prophets and the impression of Bultmann seems to be confirmed: "It was the risen (or ascended) Lord who spoke."[2]

MATTHEW 12:33–35: KNOW THEM
BY THEIR FRUITS

This Q material, though not of prophetic origin, is again brought into conjunction with traditions that have prophetic contacts by Matthew or someone in the Matthean church, as in 7:17–20 above. In verses 34, 36, and 37, the general criterion of "knowing them by their fruits," is made to apply directly to recognizing authentic Christian speech, that is, it is related more closely to the issues at the heart of Christian prophecy.

MATTHEW 13:35: PROPHETIC INTERPRETATION

Matthew's selection and interpretation of an Old Testament text is here probably influenced by the Christian prophets in Matthew's church, for it embodies several themes of Christian prophecy: the disclosure of what has been hidden, the revelation of contemporary events as part of the eschatological plan of God, the similarity to 1 Peter 1:10–12, the awareness of interpretating scripture with divinely given insight, as in the Qumran community, and the selection of a text from scripture in which Jesus could speak in the first person. Though Matthew is not a prophet himself, his use of the Old Testament is influenced by the prophets of his church. Scribal as he is, Matthew is not anticharismatic. He offers a model for noncharismatic affirmation of charismatic gifts in a pluralistic church.

MATTHEW 16:17–19, 18:18: PROPHETIC
AUTHORITY AND PRESENCE

The declaration in 18:18 could hardly be from the historical Jesus since it presupposes a post-Easter church that functions institutionally, needing some rabbiniclike procedures and structures for settling disputed issues. The saying has several indications of prophetic origin: (1) the introductory formula "amen, I say to you," (2) the legal-sounding declaration that settles a disputed issue in the community's life, expressed in (3) antithetic parallelism, similar to "sentences of holy law," and (4) the relation to John 20:23, where the saying is a post-Easter saying of the exalted Christ, from the prophetic Johannine community.

---

2 Bultmann, *History of the Synoptic Tradition,* 145.

The saying in 18:18 has an obvious connection with 16:17–19. This connection, the references to revelation from the Father and the assumed originally post-Easter setting of the story of Peter's confession have led some scholars to regard 16:17–19 as also having originated in Christian prophecy. But the matter needs to be stated more precisely. The form of 16:17–19 is not appropriate to a prophetic saying, despite the material connections with Christian prophecy: the saying pictures Jesus addressing a third party (Peter), rather than the hearer/reader. Prophets do not narrate incidents in which Jesus addressed a revered leader of the past but allow the risen Jesus to speak directly to the present.

Yet the prophetic characteristics of the passage call for explanation. It seems that the tradition developed in the following manner, in which Christian prophets played a formative role. (1) The tradition originated with the prophetic declaration 18:18 to the early Palestinian church, giving to the community (through its leaders) the power to bind and loose, i.e., regulatory power comparable to that exercised by the rabbis in the Jewish community, although its decisions were based on the charismatic utterance of prophetic figures in the community rather than on scribal tradition. (2) At a later date this logion was combined with a story narrating the risen Lord's appearance to Peter and establishing him as the foundational leader of the eschatological congregation. This accounts for both the post-Easter prophetic characteristics of 16:17–19 and the unprophetic objectifying and historicizing third-person style. (3) Matthew then combined this material with the narrative of Peter's confession in Mark, which also may have originally been a post-resurrection story.

MATTHEW 18:19–20: CONTINUING PRESENCE OF JESUS

This saying is certainly a post-Easter creation, for it gives a rule for prayer in the Christian community and represents Jesus as the cultically present Lord of the community, who takes the place of the Torah as the mediator of God's presence (cf. *Aboth* 3:2). The saying, or at least verse 20, is often considered to be the word of a Christian prophet. This may be the case, even though there are few specific indications of prophetic origin. The "amen" of verse 19 is of doubtful attestation, and otherwise the only indication of prophetic speech is the first-person form of a saying that is obviously post-Easter. But this could also readily be the literary product of a scribe or teacher who created a saying of Jesus in imitation of the Jewish saying about Torah. The presence of prophets in Matthew's church would have made this more acceptable, but not every such expansion of the tradition is prophetic.

MATTHEW 19:12: THE DECISION FOR
THE ASCETIC LIFE

This saying is not from a Christian prophet; it may even be from the historical Jesus. But its preservation in the Matthean church, and its inclusion by Matthew alone, may reflect the ascetic lifestyle of the Christian prophets, so that Matthew 19:12 is a "prophetic confession."

MATTHEW 17:20, 19:23b, 22:3:
PROPHETIC MARKS ON THE TRADITION

In 17:20 and 19:23b, material from Q and Mark respectively has the prophetic formula *"amen,* I say to you" added by the Matthean community or by Matthew himself. This does not mean that these two passages can be identified as sayings of Christian prophets, but it does mean that prophetic formulae are known and respected in the Matthean community and find their way into the tradition as it is handed on and around, and by literary imitation.

Matthew 22:3 is included in the Parable of the Great Supper, which was probably transmitted in the Q materials, but has been allegorized in the Matthean community or by Matthew. The "servants" of verses 3–6 are usually taken as intended to represent the Old Testament prophets. But Jack Kingsbury has pointed out that the "son" is already on the scene when the story opens, so these cannot be Israel's prophets.[3] He might have taken the observation one step further and noted that since all the figures in the story belong "to the eschatological age he ['the son'] has inaugurated," the "servants" must be the Christian messengers who were rejected and persecuted, namely, Christian prophets. The parable seems to have been reshaped in a community where prophecy was alive and respected.

MATTHEW 23:1–39: WOES

In this long speech against the Pharisees, Matthew incorporates the entirety of the prophetic Q speech against the Pharisees, preserving its original sevenfold pattern, appends the prophetic lamentation against Jerusalem from another context in Q, and expands the speech with material from his own tradition. What was already basically a collection of sayings from Christian prophets is amplified with other material and receives even more pronounced prophetic characteristics.

For instance, in verses 29–33, Matthew or his community has reformulated the saying in order to obtain another "prophet/righteous" pair,

---

3 *Matthew: Structure, Christology, Kingdom,* 72.

that is, a community composed of "prophets" (leaders) and "righteous" (laity), so that the phrase is a synonym for the whole church. He has increased the references to the suffering of the prophets and has made it more explicit that, just as the opponents stand in the succession of those who persecuted the true prophets of old, so he and his community stand in the succession of the true prophets themselves. And the Matthean editing of the concluding oracles in verses 34–36 and 37–39 makes them refer all the more clearly to the persecution of *Christian* prophets (and wise men and scribes), intensifying the references to persecution and replacing the ambiguous reference to the Wisdom of God with the prophetic "Behold, I send you forth . . ." (v. 34, RSV "Therefore I send you . . .").

THE RELATION OF MATTHEW'S GOSPEL TO SAYINGS OF THE RISEN JESUS

We have seen that Matthew's church and tradition are directly influenced by the presence of Christian prophets and that Matthew himself is open to the reception of sayings from Christian prophets. Matthew is suspicious of miraculous, charismatic phenomena when they are used to buttress a faulty theology or ethic but not of charismatic speech as such (7:15–22). Thus Matthew re-incorporates the Q tradition that had been rejected by Mark and strengthens and elaborates the prophetic motifs and materials in it. Unlike Mark, he has no hesitancy about allowing the risen Jesus to appear after Easter and to deliver a post-Easter speech that forms the climax of the book (28:16–20). Matthew throughout has a programmatic emphasis on the continuing presence of God with the community by means of the continuing presence of Jesus (1:23; 13:37–38; 18:18–20; 28:18–20). Unlike Luke, Matthew does not neatly contain Jesus within the framework of birth and ascension. The risen/exalted Christ does not "ascend" but remains on this earth with his church.

On the other hand, a number of items in Matthew indicate that the sayings of Jesus that he records are intended to be heard as the teaching of a historical figure of the past. Matthew adopts the Markan pre-Easter framework for his sayings, which he certainly understands in a historicizing manner, as is proven by his frequent addition of temporal connectives to Mark's rather "timeless" narrative style (e.g., "then" [*tote*] in 3:13; 4:1, 17; 9:14, 37; 15:1, 12, 28; 16:21, 24). Matthew thinks of the narrative he is relating in a there-and-then rather than here-and-now perspective. The five great discourses are specifically set off from the present as part of the historicizing narrative by the repeated formula "and when he [or Jesus] had finished these sayings . . ." (7:28; 11:1; 13:53; 19:1; 26:1). The commands of Jesus to be taught to disciples of all nations are represented by the teaching of the pre-Easter Jesus, a given body of material delivered in the past (28:18–20). The contemporizing final word of Mark's eschatological discourse (13:37) is conspicuously absent in Matthew 24:42. There is no place in the Matthean narrative, in fact, where Jesus addresses the reader directly—unlike the prophetically oriented narratives of Mark and John. The teaching of the historical Jesus is generalized to include the reader indirectly, by such formulae as "whoever" plus a verb in the subjunctive and "everyone who" plus a participle. Jesus is not presented to the reader as a prophet who addresses her or him immediately but as the supreme rabbi/teacher for the community (23:8–10), whose teaching is contained in the document at hand. This does not mean that the teaching of Jesus is a rigid new law, for the community has within it both prophetic and scribal leaders whose function it is to interpret and make relevant the teaching of Jesus (23:34; 13:52; 18:18).

Matthew seems to have both a historicizing and a contemporizing orientation to the sayings material he presents in his Gospel. How should we understand this dual thrust in Matthew? Matthew regards the sayings of Jesus that he transmits as the words of the historical Jesus, which have been preserved, amplified, and interpreted by the prophetic and scribal leaders of his community, of which he himself is one (scribe, not prophet: 13:52). The teaching of Jesus in the Gospel of Matthew is thus for Matthew basically report, not address: the word of the historicized Jesus in the narrative past, not the present word of the exalted Lord. But the sayings of Jesus are not a dead letter. The living Lord is present with his church as it transmits and interprets the teaching of its historical Lord (18:18–20; 28:18–20). The word of the exalted Lord heard in the preaching of church prophets and the contemporizing interpretation of Jesus' teaching done by church scribes must stand in historical continuity with the teaching of Jesus in the Gospel narrative and must responsibly interpret its content, though not necessarily repeat it. The prophetic phenomenon is affirmed by Matthew, but not uncritically, and all is seen through the rabbinic eyes of that scribe who has been trained for the Kingdom of Heaven and who brings out of his treasure things both new and old.

15

Prophetic Sayings of the Risen Jesus in Luke

In discussing the value of Luke-Acts as a source for the reconstruction of early Christian prophecy, I presented the general relationships between Luke and Christian prophecy. I now turn to inquire whether Luke contains sayings of Christian prophecy within the tradition of Jesus' words that he includes in his Gospel. Obviously, Luke takes over some sayings that originated as, or were shaped by, Christian prophets by virtue of using Mark and Q materials that included such sayings. But there is no indication that Luke understood these sources to contain sayings of the risen Jesus (cf. Luke 1:1–4; Acts 1:1–2). And it is a striking fact that Luke never contains the more prophetic form of a saying that he has taken from Mark or Q. This indicates that, unlike the Matthean tradition of Jesus' words, Luke's material from Mark and Q has not been reshaped in his immediate community by Christian prophets. Like the author of the Pastorals, Luke admires prophecy from a (chronological) distance but seems to have had minimal or no personal experience of the prophetic phenomenon in the church. I will now examine the peculiarly Lukan traditions, including those inserted into Markan and Q contexts, to determine whether they may contain expansions to the tradition made by Christian prophets in the earlier stage of the tradition.

LUKE 4:24–27: THE PROPHET IS
NOT ACCEPTABLE

Although Luke certainly has Mark 6:1–6 before him as he composes his programmatic scene of Jesus' rejection at Nazareth, it appears that he also has independent traditions that he works into his presentation. Some of these may have been influenced by Christian prophets in the early stage of the tradition. Luke 4:24, for instance, seems to have picked up the prophetic "amen, I say to you" in the course of the tradition. But there appear to be no further indications of influence from Christian prophets.

We seem to have a Lukan composition portraying Jesus in a prophetic role, attributing appropriate sayings to him based on Luke's understanding of Jesus as the prophet par excellence on the Old Testament model, rather than sayings from a Christian prophet incorporated by Luke. The prophetic aspect of the sayings is thus more redactional than traditional, more closely related to Luke's adoption of the prophets of Israel as his model than to Christian prophets. We shall find that this first instance of the phenomenon is typical of Luke.

LUKE 6:24–26: WOES

The four woes manifest some features of early Christian prophecy. The woe form itself is basically prophetic. The negative reference to "consolation" (paraklēsis) in verse 24 reflects the prophetic vocabulary. The eschatological orientation, including the motif of the reversal of status at the End Time, is appropriate to prophets, as is the reference to false prophets in verse 26. One could thus imagine that at some point in the developing tradition between Q and Luke, the four beatitudes in Q were taken up by a Christian prophet and expanded by adding the corresponding woes. Yet there is probably a better explanation. Since the woes are permeated with Lukan vocabulary and style, Luke himself, on the basis of some traditional elements, expands the beatitudes in his tradition, placing four "woes" in the mouth of Jesus in order to underscore dramatically the meaning of the traditional beatitudes. He does this not as a Christian prophet but as an author who exercises the right to make a literary expansion of the historicized speech of Jesus, just as he did with the speeches of his characters in Acts, and just as Josephus did in his histories. This would better account for the precise correspondence between woes and blessings; the author had the blessings before him in written form and composes the woes accordingly. This would also account for their prophetic form, for there are no features of the woes that are not readily explained on the basis of Old Testament prophecy. The content of the woes accords with the peculiarly Lukan blessing of the poor and the admonition of the rich (1:46–55; 2:8–14, 22–24 [cf. Lev. 12:2–8]; 3:11–14; 4:18; 12:13–21; 16:14, 19–31). The "prophetic" features of this text can then be seen more readily as redactional than traditional, and again we have a case of the peculiarly Lukan sayings of Jesus sounding the prophetic note because of Luke's interest in portraying Jesus as a "biblical" prophet.

LUKE 10:18: VISION OF SATAN'S FALL

This saying is unrelated to its context and appears to be a detached fragment, perhaps from some larger sayings complex now lost to us. The brevity of the saying precludes any firm decision as to its authenticity. It could derive from Jesus' own report of some visionary experience, analogous to his baptismal experience and the call-vision of a prophet, or it could represent some occasion of elation in Jesus' ministry in which he expressed his certainty of the defeat of Satan, similar to Mark 3:27. Some scholars have seen it as offering an important insight into Jesus' own self-consciousness. If the saying is from Jesus, it expresses his prophetic insight into the ultimate, behind-the-scenes meaning of his own ministry, as a response to the healings and exorcisms that he (and his disciples?) performed.

If the saying is not from Jesus, it is probably from a Christian prophet, for the nearest parallel is Revelation 12:8–9, where the seer expresses the divinely given insight that Satan has already been defeated in the heavenly world, so that the beleaguered disciples on earth can take courage. Since the saying reports a visionary experience, using eschatological language, to interpret the meaning of the present, it is more probable that the saying is of prophetic origin than from some other setting in the life of the church, if it is not from Jesus himself.

LUKE 10:19–20: THE TRUE CAUSE
FOR REJOICING

The circumstance of regarding too highly the spiritual powers of Jesus' disciples was certainly present in the early church (e.g., 1 Corinthians 12–14; 2 Corinthians 10–13); whether this was also true during Jesus' ministry is debatable, though possible. The sayings are quite appropriate to a post-Easter setting, as their similarity to the spurious ending of Mark indicates, and the reference to Jesus' "authority" is reminiscent of Matthew 28:18. The issue of the authenticity of these verses may be a borderline case, in which the relation to Christian prophecy might tip the scales in the direction of a church product.

There are points of contact with Christian prophecy in the vocabulary: "behold," "strike," "snake," and "scorpion" all occur frequently in Revelation. The saying in verse 19 was originally intended eschatologically, declaring that in the eschaton, which is already dawning, the disciples will triumph over the demonic powers that are defeated at the eschaton. The saying was not, then, intended as a promise that the disciples would survive snakebites (Acts 28:3–6; Mark 16:18); its horizon is eschatological, not historical. There is probably an allusive representation of scripture in the reference to treading on snakes and scorpions (Ps. 91:13; cf. Deut. 8:15), exhibiting the prophetic interpretation of scripture in eschatological terms. The general perspective of the saying is appropriate to Christian prophets, in that it is readily understood as a post-Easter commissioning declaration, in which the exalted Lord confers authority on his missioners, as in Matthew 28:16–20; Acts 13:1–3. Verse 20 would then fit a church setting in which charismatic phenomena were in danger of being overrated and would be the appropriate response of a Christian prophet who exhorts the Spirit-filled community not to be too impressed by signs and wonders but rather to be impressed by their election to the eschatological covenant community made known to them in the prophetic word, as in Paul (1 Corinthians 12–14), Revelation (e.g., 12:8–14), Mark 13:22–23, and Matthew 28:16–20.

LUKE 12:32: THE LITTLE FLOCK RECEIVES THE KINGDOM

This isolated saying was apparently not in Q but added to the tradition in the Q^{Lk} tradition, on the basis of the catchword "kingdom." The saying would fit well into a post-Easter situation in which the church knows itself to be the threatened "little flock" in need of assurance. The brevity of the saying makes it almost impossible to be confident of either its authenticity or its secondary origin.

The context in which the saying is presently found has been shaped by Christian prophets. The introductory formula "fear not" is a form of prophetic reassurance in Revelation 1:17; 2:10; is the address of the heavenly messenger and the risen Lord in Matthew 28:5, 10, and Acts 18:9; is the address of an angel in the context of prophetic revelation in Matthew 1:20 and Luke 1:13, 30; 2:10; is combined with the prophetic revelatory formula "I am" in Mark 6:50, Matthew 14:27, and John 6:20; occurs in Christian prophetic material in Matthew 10:26, 28, 31, and Luke 12:4, 7; and occurs elsewhere in the New Testament only as a word of Jesus. "Fear not" is thus clearly a prophetic form. The saying reflects the eschatological orientation of Christian prophecy, expressing the tension between the troubled present and the happy future that will soon be brought about by the eschatological reversal that was a theme of Christian prophecy. The behind-the-scenes decision of God, not apparent to anyone except the prophet who has divinely given insight, comes to expression in this saying, which as a whole resembles the oracle of salvation of the Old Testament prophets. Thus, if the saying is not from Jesus, it is probably from a Christian prophet or from Luke, who composes such prophetic sayings for the prophet Jesus in his narrative. A firm decision between these three is not possible.

LUKE 12:35–38: BE READY FOR THE COMING
OF THE SON OF MAN

Although these sayings have sometimes been attributed to Christian prophets, comparison with the criteria for prophetic speech fails to provide convincing evidence. One rather receives the impression from the sayings as a whole of a disparate collection of fragments that have incidentally accumulated some prophetic forms in the tradition, rather than of a unified prophetic oracle.

LUKE 19:42–44/21:20–24/23:28b–31:
THE COMING DESOLATION
OF JERUSALEM

Luke 19:42–44 has been considered the oracle of a Christian prophet and does seem to represent the prophetic insight as to what is really transpiring in history as seen from God's point of view (although the masses are unperceptive). Furthermore, it seems to express this in prophetic-predictive form, using the language of scripture (Isa. 29:1–4; Jer. 6:6–21; 52:4–5; Ezek. 4:1–3; Hos. 13:16; Hag. 2:15; Ps. 137:9), which is represented as the word of the exalted Jesus. Thus the saying could have been a prophetic oracle rewritten by Luke.

But 19:42–44; 21:20–24, and 23:28b–31 should all be considered together. In the Lukan narrative, these are three prophetic predictions by Jesus of the coming destruction of Jerusalem: the first given just before he enters the city, the second during the course of his teaching there, and the third as he leaves the city for the last time. Luke seems to have a definite interest in portraying Jesus as the last prophet to announce God's word in Jerusalem and be rejected, a prophet who gives the final announcement that God has rejected the city, which now faces the inevitable doom. The three oracles are related not only in general subject matter but in vocabulary, which suggests that they all have the same author. There is considerable peculiarly Lukan vocabulary, which has many contacts with the LXX. This suggests Lukan composition on the basis of his knowledge of the LXX; the supposed Aramaisms are most likely Septuagintisms. Peculiarly Lukan motifs occur, e.g., the resemblance of Jesus to Elisha, who also wept for the coming destruction of his people, using the identical verb from 2 Kings 8:11: *eklausen* ("he wept"). In Luke 21:20–24 we can see Luke himself rewriting the eschatological prediction of Mark 13:14–19, transforming it into the historicized *vaticinium ex eventu* that makes Jesus appear to be a prophet predicting the great historical crisis of the siege of Jerusalem during the Jewish war with Rome. This is all that is necessary to explain all three oracles of 19:42–44/21:20–24/23:28b–31. Although the possibility that Luke is rewriting material that had originally been created by Christian prophets cannot be excluded, the more likely possibility seems to be that once more Luke is himself composing prophetic-sounding sayings to place on the lips of the last great prophet, Jesus.

LUKE-ACTS AND THE SAYINGS OF
THE RISEN JESUS

As is the case in other streams of the Gospel tradition, so also in Luke, sayings of Christian prophets have made their way into the tradition of Jesus' words. But this has happened only to a minimal extent in the traditions peculiar to Luke. Christian prophets do not seem to have played a major role in the development of the sayings tradition in Luke's context. The more influential factor seems to have been the Lukan picture of Jesus as a prophet on the Old Testament model, which encouraged Luke to modify the sayings tradition redactionally so that Jesus speaks more like a prophet (of the Old Testament) in Luke than in his sources.

This minimal prophetic influence on the sayings of Jesus in Luke is strange since Luke pictures the early church as in frequent communication with heaven. The church's mission unfolds on the stage of history as it receives promptings from the heavenly world by a variety of means. Sometimes a heavenly voice, not otherwise identified, is the vehicle of the divine revelation (Acts 10:9–16; 11:7–10). Frequently the agent who instructs the church concerning the next steps in its mission is simply called "the Spirit," or "the Holy Spirit," without further description of the revelatory process (8:29; 10:19; 13:2; 16:6; 19:21; 20:22 [cf. 21:4]); once this Spirit is identified as the "spirit of Jesus" (16:7). Divine instruction is sometimes given through an "angel" (10:7, 22; 11:13), called also an "angel of the Lord" (5:19; 8:26; 12:7–11) or an "angel of God" (10:3; 27:23). The angel sometimes appears in a vision (10:3) and appears in scenes interchangeably with "the Spirit" (8:26/29; 11:12/13/15). Sometimes the various media of revelation are effected through a "vision" (9:10; 10:3, 17; 18:9; 26:19), and sometimes the vision alone is the means of revelation (16:9). Occasionally, the revelation is simply attributed to "God" (10:28) or "the Lord," in the sense of "God," not the "Lord Jesus" (10:33). It is thus clear that Luke intends the reader to see that the expansion of the early church, both geographically from Jerusalem to Rome and theologically from a Jewish sect to an inclusive worldwide religion, was directed by God from heaven, by means of heavenly voices, visions, angels, and the divine word mediated by persons inspired by the divine Spirit.

It is striking that in all this the exalted Jesus plays a minor role, and then only in the case of one person, Paul. Jesus himself speaks from heaven after the ascension only in 9:4–16; 22:6–10; 26:12–18, all referring to the one occasion of Paul's call to be an apostle/prophet, and in 18:9; 22:17–21; and 23:11. Paul is made a special case in this regard in order to authenticate him as a *witness* (26:16), since he does not qualify to be a full apostle in the Lukan understanding of the term. The exalted Jesus appears amidst the plethora of heavenly communication of Acts in only this relatively modest role and for this special purpose in connection with Paul's ministry.

A second remarkable fact is that the multitude of heavenly communications in Acts is primarily for revealing the divine strategy for the continuation of the church's mission, and for encouragement and consolation, rather than for new revelations of the will of God of the type made known in the teaching of the pre-Easter Jesus. Post-Easter revelations by voice, angel, vision, Spirit, or the word of the exalted Jesus himself do not add to the content of the revelation given in the word and ministry of Jesus of Nazareth. This is the case even in the crucial account of Peter's extension of the Gospel to the Gentiles in chapters 10–11 and the report of the Apostolic Council in chapter 15. In the first of these scenes, the church is led by an overwhelming display of divine revelations to include those who were formerly excluded. But this only makes effective what was already revealed by Jesus prior to his ascension (Luke 7:1–10; 13:22–30; 20:9–16; 21:24; 24:44–48) and was implicit in the Pentecost events and the preaching of Peter on the first day of the church's existence (Acts 2:5–11, 17, 21, 39). Neither the risen Jesus nor any other heavenly messenger reveals new increments of information concerning the divine will in Acts 10–11. Rather, the divine Spirit leads Peter and the others to realize in practice in their new situation the will of God that had already been revealed. The new insights in this regard are mediated by divine revelations and confirmed by the decision of the community that contains apostles (11:1, 18). So also in Acts 15—on the basis of reports of what God has done in the community by the Holy Spirit—the apostles and elders decide what God's will is for the present mission of the church (15:6–12, 22, 25), and the result is described as what "seemed good to the Holy Spirit and to us" (15:28). This is radically different from picturing the post-Easter community as receiving qualitatively new revelations from the risen Jesus.

By the power of the Spirit at work within it, the church continues to preach the "word of God," just as Jesus did during his earthly ministry (Luke 5:1; 8:11, 21; 11:28; Acts 4:31; 6:2; 8:14; 11:1; 13:5, 7, 44, 46, 48; 17:13; 18:11). But the "word of God" proclaimed by the church is not a continuation of, or supplement to, the preaching of the pre-ascension Jesus. Jesus himself—his life, ministry, death, resurrection, and future role as judge—is the content of the preaching of the "word of the Lord," which is simply a synonym for "word of God," rather than "word of the (risen) Lord (Jesus)" understood as a subjective genitive. The church's inspired preaching of the word of God is not for Luke a repetition of the teaching of the historical Jesus. Only in 11:16 and 20:35 is there reference to sayings of Jesus. The church's message is entirely a message about Jesus (= what God had done through him) rather than a continuation or repetition of his message.

The word of Jesus is thus strictly confined by Luke to the historical past, to the "midst of time" in which Jesus appeared and delivered his message. The sayings of Jesus are authoritative in that they were spoken by a past authority, introduced by the Lukan historicizing formula adapted from Mark (Acts 11:16; 20:35; cf. Luke 22:61 = Mark 14:72). In this the words of Jesus are not different in kind from the words of the Old Testament prophets, who are constantly cited as an authoritative word from the past. Luke intends his portrayal of Jesus as a prophet (Luke 4:16–21; 7:16; 24:19; Acts 3:22; 7:37) to be taken seriously, filling in his picture of Jesus with details and allusions from the prophets Moses, Elijah, and Elisha (e.g., Luke 4:25–27; 7:11–17; 8:49–56; 9:30 [9:36 omits the Markan John the Baptist–Elijah equation], 9:51, 54, 57–61). In 9:8, 19, Luke twice adds the word "old" prophets. The identification of Jesus as a "prophet" is not to be rejected, but the ministry of the prophet Jesus is firmly restricted to the historical past, the time before "the day when he was taken up," the time recorded in the "first book" of the Gospel of Luke, specifically dated as the fifteenth year of Tiberius Caesar (3:1–2).

The "began" of Acts 1:1 is strictly pleonastic and does not imply that Acts relates what the risen Jesus *continued* to do and teach. The relation of the power of God to the unfolding mission of the church in Acts is conceived by Luke in a different way than as the continuing ministry of Jesus, as we have seen above. The point may be seen by comparing Luke to Mark in this regard. In Mark, the "then" of Jesus' ministry is dialectically represented in the "now" of Mark's and his reader's own time. The reader is directly involved in the story, is addressed from within it, is invited to see himself or herself within the story.[1] For Luke, Jesus' word and ministry are past history. But all revelations of the Spirit, all new communications from heaven, must be judged by the recollection of the life, teaching, death, and resurrection of Jesus. God leads the Christian community forward, but not along a line contrary to God's definitive revelation in Jesus. The reader is separated from the story, to which he or she is related only indirectly.

This is clearly illustrated, for example, in the ways in which Mark and Luke respectively handle the missionary charge of Jesus to his disciples. Mark 6:8–11 changes the original radicality of the instructions to make

---

1 Norman Perrin, *Modern Pilgrimage,* 59.

them more realistically applicable to Mark's own day because he intends them to be heard as the present address of the risen Lord. The missioners are thus permitted to take a staff and to wear sandals. In Luke, on the other hand, the original radicality of the Q form of the saying is preserved in the instructions to the disciples during Jesus' ministry (9:3; 10:4) but is "corrected" by Jesus at the end of his ministry (22:35–36). The teaching of Jesus is directly applicable only during the "midst of time," the historical time when Jesus was on the earth. The teaching of Jesus is still authoritative but no longer addresses the reader directly as the word of the living Lord.

We are thus faced with the conclusion that Luke, who pictures the church as guided by the Spirit and frequently addressed by Christian prophets, does not understand these prophets to have produced new words of Jesus. Speeches inspired by the Holy Spirit do not result in sayings *of* Jesus (2:14–36; 4:8–12; 7:2–56) but proclaim the gospel *about* Jesus, reinterpreting the scriptures in the process, in accord with the post-Easter ministry of Jesus as portrayed in Luke 24:25–27, 44–47. The form of Christian prophecy in Acts is not that of "sayings of the risen Jesus" (11:28; 21:11). We have seen that this is not a result of accurate historical tradition but of Lukan theological tendency. Although Luke refers several times to "speaking in the name of Jesus" in the early church (Acts 4:17–20; 5:28; 5:40–42; 9:27–29), it is everywhere clear that for Luke this is not a description of speaking for the risen Jesus but describes the authority with which the disciples preached about Jesus and his soteriological significance (cf., e.g., 9:20–22 and 9:27–29; 4:7–12 and 4:17–18). Luke does not expect Jesus to speak through the Christian prophets of his own church. One has the distinct impression that Luke not only looked back upon the ministry of Jesus, when Jesus said what he had to say, but, like the author of Ephesians (2:20), also looked back to the ideal early days of the church, when Christian apostles and prophets under the sway of the Spirit led the church into new missionary paths.

16

A Note on Prophetic Sayings
of the Risen Jesus
in John

We have seen that early Christian prophets played a leading role in the Johannine community. But when we attempt to identify particular sayings in the Fourth Gospel as having been created or modified by Christian prophets, we find that we enter a different world from that of the Synoptics. The sayings themselves are very different from the Synoptics sayings tradition in both form and content. Here we no longer have short sayings, or even collections of such, but long and elaborate discourses, partly dialogue, but mostly monologue, and always tending to modulate from dialogue into monologue. The discourses are constructed thematically and resist analysis into separate pericope like those of the Synoptics.

The discourses of Jesus in the Fourth Gospel bear the characteristic stylistic marks of the author himself and his community. They are more like the discourse of the Johannine letters, especially 1 John, than they are like the sayings of Jesus in the Synoptics. But this does not mean the discourses were composed by the author *ex nihilo.* There are clear marks of a tradition. But it is practically impossible to distinguish layers in the developing tradition, as can be done with some readiness in the synoptic tradition. There is a kind of fusion, as though the tradition had been taken up, melted down, and reminted in the idiom of the Johannine community, and that this had been done repeatedly. It is thus very difficult to distinguish "primary" and "secondary" elements in the tradition, and then to look for prophetic characteristics in the secondary layer, as has been done with the Synoptic sayings.

When one looks at the discourses as wholes, however, one immediately notes prophetic features that characterize the tradition taken as a whole. While unlike the Synoptic sayings, the Johannine discourses bear a remarkable similarity to the discourses of the Hermetic literature common in the Hellenistic world. Hermes Trismegistus (Thrice-greatest Hermes) is the Greek designation for the Egyptian god Thoth. He is

266

represented as a sage of ancient Egypt who had been deified and who appeared in visions to his prophets, giving them revelations of the nature of the cosmos and the meaning of life. In form and vocabulary, these revelatory discourses remind one of the Johannine discourses.[1] The closest parallels to the Johannine discourses are the revelatory discourses of the risen Jesus in the apocryphal and Gnostic documents.

There are also particular points of contact between the features of the Johannine discourses and the characteristics of Christian prophets, such as the repeated introductory "amen" (RSV: "truly, truly, I say to you") and the revelatory use of "I am." Again, this does not mean that sayings that have such features are more likely to be from Christian prophets than other sayings, but that these prophetic features have come to characterize the tradition as a whole. We should most likely think of a long tradition of reinterpretation of the sayings of Jesus by preachers and teachers of the Johannine community who had come to think of the function of preaching and teaching as re-presenting the word of Jesus for the contemporary situation. Some of these transmitters and interpreters of the Johannine sayings tradition may have self-consciously exercised the role of the prophet-paraclete in the community; all of them are influenced by this model.

Likewise, the author of the Fourth Gospel, though he composes a narrative that places Jesus in the historical past, presents the discourse material within this framework in such a way that the reader is addressed out of the narrative by the continuing voice of the living Christ. Whether he knew the Gospel of Mark and understood this transhistorical dimension of the voice of Jesus in the Gospel in a manner analogous to Mark, or whether he independently devised a narrative form for the same purpose as Mark, the function of the word of Jesus in Mark and John is very similar, though the form of the sayings is different. In both cases, the continuing voice of Jesus is contained in a narrative, to keep it from floating free of its historical contact with the earthly crucified Jesus.

John has exercised more freedom than Mark in carrying out this intention, however. He characteristically begins the discourse in the there-and-then framework of the story of Jesus, who in the story line addresses the characters of the story, which the reader only "overhears." This modulates, sometimes imperceptibly, into direct address of the risen Lord to the reader. The line between report and address, tradition and prophecy grows thin. This can be seen most clearly in John 3, for example, where a past dialogue between Jesus and Nicodemus becomes the present address of the prophetic Johannine community to the reader.

---

1 See C. H. Dodd, "Hermetic Literature," in *The Interpretation of the Fourth Gospel*, 10–53. Samples of the texts themselves may be read in C. K. Barrett, *The New Testament Background: Selected Documents*, 94–103.

Both the times ("then" and "now") and the voices (the "past Jesus" and the "present Jesus speaking through the Johannine community") alternate and fade into each other without any overt indication. The paraclete-prophet respects the tradition of what the historical Jesus had said, calling it to memory (John 14:26), and gives new revelations for new post-Easter situations that the historical Jesus could not have said (16:12–13). Memory and new revelation are seen as complementary rather than competitive. But even the remembered sayings are not simply repeated but reformulated in the Johannine idiom. "Remember" does not mean simply "call past information to mind," but as 2:22; 12:16; and 13:7 show, it is the correct understanding given to the disciples only after the resurrection and the coming of the Spirit. The Fourth Gospel is composed in such a way as to frustrate any effort to distinguish between the sayings of Jesus and the voice of the prophetic/apostolic community. The prophetic phenomenon has modulated into a new narrative form.

17

Summary and Conclusions

We have seen that the influence of Christian prophets can be detected in each of the Gospels and their sources. Sayings of the risen Jesus appear in Q, Mark, "M," and "L" materials, and in the Johannine sayings tradition. But neither the number of sayings of the risen Jesus nor other influences of Christian prophets are randomly or equally distributed across the various layers and streams of the tradition and the Gospels into which they flowed. This is the result of the tension inherent between the prophetic form of "sayings of the risen Jesus" and the historicizing narrative form of the Gospels being resolved in different ways in the history of the development of the Gospels. In bold strokes that history may be charted as follows:

1. Jesus was himself a prophetic figure who initiated a prophetic community.

2. After Jesus' death the Easter experiences of his disciples were conceptualized as his having been raised from the dead and exalted to heaven as the Son of man who was shortly to come on clouds of glory at the eschaton, and who already made himself and his will known to his disciples in revelatory experiences related to the prophetic phenomena with which they were already acquainted. The Easter experiences themselves were apparently of a prophetic type, as the risen Jesus spoke in his own voice through his prophetic followers.

3. In the earliest Palestinian church, disciples who believed that Jesus had been exalted to the presence of God, and that this risen Jesus spoke through them, delivered pronouncements in his name in which he addressed the community as the exalted (and soon-to-reappear) Son of man. These prophetic pronouncements were a significant factor in the development of Christology.

4. The Palestinian-Syrian church handed on the tradition of Jesus' words but made no sharp distinction between them and sayings of Chris-

tian prophets in its midst. Christian prophets were related to the developing tradition of Jesus' words in a number of ways, of which the following may be listed:

a) A traditional saying of the historical Jesus could be taken up by a Christian prophet and re-presented in exactly the same form as a saying of the risen Jesus. Such a saying would have been proclaimed by the prophet as the present address of the exalted Lord and heard by the community as such, with a meaning appropriate to the new post-Easter situation. When this happens, there are no formal or material means of identifying the saying in our Gospels as "from" a Christian prophet.

b) A traditional saying of Jesus could be taken up by a Christian prophet, modified in ways that make it more relevant to the post-Easter church situation, and re-presented to the community as a saying of the risen Lord. This could happen without any characteristic traits of Christian prophetic speech being impressed on the saying. In this case, the saying belongs both to Jesus and to Christian prophecy, but we would not be able to identify it as related to Christian prophets, though we might be able to detect post-Easter elements in the saying.

c) A traditional saying of Jesus could be taken up by a Christian prophet, re-formed in ways characteristic of prophetic speech, and re-presented as a saying of the risen Jesus. Here, we might be able to identify the saying as "from" a Christian prophet but without denying that an earlier form of the saying originated with Jesus. In such sayings, "Jesus *or* Christian prophet?" is the wrong way of putting the question.

d) One or more traditional sayings of Jesus could be taken up by a Christian prophet, re-presented as the word of the exalted Lord, with or without modification in senses (b) and (c) above, and expanded by adding an additional saying or sayings that the prophet had created. When this happens, we might be able to identify the additions as from Christian prophets, without claiming that the whole sayings complex of which it is a part originated *ex nihilo* from Christian prophecy.

e) Without beginning with a saying of Jesus from the tradition, a prophet could deliver a new word of Jesus as an oracle from the risen Lord. Such oracles need not be seen as *creatio ex nihilo* and could use preexisting materials from the Old Testament and Christian tradition, but such traditional elements in the prophet's oracle would not have been heard previously as a saying of *Jesus,* pre- or post-Easter. If there are characteristic items of form or content present in such sayings, they can be identified as from Christian prophets. We should not expect that this will always be the case. Christian prophets may well have contributed sayings to the tradition of Jesus' words of any of the above types that did not contain sufficient typical prophetic traits of form and/or content to allow them to be identified by us. But my study has shown that a relatively large number can in fact be identified with some degree of probability.

f) Nonprophetic transmitters and shapers of the tradition between Jesus and the evangelists could have been influenced by the presence of Christian prophets in their community. Christian prophets might thus influence the tradition indirectly, as noncharismatic tradents modify the tradition in response to the presence of prophets in their community. This response could be either positive, where nonprophets reshape elements of the tradition into forms that prophets have made common, or negative, where traditional material is reshaped to oppose a certain kind of Christian prophecy.

This collection of sayings, containing sayings of both the historical and the exalted Jesus, as well as other materials attributed to Jesus, later crystallized into one or more editions of the document Q. The community that produced Q was led primarily by prophetic figures and tended to develop a prophetic understanding of the entire tradition of sayings of Jesus, so that even the sayings of the pre-Easter Jesus were heard more and more as the word of the exalted Lord, and Q began to take on the character of "sayings of the risen Jesus" in toto. Q contains a relatively large number of sayings originating from, and influenced by, Christian prophets.

5. One factor in Mark's creation of the Gospel form was his wariness of the genre of sayings collections represented by Q, in which the sayings of Jesus threatened to float free from the Jesus of history. Mark's suspicion of the Q genre accounts for the paucity of sayings of Jesus in Mark in general and the small number of sayings of Christian prophets in particular. Mark created a narrative form, "Gospel," in which the risen Jesus addresses the community only from within the framework of the pre-Easter life of Jesus. Prophecy receives a new form in the hands of Mark. But after Mark, the word of Jesus seems to have been expressed in the church in two contrary forms: "sayings of the risen Jesus," in which the living Lord of the church addressed the community directly, as one always contemporary with it (even if sayings of the historical Jesus were taken up into such an address), and the Gospel form, which was understood more and more in a historicizing manner, tending to *contain* the word of Jesus within a narrative anchored in the past.

6. Christian prophets similar to those of the Q community continued to be active parallel to the circulation of Mark in the church. In the stream of tradition in which Matthew was located, traditional sayings of Jesus were reshaped by Christian prophets and their influence, and new sayings were created. Adopting the historicizing framework of Mark as fundamental, Matthew had no hesitation about accepting the prophetic Q materials back into the tradition. But by the inclusion of Q *within* the Gospel framework, the danger Mark feared was still avoided, though no longer with the sharpness and intentionality of Mark. Matthew finds the prophetic form "sayings of the risen Jesus" congenial, so that we find a

relatively large number of sayings of Christian prophets in Matthew, but he has followed Mark in enclosing these within the life-of-Jesus framework. It is not clear that he has maintained the Markan dialectic between the historical and the exalted Jesus, and the sayings are probably all to be understood from a rabbinic rather than from a prophetic point of view, in Matthew's own eyes.

7. The peculiarly Lukan traditions contain a minimum of sayings of Christian prophets. This corresponds to Luke's own point of view, for he clearly transforms the Markan Gospel form into a life of Jesus. The Jesus of Luke's second volume still lives in heaven, but he no longer speaks to his church on earth; the Jesus of the first volume is the definitive figure of the past, but past nonetheless. For Luke, "sayings of the risen Jesus" has ceased to function as a category that has any relation to the tradition of the historical Jesus. Whatever sayings of Christian prophets appear in the Gospel of Luke as sayings of Jesus are accidental and incidental. Direct address has become report; prophecy has become history.

8. John, whether or not he knew the synoptics, is the product of an independent stream of tradition in which Christian prophecy had played a major role. The author of the Fourth Gospel has been influenced by the prophetic mode of interpreting the Jesus tradition, and, like Mark, composes a narrative that both pictures the Jesus of past history in the narrative story line and allows the risen Jesus directly to address the reader from within the narrative framework.

Theological struggles with Christian prophecy are apparent in the variety of ways that the New Testament relates the Jesus of history to "sayings of the risen Jesus." These struggles have not ceased. The church always finds itself with the double task of bearing witness to the once-for-all revelation given the world in the there-and-then event of Jesus of Nazareth, *and* of mediating the continuing voice of the living Lord. Study of the New Testament is the church's ally in this task, for it was composed in the midst of just such a struggle. In the canonical forms of Gospel and epistle, the Jesus who once spoke in Galilee and Jerusalem, and through whom God spoke in the cross and resurrection, continues to speak.

Selected Bibliography

Abrahams, Israel. "The Cessation of Prophecy." In *Studies in Pharisaism and the Gospels.* New York: KTAV Publishing House, 1967.

Aland, Kurt. "The Problem of Anonymity and Pseudonymity in the Christian Literature of the First Two Centuries." *Journal of Theological Studies* 12 (1961): 39–49.

Aune, David. "Christian Prophets and the Sayings of Jesus: An Index to Synoptic Pericopae Ostensibly Influenced by Early Christian Prophets." In *SBL 1975 Seminar Papers.* Missoula, Mont.: Scholars Press, 1975.

———. *The Cultic Setting of Realized Eschatology.* NovTSup. Leiden: E. J. Brill, 1972.

———. *Prophecy in Early Christianity and the Ancient Mediterranean World.* Grand Rapids: Wm. B. Eerdmans Publishing Co., 1983.

Bacht, H. "Die prophetische Inspiration in der kirchlichen Reflexion der vormontanistischen Zeit." *Scholastik* 19 (1944): 1–18.

———. "Wahres und falsches Prophetentum." *Biblica* 32 (1951): 237–262.

Bacon, B. W. *The Gospel of Mark: Its Composition and Date.* New Haven, Conn.: Yale University Press, 1925.

Barnett, P. W. "The Jewish Sign-Prophets, A.D. 40–70: Their Intentions and Origin." *NTS* 27 (1980): 679–697.

Barrett, C. K. *The Gospel According to St. John.* London: SPCK, 1956.

———. *The Holy Spirit and the Gospel Tradition.* New York: Macmillan Co., 1947.

———. *The New Testament Background: Selected Documents.* New York: Harper & Row, 1987.

Beare, F. W. "The Mission of the Disciples and the Mission Charge: Matthew 10 and Parallels." *JBL* 89 (March 1970): 1–13.

———. "Sayings of the Risen Jesus in the Synoptic Tradition: An Inquiry Into Their Origin and Significance." In *Christian History and Interpretation: Studies Presented to John Knox,* edited by W. R. Farmer, C. F. D. Moule, and R. R. Niebuhr. Cambridge: Cambridge University Press, 1967.

Beasley-Murray, G. R. *A Commentary on Mark Thirteen.* London: Macmillan & Co., 1957.

————. *Jesus and the Future: An Examination of the Criticism of the Eschatological Discourse, Mark 13, with Special Reference to the Little Apocalypse Theory.* London: Macmillan & Co., 1954.

Benz, Ernst. *Paulus als Visionär.* Wiesbaden: Steiner Verlag, 1952.

Berger, Klaus. *Die Amen-Worte Jesu. Eine Untersuchung zum Problem der Legitimation in apokalyptischer Rede.* Berlin: Walter de Gruyter, 1970.

————. *Exegese des Neuen Testaments: Neue Wege vom Text zur Auslegung.* Heidelberg: Quelle & Meyer, 1977.

————. "Die sogenannten 'Sätze heiligen Rechts': Ihre Funktion und Sitz im Leben." *TZ* 28 (1972): 305–330.

————. "Zu den sogenannten Sätzen heiligen Rechts." *NTS* 17 (October 1970): 10–40.

Best, Ernst. "Prophets and Preachers." *SJT* 12 (1959): 129–150.

Betz, Otto. *Offenbarung und Schriftforschung in der Qumransekte.* WUNT 6. Tübingen: J. C. B. Mohr (Paul Siebeck), 1960.

————. *Der Paraklet. Fürsprecher im häretischen Spätjudentum, im Johannesevangelium und in neugefundenen Gnostischen Schriften.* AGJU. Leiden: E. J. Brill, 1963.

Bieler, Ludwig. *THEIOS ANĒR. Das Bild des "göttlichen Menschen" in Spätantike und Frühchristentum.* Vienna: Buchhandlung Oskar Höfels, 1935.

Blenkinsopp, Joseph. "Prophecy and Priesthood in Josephus." *JJS* 25 (Summer 1974): 239–262.

Böcher, O. "Wölfe in Schafspelzen. Zum religionsgeschichtlichen Hintergrund von Matt. 7, 15." *TZ* 24 (1968): 405–426.

Boers, Hendrikus. "Where Christology Is Real." *Inter* 26 (1972): 300–327.

Boismard, E. "Jésus, le Prophète par excellence, d'après Jean 10:24–39." in *Neues Testament und Kirche,* edited by Joachim Gnilka. Freiburg: Herder, 1974.

Boman, Thorleif. *Die Jesus-Überlieferung im Lichte der neueren Volkskunde.* Göttingen: Vandenhoeck & Ruprecht, 1967.

Boring, M. Eugene. "The Apocalypse as Christian Prophecy." In *SBL 1974 Seminar Papers.* Missoula, Mont.: Scholars Press, 1974.

————. "Christian Prophecy and Matt. 10:23." In *SBL 1976 Seminar Papers.* Missoula, Mont.: Scholars Press, 1976.

————. "Christian Prophecy and Matt. 23:34–36: A Test Exegesis." In *SBL 1977 Seminar Papers.* Missoula, Mont.: Scholars Press, 1977.

————. "The Historical-Critical Method's 'Criteria of Authenticity': The Beatitudes in Q and Thomas as a Test Case." *Semeia* 44 (1988): 9–44.

————. "How May We Recognize Oracles of Christian Prophets in the Synoptic Tradition? Mark 3:28–29 as a Test Case." *JBL* 91 (1972): 501–521.

————. "The Influence of Christian Prophecy on the Johannine Portrayal of the Paraclete and Jesus." *NTS* 25 (1978): 113–123.

————. "The Paucity of Sayings in Mark: A Hypothesis." In *SBL 1977 Seminar Papers.* Missoula, Mont.: Scholars Press, 1977.

————. *Revelation: A Bible Commentary for Teaching and Preaching.* Louisville, Ky.: John Knox Press, 1989.

————. *Sayings of the Risen Jesus: Christian Prophecy in the Synoptic Tradition.* SNTSMS. Cambridge: Cambridge University Press, 1982.

————. "The Unforgiveable Sin Logion Mark 3:28–29/Matt. 12:31–32/Luke 12: 10: Formal Analysis and History of the Tradition." *NovT* 17 (1976): 258–279.

―――. "What Are We Looking For? Toward a Definition of the Term 'Christian Prophet.' " In *SBL 1973 Seminar Papers.* Missoula, Mont.: Scholars Press, 1973.

Bornkamm, Günther. *Jesus of Nazareth.* New York: Harper & Row, 1960.

―――. "Die Komposition der apokalyptischen Visionen in der Offenbarung Johannes." In *Studien zu Antike und Urchristentum,* edited by E. Wolf. Munich: Chr. Kaiser Verlag, 1959.

―――. "Der Paraklet im Johannesevangelium." In *Neutestamentliche Studien für Rudolf Bultmann zu seinem 70. Geburtstag am 20. August 1954,* edited by W. Eltester. Berlin: Alfred Töpelmann, 1957.

―――. "The Risen Lord and the Earthly Jesus, Matt. 28:16–20." In *The Future of Our Religious Past,* edited by James M. Robinson. New York: Harper & Row, 1971.

Bosold, I. *Pazifismus und prophetische Provokation: Das Grussverbot Lk 10, 4b und sein historischer Kontext.* Stuttgart: Katholisches Bibelwerk, 1978.

Bousset, Wilhelm. *Die Offenbarung Johannes.* KEK. Göttingen: Vandenhoeck & Ruprecht, 1906.

Brandenburger, Egon. *Markus 13 und die Apokalyptik.* FRLANT 134. Göttingen: Vandenhoeck & Ruprecht, 1984.

Brent, A. "Pseudonymity and Charisma in the Ministry of the Early Church." *Augustinianum* 27 (1987): 347–376.

Brockhaus, Ulrich. *Charisma und Amt. Die paulinische Charismalehre auf dem Hintergrund der frühchristlichen Gemeindefunktionen.* Wuppertal: R. Brockhaus, 1972.

Brooten, Bernadette. *Women Leaders in the Ancient Synagogue.* Chico: Scholars Press, 1982.

Brosch, Joseph. *Charismen und Ämter in der Urkirche.* Bonn: Peter Hanstein Verlag, 1951.

Bultmann, Rudolf. *The History of the Synoptic Tradition.* 1921. New York: Harper & Row, 1963.

―――. *Jesus and the Word.* New York: Charles Scribner's Sons, 1934.

―――. *Theology of the New Testament,* 2 vols. New York: Charles Scribner's Sons, 1951–55.

Bultmann, Rudolf, and Karl Kundsin. *Form Criticism: Two Essays on New Testament Research.* Chicago: Willet, Clark & Co., 1934.

Burrows, Millar. "Prophecy and the Prophets at Qumran." In *Israel's Prophetic Heritage,* edited by B. W. Anderson and Walter Harrelson. New York: Harper & Row, 1962.

Caird, G. B. *A Commentary on the Revelation of St. John the Divine.* New York: Harper & Row, 1966.

Callan, T. "Prophecy and Ecstasy in Greco-Roman Religion and in 1 Corinthians." *NovT* 27 (1985): 125–140.

Calvert, D. G. A. "An Examination of the Criteria for Distinguishing the Authentic Words of Jesus." *NTS* 18 (1971): 209–219.

Campenhausen, Hans Freiherr von. *Ecclesiastical Authority and Spiritual Power in the Church of the First Three Centuries.* London: Adam & Charles Black, 1969.

Charles, R. H. *A Critical and Exegetical Commentary on the Revelation of St. John.* 2 vols. ICC. New York: Charles Scribner's Sons, 1920.

Christ, Felix. *Jésus Sophia. Die Sophia-Christologie bei den Synoptikern.* ATANT. Zurich: Zwingli Verlag, 1970.

Colani, Timothy. *Jésus Christ et les croyances messianiques de son temps.* Strasbourg: Treuttel & Wurtz, 1864².

Collins, A. Y. *Crisis and Catharsis: The Power of the Apocalypse.* Philadelphia: Westminster Press, 1984.

Colpe, Carsten. "Der Spruch von der Lästerung des Geistes." In *Der Ruf Jesu und die Antwort der Gemeinde,* edited by Eduard Lohse. Göttingen: Vandenhoeck & Ruprecht, 1970.

———. *"Ho huios tou anthrōpou." TDNT* 8:400–477.

Conzelmann, Hans. *Acts of the Apostles.* Hermeneia. Philadelphia: Fortress Press, 1987.

———. *First Corinthians: A Commentary on the First Epistle to the Corinthians.* Hermeneia. Philadelphia: Fortress Press, 1975.

———. *Jesus.* Philadelphia: Fortress Press, 1973.

———. *An Outline of the Theology of the New Testament.* London: SCM Press, 1969.

———. *The Theology of St. Luke.* New York: Harper & Row, 1960.

Cothonet, É. "Les prophètes chrétiens dans l'Évangile selon saint Matthieu." In *L'Évangile selon Matthieu: Rédaction et théologie,* edited by M. Didier. Gembloux: Duculot, 1972.

———. "Prophétisme dans le Nouveau Testament." *DBSup* 8. Paris: Ceffonds, 1972.

———. "Prophétisme et ministère d'après le Nouveau Testament." *Maison-Dieu* 107 (1971): 29–50.

Crenshaw, J. L. *Prophetic Conflict.* Berlin: Walter de Gruyter, 1971.

Crone, Theodore. *Early Christian Prophecy: A Study of Its Origin and Function.* Baltimore, 1973.

Crossan, J. D. *In Fragments: The Aphorisms of Jesus.* San Francisco: Harper & Row, 1983.

Cullmann, Oscar. *Early Christian Worship.* SBT. London: SCM Press, 1953.

———. " 'Kyrios' as Designation for the Oral Tradition Concerning Jesus." *SJT* 3 (1950): 180–197.

———. "The Tradition." In *The Early Church,* edited by A. J. B. Higgins. London: SCM Press, 1956.

Currie, S. D. " 'Speaking in Tongues': Early Evidence Outside the New Testament Bearing on 'Glossais Lalein.' " *Interpretation* 19 (1965): 274–294.

Daniel, Constantine. " 'Faux Prophètes': surnom des Esséniens dans le Sermon sur la Montagne." *Revue de Qumran* 7 (1969): 45–79.

Dautzenberg, Gerhard. "Glossolalie." *RAC* 11 (1981): 225–246.

———. *Urchristliche Prophetie. Ihre Erforschung, ihre Voraussetzungen im Judentum und ihre Struktur im ersten Korintherbrief.* BWANT. Stuttgart: W. Kohlhammer, 1975.

———. "Zum religionsgeschichtlichen Hintergrund der *diakrisis pneumatōn* (1 Kor. 12, 10)." *BZ,* new series, 15 (1971): 93–104.

Davies, W. D. "Reflections on a Scandinavian Approach to 'the Gospel Tradition.' " Appendix 15 of *The Setting of the Sermon on the Mount.* Cambridge: Cambridge University Press, 1966.

Delling, Gerhard. "Geprägte Jesus-Tradition im Urchristentum." *Communio Viatorum* 4 (1961): 59–71.

Dibelius, Martin. *Botschaft und Geschichte: Gesammelte Aufsätze von Martin Dibelius.* Vol. 1, *Zur Evangelienforschung.* Tübingen: J. C. B. Mohr (Paul Siebeck), 1953.

———. *Die Formgeschichte des Evangeliums.* 3rd edition with a supplement by Gerhard Iber. Tübingen: J. C. B. Mohr (Paul Siebeck), 1959.

———. *From Tradition to Gospel.* 1919. New York: Charles Scribner's Sons, 1935.

Dodd, C. H. *According to the Scriptures: The Sub-structure of New Testament Theology.* New York: Charles Scribner's Sons, 1953.

———. "Hermetic Literature." In *The Interpretation of the Fourth Gospel.* Cambridge: Cambridge University Press, 1953, 10–53.

———. "Jesus as Teacher and Prophet." In *Mysterium Christi,* edited by G. K. A. Bell and Adolf Deissmann. New York: Longmans, Green & Co., 1930.

Dungan, David. *The Sayings of Jesus in the Churches of Paul.* Philadelphia: Fortress Press, 1971.

Dunn, James D. G. *Christology in the Making.* Philadelphia: Westminster Press, 1980.

———. *Jesus and the Spirit.* Philadelphia: Westminster Press, 1975.

———. "Matthew 12:28/Luke 11:20—A Word of Jesus?" In *Eschatology and the New Testament,* edited by Hulitt Gloer. Peabody, Mass.: Hendrickson, 1989, 29–50.

———. "Prophetic 'I'-Sayings and the Jesus Tradition: The Importance of Testing Prophetic Utterances Within Early Christianity." *NTS* 24 (January 1978): 175–198.

Dupont, Jacques. *Les Béatitudes,* 3 vols. Paris: J. Gabalda, 1969–73.

———. "Le logion des douze trônes (Matt. 19:28/Luc. 22:28–30)." *Biblica* 45/3 (1964): 355–392.

Easton, B. S. *The Gospel Before the Gospels.* New York: Charles Scribner's Sons, 1928.

Edwards, Richard. "Christian Prophecy and the Q Tradition." In *SBL 1976 Seminar Papers.* Missoula, Mont.: Scholars Press, 1976.

———. *A Theology of Q: Eschatology, Prophecy, and Wisdom.* Philadelphia: Fortress Press, 1976.

Ellis, E. Earle. "Luke 11:49–51: An Oracle of a Christian Prophet?" *Expository Times* 74 (1963): 157–158.

———. *Paul's Use of the Old Testament.* Grand Rapids: Wm. B. Eerdmans Publishing Co., 1957.

———. *Prophecy and Hermeneutic in Early Christianity.* Grand Rapids: Wm. B. Eerdmans Publishing Co., 1978.

———. "The Role of the Christian Prophet in Acts." In *Apostolic History and the Gospel: Biblical and Historical Essays Presented to F. F. Bruce on His Sixtieth Birthday,* edited by Ward Gasque and Ralph P. Martin. Grand Rapids: Wm. B. Eerdmans Publishing Co., 1970.

Fascher, Erich. *PROPHĒTĒS. Eine sprach- und religionsgeschichtliche Untersuchung.* Giessen: Alfred Töpelmann, 1927.

Filson, Floyd V. "The Christian Teacher in the First Century." *JBL* 60 (1941): 317–328.

Fiorenza, Elisabeth Schüssler. *The Book of Revelation: Justice and Judgment.* Philadelphia: Fortress Press, 1985.

———. *In Memory of Her: A Feminist Theological Reconstruction of Christian Origins.* New York: Crossroad Publishing Co., 1983.

———. "The Quest for the Johannine School: The Apocalypse and the Fourth Gospel." *NTS* 23 (1977): 402–427.

Forbes, Christopher. "Early Christian Inspired Speech and Hellenistic Popular Religion." *NovT* 28 (1986): 257–270.

———. "Prophecy and Inspired Speech in Early Christianity and Its Hellenistic Environment." Ph. D. diss., Macquarie University, 1987.

Forster, Werner. "Der Heilige Geist im Spätjudentum." *NTS* 8 (1961): 117–134.

Friedrich, Gerhard. *"Prophētēs." TDNT* 6:848–849.

Fuchs, Ernst. "Das Sprachereignis in der Verkündigung Jesu, in der Theologie des Paulus und im Ostergeschehen." In *Zum hermeneutischen Problem in der Theologie. Die existentiale Interpretation.* Tübingen: J. C. B. Mohr (Paul Siebeck), 1965².

Funk, Robert. *Language, Hermeneutic, and Word of God.* New York: Harper & Row, 1966.

Furnish, Victor. *The Jesus-Paul Debate: From Baur to Bultmann.* Manchester: John Rylands Library, 1965.

Gager, John. *Kingdom and Community: The Social World of Early Christianity.* Englewood Cliffs, N.J.: Prentice-Hall, 1975.

Gaston, Lloyd. *No Stone on Another: Studies in the Significance of the Fall of Jerusalem in the Synoptic Gospels.* NovTSup. Leiden: E. J. Brill, 1970.

Gerhardsson, Birger. *Die Anfänge der Evangelientradition.* Wuppertal: R. Brockhaus, 1977.

———. "Die Boten Gottes und die Apostel Christi." *Svensk Exegetisk Arsbok* 27 (1962): 110–121.

———. *Memory and Manuscript: Oral Tradition and Written Transmission in Rabbinic Judaism and Early Christianity.* Uppsala: Almquist & Wiksells, 1961.

———. *Tradition and Transmission in Early Christianity.* Lund: Gleerup, 1964.

———. "Der Weg der Evangelien-Tradition." In *Das Evangelium und die Evangelien,* edited by Peter Stuhlmacher. WUNT 28. Tübingen: J. C. B. Mohr (Paul Siebeck), 1983.

Giblet, J. "Prophétisme et attente d'un Messie prophète dans l'ancien Judaïsme." In *L'Attente du Messie,* edited by L. Cerfaux. Paris: Desclée de Brouwer, 1954.

Gillespie, Thomas W. "A Pattern of Prophetic Speech in 1 Corinthians." *JBL* 97 (March 1978): 74–95.

———. "Prophecy and Tongues: The Concept of Christian Prophecy in the Pauline Theology." Ph. D. diss., Claremont Graduate School, 1971.

Gils, F. *Jésus prophète d'après les évangiles synoptiques.* Louvain: Publications Universitaires, 1957.

Greeven, Heinrich. "Propheten, Lehrer, Vorsteher bei Paulus." *ZNW* 44 (1952): 1–29.

Grudem, Wayne. *The Gift of Prophecy in 1 Corinthians.* Washington: University Press of America, 1982.

———. *The Gift of Prophecy in the New Testament and Today.* Westchester, Ill.: Crossway Books, 1988.

Guelich, Robert A. "The Matthean Beatitudes: 'Entrance-Requirements' or Eschatological Blessings." *JBL* 95 (September 1976): 415–434.

———. *The Sermon on the Mount: A Foundation for Understanding.* Waco, Texas: Word Books, 1982.

Gunkel, Hermann. *Die Wirkungen des heiligen Geistes. Nach der populären Anschauung der apostolischen Zeit und nach der Lehre des Apostels Paulus.* Göttingen: Vandenhoeck & Ruprecht, 1888.

Güttgemanns, Erhardt. *Candid Questions Concerning Gospel Form Criticism: A Methodological Sketch of the Fundamental Problematics of Form and Redaction Criticism.* Pittsburgh: Pickwick Press, 1979.

Guy, H. A. *New Testament Prophecy: Its Origin and Significance.* London: Epworth Press, 1947.

Haenchen, Ernst. *The Acts of the Apostles.* Philadelphia: Westminster Press, 1971.

Hahn, Ferdinand. "Die Sendschreiben der Johannesapokalypse. Ein Beitrag zur Bestimmung prophetischer Redeformen." In *Tradition und Glaube: Das frühe Christentum in seiner Umwelt. Festgabe für Karl Georg Kuhn zum 65. Geburtstag,* edited by Gert Jeremias, Heinz-Wolfgang Kuhn, and Hartmann Stegemann. Göttingen: Vandenhoeck & Ruprecht, 1971.

Halliday, W. R. *Greek Divination: A Study of Its Methods and Principles.* Chicago, 1913. Reprint 1967.

Hann, R. "Post-Apostolic Christianity as a Revitalization Movement: Accounting for Innovation in Early Patristic Traditions." *JRelS* 14 (1987): 60–75.

Hanson, J. S. "Dreams and Visions in the Graeco-Roman World and Early Christianity." *ANRW* II.23.2 (1980), 1395–1427.

Hare, Douglas R. A. *The Theme of Jewish Persecution of Christians in the Gospel According to St. Matthew.* SNTSMS. Cambridge: Cambridge University Press, 1967.

Harnack, Adolf. *The Constitution and Law of the Church in the First Two Centuries.* New York: Putnam, 1910.

———. *Die Lehre der zwölf Apostel nebst Untersuchungen zur ältesten Kirchenfassung und des Kirchenrechts.* TU 2, 1/2. Leipzig, 1884.

———. *The Mission and Expansion of Christianity in the First Three Centuries.* New York: Putnam, 1904.

———. *The Sayings of Jesus.* New York: Putnam, 1908.

Hart, M. E. "Prophecy and Speaking in Tongues as Understood by Paul and at Corinth, with Reference to Early Christian Usage." Ph.D. diss., University of Durham, 1975.

Hartmann, Lars. *Prophecy Interpreted.* Lund: Gleerup, 1966.

Hasler, Victor. *Amen. Redaktionsgeschichtliche Untersuchung zur Einführungsformel der Herrenworte "Wahrlich ich sage euch."* Zurich: Gotthelf-Verlag, 1969.

Havener, Ivan. *Q: The Sayings of Jesus.* Wilmington, Del.: Michael Glazier, 1987.

Hawthorne, Gerald F. "Christian Prophecy and the Sayings of Jesus: Evidence of and Criteria for." In *SBL 1975 Seminar Papers.* Missoula, Mont.: Scholars Press, 1975.

———. "The Role of Christian Prophets in the Gospel Tradition." *Tradition and Interpretation in the New Testament: Essays in Honor of E. Earle Ellis,* edited by Gerald F. Hawthorne. Grand Rapids: Wm. B. Eerdmans Publishing Co.: 1987.

Hengel, Martin. *Judaism and Hellenism: Studies in Their Encounter in Palestine During the Early Hellenistic Period.* London: SCM Press, 1974.

———. *Nachfolge und Charisma: Eine exegetisch-religionsgeschichtliche Studie zu Matt. 8:21f und Jesus Ruf in die Nachfolge.* Berlin: Alfred Töpelmann, 1968.

Hennecke, Edgar, and Wilhelm Schneemelcher, eds. *New Testament Apocrypha.* 2 vols. Philadelphia: Westminster Press, 1964.

Henneken, Bartholomäus. *Verkündigung und Prophetie im 1. Thessalonicherbrief.* SBS. Stuttgart: Katholisches Bibelwerk, 1969.

Higgins, A. J. B. *Jesus and the Son of Man.* Philadelphia: Fortress Press, 1964.

———. " 'Menschensohn' oder 'ich' in Q: Luke 12: 8–9/Matt. 10: 32–33." In *Jesus und der Menschensohn,* edited by Rudolf Pesch and Rudolf Schnackenburg. Freiburg: Herder, 1975.

Hill, David. *"Dikaioi* as a Quasi-Technical Term." *NTS* 11 (1965): 296–302.

———. *New Testament Prophecy.* Atlanta: John Knox Press, 1979.

———. "On the Evidence for the Creative Role of Christian Prophets." *NTS* 20 (1974): 262–274.

———. "Prophecy and Prophets in the Revelation of St. John." *NTS* 18 (1972): 401–418.

Hoffmann, Paul. *Studien zur Theologie der Logienquelle.* Münster: Verlag Aschendorff, 1972.

Horsley, Richard A., with John S. Hanson. *Bandits, Prophets, and Messiahs.* San Francisco: Harper & Row, 1985.

Houston, Walter. "New Testament Prophecy and the Gospel Tradition." Ph. D. diss., Mansfield College, Oxford University, 1973.

Hubbard, Benjamin J. *The Matthean Redaction of a Primitive Apostolic Commissioning: An Exegesis of Matt. 28:16–20.* SBLDS. Missoula, Mont.: Scholars Press, 1974.

Hughs, Frank Witt. *Early Christian Rhetoric and 2 Thessalonians.* JSNTSup 30. Sheffield: JSOT Press, 1989.

Jeremias, Gert. *Der Lehrer der Gerechtigkeit.* SUNT. Göttingen: Vandenhoeck & Ruprecht, 1963.

Jeremias, Joachim. *New Testament Theology.* Vol. 1: *The Proclamation of Jesus.* New York: Charles Scribner's Sons, 1971.

———. *The Parables of Jesus.* New York: Charles Scribner's Sons, revised edition 1963.

———. *The Prayers of Jesus.* SBT. Naperville, Ill.: Alec R. Allenson, 1967.

———. "Zum nicht-responsorischen Amen." *ZNW* 64 (1973): 122–123.

Johnson, Luke Timothy. "Norms for True and False Prophecy in First Corinthians." *American Benedictine Review* 22 (1971): 29–45.

Johnston, George. *The Spirit-Paraclete in the Fourth Gospel.* SNTSMS. Cambridge: Cambridge University Press, 1970.

Juel, Donald. *Messianic Exegesis: Christological Interpretation of the Old Testament in Early Christianity.* Philadelphia: Fortress Press, 1988.

Käsemann, Ernst. "Geist und Geistesgaben im Neuen Testament." *RGG*[3]. Tübingen: J. C. B. Mohr (Paul Siebeck), 1958.

———. *Essays on New Testament Themes.* London: SCM Press, 1960.

———. *New Testament Questions of Today.* London: SCM Press, 1969.

———. *The Testament of Jesus.* London: SCM Press, 1968.

———. "Der Urchristliche Enthusiasmus." Seminarprotokol des Neutestamentlichen Seminar im Wintersemester 1964–65, University of Tübingen.

Kee, Howard Clark. *Christian Origins in Sociological Perspective.* Philadelphia: Westminster Press, 1980.

Kelber, Werner. *The Kingdom in Mark.* Philadelphia: Fortress Press, 1973.

————. *The Oral and Written Gospel: The Hermeneutics of Speaking and Writing in the Synoptic Tradition, Paul, Mark, and Q.* Philadelphia: Fortress Press, 1983.

————. *The Passion in Mark.* Philadelphia: Fortress Press, 1976.

Kingsbury, Jack. *Matthew: Structure, Christology, Kingdom.* Philadelphia: Fortress Press, 1975.

Klein, Günther. "Die Verfolgung des Apostel, Lu. 11, 49." In *Neues Testament und Geschichte,* edited by Heinrich Baltensweiler and Bo Reicke. Tübingen: J. C. B. Mohr (Paul Siebeck), 1972.

Kloppenborg, John S. "Blessing and Marginality: The 'Persecution Beatitude' in Q, Thomas, and Early Christianity." *Forum* 2/3 (1986): 35–36.

————. *The Formation of Q: Trajectories in Ancient Wisdom Collections.* SAC. Philadelphia: Fortress Press, 1987.

Kolenkow, A. B. "Relationships Between Miracle and Prophecy in the Greco-Roman World and Early Christianity." *ANRW* II.23.2 (1980), 1470–1506.

Knox, John. *The Church and the Reality of Christ.* New York: Harper & Row, 1962.

Koch, Klaus. *The Growth of the Biblical Tradition: The Form-Critical Method.* New York: Charles Scribner's Sons, 1969.

Kraft, Heinrich. "Die altkirchliche Prophetie und die Entstehung des Montanismus." *TZ* 11 (1955): 249–271.

————. *Die Offenbarung des Johannes.* HNT. Tübingen: J. C. B. Mohr (Paul Siebeck), 1974.

Kragerud, Alv. *Der Lieblingsjünger im Johannesevangelium. Ein exegetischer Versuch.* Oslo: Osloer Universitätsverlag, 1959.

Krämer, Michael. "Hütet euch von den falschen Propheten: Eine überlieferungsgeschichtliche Untersuchung zu Mt. 7, 15–23/Lk. 6, 43–46/Matt. 12, 33–37." *Biblica* 57 (1976): 349–377.

Kretschmar, G. "Ein Beitrag zur Frage nach dem Ursprung frühchristlicher Askese." *ZTK* 61 (1964): 27–67.

Kundsin, Karl. "Zur Diskussion über die Ego-eimi-Sprüche des Johannesevangeliums." In *Charisteria Iohanni Kopp. Octogenario Oblata,* edited by J. Aunver and A. Vööbus. Stockholm, 1954.

Lambrecht, Jan. *Die Redaktion der Markus-Apokalypse. Literarische Analyse und Strukturuntersuchung.* Rome: Pontifical Biblical Institute, 1967.

Lanckowski, G. "Propheten." *Lexikon für Theologie und Kirche,* edited by Joseph Höfer and Karl Rahner. 14 vols. Freiburg: Herder, 1957–65.

Leisegang, Hans. *Der Heilige Geist. Das Wesen und Werden der mystisch-intuitiven Erkenntnis in der Philosophie und Religion der Griechen.* Vol. 1 of *Die vorchristlichen Anschauungen und Lehren vom* pneuma *und der mystisch-intuitiven Erkenntnis.* Leipzig: B. G. Teubner, 1919.

————. *Pneuma Hagion. Der Ursprung des Geistsbegriffs der synoptischen Evangelien aus der griechischen Mystik.* Leipzig: J. C. Hinrichs'sche Buchhandlung, 1922.

Leivestad, R. "Das Dogma von der Prophetenlosen Zeit." *NTS* 19 (April 1973): 288–299.

Leroy, Herbert. *Jesus. Überlieferung und Deutung.* ErFor 95. Darmstadt, 1978.

Lindars, Barnabas. *New Testament Apologetic.* London: SCM Press, 1961.

Lindblom, Johannes. *Gesichte und Offenbarungen. Vorstellungen von göttlichen Weisungen und übernatürlichen Erscheinungen im ältesten Christentum.* Lund: Gleerup, 1968.

Loisy, Alfred. *The Birth of the Christian Religion*. London: George Allen & Unwin, 1948.

——. *The Origins of the New Testament*. New York: Macmillan Co., 1950.

Luedemann, Gerd. *Early Christianity According to the Traditions in Acts: A Commentary*. Philadelphia: Fortress Press, 1989.

Lührmann, Dieter. "Die Frage nach Kriterien für ursprüngliche Jesusworte. Eine Problemskizze." In *Jésus aux origines de la christologie*, edited by J. Dupont. BETL 40. Louvain: Leuven University Press, 1975.

——. "Jesus und seine Propheten. Besprächsbeitrag." In *Prophetic Vocation in the New Testament and Today*, edited by John Panagopoulos. NovTSup. Leiden: E. J. Brill, 1977.

——. *Die Redaktion der Logienquelle*. WMANT. Neukirchen-Vluyn: Neukirchener Verlag, 1969.

Luz, Ulrich. "Die Erfüllung des Gesetzes bei Matthäus (Mt 5, 17–20)." *ZTK* 75 (1978): 398–435.

——. *Das Evangelium nach Matthäus*. EKKNT. Zurich: Benziger Verlag; Neukirchen: Neukirchener Verlag, 1985.

Mack, Burton L. *A Myth of Innocence*. Philadelphia: Fortress Press, 1988.

McNeile, A. H. *The Gospel According to St. Matthew*. London: Macmillan & Co., 1915.

Manson, T.W. "The Sayings of Jesus." In *The Mission and Message of Jesus*, edited by H. D. A. Major, T. W. Manson, and C. J. Wright. New York: E. P. Dutton & Co., 1938.

Manson, W. "The *egō eimi* of the Messianic Presence in the New Testament." *JTS* 48 (1947): 137–145.

Mare, W. H. "Prophet and Teacher in the New Testament Period." *Bulletin of the Evangelical Theological Society* 9 (1966): 139–148.

Mather, P. Boyd. "Christian Prophecy and Matthew 28:16–20: A Test Exegesis." In *SBL 1977 Seminar Papers*. Missoula, Mont.: Scholars Press, 1977.

Mearns, C. "The Son of Man Trajectory and Eschatological Development." *Exp Tim* 97 (1985): 8–12.

Meyer, Paul D. "The Gentile Mission in Q." *JBL* 89 (1970): 405–417.

Meyers, Jacob M., and Edwin D. Freed. "Is Paul Also Among the Prophets?" *Inter* 20 (1966): 40–53.

Michaels, J. Ramsey. "Christian Prophecy and Matthew 23:8–12: A Test Exegesis." In *SBL 1976 Seminar Papers*. Missoula, Mont.: Scholars Press, 1976.

——. "The Johannine Words of Jesus and Christian Prophecy." In *SBL 1975 Seminar Papers*. Missoula, Mont.: Scholars Press, 1975.

Michel, Otto. "Spätjüdisches Prophetentum." In *Neutestamentliche Studien für Rudolf Bultmann zu seinem siebzigsten Geburtstag am 20. August 1954*, edited by Walter Eltester. Berlin: Alfred Töpelmann, 1954.

Miller, R. J. "The Rejection of the Prophets in Q." *JBL* 107 (1988): 225–240.

Minear, Paul. "False Prophecy and Hypocrisy in the Gospel of Matthew." In *Neues Testament und Kirche*, edited by Joachim Gnilka. Freiburg: Herder, 1974.

——. *I Saw a New Earth*. Washington, D.C.: Corpus Books, 1968.

——. *New Testament Apocalyptic*. Nashville: Abingdon Press, 1981.

——. *To Heal and to Reveal: The Prophetic Vocation According to Luke*. New York: Seabury Press, 1976.

Moore, George F. *Judaism in the First Centuries of the Christian Era.* 3 vols. Cambridge, Mass.: Harvard University Press, 1927–30.

Mowinckel, Sigmund. *Prophecy and Tradition: The Prophetic Books in the Light of the Study of the Growth and History of the Tradition.* Oslo: Jacob Dybwad, 1946.

Müller, Ulrich. *Die Offenbarung des Johannes.* Gütersloh: Gütersloher Verlagshaus Gerd Mohn, 1984.

———. "Die Parakleten-Vorstellungen im Johannesevangelium." *ZTK* 71 (March 1974): 31–78.

———. *Prophetie und Predigt im Neuen Testament. Formgeschichtliche Untersuchungen zur urchristlichen Prophetie.* Gütersloh: Gütersloher Verlagshaus Gerd Mohn, 1975.

Mussner, Franz. "Die joh. Parakletsprüche und die apostolische Tradition." *BZ* 5 (1961): 56–70.

Neugebauer, F. "Geistsprüche und Jesuslogien." *ZNW* 53 (1962): 218–228.

Neusner, Jacob. *Early Rabbinic Judaism.* Leiden: E. J. Brill, 1975.

———. "The Formation of Rabbinic Judaism: Yavneh (Jamnia) from A.D. 70 to 100. *ANRW* II. 19.2 (1979), 292–309.

Panagopoulos, John, ed. *Prophetic Vocation in the New Testament and Today.* NovT-Sup. Leiden: E. J. Brill, 1977.

Patsch, H. "Die Prophetie des Agabus." *TZ* 28 (1972): 228–232.

Peabody, David. "A Pre-Markan Prophetic Sayings Tradition and the Synoptic Problem." *JBL* 97 (1978): 391–409.

Pearson, Birger. *The Pneumatikos-Psychikos Terminology in 1 Corinthians.* Missoula, Mont.: Scholars Press, 1973.

Perrin, Norman. *A Modern Pilgrimage in New Testament Christology.* Philadelphia: Fortress Press, 1974.

———. *Rediscovering the Teaching of Jesus.* New York: Harper & Row, 1967.

Pesch, Rudolf. *Das Markusevangelium.* HTKNT. 2 vols. Freiburg: Herder, 1976–7.

———. *Naherwartung. Tradition und Redaktion in Mk 13.* KBANT. Düsseldorf: Patmos Verlag, 1968.

Piper, R. *Wisdom in the Q Tradition: The Aphoristic Teaching of Jesus.* SNTSMS 61. Cambridge: Cambridge University Press, 1989.

Polkow, Dennis. "Method and Criteria for Historical Jesus Research." in *SBL 1987 Seminar Papers.* Atlanta: Scholars Press, 1987.

Raney, W. H. *The Relation of the Fourth Gospel to the Christian Cultus.* Giessen: Alfred Töpelmann, 1933.

Reiling, J. *Hermas and Christian Prophecy: A Study of the Eleventh Mandate,* NovTSup. Leiden: E. J. Brill, 1973.

Reitzenstein, Richard. *Die hellenistischen Mysterienreligionen. Nach ihren Grundgedanken und Wirkungen.* Leipzig: B. G. Teubner, 1927³.

———. "Paulus als Pneumatiker." In *Das Paulusbild in der neueren Deutschen Forschung,* edited by K. H. Rengstorf. Darmstadt: Wissenschaftliche Buchgesellschaft, 1969.

Riesenfeld, Harald. *The Gospel Tradition and Its Beginnings.* London: A. R. Mowbray & Co., 1961.

Riesner, Rainer. *Jesus als Lehrer. Eine Untersuchung zum Ursprung der Evangelien-Überlieferung.* WUNT 2/7. Tübingen: J. C. B. Mohr (Paul Siebeck), 3rd edition, 1988.

Robinson, James M. "The Formal Structure of Jesus' Message." In *Current Issues in New Testament Interpretation*, edited by William Klassen and Graydon F. Snyder. New York: Harper & Brothers, 1962.

———. "Die Hodajot-Formel in Gebet und Hymnus des Frühchristentums." In *Apophoreta. Festschrift für Ernst Haenchen*, edited by Walter Eltester and F. H. Kettler. Berlin: Alfred Töpelmann, 1964.

———. "The Jesus Movement in Galilee: Reconstructing Q." In *Bulletin of the Institute for Antiquity and Christianity*, 14/3 (1987): 4–5.

———. "LOGOI SOPHŌN": On the Gattung of Q." In *Trajectories Through Early Christianity*, edited by James M. Robinson and Helmut Koester. Philadelphia: Fortress Press, 1971.

———. "On Bridging the Gulf from Q to the Gospel of Thomas (or Vice Versa)." In *Nag Hammadi, Gnosticism, and Early Christianity*, edited by Charles W. Hedrick and Robert Hodgson, Jr. Peabody, Mass.: Hendricksen, 1986.

———. "The Q Trajectory: Between John and Matthew via Jesus." Forthcoming.

Robinson, James, and Helmut Koester. *Trajectories Through Early Christianity*. Philadelphia: Fortress Press, 1971.

Roetzel, Calvin. "The Judgment Form in Paul's Letters." *JBL* 88 (1969): 305–312.

Rousseau, François. *L'Apocalypse et le milieu prophétique du Nouveau Testament: Structure et préhistoire du texte*. Paris, 1971.

Rowland, C. *The Open Heaven: A Study of Apocalyptic in Judaism and Early Christianity*. London: SPCK, 1982.

Saldarini, A. J. " 'Form Criticism' of Rabbinic Literature." *JBL* 96 (1977): 264–273.

Sand, Alexander. *Das Gesetz und die Propheten. Untersuchungen zur Theologie des Evangeliums nach Matthäus*. BU. Regensburg: Verlag Friedrich Pustet, 1974.

———. "Propheten, Weise, und Schriftkundige in der Gemeinde des Matthäusevangeliums." In *Kirche im Werden. Studien zum Thema Amt und Gemeinde im Neuen Testament*, edited by Josef Hainz. Munich: Verlag Ferdinand Schöningh, 1976.

Sandmel, Samuel. *The Genius of Paul*. New York: Schocken Books, 1970.

Sasse, Hermann. "Der Paraklet im Johannesevangelium." *ZNW* 24 (1925): 260–277.

Satake, Akira. *Die Gemeindeordnung in der Johannesapokalypse*. WMANT. Neukirchen-Vluyn: Neukirchener Verlag, 1966.

Sato, Migaku. *Q und Prophetie. Studien zur Gattungs- und Traditionsgeschichte in der Quelle Q*. WUNT 2/29. Tübingen: J. C. B. Mohr (Paul Siebeck), 1988.

Schelke, Karl Hermann. "Jesus: Lehrer und Prophet." In *Orientierung an Jesus*, edited by Paul Hoffmann, Norbert Brox, and Wilhelm Pesch. Freiburg: Herder, 1973.

Schlier, Heinrich. *Der Brief an die Galater*. Göttingen: Vandenhoeck & Ruprecht, 1971.

———. "Die Verkündigung im Gottesdienst der Kirche." In *Die Zeit der Kirche*. Freiburg: Herder, 1958.

Schmeichel, Waldemar. "Christian Prophecy in Lukan Thought: Luke 4:16–30 as a Point of Departure." In *SBL 1976 Seminar Papers*. Missoula, Mont.: Scholars Press, 1976.

Schmeller, Thomas. *Brechungen. Urchristliche Wandercharismatiker im Prisma soziologisch orientierter Exegese.* SBS 136. Stuttgart: Katholisches Bibelwerk, 1989.

Schmidt, Daryl. "The LXX *Gattung* 'Prophetic Correlative.'" *JBL* 96 (1977): 517–522.

Schmidt, Joseph. "Propheten (b) im NT." LTK 8:799.

Schnider, Franz. *Jesus der Prophet.* Göttingen: Vandenhoeck & Ruprecht, 1973.

Schniewind, Julius. *Das Evangelium nach Markus.* NTD. Göttingen: Vandenhoeck & Ruprecht, 1960⁹.

Schulz, Siegfried. *Komposition und Herkunft der johanneischen Reden.* Stuttgart: W. Kohlhammer, 1960.

———. *Q: Die Spruchquelle der Evangelisten.* Zurich: Theologischer Verlag, 1972.

———. *Die Stunde der Botschaft.* Zurich: Zwingli Verlag, 1970².

Schürmann, Heinz. "Beobachtungen zum Menschensohn-Titel in der Redequelle." In *Jesus und der Menschensohn. Für Anton Vögtle,* edited by R. Pesch and R. Schnackenburg. Freiburg: Herder, 1975.

———. *Traditionsgeschichtliche Untersuchungen zu den Synoptischen Evangelien.* KBANT. Düsseldorf: Patmos-Verlag, 1968.

———. "'. . . und Lehrer': Die geistliche Eigenart des Lehrdienstes und sein Verhältnis zu anderen geistlichen Diensten im neutestamentlichen Zeitalter." In *Orientierungen am Neuen Testament. Exegetische Gesprächbeiträge.* Düsseldorf: Patmos-Verlag, 1978.

Schweizer, Eduard. *Church Order in the New Testament.* SBT. Naperville, Ill.: Alec R. Allenson, 1961.

———. *EGŌ EIMI. Die religionsgeschichtliche Herkunft und theologische Bedeutung der johanneischen Bildreden, zugleich ein Beitrag zur Quellenfrage des vierten Evangeliums.* Göttingen: Vandenhoeck & Ruprecht, 1939.

———. *Matthäus und seine Gemeinde.* SBS. Stuttgart: Katholisches Bibelwerk, 1974.

———. "Observance of the Law and Charismatic Activity in Matthew." *NTS* 16 (April 1970): 213–230.

Schweizer, Eduard, et al. *"Pneuma."* TDNT 6:332–451.

Scott, Ernest F. *The Validity of the Gospel Record.* London: Nicholson & Watson, 1938.

Scroggs, Robin. "The Exaltation of the Spirit by Some Early Christians." *JBL* 84 (1965): 359–373.

Seitz, O. J. F. "The Commission of Prophets and 'Apostles,' a Re-Examination of Matt. 23:34 with Luke 11:49." In *Studia Evangelica* 4, edited by F. L. Cross. Berlin: Akademie Verlag, 1968.

Selwyn, E. C. *The Christian Prophets and the Prophetic Apocalypse.* London: Macmillan & Co., 1900.

———. *The Oracles in the New Testament.* New York: Hodder & Stoughton, 1911.

———. *St. Luke the Prophet.* London: Macmillan & Co., 1901.

Smith, D. Moody. "Johannine Christianity: Some Reflections on its Character and Delineation." *NTS* 21 (1975): 222–248.

———. "John 16:1–15." *Inter* 33 (January 1979): 58–62.

———. "The Presentation of Jesus in the Fourth Gospel." *Inter* 31 (October 1977): 367–378.

Stählin, Gustav. *"To pneuma Iēsous* (Apostelgeschichte 16: 7)." In *Christ and Spirit in the New Testament,* edited by Barnabas Lindars and Stephen Smalley. Cambridge: Cambridge University Press, 1973.

Steck, O. H. *Israel und das gewaltsame Geschick der Propheten.* WMANT. Neukirchen-Vluyn: Neukirchener Verlag, 1967.

Streeter, B. H. *The Four Gospels: A Study of Origins.* Rev. ed. London: Macmillan & Co., 1930.

Stroker, W. D. *Extracanonical Sayings of Jesus.* Atlanta: Scholars Press, 1989.

―――. "The Formation of Secondary Sayings of Jesus." Ph.D. diss., Yale University, 1970.

Strugnell, John. " 'Amen I Say Unto You' in the Sayings of Jesus and in Early Christian Literature." *HTR* 67 (1974): 177–190.

Suggs, M. Jack. *Wisdom, Christology, and Law in Matthew's Gospel.* Cambridge, Mass.: Harvard University Press, 1970.

Swete, H. B. *The Holy Spirit in the New Testament: A Study of Primitive Christian Teaching.* London: Macmillan & Co., 1910.

Taylor, Vincent. *The Formation of the Gospel Tradition.* London: Macmillan & Co., 1933.

Teeple, Howard M. "The Oral Tradition That Never Existed." *JBL* 89 (1970): 56–68.

―――. "The Origin of the Son of Man Christology." *JBL* 84 (1965): 213–250.

Theissen, Gerd. *Sociology of Early Palestinian Christianity.* Philadelphia: Fortress Press, 1978.

―――. *Studien zur Soziologie des Urchristentums.* WUNT 19. Tübingen: J. C. B. Mohr (Paul Siebeck), 1983².

―――. "Wanderradikalismus. Literatursoziologische Aspekte der Überlieferung von Worten Jesu im Urchristentum." *ZTK* 70 (1973): 245–271.

Tiede, David. *The Charismatic Figure as Miracle Worker.* SBLDS 1. Missoula, Mont.: Scholars Press, 1972.

Tödt, Heinz E. *The Son of Man in the Synoptic Tradition.* Philadelphia: Westminster Press, 1965.

Tontenrose, J. *The Delphic Oracle.* Berkeley and Los Angeles: University of California Press, 1978.

Torrey, Charles C. *The Lives of the Prophets: Greek Text and Translation.* Philadelphia: Society of Biblical Literature, 1946.

Trocmé, Étienne. *The Formation of the Gospel According to Mark.* Philadelphia: Westminster Press, 1975.

Uro, Risto. *Sheep Among the Wolves: A Study on the Mission Instructions in Q.* Annales Academiae Scientiarum Fennicae Dissertationes Humanarum Litterarum 47. Helsinki: Suomalainen Tiedeakatemis, 1987.

van der Horst, P. W. "Hellenistic Parallels to the Acts of the Apostles (2:1–47)." *JSNT* 25 (1985): 49–60.

van Unnik, W. C. "A Formula Describing Prophecy." *NTS* 9 (1963): 86–94.

―――. "A Greek Characteristic of Prophecy in the Fourth Gospel." In *Text and Interpretation: Studies in the New Testament Presented to Matthew Black,* edited by E. Best and R. McL. Wilson. Cambridge: Cambridge University Press, 1979, 211–229.

Vermes, Geza. *Jesus the Jew.* Philadelphia: Fortress Press, 1973.

Vielhauer, Philipp. "Apocalypses and Related Subjects: Introduction." In *New Testament Apocrypha,* edited by Edgar Hennecke and Wilhelm Schneemelcher. Philadelphia: Westminster Press, 1964.

Walker, William O., Jr. "The Origin of the Son of Man Concept as Applied to Jesus." *JBL* 91 (1972): 482–490.

———. "The Quest for the Historical Jesus: A Discussion of Methodology." *Anglican Theological Review* 51 (1969): 38–56.

Weber, Max. *The Sociology of Religion.* Boston: Beacon Press, 1963.

Weinel, Heinrich. *Die Wirkungen des Geistes und der Geister im nachapostolischen Zeitalter bis auf Irenäus.* Freiburg: J. C. B. Mohr, 1899.

Wellhausen, Julius. *Einleitung in die drei ersten Evangelien.* Berlin: Georg Reimer, 1911².

Wilder, Amos. "Form-History and the Oldest Tradition." In *Neotestamentica et Patristica* (Festschrift for Oscar Cullmann). Leiden: E. J. Brill, 1962.

———. *The Language of the Gospel: Early Christian Rhetoric.* New York: Harper & Row, 1964.

Wilkinson, T. L. "Tongues and Prophecy in Acts and 1st Corinthians." *Vox Reformata* 31 (1978): 1–20.

Windisch, Hans. "Jesus und der Geist nach synoptischer Überlieferung." In *Studies in Early Christianity,* edited by S. J. Case. New York: Century, 1928.

———. *Paulus und Christus: Ein Biblisch-religionsgeschichtlicher Vergleich.* UNT. Leipzig: J. C. Hinrichs'sche Buchhandlung, 1934.

———. *The Spirit-Paraclete in the Fourth Gospel.* Edited by John Reumann. Philadelphia: Fortress Press, 1968.

Wire, Antoinette Clark. "Prophecy and Women Prophets in Corinth." In *Gospel Origins and Christian Beginnings.* Sonoma, Calif.: Polebridge Press, 1990.

Wolff, Hans Walter. *Joel and Amos.* Hermeneia. Philadelphia: Fortress Press, 1977.

Zeller, Dieter. "Das Logion Mt. 8.11f/Luke 13:28f und das Motiv der 'Völkerwallfahrt,' " *BZ,* new series, 16 (January 1972): 87–91.

Zimmermann, Heinrich. "Das absolute *Egō eimi* als die neutestamentliche Offenbarungsformel." *BZ,* new series, 4 (1960): 54–69, 266–276.

———. *Die Urchristliche Lehrer: Studien zur Traditionskreis der didaskaloi im frühen Urchristentum.* WUNT 2/12. Tübingen: J. C. B. Mohr (Paul Siebeck), 1984.

Zumstein, J. "Le prophète chrétien dans la Syro-Palestine du 1er siècle." *Foi et Vie* 83 (1984): 83–94.

Index of Scripture and Other Ancient Writings

Index of Modern Authors